Hollywood
and the Female Body

Hollywood and the Female Body

A History of Idolization and Objectification

STEPHEN HANDZO

McFarland & Company, Inc., Publishers
Jefferson, North Carolina

LIBRARY OF CONGRESS CATALOGUING-IN-PUBLICATION DATA

Names: Handzo, Stephen, 1944– author.
Title: Hollywood and the female body : a history of idolization and objectification / Stephen Handzo.
Description: Jefferson : McFarland & Company, Inc., Publishers, 2020. | Includes bibliographical references and index.
Identifiers: LCCN 2019049185 | ISBN 9781476679136 (paperback) ♾
ISBN 9781476637778 (ebook)
Subjects: LCSH: Women in motion pictures. | Nudity in motion pictures. | Sexism in motion pictures. | Feminism and motion pictures. | Motion pictures—United States—History. | Motion picture industry—California—Los Angeles—History. | Women in the motion picture industry—United States—History.
Classification: LCC PN1995.9.W6 H256 2020 | DDC 791.43/6522—dc23
LC record available at https://lccn.loc.gov/2019049185

BRITISH LIBRARY CATALOGUING DATA ARE AVAILABLE

ISBN (print) 978-1-4766-7913-6
ISBN (ebook) 978-1-4766-3777-8

© 2019 Stephen Handzo. All rights reserved

No part of this book may be reproduced or transmitted in any form or by any means, electronic or mechanical, including photocopying or recording, or by any information storage and retrieval system, without permission in writing from the publisher.

Front cover: publicity still of Ava Gardner
in *One Touch of Venus* (author's collection)

Printed in the United States of America

*McFarland & Company, Inc., Publishers
Box 611, Jefferson, North Carolina 28640
www.mcfarlandpub.com*

Table of Contents

Introduction	1
Prologue	5
1. Not So Innocent: Controversy and Censorship in the Silent Era	9
2. Why Be Good? Flappers, Flaming Youth and an "It" Girl	29
3. Pre-Code, Post-Code and Non-Code: Before and After the Moral Crackdown of the 1930s	45
4. Something for the Boys: Pin-Ups and Love Goddesses of the World War II Era	62
5. "She came at me in sections": Women in Postwar Genre Movies	79
6. "Looking for trouble": Howard Hughes vs. the Production Code (Again)	95
7. Hollywood or Bust: Fifties Blondes and "Mammary Madness"	105
8. "Banned by Cardinal Spellman": *Baby Doll* and Southern Decadence	116
9. Bikini Beach: From the Fifties to the Sixties	122
10. The Nude Scene: Children Under 17 Not Admitted	148
11. Blue Movie: Coming to a Theater Near You—Pornography	176
12. Girls' Trip: The End of the Double Standard?	190
Epilogue. The Reckoning: Weinstein and the #MeToo Movement	199
Chapter Notes	209
Bibliography	213
Index	215

Introduction

> "Woman is both Eve and the Virgin Mary. She is an idol, a servant, source of life, power of darkness; she is the elementary silence of truth, she is artifice, gossip, and lies; she is the medicine woman and witch; she is man's prey; she is his downfall, she is everything he is not and wants to have, his negation and his raison d'être. She is the Other, she is Evil through which Good can exist."
> —Simone de Beauvoir, *The Second Sex*

"Men dream of women, women dream of being dreamt of," wrote art critic John Berger in *Ways of Seeing*. In four words, he summed up gender roles in visual media: *men act*; *women appear*. Movie cycles may come and go but attractive women and men with guns have been consistently present from the early days to the present.

A content analysis of 3.5 million books published in English between 1900 and 2008 supervised by Dr. Isabelle Augenstein at the University of Copenhagen found that women were more than twice as likely as men to be described in terms of appearance rather than behavior or personal qualities. The adjectives most often used for women were "beautiful" or "sexy."

The motion-picture screen has always been a battleground in the "culture wars" and an arena in which society sorted out its contradictory attitudes concerning sexuality. From its formative period in the mid-teens and well into its mid-century maturity, the American feature film was undeniably constrained by state and local censor boards.

Hollywood responded to the threat of even stricter censorship with the adoption of the Production Code in 1930. When enforcement was criticized as lax, a Production Code Administration was formed in 1934 to hold the studios to the standards they had already accepted. The Code banned nudity even in silhouette. Non-marital sex could never be shown as pleasurable unless it was followed by compensatory moral values, i.e., suffering and remorse. One thing the Code could not do was keep Hollywood from casting attractive people. Even the Code's bedrock principle, the sanctity of marriage, could be subverted by casting. No one could really blame Walter Huston's retired auto magnate in *Dodsworth* (1936) for favoring the vibrant Mary Astor over his middle-aged, flighty wife (Ruth Chatterton). James Cagney as a Huey Long–type politician in *A Lion Is in the Streets* (1953) managed a wife (Barbara Hale) and mistress (the young Anne Francis) without conflicted feelings.

The visual signifier, or what literary critics call the "objective correlative," for desire in Hollywood was the female body. Denied nudity and realistic sex, Hollywood sublimated its libidinous impulses through the three "c's" of creativity: cinematography, costume, and choreography. Directors of photography learned how to frame and light women for maximum allure. Designers developed a dialectic of exposure and concealment that emphasized the erogenous zones even as it covered them. Dance directors created eruptions of sensuality amid otherwise earthbound narratives. In spite of, or perhaps because of, the restrictions, Hollywood perfected erotic fantasy. The great French critic André Bazin even stated that the history of eroticism in cinema is the history of eroticism in American film.

Before the Second World War, Hollywood assumed that the audience was predominantly female. Young women read fan magazines, followed the love lives of the stars and went to movies to see the clothes. Some movies, such as the vehicles for Joan Crawford, were aimed at the "shop girl trade." After the Second World War, male oriented genres such as the Western and war film came into increased prominence. Women were subordinated and sometimes not present at all.

In both eras, the image of women on the screen was largely the creation of men. Women did have representation as screenwriters and film editors and in more traditional fields such as wardrobe and hair styling. There were female directors in the silent era but much of their work is lost along with their reputations. Some female stars produced their own films but, with the domination of distribution by the large companies, production became centralized as well. Between Dorothy Arzner's last film in 1943 and Ida Lupino's first directorial credit in 1950, there were no female directors in Hollywood at all. Lupino was the first female director to launch a career in the sound era. Described as "the prettiest member of the Director's Guild" by its president, Joseph L. Mankiewicz, she was, for many years, the only female director in Hollywood.

Reference is made almost entirely to mainstream, commercial or "Hollywood" films, i.e., what most people think of as "the movies." Foreign films do not really figure in unless they had an unusually large cultural impact as with *And God Created Woman* in the 1950s, *I am Curious (Yellow)* in the 1960s and *Last Tango in Paris* in the 1970s.

In the 1950s young women aspired to look like Grace Kelly, Elizabeth Taylor and Audrey Hepburn. Advance Patterns, sold exclusively by J.C. Penney, advertised in *Photoplay* so that women who could sew might re-create Hollywood fashions at home. The company shut down in the mid–1960s. By then, amid all the cultural upheavals, fashion trends originated in the street, not on the sketchpads of Paramount's Edith Head or M-G-M's Helen Rose.

The rise of the feminist movement further accelerated the trend to cheap, unisex clothing. By the 1970s, the only designer on staff was the aged Edith Head who had moved to Universal where her office was a stop on the studio tour. Most of her later credits were for retro projects that evoked Old Hollywood: *Gable and Lombard* (1976) and the posthumously-released *Dead Men Don't Wear Plaid* (1982). Interviewers may still ask stars on the red carpet, "Who are you wearing?" but, in their movies, the clothes are generally uninteresting and they are no longer style icons.

With the demise of the studio contract system, the switch to independent production and the rise of the *auteur* director, the film companies lost the capacity to create stars or any incentive to do so.

When the Production Code was replaced by the ratings system in 1968, the barriers against nudity and realistic sex fell. Eventually, there would be almost nothing that could not be shown.

The explosion of pornography in the 1970s took the objectification of women to the extreme. It raised vexing legal, political and artistic questions. Did the First Amendment always favor free expression over the right of communities to enact their values into law? Does pornography degrade women? Is there a place for explicitness or is art indirect by definition?

In recent years, there have been many more female directors. Female directors are more likely to treat women less as sex *objects* than as sex *subjects*. Stories are told from the woman's viewpoint and their female leads are more likely to take the initiative in sex.

Finally, the downfall of Harvey Weinstein and the rise of the #Me Too movement have opened up film industry sexism to public scrutiny and debate, possibly to point the way to a more egalitarian future.

Prologue

> "Begin at the beginning," said the King gravely, "and go on till you come to the end: then stop."
> —Lewis Carroll, *Alice's Adventures in Wonderland*

The affinity of the motion-picture camera for the female body can be traced not just to the beginning but before the beginning. To win a bet that a horse had all four hooves on the ground while at a gallop, California governor Leland Stanford hired photographer Eadweard Muybridge to conduct an experiment in 1878. Muybridge used a battery of still cameras. John D. Isaacs, chief engineer for the Southern Pacific railroads, rigged up a system of magnetic releases to trigger the cameras.

Between 1883 and 1886, Muybridge conducted animal locomotion studies that included human subjects at the University of Pennsylvania. In 1887, he published the book *Animal Locomotion: An Electro-Photographic Investigation of the Connective Phases of Animal Movement*. The academic affiliation, the endorsement of artist Thomas Eakins and support from the science faculty enabled Muybridge to publish images that could have been prosecuted as obscene in most jurisdictions well into the 20th century.

In 1885, in the outdoor studio of the veterinary department at the University of Pennsylvania, Blanche Epler posed for motion studies for Muybridge. She walked up and down a short flight of stairs carrying a water vessel. She repeated the action in the nude. Another model, Catherine Aimer, bathed and poured water over her head, dried herself, stepped out of the bath and put on stockings.[1] Muybridge also posed Epler and Aimer nude together. The models were identified on the plates by numbers, e.g., "Model No. 1" (Epler) or "Model No. 8" (Aimer). Their names were recorded in Muybridge's notebooks along with the hours worked and the amounts paid. The models were supplied by "Mrs. Tadd," the wife of the director of Philadelphia's School of Industrial Arts, and were probably prostitutes. Muybridge complained that their working-class origins made it hard for them to achieve the elegant posture of the women on Greek vases. Muybridge photographed "abnormal" bodies to contrast them with "healthy" ones. He photographed a 340-pound woman whose obesity was meant to inspire disgust.

Author Rebecca Solnit observes that Muybridge assigned different gender roles to his male and female models. The men, who were mostly campus athletes, tended to carry out comparatively neutral sporting and working activities, from shoeing a horse to hitting a baseball, with considerable walking, running, jumping, throwing and other basic exercises. The women were more often engaged in domestic and social activities, such as dressing, pouring tea, sweeping, waltzing, though they too walked, climbed stairs, jumped, ran and carried loads.[2]

Muybridge did not pose naked men and women together. Eakins did and was forced to resign from the Pennsylvania Academy of the Fine Arts. In one photograph, he carried a woman in the classic pose of movie monsters of the 1940s and 1950s.

Although some historians credit Muybridge as the inventor of motion pictures, movies as we know them required "film" in the form of a photosensitive emulsion on a flexible, transparent base. Celluloid, from a nitrocellulose base, was used by the Eastman Kodak Company in 1889 to democratize photography. "You press the button, we do the rest," announced the ad for the Kodak box camera. Thomas Edison's Kinetograph adapted celluloid film to motion-picture photography.

The first woman to be filmed at Edison's Black Maria studio in 1894, and therefore the first woman to appear in an American motion picture, was the internationally renowned Spanish dancer Carmencita in her "butterfly" dance. In the film, only about half a minute long when seen on the individual viewing device called the Kinetoscope, she flashed her ankle and showed some white lace underwear. *The Newark Evening News* of July 17, 1894, reported that State Senator James Bradley and Asbury Park mayor Franklin Ten Broeck attended the opening of a Kinetoscope parlor in the seaside resort and concluded that the film was unsuitable. It was replaced by *The Boxing Cats*, arguably more disturbing as two felines were forced to stand and pummel each other with little boxing gloves.[3] Two precedents were established: the authority of government to interpose itself between the exhibitor and the public and the harsher treatment given to sex than violence.

Another famous dancer who appeared for the Kinetoscope in 1894 was Annabella. The first documented instance of a motion-picture image projected before an audience was of Annabella by Charles Francis Jenkins in a tent theater at the Cotton States and International Exposition in Atlanta in 1895.

The premiere showing of the Edison Vitascope (projector) in 1896 included the "skirt dance" and the "umbrella dance."

Fatima Djemille, who performed under the name "Little Egypt" at the Chicago World's Fair in 1893, re-created *Fatima's Muscle Dance* for Edison in 1896. Edison's rival, American Mutoscope and Biograph Company, produced *Fatima*, also known as *Fatima's Coochee-Coochee Dance* in 1897. This may have been the first film to be censored in America. Some prints show Fatima's body obscured by what looks like a board ranch fence.

One of the most famous early Edison shorts was *The Kiss* (1896). It showed John Rice and May Irwin in a scene from the stage musical *The Widow Jones*. The portly, middle-aged lovers nuzzle and kiss on the lips in medium close-up. At the Kinetoscope rate of 40 frames per second, the 60-foot film lasted just 18 seconds. It was also added to the Vitascope program, where it lasted almost a minute at the lower frame rate. It caused a sensation as the first intimate moment shown on film. The Edison catalogue exaggerated what was little more than a brief peck: "They get ready to kiss, begin to kiss, then kiss and kiss and kiss in a way that brings the house down every time." The popular subject was used at the start or end of a program and remained in the Edison catalogue until 1901.

Another Edison title, *Trapeze Disrobing Act* (1903), is exactly what it sounds like. A young woman on a trapeze, the vaudeville performer Chamion discards her petticoat while cigar-chewing males watch from box seats.

A 1904 Edison had the (now) misleading title *The Gay Shoe Clerk*. A young man tidies up the store as two women come in. As the clerk fits the younger and better-looking of two, he fondles her foot and takes a more than occupational interest in her ankle and stockinged calf. He kisses her, whereupon the older woman hits him with her umbrella.

One of the more surprising Edisons was *Treloar and Miss Marshall, Prize Winners at the Physical Culture Show in Madison Square Garden* (1904). Beatrice Marshall was actually the third-place finisher, but she was willing to assume classic poses while wearing a skintight leotard that showed a curvaceous body and left her legs exposed. (The Society for the Prevention of Vice had protested the show.)

Streetcar Chivalry, a 1903 Edison, illustrates the turn of the 20th-century trend toward what would now be called fat-shaming. A slim young woman enters the streetcar and the men get up to give her their seats. When a heavyset woman gets on, they ignore her and hide behind their newspapers until she falls on them.

Slender Sarah Bernhardt, held to be ugly in her first American visit in 1880, was hailed for her beauty in 1900. There was a class element to it. The willowy women in John Singer Sargent paintings were considered elegant, while buxom showgirls appealed to lower-class men and were thought to be promiscuous. By 1900, even working-class men laughed at hefty showgirls.[4] Pornography reflected the trend; where women might once have come in different shapes, there was a preference for Anglo-Saxon features and a standardized figure, described in one account as "firm bust, tiny waist, swelling hips, massive spherical posteriors."[5]

In 1912, a young upper-class girl, seeing a portrait of the once-fashionable Lillian Russell, asked in all naïveté, "Who is that fat lady?"[6]

Magazine illustrators pushed a standardized image of female beauty. In 1865, there were several hundred titles with a total circulation of about four million; 40 years later, in 1905, there were some 6,000 magazines with a total audience of 64 million.

The Ladies Home Journal was the first magazine to exceed one million in circulation in 1903. *The Saturday Evening Post*, also from the Curtis Publishing Company, reached that figure in 1908. In the 1890s, the cover picture became a selling tool. The *Police Gazette* used actual photographs of women. As far back as the 1870s, a series called "Footlight Favorites" showed burlesque and musical comedy performers. For their lurid true crime stories, they used illustrations of women in tight-fitting or revealing clothing as victims or perpetrators.

Most magazines preferred illustrations to photography. Illustrations could be rendered in color; first in two colors and then four at a time when color photography was in its infancy. Illustrators, some of whom became quite famous, developed a style of romantic realism that produced images at once relatable and idealized. Charles Dana Gibson's Gibson Girl, tall and slender with large, firm breasts and a tiny waist, appeared in magazines such as *Collier's Weekly* and *Scribner's Magazine* in the 1890s and 1900s. She typified the ideal young woman.

New York's 23rd Street entered the language as "23 Skidoo" when the Flatiron Building opened in 1902. An American Mutoscope and Biograph Company subject *At the Foot of the Flatiron* (1903) showed the wind blowing women's skirts and men's coats. The men hold onto their hats although one black man loses his. The year before, Edison made an "actuality" called *What Happened on 23rd Street*. Not much happens on 23rd Street at first. Men in straw boaters cross the street. Electric streetcars and horse-drawn carts pass by. At the end, a young couple walks over a grate. A gust of air lifts the woman's skirt; she brushes it down and laughs it off. The scene was actually staged with actors from other Edison productions.

The prolific A.E. Weed of American Biograph and Mutoscope Company made several films about burlesque performers. *From Show Girl to Burlesque Queen* shows a woman discard her dress; she steps behind a screen to emerge in the costume of a Roman centurion. (Burlesque at this stage meant spoof rather than striptease.)

Several Biograph films of 1903 showed young women of the theater outwitting reformers. In *The Chorus Girls and the Salvation Army*, two chorus girls resist the efforts of a Salvation Army "lassie" to keep them from smoking and drinking and chase her away. An earlier Biograph poked fun at the "lassies." In *Soubrettes in a Bachelor's Flat*, a young man carouses with chorus girls. When the police come, the undressed women change into Salvation Army uniforms. The Gerry Society was the popular name for the New York Society for the Prevention of Cruelty to Children. Its role was to keep underage girls off the stage. In *The Gerry Society Makes a Mistake*, a proper-looking gentleman and a policeman enter a dressing room where four young actresses are in state of undress. Papers are shown to the youngest girl, who produces a wedding ring from a costume trunk. The officer appears to know the women and they all laugh and celebrate after the Society's man is foiled.

With state and local censor boards still in the future, early filmmakers could mock reformers. Soon they would turn to the reformers to save them.

1

Not So Innocent

Controversy and Censorship in the Silent Era

NBC's *Project XX* series produced a series of narrative compilation documentaries that, taken together, formed a visual history of American life in the first half of the 20th century: *The Jazz Age, Life in the Thirties* and *Not So Long Ago* (1945–50). The first in the series chronologically, though not the first to be aired, was *The Innocent Years* (1957); it covered the period 1900–1917. *The Movies in the Age of Innocence* was the title of a popular 1963 history of the silent film by Edward Wagenknecht.

The Age of Innocence was an Edith Wharton novel published in 1920 that depicted New York society in the 1890s. She may have gotten the title from a French painting of 1785. The Age of Innocence is always just far enough in the past that most living people do not remember it. To judge by what was said and written at the time, every age is the Age of Anxiety (the title of a 1947 poem by W.H. Auden and a 1949 symphony by Leonard Bernstein). Only in retrospect does the past seem more innocent than the present.

No event captured the cultural confusions of early 20th-century America more than the so-called Trial of the Century. On June 25, 1906, Harry K. Thaw shot and killed architect Stanford White in the rooftop theater of the original Madison Square Garden, designed by White himself. White had seduced Thaw's wife, the former artist and photographer's model turned *Floradora* girl, Evelyn Nesbit, when she was just 16. Thaw shouted, "You ruined my wife!" or, possibly, "You ruined my life!" Within a week of the shooting, Edison had *Rooftop Murder* in nickelodeons. Biograph had *The Thaw-White Tragedy* (July) and *In the Tombs* (August).

The most important Thaw-White film was *The Unwritten Law*. Even by the low standards of 1907, it was no great shakes as cinema. Made in Lubin Manufacturing Company's cramped studio in central Philadelphia, the flimsy interiors, with painted rather than three-dimensional details, comported uneasily with exteriors filmed on real streets. The film presumed that the audience was familiar with the story, so there is little exposition and no real attempt to introduce the characters. The Nesbit character was shown modeling for an artist, then put on stage by White (called "Black" in the film). Titles introduce "The Room with the Red Velvet Swing," where White's conquests swung in the nude. The young woman is then taken upstairs to "The Boudoir with a Hundred Mirrors," where she is plied with drink. She staggers around the room as if drugged. White/Black pulls a curtain across the door and discreetly shields the passed-out girl. This is followed by Nesbit's marriage to Thaw, filmed outside a real church.

The shooting in the rooftop theater leads to a scene introduced by a title, "In the Tombs," with Thaw in his cell in the old Criminal Courts building. In the film's one stab at cinematic imagination, the window of the cell becomes a screen on which the shooting is reenacted. In the final scene, Thaw is tried and acquitted. The film was released in March 1907 before the real trial was over. (The film was part of a media campaign waged by Thaw's mother, who financed and directed his defense.) The actual jury deadlocked, with the majority in favor of a guilty verdict. In a second trial, the insanity defense was successfully employed, widely considered a travesty enabled by Thaw's wealth and position. Some sources claim that Evelyn Nesbit played herself, but the woman on-screen is heavier and lacks Nesbit's delicate beauty. After she was cut off by Thaw's family, Nesbit did appear in about a dozen movies between 1913–1920 that exploited her notoriety.

By 1907, motion pictures moved away from peep shows, arcades and vaudeville houses to theaters built for the purpose. Pittsburgh's Nickelodeon (1905) was not actually the first, as is sometimes cited. (Thomas Tally's Electric Theatre in Los Angeles preceded it in 1902.) It did serve as a model for the storefront theaters that quickly proliferated. In the effort to attract a family audience, risqué material was de-emphasized.

Lubin claimed that *The Unwritten Law* was clean and could be exhibited in any situation, but the recently formed trade paper *Moving Picture World* deplored the picture. The *Chicago Tribune* waged an editorial crusade against the film. They claimed that teenaged girls, especially, would be attracted to the nickelodeons, where they might be molested. Rival newspapers noted that the *Tribune* had quite happily published all the salacious details revealed in the trial. However hypocritical, the campaign had results. Chicago established the Police Board of Censors in 1907, although it was not really operational until 1909. It was the first such governmental body in the U.S.

Films about the Thaw-White case also provoked a censorship crisis in New York City. In 1907, after a raid by agents of the Children's Aid Society, the proprietor of a nickel show on Third Avenue near 34th Street was fined $100 because he had imperiled the morals of young boys by admitting them to *The Unwritten Law*.[1] Theodore Bingham, the imperious police commissioner, recommended that the operating licenses of the city's 600 nickelodeons be lifted because of obscene pictures and violations of health and fire laws. He was supported by Canon William Sheafe Chase, head of the New York Civic League, and theologian Wilbur Crafts, founder of the International Reform Bureau, a Prohibitionist organization. Not all clergy were as hostile to movies as Chase and Crafts, but many wanted an end to Sunday movie showings that they thought corrupted the "Lord's Day." On Christmas Eve of 1908, Mayor George B. McClellan, Jr., acted and closed the theaters.

To save itself, the infant movie industry turned to the People's Institute, a reform organization based at the tuition-free college Cooper Union. A New York Board of Censorship (later renamed the National Board of Censorship) was formed with a membership of prominent persons. The members believed that movies could be a force for good. While some reformers saw movie theaters as a place of sin, others observed that working men, instead of getting drunk at the corner saloon and going home to brutalize their wives and children, would take them to the movies instead. Despite the threat of "movie mashers," the theaters were more wholesome than dance halls where young women were recruited for prostitution. The board was financed by the Motion Picture Patents Company, a combine of nine outfits that strove to maintain its oligopoly over production.[2]

In an era when many people worked six days a week, the ban on Sunday amusements was unpopular. Because the relevant legislation dated from 1860 and covered only live entertainment, theater owners led by William Fox were able defeat the ban on Sunday movies in court. Under McClellan's successor, Mayor William Gaynor, popular entertainment of all kinds flourished.

Because of its ties to the industry and the fact that its members were cultured people inclined to be lenient with films that had artistic merit, the National Board did not satisfy those who wanted stricter censorship.

The first state censor board was established in Pennsylvania in 1911. Ohio followed in 1913, and Kansas in 1914.

Harry E. Aitken of Mutual Film Corporation challenged the Ohio board in what became a landmark case. At issue was the *Mutual Weekly*, an early newsreel, something that would seem to have a plausible claim to Freedom of the Press. Its content was not the issue. Aitken claimed that the review process hindered topicality.

There was an adversarial relationship between distributors and exhibitors and a rivalry between the companies inside the trust and those outside of it, of which Mutual was one of the leaders. The nascent film industry thus did not mount a unified response to the threat posed by the Mutual case. The Motion Picture Patents

The Unwritten Law was the most popular of several films about the Thaw-White murder. In an ad in *The New York Clipper*, a show-business weekly similar to *Variety* and *Billboard*, Lubin marketed it as sure-fire at the box office. The controversy it created led to the establishment of film censorship. In those days, films were sold outright instead of rented.

Company's distribution arm, General Film Company, tied up in its own battle with antitrust laws, complied with Ohio's demand for review and actually rooted for Mutual to fail.

The U.S. Supreme Court ruled in *Mutual Film Corp. v. Industrial Commission of Ohio* that motion pictures did not enjoy First Amendment protection but were simply a somewhat noisome business that could be regulated in the name of public health and safety. The ruling was unanimous, so there was no prospect of a reversal anytime soon. (It would take nearly four decades.)

A new association, the Motion Picture Board of Trade, was formed in 1914 at the behest of William Fox, who would soon go on to found Fox Film. The group managed to get President Woodrow Wilson to speak at its first banquet. It merged with the Moving Picture Exhibitors' League of America to form the National Association of the Motion Picture Industry (NAMPI) in 1916.

The group was able stop passage of a Federal censorship bill sponsored by Senator Hoke Smith and Representative Dudley Hughes, Democrats of Georgia. The bill was reintroduced in 1918 and there would be additional attempts in the 1920s. NAMPI attempted to stop the passage of new state restrictions in the name of "freedom of the screen" but the political/legal climate was not favorable.[3] In the year of its founding, Maryland established a state censor board. NAMPI could not even stop the establishment of a licensing board in its home state of New York in 1921. Florida did not establish a censor board, but it did require in 1919 that theaters play only films passed by the National Board.

One of the more interesting personalities in the cinema world of the 1910s was the actress and director Lois Weber. *Suspense*, the 1913 film in which she starred and codirected with her husband Phillips Smalley, was the tautest and tightest 10 minutes of the one-reel era. A young mother with an infant child (Weber) is left alone when her servant quits without notice and, unknown to her, goes out the door. Weber finds a note from the servant that complains the house is too isolated and that she has left the key under the mat. A vagrant sees the servant leave and approaches the house. In an early use of the split screen, we see the vagrant find the key under the mat, Weber on the phone to her husband and the husband in his office. The husband steals a car and is pursued by the owner and the police in a second car. The vagrant feeds himself in the kitchen, finds a knife and makes his way upstairs as the wife barricades herself in the bedroom. The husband and police arrive in the proverbial nick of time. In an era of dull camera setups, the film was visually striking. There was an overhead shot of the vagrant from the point of view of the woman from an upstairs window that has him look up as he realizes she has seen him. As he climbs the stairs, he moves toward the camera in an extreme close-up. The pursuing car is seen in the side mirror of the first car. Because the same basic situation was used by D.W. Griffith in *The Lonely Villa* (1909) and *An Unseen Enemy* (1912), it is possible to do a direct comparison. The Weber-Smalley execution is at least equal to Griffith's. The film's only defect was that it began inside the house and lacked the establishing long shot needed to demonstrate its isolation.

The woman in jeopardy became a cliché so quickly that even in 1913 it was the stuff of parody. In Mack Sennett's *Barney Oldfield's Race for a Life*, Mabel Normand was tied to railroad tracks in a variation on a plot device used seriously in several earlier films.

Between 1890 and 1920, journalists regularly proclaimed the emergence of the New Woman. The signature activity of the New Woman was bicycling. Women shed long skirts and petticoats for bloomers. In 1896, Susan B. Anthony told Nellie Bly of *The New York World* that bicycling had "done more to emancipate women than anything else in the world."[4] Nellie Bly (Elizabeth Cochrane, 1864–1922) was herself the archetype of the New Woman. The intrepid journalist got herself committed to an insane asylum to expose conditions in 1887 and one-upped Jules Verne when she went around the world in just 72 days in 1890.

For most young women, the jobs available—typist, telephone operator, sewing machine operator—were repetitive and dull. In movies, they could do exciting things.

In *The Grit of the Girl Telegrapher* (1912), Anna Q. Nilsson captured a robber at gunpoint after a chase on top of a moving train. Contemporary critics noted that audiences seemed to prefer courageous and athletic females to "clinging vine" types. It was a short step to the first serial queen, Pearl White. In *The Perils of Pauline* (1914), White as Pauline survives multiple attempts on her life intended to keep her from an inheritance. In the first episode, a balloon ascent at Palisades Amusement Park goes awry when a faked accident causes the balloon to be released prematurely with Pauline instead of the balloonist in the gondola. White arrests the runaway balloon by casting an anchor to the cliffs on the New Jersey side of the Hudson River. She climbs down the rope. She is abducted and held prisoner in a house which is then set on fire and she has to escape as flaming timbers crash around her. White did her own stunts until accumulated injuries made that impossible. White posed for department store advertisements that affirmed, for all her feats of daring, she retained her femininity with an interest in hats, clothes and shoes.

Theda Bara's status as the screen's first *femme fatale* must be taken largely on faith. Only two of the 49 films she made for William Fox between 1915 and 1919 survive in any form and only her first, the rather primitive *A Fool There Was*, is complete. Still photographs show a rather unhappy-looking woman with too much eye makeup in poses more awkward than seductive. The name "Theda Bara" was concocted by the director of *A Fool There Was*. "Theda" was said to be an anagram for Death, while "Bara" was Arab spelled backward. (She was actually Jewish, born Theodosia Goodman in Cincinnati.) In reality, Theda was a diminutive of Theodosia, while Bara came from the middle name of her maternal grandfather, Francois Baranger de Coppet. At a press conference called to introduce the new star, Fox publicists claimed that her mother was an Arabian princess and her father an Italian sculptor. She was supposedly born in an oasis in Egypt and raised in the shadow of the Pyramids. She was alleged to have acted at the Grand Guignol in Paris before she fled to the United States after the outbreak of war. That the assembled reporters believed any of this is doubtful, but the time was ripe for a departure from the goody-goodys (Lillian and Dorothy Gish, Mary Pickford, Mae Marsh) who dominated the era.

A new character, the vampire, or vamp, emerged. ("Vamp" had become a verb as early as 1912.) Publicity for *The Devil's Daughter* (1915) described Bara "as the wickedest woman in the world," while for *Sin* (1915) she was called "Destiny's Dark Angel." Publicity pictures posed her with skeletons. Once the image was established, she was able to vary her roles and even managed a credible Juliet in *Romeo and Juliet* (1916).

Bara's ultimate vamp role in *Cleopatra* (1917) was lost as a result of a 1937 fire at a Fox vault in Fort Lee, New Jersey, that destroyed many early films. A fragment, lasting only 20 seconds, was restored by George Eastman House that showed Bara in one of her many costumes. (The scenario for Bara's *Cleopatra* did survive. When producer Walter Wanger proposed a new *Cleopatra* to 20th Century–Fox President Spyros Skouras in 1958, Skouras had his secretary retrieve a script as fragile as ancient papyrus. Skouras thought it could be remade with just a little updating.)

Still photographs show Bara in a variety of costumes skimpier than those worn by Elizabeth Taylor years later. One costume had her breasts covered by a design of two coiled snakes with eyes in the center.

In Lois Weber's *Hypocrites* (1915), a minister preaches a sermon on "Hypocrisy" to a bored congregation, some of whom are half-asleep while others squirm. Even the choir director and his assistant sneak a look at the Sunday paper. Some congratulate him on a good sermon, but a group of wealthy laymen plans to ask for his resignation. The minister is given the offending newspaper and sits down to read it. He sees a headline "Why the Truth Has Startled Wicked Paris." In a reverie, he imagines himself as Gabriel, the Ascetic, a monk of the Middle Ages, who is also a sculptor. Gabriel creates a statue that portrays Truth as a naked woman. The populace turns on him and his creation. He is stabbed with a spear. "Truth" vanishes from her pedestal, which is then reduced to rubble.

Back in the present, Gabriel assumes corporeal form even though he is dead. He is accompanied by the spirit of "Truth," the statue come to life. An allegorical figure of a real naked woman was seen in double exposure (Margaret Edwards, an 18-year-old physical-culture enthusiast). Truth carries a mirror that she holds up to reveal assorted hypocrites. Politicians who campaign on a platform of honesty are shown

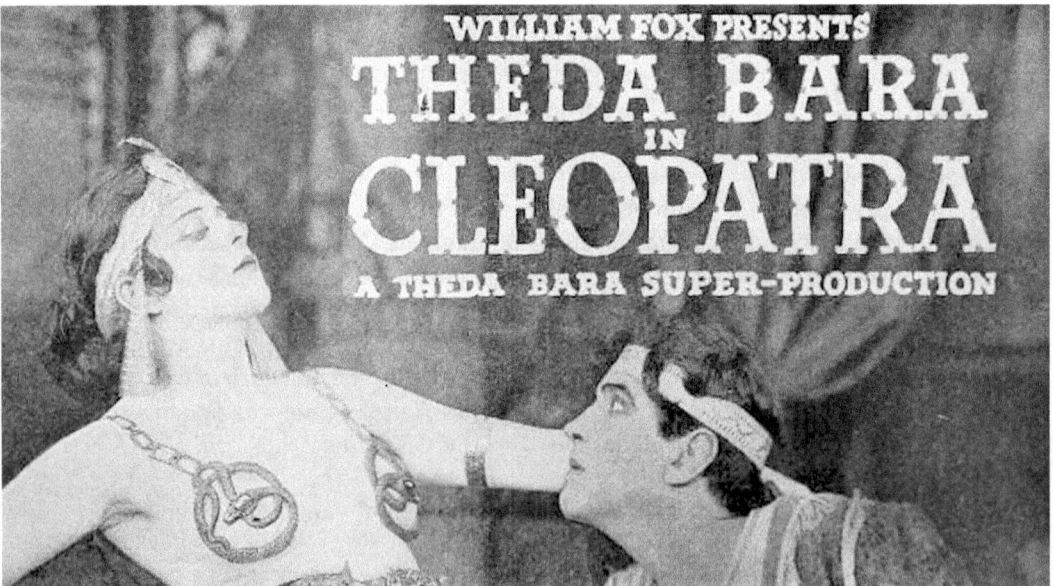

The Theda Bara version of *Cleopatra* was one of her most lavish vehicles and now one of the most sought-after of "lost" films. 20th Century–Fox thought it could be remade with just a little updating.

taking bribes. Lovers who promise fidelity turn out to be faithless. The seemingly devoted family of a dying child includes a brother who reads a fat tome titled "Sex." The minister is found dead and, in a final irony, he is portrayed as the hypocrite. The headline of the Monday morning paper reads, "Prominent Minister Expires in Church after Preaching a Sermon on Hypocrisy," with a subhead reading "It was most unfortunate that he was found with a newspaper in his hand. The congregation was most shocked."

Hypocrites was more sermon than drama. Even as a sermon it was not all that focused. Why was it hypocritical to go to the beach in bathing suits rather than robes as introduced by the title "Modesty"?

Variety wrote, "There is no other picture like this, there has been no other and it will attract anywhere."[5] The nudity caused the film to be banned in Chicago, Minneapolis and the state of Ohio. In Boston, clothes had to be drawn frame by frame onto Naked Truth. Where it could be shown, there were sold-out shows, extended runs and return engagements. *Hypocrites* was not actually the first film to use nudity allegorically. *The Temptation of St. Anthony*, made by Biograph in 1900, had a graceful nude (probably in a body stocking).

A nude Margaret Edwards as "Truth" holds the mirror of truth in Lois Weber's *Hypocrites*. A minister (Courtenay Poole, rear) imagines himself as the reincarnation of a medieval monk. Weber was the leading female director of the time and briefly rivaled D.W. Griffith in her command of the medium.

The ill-fated Audrey Munson succeeded, and in some ways surpassed, Evelyn Nesbit as the Girl of the Moment in early 20th-century New York City. While Nesbit's career is buried in bound volumes of old magazines in library stacks, Munson's legacy is still visible in Manhattan. She graces the fountain opposite the Plaza Hotel and greets visitors to the Metropolitan Museum of Art in the form of *Memory* by sculptor Daniel Chester French. Munson began her career in 1906, the same year that White was shot. There is an indirect association. She was the model for the 24-foot statue, the tallest in New York City, atop the Municipal Building (designed by Mead, McKim & White after White's death) and possibly inspired by the statue of Diana on the tower of White's Madison Square Garden.

For all her visibility in Manhattan, it was the Panama–Pacific International Exposition in San Francisco in 1915 that made Audrey Munson famous. She was the model for Alexander Calder's *Star Maiden*, reproduced in 90 plaster copies. A dozen sculptures for which she had modeled in New York were shipped to the site. She was four allegorical figures: Earth, Wind, Air and Fire. She was also on the poster and the commemorative medal.

Inspiration has been described as the first American film with nudity. *Variety* recalled that, "*Hypocrites* caused some comment with its nude figure flitting here and there in a semi-seeable manner, but in this there is no doubt that one is seeing the real thing."[6]

The five-reel film was made by the Thanhouser Company of New Rochelle, New York, in a former skating rink. Thanhouser, founded in 1909 by Edwin Thanhouser, was known for productions of higher than usual artistic quality. The story: A young sculptor despairs of finding the perfect model, until his friends bring a poverty-stricken young waif to him. She falls for the sculptor as he creates his masterpiece called *Inspiration*. After posing, she disappears but leaves behind a note. After a fruitless search takes the sculptor to actual monuments for which Munson posed, he finds her in a bedraggled heap at the base of the Maine Monument in Columbus Circle. They reunite in marriage. The story wasn't much, but in reel three Munson was nude from the feet up to illustrate the process of casting. At the end, she had cotton in her ears and a breathing tube in her mouth as plaster was applied to her face and the back of her head and a bucket poured over her head. Once the plaster was removed, it was reconstituted into a mold from which the actual sculpture was cast. Audrey's *poses plastique* were shown in conjunction with the famous statues for which she posed. Daniel Chester French's sculpture *Evangeline* dissolved into her nude body.

Thanhouser denied that he intended to create a precedent for nudity on the screen. The purpose was entirely artistic and educational. The National Board of Censorship passed it as it had with *Hypocrites*.

In Los Angeles, *Inspiration* packed a 10,000-seat theater nine shows a day for two weeks. In New Rochelle, where it was made, a committee of clergy persuaded a theater manager not to show the film. In Ossining, New York, the manager of a theater withdrew it under pressure from the Civic League.

Munson's second film, *Purity* (1916), was a much bigger production, seven reels long, made in Santa Barbara, California, by the American Film Company, also known as the "Flying A." *Purity* tells two stories. The first is an allegory set in ancient Greece where Munson is the goddess Virtue. A modern story set in New York has Munson as the fiancée, named Purity Worth, of a struggling poet. They cannot marry because

Audrey Munson, the foremost artist's model of the early 20th century, starred in *Inspiration* (1915). The subject of many of New York City's most prominent public sculptures and multiple works in the collection of the Metropolitan Museum of Art came to a sad fate.

of his poverty, so she secretly poses nude for an artist to get $500 to subsidize the publication of his poetry to great acclaim. When he discovers that Purity posed in the nude, he breaks off their engagement. When the publisher informs him that Purity financed the publication of his book, he is overcome with remorse and begs her forgiveness.

The National Board of Censorship had recently changed its name to the National Board of Review and adopted new guidelines: "All such representations of the NUDE or the practically NUDE will receive in the future the most critical consideration and will only be favorably acted on when extraordinary reasons for the presentation of such figures appear to exist as an essential element of a drama the nature of which requires such presentation."[7]

The Board invited an audience of 38 men and 16 women to a screening in New York City. The group voted 32–20 against approval for general release, but 50–4 in favor of its showing to age-restricted audiences. Prominent artists for whom Munson posed spoke in the film's defense. In the end, the Board decided neither to "pass" nor "deny" the film but to seek state and local reaction. Ten cities banned it altogether. In New York City, the license commissioner demanded about three minutes of cuts. Where it could be shown, initial business was strong, even standing room only. Its opening day surpassed D.W. Griffith's epic *The Birth of a Nation* (1915), but, of course, it didn't have the same "legs."

Purity is the only one of Munson's films that still exists. A copy of the French release print was acquired by a collector of erotica and eventually discovered in the French national archive, Centre National du Cinéma et de l'Image Animée, in 1993. It has had a few showings, including one in 2005 in Santa Barbara where it was made.

After *Purity* was made, Munson flew by "heavier-than-air" craft (piloted by Alan Lockheed) to Catalina Island for *The Girl o' Dreams*. In it, a cad who desires a young convent-raised girl (Munson) persuades her mother that they should all go on a cruise on his yacht. The yacht catches fire and Munson is conveniently washed ashore on a desert island, where a millionaire sculptor disconsolate over the death of his young wife has sought refuge. The trauma of the shipwreck has left Munson with no memory of the event and reduced her to a childlike state. She becomes the model for the sculptor. The sculptor sends a picture of his work to a friend in New York, where it is seen by the cad. The cad travels to the desert island and tries to rape Munson but is thrown off a cliff in the struggle. Miraculously, she regains her memory. The millionaire sculptor nobly sends her back to New York. As he admires his sculpture of her, she appears from behind the form. She did not take the boat, after all, and they are happily united. The film was not registered for copyright until 1918, and appears never to have been released in the U.S.

In 1919, 65-year-old Dr. Walter Wilkins was arrested for the murder of his wife at their estate in Nassau County, Long Island, New York. He had been Audrey Munson's doctor and she lived briefly in a brownstone he owned on West 65th Street in Manhattan. A picture postcard of her was in his possession. Although she was never implicated, the fact that Munson stayed in Canada while her testimony was sought created suspicion. To cash in on the notoriety, *Inspiration* was rereleased as *A Perfect Model*. Wilkins was found guilty and sentenced to die in the electric chair but hanged himself first.

Munson's modeling work dried up. Her association with American Films, already dormant, was terminated. Munson signed in 1919 with William Fox for personal appearances at his theaters in Chicago and Detroit in conjunction with the showing of the film *Purity*. By 1920, the money from that was gone and she was penniless, unable get even cashier or waitress jobs. News stories that described her as "down and out" generated some sympathy, and she made some additional "living picture" appearances in October and November of 1920 accompanied by showings of *Purity* or *A Perfect Model*. An offer for a new movie came along. An ad appeared in the trade press that showed a check for $7,500 made out to Audrey Munson; it notified everyone that Perry Plays, Inc., had secured exclusive rights to "The Story of Audrey Munson."

The release of the film, now entitled *Heedless Moths*, was promoted with a ghostwritten series of articles by the "Queen of the Artist Studios" that appeared in the Hearst newspapers. In the midst of production, an urgent casting call went out and a look-alike named Jane Thomas was hired for the story scenes. Both shared billing as "Audrey Munson." One review stated that Munson was "posed in a few brief scenes undraped but only in the dim distance." Another reviewer noted the "aphrodite depressions on either side of the base of her spinal column," for which Munson was famous, to prove that it was really she in the film. Munson sued the producers who, in reply, claimed that she hadn't shown up for work.

In the film, "Audrey Munson" is hired by a dilettantish Greenwich Village painter to pose but runs away to escape what the ad copy called "the distressing tragedies of the pretty models who lacked moral balance to safeguard them from the intimate atmosphere of the studios." A kindly old artist, "The Spirit of the Arch," finds her wandering in a storm and introduces her to a young sculptor; she poses nude for his masterpiece *Body and Soul*. The sculptor's jealous wife takes up with a libertine painter. "Audrey" goes to the painter's studio herself so that the sculptor discovers her and not his errant wife. Disillusioned, he destroys his work. The selfless "Audrey" reconciles the sculptor and his wife. Her noble act of self-sacrifice so inspires the libertine that he reforms and marries his former mistress. No one took credit for the screenplay.

Heedless Moths was lambasted by the critics. Munson's last film was especially savaged by *Photoplay*, not yet the fan magazine it later became but then an important arbiter of taste:

> "Heedless Moths" despite whatever claim it may make as a story or dramatic photoplay, is a bold bid to indecency. Produced by Perry Photoplays, it is the characteristic exhibition of certain new producers who bring nothing into the field but an insincere vehicle to make a little tainted money. Its star is Audrey Munson, who may or may not be remembered in an undraped celluloid demonstration satirically called "Purity," "Heedless Moths" had to have a story and this one is laid in Greenwich Village, that over-rated and so-called artistic quarter of New York City. It is not an interesting story. It is a tiresome play. And let us hasten to add, in order that no craven pulse may quicken with anticipation, it does not even purvey the prurient thrill which is its thinly-veiled pretense. No one knew better than its producers that downright uncleanliness could not be shown at all. So all that we have left is mock sentimentality, lachrymose titling, a considerable extent of unnecessary and unstimulating epidermis, and—boredom. Don't patronize it, for it is not worth your attention from any angle. If you do patronize it, you are adding fuel to the intolerant flame of censorship.

As the Fatty Arbuckle scandal (q.v.) was still in the future when *Heedless Moths* debuted in June 1921, that last reference was probably to the "Lusk bill" that established censorship in New York State despite the efforts of theater owners to stop it.

Munson continued to tour and make personal appearances, at the end of which she would disrobe with her back to the audience. In St. Louis in October 1921, she was arrested on a morals charge; she demanded a jury trial and was acquitted in 27 minutes. The movie on the program was called *Innocence*. This was most likely *Purity* under a different title, as there is no record of any film by that name. A newspaper ad in Duluth, Minnesota, in 1922 announced her appearance in conjunction with *Innocence*.

The rest of the Munson story is quite sad. She attempted suicide in 1922 and in 1931 was committed to an asylum where she spent the next 65 years. When her death at the age of 104 was announced in 1996, few people knew that she had been alive all along.

Australian swimmer-turned-vaudeville-performer Annette Kellerman made headlines in 1907 when she was arrested at Boston's Revere Beach over a formfitting one-piece bathing suit of her own design. Her career got a boost when Harvard professor Dr. Dudley Allen Sargent, director of the Hemenway University Gymnasium, undertook a study of the figure of "the modern woman," completed in 1910. He studied the proportions of 10,000 female students from women's colleges such as Mt. Holyoke,

Smith, Wellesley and Bryn Mawr and the coeducational Oberlin and Swarthmore over the previous 20 years, apparently to address fears that physical exercise was making women more masculine. He declared that any changes had been for the better: "The American woman of today is becoming more like the Greek ideal of the beautiful. She substitutes harmonious curves and symmetry for exaggeration of the distinctly feminine characteristics." Having seen Kellerman perform, he invited her to Harvard to be measured. While he acknowledged that no one person could meet the ideal, he declared Kellerman was "nearest to the perfectly proportioned woman." The ad for *Neptune's Daughter* (1914) slightly distorted this to bill her as "The Perfect Woman" with "measurements that almost surpass belief," and compared Kellerman's measurements in 12

Swimmer Annette Kellerman was nude in *A Daughter of Gods*. The ads (facing page) compared her measurements to Cleopatra and the Venus de Milo. She was known as "The Perfect Woman."

categories to those of the Venus de Milo and an unspecified version of Diana. Both were 5'4" tall. Kellerman's chest, waist and hip measurements were 33.1-26.2-37.5 against Venus at 33-26-35. That her weight was measured by Dr. Sargent as 134 pounds was not mentioned in the ad. (Kellerman had been billed as "The Diving Venus" as far back as 1908.)

Largely because of its prominent position in The Louvre, the Venus de Milo came to represent the classical ideal against which women were measured. In reality, the statue is not from the classical period at all but from about 130 B.C. and may not even represent Venus but some local deity.

The first and greatest life-size female nude of antiquity was the *Aphrodite of Knidos*, created by Praxiteles (c. 330 B.C.). Greek sculptors had long depicted the idealized

male physiques of athletes or warriors in the nude. Because of the near-exclusion of women from public life, there were no female subjects other than goddesses. Perhaps also because of the reluctance of female models to pose nude, women had always been draped. The model for the *Aphrodite of Knidos* was Phryne, a famous courtesan and the artist's mistress. Legend has it that she was put on trial, but her lawyer had her shed her clothes to show that the gods would not have made a woman with such beautiful breasts if they had wanted her punished. (Artist William de Leftwich Dodge portrayed Audrey Munson as Phryne for a mural in a Fifth Avenue ballroom.)

The classicist Mary Beard cites an account from 300 A.D. that claimed a little mark in the marble on the statue's inner thigh near her buttocks was actually a semen stain left by a young man who copulated with the statue, went mad and jumped off a cliff. For Beard, the work "established that edgy relationship between the statue of a woman and a presumed male viewer that has never been lost from the memory of European art."[8]

If Annette Kellerman embodied a classical ideal, she was also thoroughly modern. One writer compared her sleek physique to the 20th Century Limited, the express train between New York and Chicago.

Neptune's Daughter contained a seeming nude scene actually accomplished with a "fleshling," or flesh-colored body stocking, as the mermaid shed her tail for a dive. This is one of the few scenes of the film that survives.

Kellerman's next film, *A Daughter of the Gods* (1916), is one of the most sought-after "lost films." It had actual nudity in addition to a body stocking. "Audrey Munson exhibited in the short-lived *Purity* has nothing on Miss Kellerman and, as it has been observed elsewhere, neither has Miss Kellerman," wrote *The New York Times* reviewer.

Kellerman may have been the indirect inspiration for Mack Sennett's Bathing Beauties. In the 1912 half-reel *A Water Nymph*, Sennett had his costar Mabel Normand emerge from the bathhouse "where ladies dress in straitjackets popularly called 'bathing suits.'" In a formfitting suit similar to the one that got Kellerman taken to court, Mabel performs a couple of dives. Sennett's own account says that he got the idea of the Bathing Beauties in 1914 from a newspaper story of a woman involved in car accident. There was three-column-wide photography of the young woman with her knees exposed. Sennett called in his staff: "Boys take a look at this. This is how to get our pictures in the papers. Go hire some girls, any girls, so long as they're pretty, especially around the knees. Sure, I know they can't act, but they don't have to act. Put them in bathing suits and just have them around to be looked at while the comics are making funny."

The assumption was that comics would be male. Sennett's first star, Mabel Normand, was pretty enough to have been a Gibson Girl, but could throw a custard pie or take one in the face. The two roles diverged. Sennett comedians not only did funny things, they were funny-looking; so were the women, fat Marie Dressler or homely Louise Fazenda. Attractive women became eye candy—not just the Bathing Beauties, usually shown in a group of 10, but the female leads. In *A Bedroom Blunder*, a pretty newlywed (Mary Thurman), described in the film's publicity as "the chief wigglette of Wigglesville," wiggles her bottom as she adjusts her bathing suit to give hotel clerk Ben Turpin good reason to do his trademark cross-eyed stare. She also inspires adulterous thoughts in a middle-aged man staying at a beachfront hotel with his hefty wife. Despite her looks, Thurman is not exempt from being knocked about and is folded up in a Murphy bed. In an earlier scene, the married man looks longingly out the window of the hotel to see a group of attractive women playing with a beach ball. When his wife exhibits her ample rump in the open window, one of the girls aims the ball at the inviting target. Male and female posteriors in Sennett films were slapped, kicked, even bitten by geese.

Such vulgarity caught the attention of the Chicago Police Board of Censors, then under the leadership of the imposingly named Metellus Lucullus Cicero Funkhouser. The Board demanded cuts in 57 Sennett films made between 1914 and 1916. *Tillie's Punctured Romance* (1914) alone inspired 28 demands for cuts:

> All scenes of men kicking women and vice versa; all scenes of woman bumping into men and women; two sets of men wiggling back in vulgar manner; man poking girl with cane in vulgar manner; man lifting tail of girl's coat in vulgar manner; woman lifting her dress to above knees, man lifting woman's dress above knees; girl falling over couch and exposing her legs; woman doing wiggle dance; man kicking woman in the abdomen.

Sennett relished the complaints. "The sight of the most curvaceous girls I could get caused a riot," he recalled. "Women's clubs, reformers and the police gave us a million bucks worth of publicity." *Hula Hula Land* (1917) provoked outraged letters but also ticket sales.

Curiously, there was more nudity on the screen in the "innocent" years of the teens than in the supposedly "roaring" Twenties. There were not as many state and local censor boards. With the decline of the Motion Picture Patents Company and the rising demand for feature-length films, entry into the industry was relatively easy, with some 40 to 60 companies active in the 1914–18 period. Directors enjoyed more autonomy than they would after the reconcentration of the industry after the First World War and the emergence of the "studio system" turned them into employees. Late Victorian academic artistic ideals, rooted in admiration of classical Greek and Roman sculpture, had not yet been displaced by the modernist *avant-garde.* There would be no industry-wide guidelines for content until 1921.

More controversial than the films with nudity was the "white slave" cycle. The foundation was *Traffic in Souls* (1913), one of the earliest American features. The film is somewhat confusing due to the lack of exposition. A wealthy and socially ambitious man, Trubus, becomes head of the International League for Purity and Reform. His office is on a different floor of the same building as the headquarters of a prostitution ring. What no one knows is that he is secretly involved himself. The two offices are connected by a Dictograph listening device that allows him to monitor the business.

The vice ring tries to recruit immigrant girls. Two Swedish girls are met by their brother at Ellis Island. An agent of the ring provokes a fight that results in the brother's arrest. He takes the girls to a "Swedish Employment Agency" that is actually a brothel. An honest cop rescues the girls, but the brothel is not shut down. The cop is the boyfriend of a young woman who works with her somewhat lazy and flighty sister in a candy store. The vice ring kidnaps the sister and takes her to the brothel, where she is threatened with a whip. The cop's girlfriend is fired from her job—rather unjustly—and manages to get another job as the secretary to Trubus. She makes use of the office's state-of-the-art 1913 technology and connects the intercom to a Dictaphone to make cylinder recordings of conversations that can be used as evidence. She, her boyfriend and a squad of police raid the brothel and free the sister. In a scene that would be repeated many times in the future, there is a gun battle that turns into a rooftop chase.

Trubus is arrested but freed on bail. His wife dies of shame; his daughter, due to be married, repudiates him and he commits suicide.

The interior sets are artificial and cheap-looking. The real shots of Ellis Island, the newly opened Pennsylvania Station and New York City streets filled with streetcars come as a relief. *Traffic in Souls* was not the first feature produced by Universal Pictures, formed in 1912, but it put the company on the map.

The Inside of the White Slave Traffic (1913) was the first of many imitators and an improvement on the original. The sets were better and there was extensive location work. A young woman, Annie, works as a sewing machine operator. She is enticed into a sham marriage to a man who abandons her to the care of his "friends." The friends send Annie to a brothel in New Orleans, where she is treated like a slave. She escapes to Denver but discovers that the syndicate controls prostitution everywhere and she cannot work independently. She pawns her wedding ring and travels to Houston but cannot work there either. A novel feature of the film is an on-screen glossary of underworld argot, e.g., a girl is a "Gillette blade." There is a subplot with an immigrant girl lured into prostitution.

Annie spends her last dollar on a night's lodging. She returns to New Orleans and works again for the syndicate. Annie solicits a man on the street and is arrested. There is, as the title says, "one law for the man, another for the woman." Upon release from prison, she gets a job as a shopgirl, but her pay is so little that she goes back to prostitution. In a fantasy, she imagines the happy life she might have had with a son and the approval of her parents. Annie dies, possibly a suicide, and is buried in a numbered grave in a crowded Potter's Field.

The film was produced under the banner of the Moral Feature Film Company by Samuel London, who had been head of the U.S. Secret Service and research director for the Rockefeller Commission that investigated vice in New York City. It carried endorsements from 12 prominent reformers. In spite of all this and the fact that the film did turn away business, New York City shut the film down. It never played in Chicago at all. The controversy was due entirely to the subject matter. There was no sex in the movie. As with *Traffic in Souls*, any interaction between the prostitute and her clients was kept off-screen.

Lois Weber made a high-minded contribution to the white slave cycle with *Shoes* in June 1916. Based on a *Collier's* magazine story in turn derived from a paragraph in a book by reformer Jane Addams, it told the story of a shopgirl who spends all day on her feet selling things but cannot buy a decent pair of shoes for herself. Her salary of five dollars a week must support her whole ungrateful family while a new pair of shoes costs three dollars. In the end, her lazy father gets a job and buys her a pair of shoes but not before she sells her virtue. Weber, once again, was ahead of her time visually. The camera concentrates on the girl's feet and follows as she walks the rain-soaked sidewalk in her shabby shoes, the sort of camera movement one would expect to find in a German film of the 1920s.

The white slave cycle received a blow when the New York City Commissioner of Licenses threatened to pull the license of the Maxine Elliott's Theatre over the showing of *Is Any Girl Safe?* in September 1916. The producers, the Anti-Vice Film Company, portrayed the film as a cautionary tale. Clergy were not convinced and denounced the film as exploitation. In December, the National Board declared that, "No picture hereafter will be passed by the National Board of Review which is wholly concerned with the commercialized theme of 'White Slavery' or is so advertised as to give the impression that it is a lurid 'White Slave' picture."

The prostitution, street crime and labor strife of early 20th-century America are all present in the "modern" story of D.W. Griffith's four-part epic *Intolerance: Love's Struggle Throughout the Ages* (1916). Jenkins, a mill owner, is alarmed when an employee dance goes past 10 p.m. They should know that they have to work the next day. He listens to the demands of his old maid sister who wants him to finance her "reform" movement. The bars and dance halls are closed down. A police raid on a brothel is preceded by a line that bears the claw marks of Anita Loos, hired by Griffith as title-writer: "When women cease to attract men they often turn to Reform as a second choice." Jenkins spends so much money on reform that his profits drop. The industrialist orders a 10 percent cut in wages. This provokes a strike that is quickly crushed by the militia. The striking workers are replaced by strikebreakers.

Several of those displaced by the strike find their way to a nearby city where their lives become entwined. The Friendless One (Miriam Cooper) becomes a prostitute for the "Musketeer of the Slums." There's a voluptuous nude statue in the Musketeer's office and prints of fleshy women on the wall. (This reflected the touch of Erich von Stroheim, employed by Griffith as a bit actor and jack-of-all-trades, according to Stroheim expert

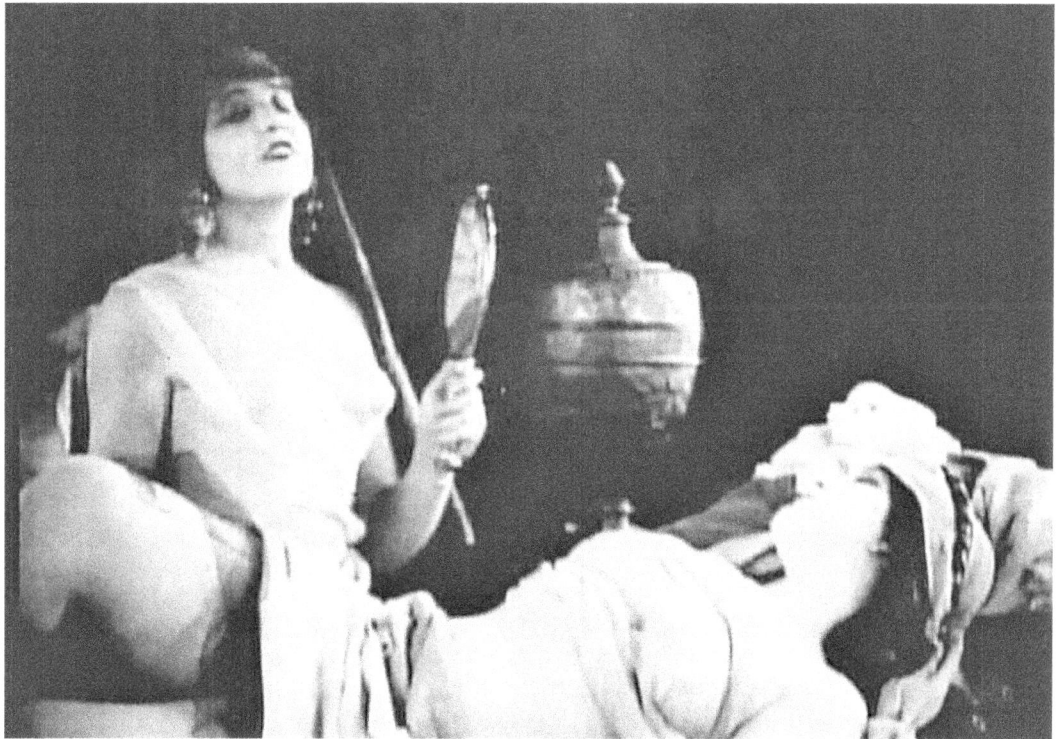

The Temple virgins in the Babylonian sequence in D.W. Griffith's *Intolerance* included at least one nude.

Richard Koszarski. It was a foretaste of Stroheim's own films.) The Musketeer makes a thief out of The Boy (Robert Harron), whose father died in the strike. The Little Dear One (Mae Marsh) naively emulates the saucy carriage of streetwalkers to become popular with men. She attracts the attention of The Boy, but her father warns her never to bring a man into the house. Her father dies. After a date, The Boy tries to follow her inside. She closes the door, looks Heavenward and implores, "Help me to be a strong-jawed Jane." She and The Boy are married, but after a flawed trial he is convicted of murder and her baby is taken from her.

In the Babylonian sequence of *Intolerance*, Griffith serves up some risqué material. A title reads, "In the Love Temple, Virgins of the sacred fires of Life." The scantily clad women don't look very virginal, more like French postcards. One is nude.

Intolerance aside, nudity in movies of the teens did not attempt to incite lust. It was allegorical in *Hypocrites*, associated with athleticism and nature in *Daughter of the Gods* and with art in the Audrey Munson pictures. Canadian actress Nell Shipman swam nude in *Back to God's Country* (1919), but it was just a body stocking. An ad for the movie with a line drawing of Shipman nude asked, "Is the Nude Rude?" and answered in the negative, "But in this picture, the nude is artistic and art is not rude." (They were presumably unaware that Marcel Duchamp had presented a urinal as sculpture in 1917.) In a Lon Chaney vehicle, *The Penalty* (1920), a female sculptress works with a nude model that steps down from the podium and hides when a male visitor comes to the studio.

In February 1921, Adolph Zukor, president of Paramount Famous Players-Lasky

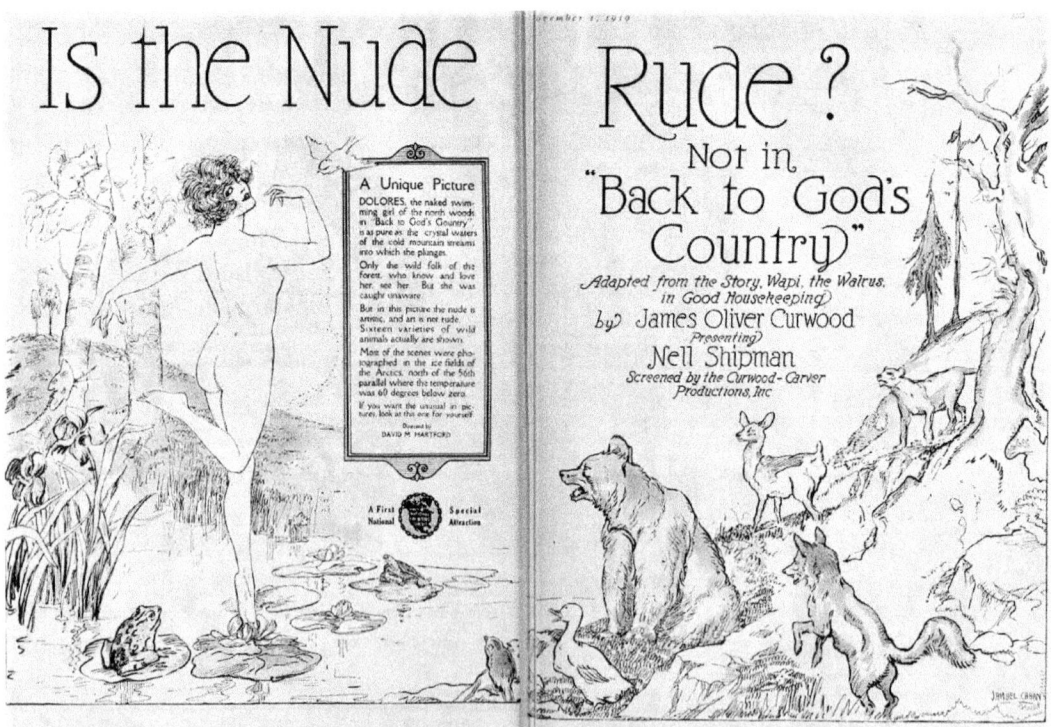

The ad for *Back to God's Country*, a Canadian production distributed by First National, asked "Is the Nude Rude?" and answered in the negative.

Corporation, by then the industry leader, convened a meeting of fellow movie moguls in New York. Possibly with President Wilson's statement of war aims in mind, they came up with their own Fourteen Points:

1. No sex attraction in a suggestive or improper manner.
2. No white slavery pictures. These were justifiable only when that evil was present.
3. No stories with illicit love affairs as a theme unless they convey a moral lesson.
4. Nakedness is banned, except for long shots of small children.
5. No inciting dances, no close-ups of stomach dancing.
6. No unnecessarily prolonged passionate love scenes. No "manhandling."
7. No stories predominantly concerned with crime unless part of the essential conflict between good and evil.
8. No drunkenness or gambling should be made attractive.
9. No pictures which instruct morally feeble in crime-committing methods.
10. No needless religious offenses.
11. No disrespect for religion.
12. Suggestive comedy business eliminated, including winks, gestures, postures.
13. No unnecessary bloodshed, close-ups of bloody faces or wounds.
14. No salacious stills, titles and ads.

NAMPI embraced a slightly different version of the guidelines in March 1921. Zukor had wanted the guidelines to remain a trade secret, but his partner, Jesse L. Lasky, leaked them to the press in an effort to preempt demands for censorship. Once the guidelines were made public, the industry found, somewhat to its surprise, that it was actually expected to live up to them.

In 1919, there were some 3,000 strikes involving four million workers. After the hyper-patriotism of the First World War, the Bolshevik Revolution and a wave of bombings blamed on anarchists, sympathy for striking workers belonged to another era. Griffith's *Orphans of the Storm* (1921) tells the story of "two little orphans who suffer first through the tyranny—selfishness of Kingly bosses, nobles and aristocrats." This is the old Griffith who identifies with the downtrodden (and shows the decadence of aristocracy with seminude women bathing in fountains). He hastens to add: "The French Revolution RIGHTLY overthrew a BAD Government but we in America should be careful lest we with a GOOD government mistake fanatics for leaders and exchange our decent law and order for Anarchy and Bolshevism."

There was a brief cycle of antiradical films in 1919–20 that included such titles as *Bolshevism on Trial* (1919). Bolshevism terrified the American middle class, not just because of the threat to private property, but because political radicalism was associated with sexual radicalism. In *Dangerous Hours* (1919), a recent college graduate comes under the influence of a foreign-born female radical, "a rebel against every convention and law that civilization has found necessary." In the end, he comes to his senses and marries the 100 percent American daughter of an industrialist.

The Labor Film Service, established by a consortium of New York unions allied with the Socialist Party in 1920, set out to fight the absorption of the motion-picture medium by "moneyed interests and reactionary forces." It proposed to fight for labor with "news reels, pictorials, travelogues, and scenics that depicted the worker's life in the mines, in the slums, on farm, railroads, the picket lines, etc." Its one feature, *The Contrast* (1921), dramatized a mine strike in West Virginia where railroad workers supported the strikers. The "contrast" was between the hedonistic lives of the mine owners and the poor; a starving girl steals food a dog has rejected. Trade papers advised theater owners not to show it in order not to alienate middle-class patrons. The depression of 1921 produced a new round of wage cuts and more strikes. Even the movie industry saw cutbacks in studio personnel.

Both pro- and anti-labor films faded after 1922 with the formation of the Hays Office and its desire to avoid controversy. The "social" film gave way to the "society" film.

2

Why Be Good?

Flappers, Flaming Youth and an "It" Girl

Women got the vote nationally in 1920—they had already had it in 12 states—and used it to cast ballots for Warren G. Harding in roughly the same percentage as men. With its immediate objective achieved, the feminist movement went into eclipse, divided between those who wanted equality in everything and those who believed that women needed special protection in the laws. Younger women were not much drawn to these debates. Their main concern was to make themselves attractive to men. Even if they had to share their employment earnings with their parents or pay board, they had enough left over to spend on clothes and cosmetics. That the causes and crusades of the Wilson era no longer excited the young was evidenced by a 1920 editorial in the *Cornell Sun*: "The American public is weary of persons who seek to better the world… and sometimes wish that among all the efforts at uplift and betterment, some comfortable souls would get together and organize a society of down-pullers to even things up a little."[1]

War in the short term inspires a reaffirmation of traditional values. Flags fly. Ministers of religion beseech God for victory. Longer term, the impact is ambiguous. Marriages are disrupted, venereal disease spreads. As casualties mount, disillusionment sets in and official pronouncements are met with cynicism. America's involvement in the First World War was comparatively brief, so the war did not have the same impact as it did in Europe. Nevertheless, the war did change movies, seen most visibly in the turn taken by the career of Cecil B. DeMille. DeMille's own tastes had run to historical, religious and patriotic subjects. He contributed to the war effort with the propagandistic *The Little American* (1917) that pitted Mary Pickford against sadistic Germans.

Paramount's New York office demanded contemporary material in touch with modern attitudes that would showcase luxurious settings and fashionable clothes. In DeMille's *Old Wives for New* (1918), a middle-aged but still vital businessman leaves a fat wife who eats candy while reading magazines. This was followed by *Don't Change Your Husband* (1919) and *Why Change Your Wife?* (1920). In these, marriages are rescued from threatened adultery when the husband, too involved with business, or the wife, obsessed with social climbing, changes to satisfy their spouse's needs. It is probably no coincidence that Theda Bara declined as DeMille flourished. In DeMille's films, the erotic was no longer a threat but a necessary component of marriage.

In 1919, DeMille made *Male and Female*, the most commercial title to that time or, possibly, ever. It was based on James M. Barrie's play *The Admirable Crichton*. Jesse L. Lasky worried that the public would pronounce the title as *The Admiral Crichton* at a time when the abrupt end of the World War made military subjects a drug on the market. Barrie agreed to the change and expressed regret that he had not thought of it himself.

Crichton (Thomas Meighan) is the indispensable butler to Lord Loam. He heads a household staff that attends to every need of the Lord's family, who is incapable of doing anything for itself.

At a time when many American households lacked indoor plumbing, DeMille concocted a scene in which the Lord's eldest daughter, Gloria Swanson, had her servants draw a bath that she took in a sunken tub filled with rose water heated to 90 degrees.

In the Lord's library, Crichton opens a book of poems by William Ernest Henley and reads aloud the line, "I was a King in Babylon and you were a Christian slave." Crichton harbors a secret desire for Swanson, but she tells a friend who has fallen in love with her chauffeur that the classes can no more mix than can species of birds.

The family takes their yacht on a cruise to the tropics. The boat hits a rock and takes on water. When they take refuge on an island, class distinctions start to erode. At first, the family resists Crichton's assertion of leadership, but he is able to make a shelter, start a fire and feed himself as they shiver and starve. A title tells us that Crichton no longer regards Swanson as a great lady but just a woman. She comes around. When she is menaced by a leopard, he kills it with a bow and arrow. This initiates a flashback to ancient Babylon that owes a lot to *Intolerance*.

As the King, Meighan and his sexy consort wear costumes that recall those of Belshazzar and the Princess Beloved, while Swanson's performance as a feisty Christian slave recalls Constance Talmadge as the rambunctious Mountain Girl in the Griffith film. The slave girl is given a makeover and a choice: yield to the King or be fed to the lions. She chooses martyrdom. The actual mauling takes place off-screen, to which the King and his consort are seen to react. The lion hovers over Swanson's prone body. DeMille shot the scene, gun in hand, while the terrified actress felt the lion's paws on her bare back and its hot breath on her neck. She was promised a tame lion, but two weeks later the lion nearly killed somebody. (Babylon had ceased to be important well before the Christian era, so the poet's imagined meeting of King and slave girl would not have happened.)

Crichton builds a signal fire and the group is rescued. Back in England, class distinctions reassert themselves. Swanson is ready to give it all up for Crichton, but he announces his marriage to the scullery maid. They move to America and start a new life.

DeMille's main rival in letting viewers into the lives of the rich was Erich von Stroheim. In *Foolish Wives* (1922), he created a plum role for himself as Count Karamzin, an exiled Russian aristocrat who wears a monocle, clicks his heels and eats caviar for breakfast, clad in a silk dressing down. The Count lives in a rented villa in Monte Carlo with two "cousins," one of whom may be his mistress, and who go by the title "Princess" or "Her Highness." They are all frauds and live off of gambling winnings made possible by the counterfeit money they get from an Italian engraver.

Karamzin is an inveterate seducer. He even eyes the retarded daughter of the engraver. When he reads in the newspaper that a new American envoy is to come to Monaco, he makes plans to ingratiate himself with the man and his wife. He cannot help himself and immediately tries to seduce the envoy's wife.

In a touch that would now be called "meta," Karamzin hands the woman a book titled *Foolish Wives* "by Erich von Stroheim" and points out a passage: "To the average

American, written and unwritten codes of honor and etiquette are unessential as, in his tiresome chase after the dollar, he has no time to cultivate that for which the European mainly lives." The passage is ironic. It is Karamzin who cares only for money and his code of honor is bogus.

Universal turned Stroheim's extravagance to its advantage with ads that enumerated the ever-mounting production costs that eventually reached over a million dollars—the most expensive picture in the company's history. The biggest expense was for the set of Monte Carlo built at Universal City, California, so large and detailed that it could have passed for the real place.

The reviewer for *Motion Picture Classic* wrote, "Von Stroheim has taken the one real theme of life—sex—and ... looks upon it with the worldly and half cynical, half humorous Viennese viewpoint of a Schnitzler." The review lamented that Stroheim had not filmed *The Affairs of Anatol* (1921) from the Schnitzler play that DeMille Americanized and sanitized beyond recognition.

Photoplay, however, denounced *Foolish Wives* as "a photoplay that is unfit for the family to see, that is an insult to American ideals and womanhood" and complained of "sly little thrusts at our traditions and sentiments."

The two reviews reflected Americans' contradictory attitudes toward the outside world. A cosmopolitan aspiration to Continental sophistication coexisted with nativism of the crudest kind. A favorable exchange rate (25 francs to the dollar) and the absence of Prohibition lured Americans to Paris. At home, the resurgent Ku Klux Klan defined American identity as white, Anglo-Saxon, Protestant and native-born. Millions of women swooned over the Italian-born Rudolph Valentino even as legislation moved through Congress to cut off immigration from Southern and Eastern Europe. The Hollywood branch of the American Legion protested Germany's *The Cabinet of Dr. Caligari*, imported by Samuel Goldwyn, for "foreignness." *Caligari* was also blamed for taking film-industry jobs that should go to Americans.

A major scandal rocked Hollywood in September 1921 when a woman named Virginia Rappe died during a wild party in San Francisco where comedian Fatty Arbuckle was present. Although Arbuckle was acquitted in all three trials in which he was a defendant and even got an apology from the last jury, Hollywood was portrayed as "Sodom by the Sea" and Arbuckle's career was ruined. There were rumors that the popular star Wallace Reid, a fine specimen of American manhood who resembled a real-life Arrow Collar ad, was addicted to drugs. (The rumors were true. Reid had been given morphine after an injury on location and was given more to keep him going through seven films in 1921 and eight in 1922 before he checked himself into a sanitarium.)

A group such as NAMPI, composed only of industry insiders, did not have the credibility to clean house. After the Black Sox scandal of 1919, Judge Kenesaw Mountain Landis was made Commissioner of Major League Baseball. Perhaps a "czar" was needed to oversee the movie industry. The idea to approach Will H. Hays appears to have originated with Lewis J. Selznick, father of producer David O. Selznick and an important producer of the day himself. Hays had managed Warren G. Harding's campaign in 1920 and was appointed Postmaster General. He brought influence in Washington and was an elder in the Presbyterian Church, no small asset in an era when the movies were seen as a "Jewish" business.

A new organization, the Motion Picture Producers and Distributors of America, was formed with Hays as president in January 1922. One of Hays's first acts was to direct that all Arbuckle films be withdrawn from circulation and destroyed. As this was clearly unjust, he backed down. Hays had to contend with a new scandal, the murder of director William Desmond Taylor in March 1922 (probably by the mother of actress Mary Miles Minter, although the case is officially unsolved).

Hays had to navigate between the producers who paid his $100,000 salary, enormous for the time, and who wanted a free hand in the selection of material, and the churches, women's clubs and civic groups that had to be placated. Hays's main goal was to stop the creation of any new censor boards. Canon Chase led a renewed effort to have the U.S. Congress pass legislation that would establish a Federal Commission on Motion Pictures. (He claimed that his goal was "regulation, not censorship.") He would try again with Congressional hearings in 1923, 1926, 1929 and 1934. New York had established a censor board in 1921. With Hays new in his position, Virginia established what turned out to be last state censor board in 1922. (The Virginia board was part of a broader effort at purification that included a strict anti-miscegenation law and the sterilization of mental defectives. It was especially concerned that the races not mix as equals and that black characters be seen only as menials, clowns or criminals.)

Massachusetts was the only state to put the creation of a censor board to a popular vote. It was voted down in 1922 by a more than two-to-one margin. Hays's adroit political maneuvers could claim some credit, but the outcome also confirmed the contention of Pare Lorentz and Morris L. Ernst in their 1930 book *Censored: The Private Life of the Movie* that demands for censorship never emanated from aggrieved moviegoers but from pressure groups and their political allies.

In 1919, Paramount became the first motion-picture company to be listed on the New York Stock Exchange. A stock issued by Kuhn, Loeb & Co. enabled Paramount to build and buy a chain of theaters that eventually grew to nearly 1,500. The main studio on Melrose Avenue in Hollywood, with its famous monumental gate, and a second one in Astoria, New York, turned out a combined total of over a hundred features a year. Its distribution arm divided the nation into five regions with branch offices in the major cities of each. It was, to paraphrase Gilbert and Sullivan, the very model of a modern major studio. Its dominance was such that its business practices drew scrutiny from the Federal Trade Commission.

Paramount hit the trifecta of Hollywood scandals. They had released the films of Arbuckle and Desmond Taylor. Wallace Reid was a contract star and the lead in DeMille's *The Affairs of Anatol*. It was in this climate that DeMille, the company's top director, responded with the moralistic melodrama *Manslaughter* (1922). A district attorney (Thomas Meighan, again) is in love with a spoiled, thrill-seeking society girl (Leatrice Joy). A lawn party with young women prancing on pogo sticks reminds him of the debauchery that led to the downfall of the Roman Empire. Joy, previously warned about speeding, drives her roadster so recklessly that she causes the death of a motorcycle cop. Meighan does his duty and prosecutes her. His summation to the jury invokes the decadence of Ancient Rome. In a flashback, we see revelers exhausted from a drunken orgy. Meighan and Joy appear in costume. Meighan is the conqueror that exhorts his followers to "Loot, Plunder and Kill!" Joy is the deposed queen he drags along the floor. His men carry women, kicking and screaming, off to be raped. The defense counsel objects, quite rightly, that this is all irrelevant.

Joy is convicted. In prison, she reforms and resolves to do only good upon release. Meighan turns to drink, loses his job and falls on hard times. When he turns up among the homeless men fed by her charity on New Year's Eve, Joy makes it her project to rehabilitate him so that he can run successfully for governor. It was all hokum and DeMille knew it. He told Leatrice Joy, "I want you to be a lady in this, but I don't want you to be a *real* lady, I want you to be what a housemaid *thinks* a lady is."

Manslaughter is not a good film, but it was notable as the one in which DeMille showed his ability to have it both ways—to make the decadence of the pre–Christian era exciting, but also something fit to condemn—that would serve him well in the future. It was also the point where critical and popular views of DeMille sharply diverged. Critics mocked the mechanical acting and the absurd theatricality that DeMille passed off as spectacle. The public ate it up and there were lines even at matinees.

Comedy was less central to the moviegoing experience of the 1920s than might be surmised from later compilations, such as Robert Youngson's 1961 *Days of Thrills and Laughter*. As theaters got more elaborate with thousands of seats, symphonic orchestras and atmospheric décor, they demanded larger-than-life characters of the sort played by Douglas Fairbanks and John Barrymore to go with them.

In their classic 1927 *Middletown*, a study of a midsize industrial city (Muncie, Indiana), sociologists Robert and Helen Lynd found nine movie theaters. "Society" films were popular, but Middletown wanted more comedies than the industry would provide.

What comedy meant to audiences in the 1920s was captured in King Vidor's 1928 *Show People*. A preview audience is bored by an elaborate costume drama, Vidor's own *Bardelys the Magnificent* (1926). One audience member (Vidor himself) is actually asleep. As a two-reel comedy comes on, the audience becomes awake and engaged. Just as *Show People*'s female lead Peggy Pepper (Marion Davies) became Patricia Pepoire to erase her background in two-reel comedies, the bigger studios developed a snobbish disregard for slapstick. They were willing to leave comedy to low-budget producers such as Hal Roach, who had displaced Mack Sennett as the leading supplier of two-reelers.

The true comic geniuses were too individualistic to fit into the factory system. After *The Kid* (1921), Charlie Chaplin made only two more shorts. *The Gold Rush* (1925) and *The Circus* (1928) each took three years to make. Buster Keaton was more prolific, with an average of two features per year between 1923 and 1928, but was a little too dour and ironic. He is more appreciated today than he was in his own time. Harold Lloyd, the go-getter always ready to shake hands and introduce himself, was Middletown's great favorite.

Amory Blaine, the protagonist of F. Scott Fitzgerald's 1920 *This Side of Paradise*, witnessed the petting parties and automobile romances unthinkable before the War and declared, "the cities between New York and Chicago as one vast juvenile intrigue."

There was actually a movie called *The Flapper* (1920). It offered little of what we think of as the flapper era. The title character is only 16, although she pretends to be older. She has a full head of hair instead of the helmetlike bob and spends much of the film in the middy blouse uniform of a boarding school. Only in one scene in an expensive restaurant does she wear the headband and beaded dress we associate with the flapper era. The movie is interesting primarily for its scenes of 1920 New York City as seen from an open-air Fifth Avenue bus. It was also one of the last appearances of its young star, Olive Thomas, whose death under disputed circumstances was the first of several scandals that brought unwelcome attention to the movie industry.

Notwithstanding the 1920 film, Colleen Moore claimed that it was with her film *Flaming Youth* (1923) that a new word entered the American vocabulary—"flapper."

Flaming Youth was based on a popular novel by "Warner Fabian," a pseudonym for Samuel Hopkins Adams. Colleen Moore campaigned for the role of Patricia over the objections of the First National executives who thought she was wrong for the part. (She got it as a wedding present when she married the producer.) For the role, Moore cut her hair Japanese style with bangs.[2]

Moore in her autobiography wrote, "College girls everywhere cut their hair in Dutch bobs. They copied my clothes. No longer did a girl have to be beautiful to be sought after. Any Plain Jane could become a flapper."[3]

Flaming Youth was not as wild as the title and its ad campaign suggested. To inaugurate a new swimming pool at their residence, a wealthy couple throws a party. A hired hula dancer is carried off by a man who walks fully dressed through the pool and emerges dipping wet. Colleen Moore tells her married date, "Don't be alarmed if I go all smash on your hands. I'm not responsible when I'm listening to wonderful music." When the pool is lighted, people strip down to their underwear.

Music historian David Hajdu claims that the Charleston craze of the 1920s from the song of the same name by James P. Johnson brought "angular limb-twisting movements derived from the African-American juba dances of the slave period," and he quotes the *New York Herald Tribune* in 1925: "Unless it is suppressed or modified, it may be a great force toward the impairment of collegiate morals."[4]

Flaming Youth, *Black Oxen* and *Three Weeks* all caused Hays to come under criticism. The problem was not the movies themselves, which were bland, but that they were based on mildly notorious novels. Hays responded with the creation of "The Formula," which required that plays and books be vetted by his office before production. This was followed by the "Do's, Don'ts, and Be Carefuls" of 1927.

The Lynds found that what Middletown wanted was "Heart Interest" or, in other words, sex appeal. The recently formed Warner Bros. took the unusual step of giving theater owners a choice of titles for the same picture in 1923. They could run it as *Lucretia Lombard*, the title of the Kathleen Norris novel on which it was based, or as *Flaming Passion*. (There really wasn't that much passion, but there was a forest fire for the climax.) *Lucretia Lombard* flopped; *Flaming Passion* did business.[5]

The recession of the early 1920s was sharp but brief. By 1923, the economy was growing again. Not even the death in office of President Harding could slow things down. Between 1922 and 1928, industrial production rose by 70 percent, gross national product by over 40 percent, per capita income by 30 percent and real wages by 22 percent.[6] The real estate and stock market booms of the Calvin Coolidge era caused the Twenties to roar. Between 1924 and 1929, the Dow Jones Industrial Average increased by 216 percent. Between 1924 and 1927, tax returns that showed an income of more than a million dollars a year grew from 75 to 283. The fruits were not evenly distributed. By the end of the decade, 1 percent of the population owned 40 percent of the wealth. Sarah Churchwell, in her book *Behold, America*, even claims that, "between 1923 and 1929, 93 percent of the country experienced a drop in per capita income."[7] The way of life shown in the "society" films with their lavish parties in big suburban houses was really available only to a few.

Although Wallace Reid's struggle with drug addiction was well known, his death in January 1923 still shocked the country. His widow, actress Dorothy Davenport, conceived, and appeared in, *Human Wreckage* (1923), the first of a number of social-problem films presented by "Mrs. Wallace Reid." (The film had sequences from the point of view of a drug-crazed man. Unfortunately, it is considered lost.)

"Mrs. Wallace Reid" was only producer with the moral authority to address the taboo subject of prostitution in *The Red Kimono*. She made an expensive mistake when she used the real name of the woman on whose story the script was based.

Unlike DeMille, who enjoyed the sybaritic a little too much for his denunciations to be entirely convincing, no one questioned Mrs. Reid's moral authority or earnestness. *The Red Kimono* (1925) dealt with prostitution, a subject largely taboo after the "white slave" cycle of the previous decade was suppressed. In the opening sequence, Davenport-Reid appears on-screen in an expressionistic newspaper morgue, where she opens a huge bound volume that contains the true story of a young woman who turned to prostitution during the First World War. The red kimono of the title and the red lantern that indicated a house of prostitution were hand-colored for heightened effect. Mrs. Reid took veracity a little too far. She used the actual name of Gabrielle Darley, who had since recovered from her experiences and was happily remarried (if not as the madam of a brothel in Prescott, Arizona, quite the upstanding citizen she claimed to be). Darley sued Reid for $50,000 in damages. Screenwriter Adela Rogers St. Johns was not named in the suit, probably because her father, legendary defense attorney Earl Rogers, had gotten Darley acquitted in the murder of her pimp. The courts initially ruled that Darley's story was in the public domain, but an appeals court found that the use of her real name violated her right to privacy.[8]

The quest for an American Venus continued. At the Physical Culture Show and beauty contest held at New York City's Madison Square Garden in October 1922, the judges—five sculptors, all men—examined the contestants in the nude. They selected 18-year-old Dorothy Knapp. Knapp appeared onstage in the *Ziegfeld Follies* and for Earl Carroll, who proclaimed her "the most beautiful girl in the world." One Ann Hyatt disputed the choice. She hired a lawyer and threatened to have a life-size statue of the Venus de Milo brought to court against which she would be measured.[9]

Paramount's East Coast studios contributed to the search for the American Venus, fittingly, with *The American Venus* (1926). This was a joint venture between the studio and the organizers of the Miss America pageant. The film, unfortunately, is not known to exist but two versions of the trailer do. The trailer gives the measurements of the Venus de Milo: "Bust 34¾, Waist 28½, Hips 36."

Atlantic City, New Jersey, came up with the idea of a September beauty contest to extend the tourist season beyond its Labor Day finale. The Miss America pageant did not assume its modern form until the mid–1930s. In the beginning, it was not even called "Miss America" but the "Inter-City Beauty Contest." Professional models and actresses could enter, among them the aforementioned Dorothy Knapp.

The American Venus promised to be mutually beneficial. The pageant got enhanced visibility. (It was also broadcast on radio for the first time.) Paramount got what a trade paper called a "shape show" at minimal cost, as most of the entrants were nonprofessionals.

The film's director, Frank Tuttle, was one of the judges for the 1925 competition. The winner was to be cast in the movie. Several unsuccessful aspirants claimed that the contest was fixed, a charge reinforced by an article (later retracted) by Bernarr Macfadden in the *New York Evening Graphic*. The winner was Miss California, Fay Lanphier, the first contestant to represent an entire state.

Lanphier had the title role but not the leading role. (In the movie, she plays "Miss Alabama.") Paramount's new star, pretty blonde Esther Ralston, played the daughter of a cosmetics manufacturer engaged to the son of her father's main competitor. A public-relations man encourages her to enter the Miss America contest so that she can endorse her father's cold cream should she win. She breaks off her engagement. When it appears that she might win, she is tricked into quitting by a false report that her father is dying. All ends happily. The winner of the Miss America title (Lanphier) attributes her success to the cold cream made by Ralston's father. Ralston and the P.R. man get married. The film marked the first important role for Louise Brooks, cast as "Miss Bayport," the mistress of the rival cosmetics tycoon. (The British Film Institute discovered a three-second fragment of Brooks in costume and in color in 2018.)

There were three sequences in two-strip Technicolor: a prologue, the actual pageant filmed on location in Atlantic City and a fashion show filmed at Paramount's Astoria Studios. The trade paper *Harrison's Reports* (January 30, 1926) warned that some of the tinted scenes "will no doubt prove offensive to churchgoing people, especially in the smaller communities, because of the fact that women's legs, backs, sides and the abdomens as low as below the navel, are shown aplenty." The reviewer, P.S. Harrison, went on: "Women in tights have been shown in his pictures by Mack Sennett but he has never been so 'raw'; at least he had the girls wear brassieres, whereas Jesse Lasky has the girls wear nothing under the bathing suits with the results that the women's outlines of their breasts are clearly seen. In places, there isn't even the thin cloth of the bathing suit to cover the flesh." The *Washington Herald* reported that the exposure of skin in the fashion revue "drew forth gasps from the audience, whether from shock or admiration, we cannot say." Lanphier and the actual contestants were not shown in the risqué costumes, but the artist Howard Chandler Christy, one of the judges, unveiled a nude statue of "Miss America 1925" that resembled Lanphier. She had not actually posed for it, but it fed the criticism from churches and women's groups that caused the pageant to go on hiatus in 1928.

Promotional material for *The American Venus* included a herald to be given out at theaters that had a picture of Lanphier with her measurements. There was a space on the back for women to fill in their own measurements and a message: "The lady turning in measurements nearest to The American Venus will be given ten tickets to this theatre. Measurements must be turned in on playing date—at the box office."

After the failure of *Heedless Moths* and the formation of the Hays Office, nudity disappeared from mainstream commercial features. The introduction of the Cine Kodak camera with an accompanying projector in 1923 popularized home movies and established the 16mm format for nontheatrical films. A short item in the December 1927 issue of *Movie Makers* magazine announced that Cine Art Productions of Hollywood would henceforth produce for the home market. Most of the items in the Cine Art library were innocuous—*Rapids in the Rockies, Missions of California*—but they also produced a series of short films, about five minutes long, in 1928 (not listed in the ads) that featured female nudity. These were not "stag" films or pornography. Either there were no men, or when men appeared the women turned the tables on them. *Sirens of the Sea* showed two nude women cavorting. *Desert Nymphs* had three nudes in Joshua Tree National Monument. In *Hollywood Sand Witches*, two nude women play with an umbrella. A nerdy young man is so engrossed in a book that he doesn't notice until he literally bumps into them. He peers under another umbrella only to find out the woman under it is a heavyset black woman. He runs, horrified, into the sea. The best of them, *Betty's Bath*, offered a Clara Bow look-alike who undresses for the bath. She sees a rat and screams for help. A male passerby on an otherwise deserted street of stucco bungalows comes in, wraps the rat in a towel and takes it outside, but not before getting

Esther Ralston and Lawrence Gray, stars of *The American Venus*, with director Frank Tuttle (right) and the inevitable Venus de Milo. Fay Lanphier, Miss America 1925, was featured in the film and the ads (facing page) touted her measurements.

an eyeful of the comely Betty. He sits himself in her living room as Betty, now dressed, comes out. He wants to become better acquainted and undresses her with his eyes. She, in turn, superimposes the face of the rat onto his. She summons her dog, who scares him away.

The photographer Albert Arthur Allen was the leading exponent of the female nude. He was plagued by a physical handicap and financial hardship. Although his work is now sought by collectors and museums, he was tried several times for obscenity and convicted in 1925. He established Classic Motion Picture Productions to make films but had to file for bankruptcy after its only production, *Forbidden Daughters*, in 1927. Much of the 13-minute running time was devoted to naked women. Alva, a wealthy New York City woman, receives a cable from a detective agency that her errant artist husband, Russell, is in Africa and has taken up with a Princess Loma. She decides to pursue him, although not before opening her dressing gown to reveal the body she will use to lure him back. She pursues him through African villages, where women are shown nude.

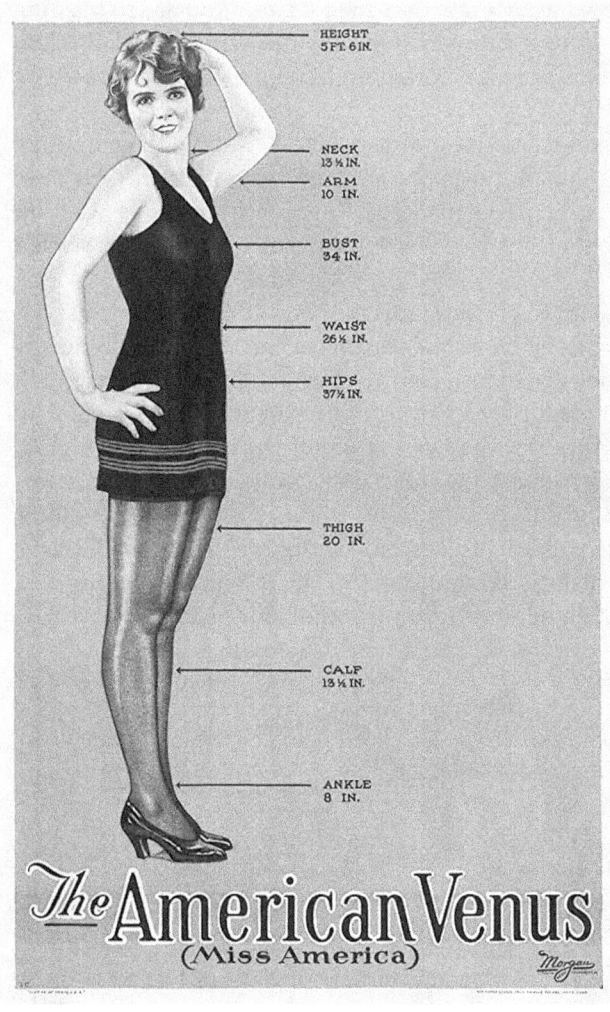

(Allen was one of the few photographers to shoot nonwhite women.) A wealthy East Indian trader Rajah Sana has a harem of white women. A jealous dancer stabs the harem favorite. Alva is blamed and sent to a dungeon, where more nude women are chained. She escapes and makes her way through the jungle. The Dance of the Forbidden Daughters provides still more naked native women. Finally, she finds Russell in the arms of Princess Loma. She strips naked to reveal a beautiful body (and shaved pubis). She forces him to choose and he embraces her.

What people know about Clara Bow is that she was the "It" Girl (true), had sex with the entire USC football team (not true) and was one of the silent film personalities who failed to make the transition to sound (it's more complicated).

Bow became a star without a starring role. In *Black Oxen* (1924), in a supporting role, she was a teenager who responds to Conway Tearle's threat to spank her with "Can I depend on that?" About *Mantrap* (1926), *Variety* wrote, "It should do as much for this corking little ingénue lead as *Flaming Youth* did for Colleen Moore." The enthusiastic reviewer marveled "how she vamps with her lamps." She was not a vamp in the Theda Bara or Nita Naldi mode. David Thomson called her the first sexy star who is not ridiculous.

Such was Bow's growing popularity that B.P. Schulberg, whose Preferred Pictures held her contract, was able to sell her, the company and himself to Paramount where he became head of West Coast production in 1926.

In 1926, Elinor Glyn wrote a novelette called *It*. As put forth by Glyn, "It" wasn't just sex appeal, but a mixture of charisma, confidence, animal magnetism and star quality.

It even inspired a song in the 1926 operetta *The Desert Song*: "In a word, she defined the indefinable thing. She called it 'It,' just simply 'It.' That is the word we're using now." ("It" became a tap riot by Ann Miller with a chorus in *Deep in My Heart*, M-G-M's 1954 Sigmund Romberg portmanteau.)

Paramount arranged for "Madame" Elinor Glyn to meet Bow, and to proclaim, in return for $50,000, that "Clara Bow has 'It.'" She informed Clara, "You are to play the leading role in my story." Although she got screen credit for the story and adaptation, a new script was written by the team of Hope Loring and Louis Lighton to showcase Clara.

Bow's character in *It* was flirtatious but not promiscuous. As a shopgirl who wants to marry the store owner's son (Antonio Moreno), she stretches across his desk. He does take her out to Coney Island. When he parks his Rolls-Royce in front of her walk-up apartment and attempts a kiss, she slaps his face and runs upstairs carrying the stuffed animals she has won.

The only Bow film with any claim to classic status is *Wings* (1927), in which she is just the icing on the cake. In one scene, Military Police come in and she hurriedly covers her breasts. Thereafter, risqué scenes would be a feature of Bow's films. In *Hula* (1927), she bathed nude in a waterhole, though only the tops of her breasts were visible. Her character was named "Hula," so, of course, she has to toss off her clothes, don a grass skirt and "show them what my name means." *Red Hair* (1928) had sequences in the two-color Technicolor process.

M-G-M spent a full year in preparation of a custom-tailored vehicle, *Anna Christie* (1930), before it could make the historic announcement: "Garbo Talks." Paramount, with no preparation, put Bow through her customary paces of four pictures per year.

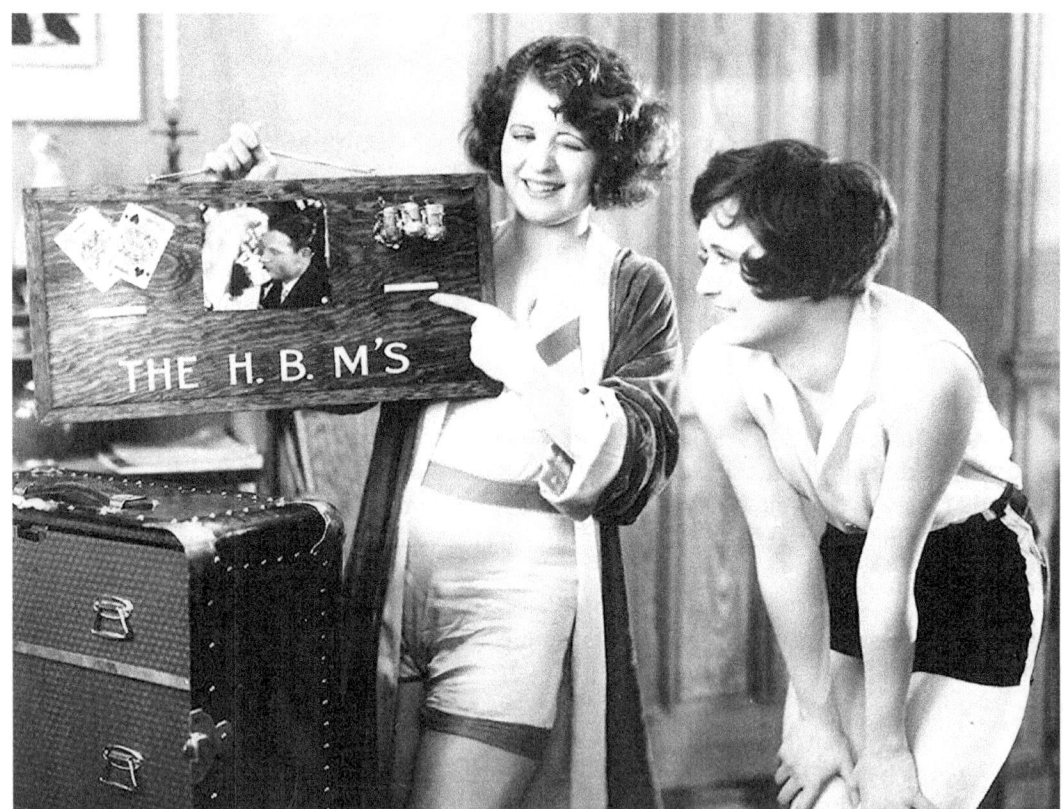

Clara Bow's talkie debut in *The Wild Party* was guided by Dorothy Arzner, for many years the only woman director to be employed by Hollywood studios. Bow explains to college roommate Marceline Day that H.B.M. stands for "Hard Boiled Maidens." MCA.

The problem with Bow's sound films is not that she was bad but that she was no longer special. She overcompensated for mic fright with the loud and emphatic delivery that sound engineers wanted, but she lost the subtlety of her facial expressions in silent films. She hated the microphone and once took a swat at it. That she had to stay in microphone range frustrated her uninhibited physicality. She had put on weight and was up to 132 pounds. There was also unfavorable publicity over a broken engagement, gambling debts and an embezzlement scandal involving a personal assistant that caused B.P. Schulberg to call her "Crisis-a-day Clara." She battled schizophrenia and was admitted to a mental hospital in Glendale after a nervous breakdown in May 1931. Paramount dropped her. The main impact of sound on Bow's career was the emergence of a new crop of female stars in 1929–31, such as Barbara Stanwyck, Jean Harlow and Marlene Dietrich, against whom Bow, in movies since 1922, seemed like yesterday's news.

As a young producer at Paramount, David O. Selznick witnessed the studio's mishandling of Bow. As production head of RKO, he planned to offer her the lead in *What Price Hollywood?* (1932). The part went to Constance Bennett. Bow accepted a better-paying offer from Fox. Her "comeback" picture, if someone who was off the screen for only a year and a half can be said to make a comeback, was *Call Her Savage* (1932). It had enough plot for five movies and its share of absurdities. It began with an Indian attack on a wagon train—stock footage from *The Big Trail* (1930)—that Bow's mother survives as a little girl. (As Bow's character was born 18 years later, in the early 20th century, the time period of the Indian attack is at least 30 years too late.)

A visit to New York takes her to a Greenwich Village restaurant, where mincing homosexuals who wear aprons and wield feather dusters provide the entertainment. Bow goes from wealth—via marriage to a playboy whom she steals from his mistress but who turns out to be a sadist—to poverty after she gives birth to his son. At her lowest point, she goes out on the street to solicit men in order to buy medicine for her sick son, placing the film squarely in the "fallen women" cycle of 1931–32. She returns home to find the building engulfed in flames and her son suffocated. Soon after, she learns that she has been left an inheritance and is rich again. At the film's end, she finds out that she is the illegitimate offspring of her mother's affair with an Indian. This makes her a suitable mate for the "half-breed" Gilbert Roland with whom she shares "savage" blood. Although Bow was only 27, she looked older.

Her second Fox film, *Hoop-la* (1933), was neither good enough to prolong her career nor bad enough to end it. It had the inevitable undressing scene, this time in a train compartment. It was discreet and provocative at the same time. Director Frank Lloyd dollied into Bow's face as she removed her undergarments and then out again as she was covered by a nightgown. She chose to retire and concentrate on her marriage to Rex Bell, cowboy star and later lieutenant governor of Nevada.

"The Decline of D.W. Griffith" is such a well-established theme of film history that *The Battle of the Sexes* (1928) comes a pleasant surprise. Unpromisingly, it was a remake of a five-reeler that Griffith himself made in 1914. If the old man (all of 53, younger than many of today's directors) was no longer an innovator, he was not an anachronism either. Aided by new collaborators—the great production designer William Cameron Menzies and cinematographer Karl Struss, fresh from the triumph of *Sunrise*, who joined Griffith's regular cameraman Billy Bitzer—he came up with a polished piece of contemporary entertainment. A married, middle-aged businessman (Jean Hersholt) becomes infatuated with a young woman (Phyllis Haver) who is so aggressively modern that she has her mane of frizzy blonde hair cut in the same barbershop that he goes to. Hersholt's wife is so depressed over her husband's affair that she contemplates suicide by jumping off the roof of their apartment building. This is imaginatively staged; as she approaches the railing, there is an overhead shot in which miniature moving cars are shown in perspective on the street below. She is rescued by her daughter, the vivacious Sally O'Neil, who goes on to break up her father's affair and bring him back to his family.

Why Be Good? (1929) was advertised as "*Flaming Youth*, 1929 model." The Moore character, "Pert Kelly" says, "This isn't 1889, it's 1929." Pert Kelly enters dance contests and kisses men whom she has just met. A man (Neil Hamilton) takes her to a roadhouse in the expectation that they will spend the night. In something of a proto-feminist attack (via title cards) on the double standard, Colleen Moore's character asserts that she dresses and acts the way she does because men find it sexy. She's more smoke than fire. She turns him down to prove that she is "good," i.e., a virgin. Although the 13 years that separate *Why Be Good?* from *Intolerance* at first seem more like a century, Pert Kelly and Mae Marsh's "strong-jawed Jane" are perhaps not so different after all. *Why Be Good?* also shows the growing sophistication of motion-picture art direction. The art deco Manhattan penthouse of Hamilton, a rich man's son, and the outer-borough frame house of Moore's stolid, lower-middle-class parents serve to situate the characters socially. Made at the very end of the silent era, the recorded musical accompaniment was synchronized so closely that when a character on-screen adjusted the volume on the radio, the soundtrack came up with it.

Women of the 1920s enjoyed a level of sexual freedom that would have shocked or delighted people less than a decade earlier. A study in the 1930s by psychologist Lewis M. Terman found that for women born before 1890, 90 percent were virgins at the time of marriage compared to 74 percent for those born between 1890 and 1899, 51 percent between 1900 and 1909, and just 32 percent of those born after 1910. His sample was small and select and his findings have come under criticism but it is likely that something changed. As summarized by William O'Neill in *Feminism in America*, "it appears that these women usually lost their virginity to fiancés, actual or intended.... Previously, women had saved themselves until marriage; now an engagement ring would do."[10]

O'Neill confirms that the flapper was more smoke than fire. No young woman wanted to be considered "fast." Outside of bohemian circles and Hollywood itself, sexual adventurousness was not really possible even for a woman so inclined. Abortion was illegal in every state. Contraceptives were not widely available. Before antibiotics, treatment for venereal disease was expensive and unreliable. The double standard was very much in force and there were few jobs that could enable a woman to live independently of a man.

Another morality play from Mrs. Wallace Reid, *The Road to Ruin* (1928), illustrated the limits of the tentative sexual freedom of the 1920s. A teenage girl (Helen Foster) falls under the influence of her more sophisticated friend. On a sleepover, they read steamy passages from a novel. New York State Senator and future New York City Mayor James J. Walker famously deflected a 1923 "clean books" bill with the line, "I have never yet heard of a girl being ruined by a book." He might have had his mind changed here. "Don't be a flat tire," says the friend as Foster is introduced to jazz, smoking and alcohol. As depicted by Mrs. Reid, the road to ruin is an expressway with no exit ramps. On a double date, Foster loses her virginity to her boyfriend and immediately regrets it amid many tears.

The ad for Colleen Moore's *Why Be Good?* noted the addition of "Vitaphone," but it was really a silent film with a synchronized musical accompaniment. Warner Bros.

The 1928 silent was remade with sound in 1934 with essentially the same story and even the same female lead. (Helen Foster was by then 27, a little long in the tooth to play a teenaged innocent.) Seated with her boyfriend at a roadhouse, the all-purpose sin spot in these things, she catches the eye of the lecherous owner. He seduces her with rides in his expensive car, booze, drugs and an empty promise of marriage. While they are sprawled on a couch, the camera pans away and tilts up to show the man's hand turning out the light. (The New York censors called for deletion of this shot, as it obviously portended intercourse.)

Now completely given over to licentiousness, Foster is at a wild party marked by undressing games. (In the silent version, it was strip poker; in the sound version, a dice game.) Helen's friend is completely nude, partially hidden by a screen. The drunken revelers end up in a swimming pool whereupon the neighbors call the police. Helen is classified as a "Sex Delinquent," although a notation or her record informs us that the Wassermann test was negative. Her friend was not so lucky and tested positive for syphilis. Helen informs her seducer that she is pregnant. He arranges an abortion, but she dies of complications. The silent version ends with the words "The Wages of Sin Is Death" in fiery letters. That abortion, even when it was illegal, was less risky than childbirth was, of course, not acknowledged. Although it was released before the creation of Production Code Administration, the 1934 *Road to Ruin* was marketed as an "adults only" film despite its anti-sex message. The ads featured a leggy Helen Foster and promised lurid thrills.

3

Pre-Code, Post-Code and Non-Code

Before and After the Moral Crackdown of the 1930s

In theory, the coming of sound raised the possibility that the *Mutual* decision might be overturned and censorship eased. If movies could talk, could they not claim to be constitutionally protected speech? In anticipation of a possible defeat in court, the Pennsylvania censors stopped vetting newsreels in 1930.[1]

In practice, the advent of sound intensified the pressures for censorship. Sound brought cynical, wisecracking humor of the Broadway type and double *entendres*. *The Cock-Eyed World*, the sound sequel to his silent classic *What Price Glory* (1926), was directed by Raoul Walsh for Fox in 1929. It was set in Nicaragua during the U.S. Marine occupation. Ordered by Captain Flagg (Victor McLaglen) to get the "lay of the land," Swedish dialect comedian El Brendel returns with a map in one hand and a brunette senorita in the other.

Hays and his appointees were attacked in the pages of *The Churchman*, an evangelical Anglican quarterly, in 1929 as "men whose occupation it is to shield, for enormous salaries, the panderers who have made their millions selling vice, crime and sexual suggestion to a public that is in the main composed of the immature."

The early talkie era saw an avalanche of what film historian Benjamin Hampton in 1931 called "girl pictures," i.e., musicals. The first talkie, *The Jazz Singer* (1927), had been a musical of sorts. Although synchronized sound accounted for a little more than ten minutes of what was otherwise a silent picture, Al Jolson managed to squeeze in five songs. Musicals quickly flooded the screen in a variety of subgenres. There were backstage stories such as *The Broadway Melody*, the Oscar winner for Best Picture in 1929. There were revues such as Warner Bros.' deadly *The Show of Shows*, M-G-M's *The Hollywood Revue*, *Fox Movietone Follies*, all in 1929, and *Paramount on Parade* (1930), in which contract stars sang, danced and performed in comedy or dramatic sketches. These were advertised as "All Talking-All Singing-All Dancing" (and, in the opinion of the theatrical *grande dame* in 1930s *The Royal Family of Broadway*, "all terrible"). The newly formed RKO added songs to what had been planned as a straight comedy, *Tanned Legs* (1929). Pretty June Clyde displayed some appealing frontal topography as she addressed her song "Come in the Water, the Water Is Fine" directly to the audience in a swimsuit. As Teri Hatcher would say in a classic *Seinfeld* episode, "They're real and they're spectacular."

Just about every hit Broadway musical of 1925–29 came to the screen in 1929–30.

The first was *The Cocoanuts*, a mixture of Marx Brothers *shtick* and antique (even then) musical comedy elements. At a time when directors positioned the camera from the viewpoint of a theatergoer in the center orchestra, codirector Robert Florey tried to break free of the proscenium. As Mary Eaton danced in the "Monkey Doodle Doo" number, he fastened the camera on her panties in a crotch shot. (He used negative film of the number under the opening credits to turn white chorus dancers black.) For the ballet sequence, he mounted the camera in the rafters of a stage at Paramount's Astoria Studios and pioneered the overhead shot of dancers in a floral pattern that came to be identified with Busby Berkeley.

Berkeley himself came to Hollywood in 1930 as a result of one of Florenz Ziegfeld, Jr.'s periodic fiscal crises. Ziegfeld was a gigantic presence on Broadway. The program for the 1922 edition of his famous *Follies* proclaimed it "A National Institution—Glorifying the American Girl." He was also responsible for "book" shows such as *Rio Rita* and the historic *Show Boat* in 1927. In need of money, the Great Glorifier sold his 1928 hit *Whoopee!* to Samuel Goldwyn in a package that included the sets, costumes and the services of star Eddie Cantor and dance director Berkeley. Goldwyn was leery of Berkeley's reputation for drinking, but Cantor vouched for him. Ziegfeld and Goldwyn shared presentation credit for the movie version.

Berkeley's work on *Whoopee!* was simple and straightforward compared to what came later, but some of his signature elements were already present. In addition to the overhead shots, he had the dancers spread their legs and hop forward to straddle a camera placed on the floor. In later films, the camera, mounted on a monorail, would itself move between the dancers' legs in what became known as "the dolly 'neath the dollies." In the "Ten Gallon Hat" number, the girls pass in front of the camera and each one gets a close-up. "The Song of the Setting Sun" was typical Ziegfeld pageantry. Showgirls in feathered headdresses, wrapped in blankets, descend a stylized mountain. As they approach the camera, they unfurl the blankets to reveal John Harkrider's "Indian" costumes. Indian braves lead semi-naked maidens on horseback down the mountain trail.

Whoopee! is probably the best extant example of the two-color Technicolor process. A number of musicals were made in color. Even more common were Technicolor sequences, typically for the most lavish numbers, where it was used to show off the costumes or the relative lack of costumes, as in the finale of *Glorifying the American Girl* (1929) or the "Dancing the Devil Away" number in *The Cuckoos* (1930).

Most of the early sound musicals are of minimal interest cinematically. Their value is that they preserve the stagecraft and performance styles of late–1920s Broadway. The legendary Ziegfeld dancer Ann Pennington can be seen as a guest star, playing herself, in *Tanned Legs* and in the "Snake Hips" number in *Happy Days* (1929).

Fox's *Sunny Side Up* (1929) was advertised as the first original musical comedy created for the screen. It disproves the cliché repeated by even so knowledgeable an observer as Kenneth Macgowan, himself a former Hollywood producer and a professor of theater history at UCLA, in his book *Behind the Screen* that Hollywood between 1928 and 1930 "all but took the motion out of motion pictures." The film begins with a three-minute unbroken take that starts with children playing in the street of a New York tenement neighborhood. The camera passes by the windows to survey life on one side of the street and then the other. Most of the little vignettes also have dialogue. In the last one, a well-dressed woman offers "The Birth Control Review" to a stout matron with an Irish brogue who sits on a stoop surrounded by children, including a daughter who is pregnant herself. It was quite a feat of staging, camerawork and sound recording for any period, let alone 1929.

Less imaginatively staged, but striking in its eroticism, was the "Turn on the Heat" number, performed as part of a charity show at a Long Island estate. Girls emerge from behind igloos. The igloos melt. The arctic village turns into a tropical island. The girls toss off their Eskimo parkas to reveal scanty two-piece bathing suits. They summon banana trees that rise from the earth. As the girls writhe on the ground, smoke and flames rise from the earth to engulf the island. The girls dive into the moat that surrounds the stage to escape.

Robert Benchley, theater critic of *The New Yorker* in the 1920s, wrote that it was possible to leave a Broadway musical after the first act, go to another theater during the intermission, catch the second act and not feel that one had missed anything. The surfeit of movie musicals soon exhausted audiences. Musical numbers were cut from completed films. Most of Irving Berlin's songs were cut from *Reaching for the Moon* (1931), and he was so angry that he didn't write for Hollywood again until *Top Hat* in 1935. Increasingly, songs were taken out before production, with the possible exception of the one or two of the best known. This gave audiences the worst of both worlds; they got the silly stories without the songs that had made them bearable. Warner Bros. were the most prolific producers of musicals and operettas. When the musical tide went out, they had to work the hardest to adjust. They developed a new house style in the early 1930s with pictures that moved fast and talked fast, built around a stock company of decidedly urban types.

Maurice Chevalier at Paramount and Eddie Cantor at Goldwyn carried the banner for musicals through what film historian Miles Kreuger has called the "Moratorium Years" of 1931–32. Ernst Lubitsch cast Chevalier as a walking penis in *The Smiling Lieutenant* and *One Hour with You*. The Cantor films kept Busby Berkeley active prior to the major phase of his career at Warner Bros. In the "But We Must Rise" number in *The Kid from Spain* (1932), he broke up the vocal so that each of The Goldwyn Girls in the dormitory, among whom Eddie Cantor hides, gets to sing part of it in medium close-up. (A 16-year-old Betty Grable takes the first part.) The number also has a water ballet and some nudity in silhouette as the girls undress behind translucent screens, ideas that he would expand on later. For a comparatively minor assignment, *Night World* (1932) at Universal, Berkeley staged a floor show in which the girls had necklines that plunged to the waist. (On closer examination, the cleavage was partially covered by fabric.)

Berkeley's *annus mirabilis* was 1933. His work on Warner Bros.' *42nd Street* precipitated the revival of the musical. He followed it with *Gold Diggers of 1933* and *Footlight Parade*, both of which had even more elaborate numbers. Berkeley's love of daring camera angles and use of the then-new optical printer took his sequences ever further into the realm of abstraction and away from the proscenium. Berkeley was not a dancer himself. His background was as a drill instructor in the Army. Aside from some tap dancing by Ruby Keeler and hoofing by the chorus, dance was not the major part of what he did. It was really patterned movement. Women were literally objectified, turned into graphic elements, but also rehumanized. Several of his girls followed him from film to film and were rewarded with close-ups. Some became minor celebrities, such as the creamy blonde Toby Wing, the former Goldwyn Girl to whom Dick Powell sang "I'm Young and Healthy" in *42nd Street*.

Berkeley resumed his flirtation with nudity in silhouette in the "Pettin' in the Park" number of *Gold Diggers of 1933*. After they are caught in the rain, the dancers take refuge behind a translucent muslin screen through which they are seen to take off their wet clothes. An impish, voyeuristic toddler, played by the dwarf Billy Barty, pulls a rope and partially raises the screen to expose the undressed women.

Berkeley's numbers took on a narrative element and became movies unto themselves. The "Shanghai Lil" number in *Footlight Parade* was possibly inspired by Josef von Sternberg's *Shanghai Express* (1932) at Paramount, in which Marlene Dietrich rendered

The then-unknown Lucille Ball appeared in *Roman Scandals*. The "Goldwyn Girls" were nude except for long, blonde tresses in the "Love No More" number. Busby Berkeley filmed the sequence at night to limit the number of prying eyes. Samuel Goldwyn Company.

the line, "It took more than one man to change my name to Shanghai Lily." The Chinese girl (Ruby Keeler) involved in a romance with American sailor James Cagney is pretty obviously a prostitute. A white hooker sings, "That oriental/dame is detrimental/to our industry." Other prostitutes are spaced out on opium. A black man at the bar touches the arm of a white woman.

Berkeley somehow found time for his last Goldwyn job, *Roman Scandals* (1933), remembered for a slave market scene in which women, naked except for the long, blonde tresses that cover their breasts, are chained to a wall. (One of them was the young Lucille Ball.) The "Keep Young and Beautiful" number had The Goldwyn Girls in a steam bath attended by Nubian maidens with Cantor in blackface.

For the "Did You Ever See a Dream Walking?" number in Paramount's *Sitting Pretty* (1933), Larry Ceballos emulated Berkeley's overhead shots and put his dancers in costumes that exposed their backs and barely covered their breasts. In a possible tribute to the fan dancer Sally Rand, a sensation of the 1933 Chicago World's Fair, Ceballos had his dancers wave huge feathered fans. The next year Berkeley imitated his imitator. For the "Hall of Human Harps" number in *Fashions of 1934*, nearly nude women form the pillars of the harps played by seated women. Huge feathered fans make their appearance, wielded by the girls of the ensemble. Their navels are exposed, albeit shown only briefly or in long shot.

Seven of the purported "one hundred Hollywood honeys" in the "Did You Ever See a Dream Walking?" number from Paramount's *Sitting Pretty* (1933) take a time-out. In reality, it was closer to 50. The fabric outline of the dancers' costumes is visible; on-screen, they appeared to be nearly nude. Tenor Arthur Jarrett and emerging star Ginger Rogers duetted on the vocal. Lyricist Mack Gordon (right) appears to take a handheld vacuum cleaner to Ginger's foot for some reason. MCA.

Not only were their bodies sexualized, the dialogue characterized chorus girls as readily available. The young Ginger Rogers in *42nd Street* played a character called "Anytime Annie." The dance director of the show within the movie (George E. Stone) asks the director (Warner Baxter) if he is going to keep an aspirant to the chorus line. He replies, "If I don't keep her, you'll have to." In *Flying Down to Rio*, a female member

"I didn't raise my daughter to be a human harp," was how Richard Griffith and Arthur Mayer captioned this scene in their classic tome *The Movies*. "The Hall of Human Harps" in *Fashions of 1934* was one of Busby Berkeley's more bizarre inspirations. Warner Bros.

of bandleader Gene Raymond's troupe, jealous of the attention he pays to a Brazilian beauty (Dolores del Rio), asks, "What have these South Americans got below the Equator that we haven't?"

Berkeley alluded to the gathering clouds of censorship. The "We're in the Money" number in *Gold Diggers of 1933*, sung by Ginger Rogers in a costume that had a cluster of gold coins to cover her crotch, was shut down by the sheriff. (In his book *Incorrect Entertainment*, Anthony Slide contends that the costume implies that her lady parts are for sale or, at least, for rent.) Comic actor Hugh Herbert portrayed a censor in *Footlight Parade* who tries to inhibit James Cagney until Cagney kicks him out. Herbert essentially repeated the role in *Dames* (1934) as the eccentric millionaire creator of a foundation to improve public morals. The real-life censors would not prove so funny, nor so easily outwitted.

The Trial of Mary Dugan in 1929 aroused the wrath of Father FitzGeorge Dineen. The courtroom drama had a *Follies* showgirl (Norma Shearer in her first talkie) stand trial for the murder of her sugar daddy. It is revealed that she had multiple lovers and once sold herself for $100 before becoming a kept woman. Dineen was a friend of Martin Quigley, a prominent Catholic layman and publisher of the trade paper *Exhibitors Herald-World*, later known as the *Motion Picture Herald*. Dineen met with Quigley at the Chicago Athletic Club and suggested they bring in Father Daniel Lord, professor of dramatics at St. Louis University, to write what became the Production Code.

Catholic clergy, unlike some Protestants, had not pushed for censorship of motion pictures. As many of their parishioners were working class with limited leisure time, Catholic clergy had never attempted to restrict Sunday movies. The Church was not indifferent to the moral content of movies—quite the opposite. Where the censor boards were concerned to keep things *out* of movies, the Catholic authors of the Production Code wanted the screen to show the world, not as it was, but as it might be if Christian values prevailed. The Quigley-Lord Code restated most of the Fourteen Points of 1921 and the "Do's, Don'ts, and Be Carefuls" of 1927, but with a philosophical rationale that the industry's own guidelines lacked. The section on "General Principles" or "Reasons Supporting the Code" was as long as the Code itself. The first principle stated, "No picture shall be produced which will lower the moral standards of those who see it." Though Protestants greatly outnumbered Catholics, Catholics were concentrated in the urban centers of the Northeast and the industrial Midwest that were also the most important movie markets. The hierarchical nature of the Church gave it a capacity for unified action that the numerous Protestant denominations, divided on doctrinal issues and only loosely connected through the Federal Council of Churches, could not match. The movie industry was well aware of the Church's power and the MPDDA accepted the Production Code in March 1930.

What film historians call "the pre–Code era" began, paradoxically, with the adoption of the Production Code. Technically, any movie made before March 1930 is also "pre–Code," but no one speaks of them that way.

Now that the files of the MPPDA have been made available to scholars, the old view that the Code was not enforced before 1934 has had to be revised. In 1931, Hays required that all scripts be submitted to the Studio Relations Committee headed by Colonel Jason S. Joy. Joy would write letters to the studios recommending changes to productions. The producer could then appeal to the 15-member committee. The committee would refer the matter to a three-member rotating panel of senior studio executives. They never ruled against the producers. Theoretically, Joy could appeal to the full board of the MPDDA but never did. The system was thus dependent on self-restraint on the part of the producers.

Ultimate authority rested with the eight state censor boards and over 250 local boards, whose combined jurisdiction covered about 60 percent of the audience.

Some writers have portrayed the pre–Code era as a wonderland of sexual freedom and artistic creativity. Pre–Code movies are indeed striking if one comes to them with a broad familiarity with studio movies of the later 1930s, 1940s and 1950s. The sexual frankness is surprising, as are the racial and ethnic stereotypes. The more movies from the era that one sees, the more obvious it becomes that they were trapped in their own clichés and conventions: the kept women in their art deco apartments, the reporters who will do anything for a story, the brassy blonde chorus girls, the dumb flatfoot Irish cops, the effeminate hairdressers with penciled mustaches and marcelled waves.

The Internet Movie Database shows only one feature film with the word "Blonde" in its title and just two with "Blondes" before 1931. Then came *Platinum Blonde* (Jean Harlow) and *Blonde Crazy* (James Cagney and Joan Blondell). The trickle became a flood with *Cheating Blondes, Dangerous Blondes, Don't Bet on Blondes, Blonde Comet, The Bamboo Blonde, Incendiary Blonde, Blonde Ice*, et al. The change can mostly be attributed to Jean Harlow. To show her alabaster skin and silver/white hair, Howard Hughes incorporated an eight-minute ball scene in two-color Technicolor into his 1930 air epic *Hell's Angels*. (It was actually filmed in Multicolor, a process that Hughes owned, but only Technicolor had the ability to turn out prints in quantity.) Harlow's gown was designed by Howard Greer, whose atelier was a favorite of the movie colony. According to actress Colleen Moore, "His were the first untheatrical clothes used in movies. Conservative, elegant, subtle in design, they started a new trend on screen and off of it." The film reverts to black and white and Harlow delivers to Ben Lyon the famous line, "Would you be shocked if I put on something more comfortable?"

The 19-year-old Harlow's performance as an English noblewoman was mocked for its amateurish ineptitude. Nonetheless, she made an impression. Still under contract to Hughes, she made five pictures in 1931. In Frank Capra's *Platinum Blonde*, retitled to capitalize on her growing celebrity, she played a wealthy heiress who lived in a Fifth Avenue mansion. Her other roles were stereotypic gold diggers and floozies. As the wife of boxer Lew Ayres in *Iron Man* at Universal, her appetite for luxury causes him to neglect training and lose his title. In Fox's *Goldie*, she was described as a "tramp." In *The Public Enemy*, her acting was considered so poor that her scenes were reduced. Nevertheless, the public responded to her. Her personal appearances drew huge crowds. M-G-M took notice and bought her contract.

Her first M-G-M picture was *Red-Headed Woman* (1932), a troubled project that the Studio Relations Committee had advised against. After an indifferent preview in Glendale, California, production chief Irving Thalberg tapped Anita Loos to rewrite the script to make it a comedy in the style of her novel *Gentlemen Prefer Blondes*. New opening scenes were added. In a self-referential joke, Harlow asks a barber, "So gentlemen prefer blondes, do they?" (Harlow played the role with a red wig.) In the next scene, Harlow asks, re her skintight dress, "Can you see through this?" "I'm afraid you can, Miss," says the off-screen salesgirl. "Then, I'll take it!" As Harlow tells a girlfriend of her intention to seduce her boss, there is a close-up of her shapely leg as she slips the boss's picture into a dime-store garter. *Red-Headed Woman* got Harlow her first good notices.

3. Pre-Code, Post-Code and Non-Code   53

Jean Harlow gets a massage in Frank Capra's *Platinum Blonde*, one of five movies she made in 1931 while still under contract to Howard Hughes. Columbia Pictures/Sony.

The *New York Daily Mirror* compared her to Clara Bow, but "outbowing the famed Bow as an exponent of elemental lure and crude man-baiting techniques."

Red Dust (1932) was an ever-bigger hit, with Harlow taking a bath in a rain barrel. Though not as popular as *Red Dust*, *Bombshell* (1933) was arguably the definitive Harlow vehicle. As movie star Lola Burns, she is scheduled to do a scene in a rain barrel with the unseen Clark Gable. Victor Fleming, who directed both movies, put himself on-screen in the person of Pat O'Brien.

Harlow was not the only popular blonde of the era. Warner Bros. had the aptly named Joan Blondell, the good-hearted gold digger of its musicals, and tough-as-nails Glenda Farrell. Although she never got higher than fourth or fifth billing, Thelma Todd's elegant beauty and willingness to pose in lingerie made her a foil for almost every comedian and comedy team of the era: Buster Keaton, the Marx Brothers, Laurel and Hardy, Wheeler and Woolsey. Todd did share star billing in a series of comedy shorts that teamed her with ZaSu Pitts and, later, Patsy Kelly.

Female stars of the early 1930s went braless and iced their nipples to make them more prominent. Lilyan Tashman, sophisticated star of *Girls About Town* and *Murder by the Clock*, lauded by Colleen Moore as "our best-dressed woman,"[2] was known for her derriere-clinging gowns.

Upon arrival in Hollywood in 1932, Mae West derided the "starved ingénues ... so flat you can't see which way they are goin." However, a March 1931 *Photoplay* feature "Who has the best figure in Hollywood?" claimed that "the general notion of what is a good figure is no longer what it seemed a year or more ago when influenced by the unsound fad which glorified boyish forms" when actresses had "survived on lamb chops and pineapple, oranges and lettuce." Dolores del Rio was selected for "her roundly tuned and warmly curved figure." With only a 33-inch bust, del Rio wouldn't have rated a second look a decade later. When the original *The Mummy* (1932) was sold to television in the late 1950s, teenaged boys were no doubt surprised and disappointed that when Boris Karloff brought his dagger to Zita Johann's breasts, she seemed to have none. The then-contemporary *Horror of Dracula* (1958) took a sadistic glee in the staking of bosomy female vampires in an intimation of intermammary intercourse.

West was nearly 40 years old, more matronly than shapely, and evoked the era of parasols and spittoons. She must have had an impact though. Warner's (the lingerie makers, not the studio) introduced the "Gay Deceiver" line of padded bras in 1934.

There had been silent gangster movies such as *Underworld* (1927) and *The Racket* (1928), but sound gave car crashes and machine-gun fire enhanced realism. The 30 or so gangster movies released in 1931 spurred indignation from editorial writers, police chiefs and politicians who claimed that they glamorized crime and were a bad influence on young urban males. Despite the recent popularity of *The Public Enemy*, the Board of Directors of the Association of Motion Picture Producers, the West Coast division of the MPPDA, passed a resolution in September 1931 that prohibited production of further gangster pictures.

Howard Hughes' *Scarface*, held up by production delays and controversy, still awaited release. It was intended as the gangster movie to end all gangster movies and, for some years, it did. It stood out for its violence, with some 15 killings and a re-creation of the St. Valentine's Day Massacre. There was more than a hint of an incestuous relationship between the Al Capone–like Tony Camonte (Paul Muni) and his sister Cesca (Ann Dvorak).

The gangster did not entirely disappear, but he became a secondary character or even a comic figure in *Lady for a Day* (1933) and other adaptations derived from the popular writer Damon Runyon. The kidnapping of the Lindbergh baby in March 1932, initially blamed on gangsters, turned public opinion decisively against them. In Cecil B. DeMille's *This Day and Age* (1933), high school students kidnap and torture a gangster (Charles Bickford), while in *Gabriel Over the White House* (1933), President Walter Huston ordered them summarily executed.

As they turned away from crime, movies increasingly embraced sex. This had been anticipated by Colonel Joy in December 1931 when he wrote Will Hays's new executive assistant, Joseph Breen:

> With crime practically denied them, with box office figures down, with high pressure methods being employed back home to spur the studios on to get a little more cash, it was almost inevitable that sex, as the nearest thing at hand and pretty generally sure-fire, should be seized upon. It was.[3]

The Sign of the Cross (1932) marked Cecil B. DeMille's triumphant return to Paramount. The cruelties of the Babylonian sequence in *Male and Female* and the Roman orgy of *Manslaughter* now filled an entire two-hour spectacle. Christians were fed to lions. As played by a rouged Charles Laughton, Nero was obviously homosexual, with a near-naked young male admirer always at his side. A Christian girl (Elissa Landi) is mocked at a party by a lesbian (Joyzelle Joyner), who performs her Dance of the Naked Moon in an attempt at seduction. In an opinion that DeMille himself could have written, Col. Joy of the Studio Relations Committee justified the "kootch" dance on the grounds that it showed the contrast between paganism and Christianity. As the immoral Poppaea, Claudette Colbert bathed in a pool of asses' milk. (Under the hot lights, it curdled and turned to cottage cheese.) DeMille ignored all demands for changes, confident that the mask of pro–Christian propaganda would neutralize any criticism.

Dolores del Rio swam nude in *Bird of Paradise* (1932), joined by Joel McCrea (in trunks), and performed a dance in which her breasts were covered only by a lei, taped in place. Her navel was exposed, something that would not be seen again, at least not from a female lead, for 30 years.

A popular misconception is that Depression–era audiences were so hungry for escapism that the movie business flourished; it has even been erroneously characterized as the fourth- or fifth-largest industry in America. In reality, box-office receipts dropped by one-third between 1930 and 1933. Some of the decline was inevitable. The 1930 figures were inflated by the novelty of sound and represented a big jump over 1929. By 1932, people were watching their pennies. All the big studios, save for M-G-M, lost money in 1932–33. The Fox Film and Paramount Publix bankruptcies were the largest industrial failures in the United States to that time.

As desperation took hold, studios tested the limits. Warner Bros. most often ran afoul of the Code, with cynical movies such as *Female, Employees' Entrance* and *Ex-Lady* in 1933,

The Navel Academy, Part I: Dolores del Rio's exposed belly button in *Bird of Paradise* was the last that would be seen on a leading actress for the next 30 years. RKO.

in which women used their sexual wiles to get ahead. (In its defense, Warner Bros., whose movies were mostly shot on 17-day schedules and who took pride in their "from the headlines" topicality, claimed the processes of the Studio Relations Committee were too slow moving.) Even Paramount, formerly cooperative, turned to notorious properties such as Noel Coward's *Design for Living* with its *menage a trois*, brought to the screen by Ernst Lubitsch, and Mae West's play *Diamond Lil*, filmed as *She Done Him Wrong*. William Faulkner's *Sanctuary* (retitled *The Story of Temple Drake*) reached the screen in 1933.

Several 1933 films have been put forward as the final straw. Was it *She Done Him Wrong* in which Mae West sang, "I know a guy what takes his time"? Was it *Baby Face* in which Barbara Stanwyck slept her way to the top? Was it *Queen Christina* in which Greta Garbo kissed a woman and spent the night with a man, albeit dressed as a man herself? Perhaps it was *Convention City*. We'll never know, as it was one of the few films for which not only the prints were withdrawn from circulation but the negative destroyed as well. (In 2013, New York's Film Forum staged a reading of the script in conjunction with a pre–Code Warner Bros. series.) Even Jack L. Warner thought a brassiere should have been put on Joan Blondell in *Convention City* to cover her breasts, "otherwise we are going to have these pictures stopped in a lot of places." He warned production head Hal Wallis, "I believe in showing their forms, but for Lord's sake, don't let those bulbs stick out."[4]

The Catholic bishops were increasingly furious over the industry's betrayal of its commitment to the Production Code. In 1933, they formed the Legion of Decency. The threat of condemnation from the pulpit was potent. Parishioners were urged to sign pledge cards to boycott immoral pictures. The bishops got a boost from the 1933 publication of *Our Movie Made Children*. This was a crude, popular summary of the "Payne Fund Studies," a sociological investigation of the effects of motion pictures on children conducted by academics but funded by a private foundation.

Joseph Breen, an active Catholic layman, had come to Hollywood in 1932 and became a power on the Studio Relations Committee. He played a double game. While on the payroll of the MPPDA, he advised Catholic clergy on the best way to pressure his employer. It was to hit them at the box office. Cardinal Dennis Dougherty of Philadelphia ordered a boycott of all movies. As intended, this particularly hit Warner Bros., who owned several theaters there. It was said that you could fire a cannon and not hit anybody. The impact was muted by the overall increase in box-office receipts in 1934 as the national economy recovered, but the muscle flexing made its point. A Production Code Administration (PCA) came into being in July 1934 with Breen as its head.

Murder at the Vanities, with the kind of seminudity associated with showman Earl Carroll, got in under the wire. So did another Paramount picture, *Search for Beauty*, unusual for its *male* nudity, as Larry "Buster" Crabbe and other athletes exposed their buttocks in the locker room.

Some other movies from the first half of 1934 demonstrated what would soon be gone. In *The Scarlet Empress*, four bare-breasted women were tied up and engulfed in flames. (It was nevertheless awarded a Code seal—Certificate No. 16—probably because it was already completed.) *Tarzan and His Mate* had Maureen O'Sullivan as Jane in a costume that exposed her hips and thighs. The now-famous nude swimming scene with Johnny Weissmuller and Sullivan (doubled by Olympic swimmer Josephine McKim) was found in the vault in 1996 by Turner Classic Movies and restored for cable television and home video. It was cut before the release of the film in April 1934 and not seen by anybody except studio executives. (Cedric Gibbons, longtime M-G-M supervising art director, was credited as the director of *Tarzan and His Mate*, although he was actually taken off of the picture. The ostensible reason was that it conflicted with other responsibilities, but more likely it was that he spent a lot of time and money on nude swimming footage that couldn't be used. Gibbons was married to Dolores del Rio, whose nude swim in *Bird of Paradise* may have been his inspiration. The scene in *Bird of Paradise* took place at night, so the water was darker and the nudity less visible.)

The Hell sequence in *Dante's Inferno* (1935), based on the engravings of Gustave Doré, showed breasts and (mostly male) buttocks in long shot, likely permitted for its moral lesson.

Even cartoons came under the Code. *Betty Boop's Rise to Fame* (1934) used the framing device of an interview of cartoonist Max Fleischer by a reporter to reprise big chunks of earlier cartoons. At one point, Fleischer's pen assumes the shape of Betty's nude buttocks. The Code turned Betty into a housewife and she lost popularity.

Under Breen, both screenplays and finished films were scrutinized. For the first year, the oval Code Seal, with the word "Approved" and the certificate number, occupied a full frame and was the first thing seen on the screen ahead of the main title. Breen got wind that audiences in the Los Angeles area booed it, something he blamed on studio employees in the audience. It came to be buried in the credits along with the "bug" logo of the International Alliance of Theatrical Stage Employees union and the credit for the sound system.

The Production Code took some of the freewheeling vitality out of movies. On the plus side, the need to gain approval of scripts in advance of production enhanced the importance of the screenplay and, thus, the status of writers. In 1938, the National Labor Relations Board certified the Screen Writers Guild as their sole bargaining agent, although the first contract with the producing companies would not be signed until 1941.

The Shirley Temple doll was a big seller for Christmas 1934. By 1936, the child whom 20th Century–Fox publicity called "the dimpled darling of the Universe" was the No. 1 box-office star.

Variety wrote in 1936, "It is difficult today, when one sees the lines in front of the box offices and nearby parking spaces jammed, to appreciate how great was the fall and how fast the rise has been." This was a reference to the 1932–33 period. They went on to claim that "the quality of films has improved immeasurably, due entirely to intra-industry precautions and regulations."

The PCA's moral cleanup was so complete than only one film, the independently

Murder at the Vanities **got in under the wire just before the implementation of the Production Code in July 1934. It was based on a stage production by Earl Carroll, whose theater in New York carried the motto, "Through These Portals Pass the Most Beautiful Girls in the World." MCA.**

produced *Damaged Goods* (about venereal disease), was condemned by the national Legion between 1934 and 1940. The state and local censor boards had less to do.

Those aspects of female topography that Joe Bob Briggs, host of cable television's *Joe Bob's Drive-In Theater*, would call "the groceries" disappeared except in a few unlikely places.

In Universal's first *Flash Gordon* serial (1936), Dale Arden (Jean Rogers) relied on hunky Buster Crabbe to protect her innocence from lewd Emperor Ming. Princess Aura, Ming's lusty, busty daughter (Priscilla Lawson), looked to him to take hers. Both went around in halter tops, bare midriffs and clingy skirts that stirred 12-year-old boys to unfamiliar longings.

Jane Wyatt (or her double) offered her nude behind in extreme long shot in *Lost Horizon* (1937). For the finale ("Speak Your Heart") of *Radio City Revels* (1938), ensemble director Hermes Pan had the female dancers wear skirts slit on both sides. Fifteen-year-old tap dancer Ann Miller opened her skirt to reveal the legs that would be seen in musicals for years to come. With Busby Berkeley sidelined to straight drama after straining for effect in *Gold Diggers of 1937*, the sexiest number to come out of Warner Bros. was in *Knute Rockne, All-American* (1940), as Pat O'Brien studied chorus girls who put the backfield in motion as inspiration for football plays.

The most extensive content analysis of the Hollywood studio era was published by Dorothy B. Jones in 1950. Her findings, based a study of 1,026 features from the output of an unnamed studio from 1917 to 1947, were summarized by I.C. Jarvie as follows:

> Whom are the films about? Men to women 2:1. Three out of five were "independent adults" (rare in real life). What are the films about? Boy meets girl. Four of the five wanted safety, income or deference. Sixty-eight percent wanted love; 26 percent fame, reputation, prestige; 18 percent safety; 14 percent a way of life; 10 percent money or goods; 9 percent to do their duty. Sixty-one percent get it; 10 percent do not; 14 percent get some, not others.

Given the centrality of heterosexual romance to movie plots and the presumed attraction between good-looking people, writers adapted to the strictures of the Production Code by inventing obstacles and complications. It is probably not coincidental that 1934, the year in which the Production Code Administration was established, also saw the two films, *It Happened One Night* and *Twentieth Century*, that launched the cycle of sophisticated comedies that continued into the first year or so of World War II with *The Talk of the Town*, *Woman of the Year* and *The More the Merrier*. (All were all directed by George Stevens, who would never make a comedy again.)

A famous scene in *It Happened One Night* had Clark Gable and Claudette Colbert forced to share an auto-court cabin, space divided between them by a blanket thrown over a clothesline known as the "Walls of Jericho." The "Walls of Jericho" finally fell at the end in an implied consummation. If Gable and Colbert turned into just another bickering married couple, it was after the fade-out.

The formula of "boy meets girl, boy loses girl, boy gets girl" operated in the Fred Astaire–Ginger Rogers classic *Top Hat* (1935). They "meet cute," in the parlance of the story conference. Astaire tap-dances in his hotel room in the film's first number. This awakens Rogers, who is nearly hit by falling plaster. She goes to his room to complain. He pursues her by impersonating a hansom cab driver. Their first number together, "Isn't This a Lovely Day (To Be Caught in the Rain)," danced in a jigsawed pavilion in the park ends on a note of reconciliation. A flimsy device of mistaken identity introduces the "boy loses girl" phase when Rogers believes Astaire, not Edward Everett Horton, is the husband of her

friend (Helen Broderick). She marries the dress designer for whom she models (Erik Rhodes). At the end, it is revealed that the marriage is not legal, as it was performed by Horton's butler (Eric Blore) who turned his collar around and pretended to be a clergyman. Astaire is not really married. "Boy gets girl" after all.

Ben Hecht, one of the most in demand of Hollywood screenwriters, recounted how he solved a plot problem brought to him by a desperate producer:

Emperor Ming (Charles Middleton) lusts after Dale Arden (Jean Rogers) in Universal's *Flash Gordon* serial from 1936. Ming's daughter, Princess Aura (Priscilla Lawson, left and bottom right), regards her dismissively, confident that her larger breasts will lure Flash away from Dale. The bare midriffs would vanish from the two later *Flash Gordon* serials. King Features.

The hero and heroine fall madly in love with each other—as soon as they meet. What we need is some gimmick that keeps them from going to bed right away. Not a physical gimmick like arrest or getting run over and having to go to the hospital. But a psychological one. Now what reasons do you know that would keep a healthy pair of lovers from hitting the hay in Reel Two?

Hecht's solution: "I answered that frequently a girl has moral concepts that keep her virtuous until after a trip to the altar. And that there are men who also prefer to wait for coitus until after they have married the girl they adore."

The producer was delighted: "We'll try it!" He had never thought of that before.

The Production Code didn't just regulate the treatment of subjects, it banned some subjects altogether. This created an opening for "exploitation" pictures. Most theaters wouldn't play them, so the Legion of Decency didn't bother to condemn them. As they were necessarily low- budget, no big names appeared in them and they did not produce future stars. They did have has-beens from the silent and early talkie eras: Betty Compson, Clara Kimball Young, Wheeler Oakman (who had uttered the immortal line "take him ... for ... a ... ride" in Warner Bros.' first all-talkie *Lights of New York* in 1928) and some faces familiar from "B" Westerns or serials.

Disheartened by the sleazy way the second version of *The Road to Ruin* was marketed, Mrs. Wallace Reid parted company from producer Willis Kent and gave up preachment against the sins of the world. By then billed as "Dorothy Reid," she went on to write conventional movie and television scripts into the late 1950s. Kent, on his own, produced titles like *The Pace That Kills*, a.k.a. *Cocaine Fiends* (1935). One of his films, *Race Suicide* (1938), dealt with the taboo subject of abortion. It actually showed a woman fully nude from the rear as she disrobed and changed into a hospital gown. In 1943, Kent released *Confessions of a Vice Baron*, a sort of Greatest Hits compendium. Gangster "Lucky" Lombardo (Willy Castello), facing execution, recounts his crimes to the prison chaplain. This occasions large chunks of earlier Kent productions in which Castello appeared, with and without mustache, made between 1935 and 1940.

Another prolific producer was J.D. Kendis. His film *Guilty Parents* (1934) feigned an educational stance. A foreword began: "Sex ignorance, the black plaugue [sic] of adolescence, continues to augment the mass of innocent youth in the abyss of despair." An innocent is seduced, has an abortion and, of course, dies. Subsequent Jay-Dee-Kay (or JDK) Productions all had basically the same story. A gambling den, nightclub or model agency is a front for prostitution. In *Gambling with Souls* (1936), a doctor's wife is initially excited when she is allowed to win at gambling but soon runs up big losses that she has to pay back with her body. Shots of blonde Martha Chapin undressing for bed or nude in silhouette before sex resulted in an "adults only" label. When her kid sister is ensnared and dies from an abortion, Chapin shoots the owner of the gambling den. More usually, a young woman is ensnared but, before she travels the full road to ruin, is rescued at the end by her boyfriend and/or the authorities who have been keeping an eye on the place. *Slaves in Bondage* (1937) was typical. It was the kind of "B" crime picture that might have been made by Monogram Pictures but with the lingerie and seminudity of the pre–Code era. An initiate is taken on a tour of rooms that cater to the varied tastes of male clients. One of the cubicles has two young women who spank each other in a suggestion of kinky sex and a possible threesome.

The Kendis productions were padded with obscure crooners, knife-throwing acts and the future Cyd Charisse as a Flamenco dancer in *Escort Girl* (1941). Several of these movies were directed by Elmer Clifton, a D.W. Griffith protégé whose career peaked with *Down to the Sea in Ships* (1922), the film that introduced Clara Bow. He went on to helm Don "Red" Barry Westerns at Republic in the 1940s and was the nominal director of *Not Wanted* (1949), Ida Lupino's first independent production.

Dwain Esper was one of the most successful entrepreneurs of outlaw cinema. His film *Narcotic* (1933) invited the audience to peek into a previously hidden world: "Very few people, other than professional investigators, have ever really witnessed a 'dope' party." The film sought to remedy that with authentic depictions of the "weird and revolting behaviour" of addicts. The party includes three well-dressed men and three women in slinky gowns. One woman sniffs cocaine from a little spoon. A man injects heroin into his arm (in close-up). Another woman smokes a marijuana cigarette. The weird and revolting behavior consists of the women lifting their skirts and telling bad jokes, e.g., "The next guy who steals my brassiere, I'm gonna sue for non-support." Esper's demented *Maniac* (1934) exposed a woman's breast. His biggest successes came with films to which he acquired the reissue rights. He bought Tod Browning's *Freaks* (1932) from M-G-M in 1947. They were willing to let it go as it got few bookings after a disastrous preview in San Diego, during which a woman ran screaming up the aisle. He also acquired the film originally called *Tell Your Children* (1936), later known as *Reefer Madness*, a midnight showing and campus favorite in the 1970s.

One of the most unusual exploitation pictures, *Child Bride* (1938), was based on a true story about a girl who was married at the age of nine. Although concealed by foliage and the brevity of the shots, the budding breasts of 11-year-old lead actress Shirley Mills are clearly visible. Because Mills could not swim, she was doubled by a local 13-year-old, whose nude body, backside only, is shown at length. A potentially lurid wedding-night scene is interrupted when the groom is shot and killed by the girl's 12-year-old boyfriend. He promises to marry her when both are old enough and so he literally gets away with murder.

The industry's ebullience of 1935–36 was tested by the "Roosevelt Recession" of 1937–38. The drop in attendance was not only due to economics. There was widespread discontent with the routine quality of the pictures. The rapid spread of the double feature policy in 1935–36 that eventually encompassed 85 percent of the nation's theaters accelerated a trend toward polarization of the product that was already underway. In order to make the big pictures bigger (and longer), the small pictures got smaller. As the studios invested resources into their most important stars and story properties, low-budget "B" pictures with a typical running time of 70 minutes were intended for the bottom half of the double bill. (The most formulaic of them all, the series pictures built around characters such as Charlie Chan and Dr. Kildare, were actually the most popular.) To combat public apathy, the industry launched a massive public relations campaign that proclaimed l938 as The Movies' Greatest Year. The original slogan was "Movies Are Your Best Entertainment." When cynics pointed out that this might be reduced to the acronym MAYBE, it was changed to "Motion Pictures Are Your Best Entertainment." The pressure for better films paid off in 1939, a year that many have proclaimed as Hollywood's greatest. The trend toward more adult and ambitious subjects was typified by Lewis Milestone's production of John Steinbeck's *Of Mice and Men*. In the next decade, producers would show a greater willingness to challenge the Breen Office.

4

Something for the Boys

Pin-Ups and Love Goddesses of the World War II Era

Million Dollar Legs was a title used by Paramount twice in the 1930s. The second one (1939) starred Betty Grable, who would displace Marlene Dietrich as the possessor of filmdom's most glamorous gams. The shift of erotic emphasis to the breasts, not that legs were neglected, probably started in earnest with Lana Turner in 1937's *They Won't Forget*. Men liked the new look. Ann Sheridan (christened the "oomph" girl by Warner Bros.' publicity) in *They Drive by Night* (1940) and newcomer Veronica Lake joined the sweater brigade. The era of the Sweater Girl caused Breen some grief. Even worse, Breen wrote to MPPDA boss Will Hays in March 1941, was "a marked tendency to more and more undrape women's breasts." He claimed that in just the previous two and a half weeks 10 pictures had to be trimmed of "breast shots." Breen decreed that breasts had to be fully covered at all times. Sweaters could do that, but there was nothing in the Code that dictated the size or shape of breasts. In October 1941, U.S. Patent No. 2,258,277 was granted to the A. Stein & Co. for the design of a new brassiere with stitched concentric circles in the cups and sold under the name Perma-Lift. Protuberance had come to stay.

When a movie called *Sweater Girl* appeared in 1942, it starred June Preisser, sweetheart of "B" campus musicals. Turner had attained big star status as the eponymous *Ziegfeld Girl* (1941). With his biggest budget in years, Busby Berkeley could once again show what he and Ziegfeld, his onetime boss, were famous for. "Girls! Hundreds of 'em!" promised the trailer, although there were no more than 25 on-screen.

Ziegfeld Girl had a multi-star cast: James Stewart, Lana Turner, Hedy Lamarr and Judy Garland. Only Garland qualified as a musical star. A new song, "You Stepped Out of a Dream," sought to emulate, even if it could not hope to outdo, the jaw-dropping "A Pretty Girl Is Like a Melody" number from *The Great Ziegfeld* (1936). Hedy Lamarr climbs the stairs as Tony Martin croons. Like her character, the real Hedy, a student of Max Reinhardt who was currently involved in experiments that led to a U.S. patent for a radio-controlled torpedo, seems embarrassed at being "glorified." In a costume from which stars protrude on feelers, she strikes a pose. This may be the source of her oft-quoted remark, "Any girl can be glamorous. All you have to do is stand still and look stupid." Her émigré husband, a classical violinist (Philip Dorn), shared her discomfort while seated in the audience. A parade of lovelies wore everything from ostrich feathers to candelabras. Lana Turner was more at home in this context. She descends the staircase in a below-eye-level shot that emphasizes her body as, from the balcony, Jackie

Cooper drools and James Stewart looks on in dismay. Later on, as an alcoholic, she will descend the stairs again and collapse at the base.

Except for a part as a Moscow streetcar conductor involved with an American reporter (Clark Gable) in *Comrade X* (1940), an anti–Communist satire in the tradition of *Ninotchka* (1939), Lamarr was not well utilized by M-G-M. *Ecstasy*, a German-Czech production, made in 1933 when she was 19, was imported into the U.S. in 1937. It played for years as the only film in which a big-name star could be seen in the nude. (It was also the first film to portray orgasm, which director Gustav Machaty achieved by sticking the actress with a pin.)

To capitalize on Lamarr's sexy aura, she was put in *White Cargo* (1942) from a campy old stage melodrama. Her dark makeup skirted the Code ban on miscegenation. Dialogue characterized her as half–Arab, half–Egyptian. She uttered the immortal line "I am Tondelayo" in a Viennese-African accent. *The Heavenly Body* (1944), in which she was the wife of an astronomer, marked the first use of the word "body" in the title of a U.S. feature film, an obvious double *entendre*.

"A wartime product created for the benefit of American soldiers warming to a long exile at the four corners of the world, the pin-up girl soon became an industrial product," wrote critic André Bazin, future editor of France's leading film magazine *Cahiers du Cinéma*. He noted that "this American Venus is a tall, vigorous girl whose streamlined body splendidly represents a tall race." She was characterized by narrow hips ("the pin-up girl does not evoke motherhood") and "the firm opulence of her bosom." The essential elements of what we think of as iconic wartime popular culture actually predate the U.S. entry into World War II. Although "cheesecake" has been traced back to 1915, the first documented use of the term "pin-up" dates from 1941.

The first pin-up girls were not movie stars; they were not real women at all. The "Varga Girl" became a monthly feature in *Esquire* in October 1940 after illustrator George Petty, whose "Petty Girl" had been a feature from the magazine's inception in 1933, left in a money dispute. Alberto Vargas had produced stylish illustrations of women for over 20 years. He did a famous poster of Barbara Stanwyck for *Ladies They Talk About* (1933), but his movie opportunities diminished once the Code came in. At *Esquire*, Vargas flirted with nudity, especially from the rear, scarcely concealed by sheer, almost transparent negligees. Actual photographs of nude women, especially if they showed nipples or pubic hair, could only be sold clandestinely.

The 1941 *Esquire* calendar illustrated by Alberto Vargas was a supplement to the December 1940 issue and was also available by mail for 25 cents. It became the best-selling calendar up to that time with 320,000 copies.

Robert Landry's 1941 photograph of Rita Hayworth in *Life* magazine in which she kneeled on a bed in a black nightgown provided a real-life Varga Girl. *Life* also ran a feature on the measurements of Hollywood actresses. Hayworth was on the list, as was Carole Landis with an impressive 36½-24-35. Betty Grable, despite a recent hit in *Moon Over Miami*, wasn't a big enough name yet. That something like this would appear in the largest-circulation general-interest publication and not a fan magazine was a sign of the times. The pin-up girl, "standardized by Varga, sterilized by censorship" (Bazin), was ready to enlist.

The American public was not so overwhelmingly isolationist as is sometimes thought. The fall of France in June 1940, and, especially, the London Blitz that commenced that September, shifted popular sentiment. A Gallup poll in April 1941 showed that 82 percent of the public expected the United States would become involved in the European war and that 79 percent favored sending part of the Army to help Britain. Isolationism's real bastion was the United States Senate, where North Dakota's Gerald Nye and Montana's Burton K. Wheeler wielded influence out of all proportion to the sparse populations of their states. Their investigation into war propaganda in Hollywood movies was cut short by the attack on Pearl Harbor. Comedies such as *Buck Privates* with Abbott and Costello, *Caught in the Draft* with Bob Hope and the semi-musical *Navy Blues*, released in early-to-mid 1941, conditioned the public to accept the coming war better than the serious anti–Nazi dramas that concerned the Senators. Rita Hayworth's first starring musical, *You'll Never Get Rich* (1941), set on an Army post, put Fred Astaire in uniform and had a military-themed finale.

Patriotism and pin-ups converged in a new character, Wonder Woman, at the end of 1941. According to Jill Lepore's book *The Secret History of Wonder Woman*, she got the body of the July 1941 Varga Girl and the costume of Captain America (albeit scantier). The star-spangled cheerleader skirt of her first appearance gave way by the second outing to hip-hugging panties. Wonder Woman also bore a more than passing resemblance to Jane Russell.

Earlier in 1941, George Hurrell had ordered a half-ton of hay for a rickety loft in his studio to make the publicity photographs of Russell in Howard Hughes's *The Outlaw*. He was paid $4.000, an enormous sum for the time but well worth it. When

Hedy Lamarr (left and top of facing page) and Lana Turner (right and bottom of facing page) show their costumes for the "You Stepped Out of a Dream" number in *Ziegfeld Girl*. They appeared on-screen with Tony Martin (center). Turner.

Hurrell entered the service in 1942, he saw his pictures on barracks walls. Russell is probably the first example of someone who became a star, or least a celebrity, via picture magazines, even though there was no movie to promote and wouldn't be for two years.

Fortuitously, Rita Hayworth not only embodied the emergent ideal but was also an accomplished dancer at a time when musicals were back in vogue. Lavish musicals of the *Rosalie* type were considered passé after 1937 and replaced by comedies with a few songs of which the Astaire-Rogers *Carefree* (1938) was typical. The approach of war and the popularity of the Big Bands (whose leaders often appeared as guest stars) produced a resurgence of musicals in 1941. Wartime material restrictions limited skirt lengths to 17 inches above the floor and the popularity of the jitterbug called for a "swing skirt," as worn by Hayworth in the "Shorty George" number in 1942's *You Were Never Lovelier*, her other film with Astaire.

Columbia Pictures not only gave the former Margarita Cansino a new name. They padded her hips for a shapelier figure and forced her to undergo painful electrolysis to raise her hairline. They dyed her hair red.

Hayworth's first color musical *My Gal Sal* (1942), made on loan out to 20th Century–Fox, was one of that company's many portrayals of Gilded Age theatricals. The "On the Gay White Way" number had Hayworth as a showgirl surrounded by a bunch of stage-door Johnnies in top hats. It was the Thaw-White-Nesbit milieu sanitized as a nostalgic Cinderella story. Having danced with Astaire, she now danced with his longtime associate Hermes Pan, who would make a few on-screen appearances in 20th Century–Fox musicals.

The Gilded Age also figured prominently in *Cover Girl* (1944). Hayworth's character, Rusty Parker, enters a contest to be a "cover girl." She catches the eye of a publisher (Otto Kruger), who sees her as the spitting image of the showgirl he wanted to marry 40 years earlier, only to have her abandon him at the altar. Hayworth plays both parts and, in a flashback, performs the period song "Poor John."

One of the numbers had Hayworth in a Yellow Cab cap, a comment on the wartime labor shortage and the emergence of women in male jobs. Female cab drivers also appeared in *The Big Sleep* (released in 1946 but made at least a year earlier), *Jealousy* (1945) and, by then anachronistically, in the 1949 film version of Broadway's 1944 *On the Town*.

The title number in *Cover Girl* followed a succession of covers from now long-defunct publications. It offered a 1944 Technicolor vision of paradise. Hayworth descends from the clouds down a ramp to consort with identically tuxedo-clad suitors, only to ascend out of reach to a presumed Heaven. In *Gilda* (1946), she performed a striptease that consisted of the removal of one glove. Some writers have traced the black satin

Photographer George Hurrell turned his studio into a hayloft for the photo session that made Jane Russell famous even before she had been seen in a movie.

gown by Columbia's star designer Jean Louis for the "Put the Blame on Mame" number to the dress in John Singer Sargent's *Portrait of Madame X*. Both have bows at the side, but they also differ. Hayworth's dress is strapless, held up by a hidden plastic frame. The top of the dress thus lacks the dramatic "V" shaped dip of the bodice in the Sargent painting. Hayworth's dress, of course, has a slit to reveal her legs.

A subsequent vehicle, *Down to Earth* (1947), was a flop in its time. It went over budget. Audiences may have thought they had seen it before. The supernatural "Mr. Jordan" from 1941's *Here Comes Mr. Jordan* (with Roland Culver in the old Claude Rains role) returned along with "Max Corkle" (James Gleason). Larry Parks' show promoter was even named "Danny" like Gene Kelly in *Cover Girl*. George Macready from *Gilda* was the villain. Hayworth again danced with Marc Platt, her partner in *Tonight and Every Night* (1945). However, she never looked or danced better. A 1947 *Life* magazine spread proclaimed Hayworth the "Love Goddess." In the movie she was a real goddess, Terpsichore, sent to earth. The *Life* feature posed Hayworth with the Venus de Milo.

Down to Earth was likely intended to beat out *One Touch of Venus*, the 1943 stage musical the movie rights to which had been sold in 1945. It reached the screen in 1948 in a modest black-and-white production starring the rapidly ascending Ava Gardner. All but three of Kurt Weill's songs were thrown out and the book radically simplified. Gardner actually posed for the statue of Venus that appeared in the film on display in a department store, where it was brought to life by the kiss of a window dresser (not yet a stereotypically gay profession) played by Robert Walker. In truth, as Bazin anticipated, Hollywood goddesses Gardner and Hayworth supplanted the Greek and Roman originals with their shorter legs and torsos.

Hayworth was off the screen for three years amid a highly publicized affair with Prince Aly Khan. When she returned to work, she was 34 and looked it. Columbia was eager to capitalize on her notoriety: "You've read about her! You've talked about her! You've wondered about her." Studio boss Harry Cohn wondered whether she was still box-office. *Affair in Trinidad* (1952), in black and white, was an obvious rehash of *Gilda*, again with Glenn Ford, and hastily thrown together. "Trinidad Lady," choreographed by Valerie Bettis, provided the obligatory torrid solo.

"Single men in barracks do not grow into plaster saints," as Rudyard Kipling once wrote. Members of the American Volunteer Group, better known as the "Flying Tigers," installed an old 16mm projector in the mess hall of their outpost in China. During *The Ghost Breakers*, a Bob Hope comedy of 1940 that featured Paulette Goddard "in various stages of undress, the moans and howls of those watching could be heard all over the base."[1] They must have been pretty desperate. In one scene, Goddard takes off her dress to reveal lingerie before she covers up with a bathrobe. In another, she catches her skirt on a banister and it is pulled off as she runs upstairs to escape a zombie.

In *Star-Spangled Rhythm* (1942), homesick G.I. Johnnie Johnston sang "That Old Black Magic" to his framed, autographed picture of Paramount star Vera Zorina. After he dozes off, the picture comes to life in a dance choreographed by George Balanchine. She steps down from the frame but when he awakens and tries to embrace her, she vanishes.

Yank magazine, published by the U.S. Army and edited by and for enlisted men, always included a picture of a Hollywood female. The bigger names appeared in evening gowns, but minor figures revealed more, e.g., Chili Williams, seen mainly in unbilled parts, in her trademark two-piece polka-dot bathing suit. Ramsay Ames—who as the reincarnated Princess Ananka in *The Mummy's Ghost* (1944) excited overage college student Robert Lowery, the priest charged with bringing her back to Egypt (John Carradine) and the ever-ardent 3,000-year-old Prince Kharis (Lon Chaney, Jr.)—displayed her curvaceous body in a sultry pose. Anne Gwynne, a regular in Universal horror movies, appeared in *Yank* several times and, according to a *Life* magazine article in 1943, led all the big stars in picture requests from servicemen.

The famous rear view of Betty Grable, taken in 1943, was somewhat ahead of its time in its Kardashianesque display. (In 1974, sculptor Lynda Benglis dropped her pants for a photograph by Annie Leibovitz to appropriate it as a critique of art-world sexism.) A version of it served as the title art for *Pin-Up Girl* (1944) and was on the cover of her biography. It was sometimes erroneously claimed that Grable was shot from the rear because she was pregnant. It was actually just one of several shots made that day and was shot almost as an afterthought by Fox stills man Frank Polowney, who recalled:

> She tried several bathing suits in different colors and they weren't exactly right. Finally, she put on the white one and we made a couple of shots. She started to walk away and glanced back over her shoulder. It looked pretty good so I asked if she would come back and do it again. She struck the pose, and then said, "Is this what you want?" I shot it and that was that.

Given Grable's rapid ascent from 1940 on, her path to stardom was slow. In Columbia's *What Price Innocence?* (1932), one of the few sex-education pictures released by a mainstream company, she had her first billed part as the wised-up friend of a high school girl (Jean Parker) so naïve that she apparently didn't connect sex and pregnancy and, in disgrace, drowned herself in the river. A featured spot in the popular Fred Astaire–Ginger Rogers picture *The Gay Divorcee* (1934) put her in silk pajamas to perform "Let's K-nock K-neez" with comic actor Edward Everett Horton; this got her an RKO contract but did

The black dress by Columbia Pictures designer Jean Louis for Rita Hayworth in *Gilda* reminded some of a classic John Singer Sargent painting. Columbia Pictures/Sony.

her less good than might be expected. Two years later, she was still part of a girl trio that backed Ginger Rogers in another Astaire picture, *Follow the Fleet*. A loan-out to her future home studio 20th Century–Fox put her as a coed in *Pigskin Parade* (1936), chiefly remembered as Judy Garland's first feature. This led to a Paramount contract and more campus fluff. She was an usherette in *This Way Please* (1937). In *Campus Confessions* (1938), she was top-billed for the first time. *Million Dollar Legs* (1939) referred not to hers but a winning horse. (In a publicity stunt, her new employers at 20th Century–Fox insured her legs with Lloyd's of London for one million dollars.)

Grable's movies were pretty much assembly-line affairs but highly profitable for Fox. One of her first starring roles, *Tin Pan Alley* (1940), in which she was costarred with Alice Faye, ran afoul of the Breen Office, because of the costumes in the "Sheik of Araby" number. The number caused the film to be denied a Seal. An appeal was turned down and the number had to be reworked.

For *Footlight Serenade* (1942), Hermes Pan devised a number, "I Heard the Birdies Sing," in which Grable in boxing gloves and shorts sparred with her silhouetted self and took a kick to her shapely rear. (This was likely inspired by Pan's memory of the "Bojangles of Harlem" number in 1936's *Swing Time*, wherein Fred Astaire danced with a shadowy version of himself in triplicate.)

Vincente Minnelli recalled that during the preparation of *An American in Paris* (1951) at M-G-M, he was told at a gathering held by the aging and soon-to-be gone Louis B. Mayer, "You should copy the color in *Coney Island*, Vincente. In fact, all our color films should have that look." Pandro S. Berman, one of the studio's top producers, overheard this and whispered to Minnelli, "That picture has the most garish and vivid and ugly color in the history of the movie business."

Coney Island (1943) may have been vulgar, but it offered escape from wartime realities. It was followed by *Sweet Rosie O'Grady* (1943), an old script from the Alice

Ava Gardner contemplates a model of the Venus de Milo in a publicity photograph for *One Touch of Venus*. Universal/MCA.

"B" Actress Ramsay Ames displays a curvaceous figure and a rather fearsome visage for the readers of *Yank*, the Army's magazine for enlisted men, in 1944.

Faye era. The trick with star vehicles was to vary the formula enough to maintain interest, but not so drastically as to disorient the audience. With Grable's postwar films, Fox did some of both. *The Shocking Miss Pilgrim* (1947) had a stronger than usual story. As the first female "typewriter" in an all-male shipping office, she was subjected to discrimination and harassment and even joined the suffragist movement. It was criticized by fans who complained that it did not show off her legs, hidden under petticoats. This was corrected in *Mother Wore Tights* (1947), her personal favorite and the first of five films with Dan Dailey. *That Lady in Ermine* (1948) was begun by Ernst Lubitsch, but Lubitsch died, and the film was finished by Otto Preminger. The day of Ruritanian comedy in the style of Lubitsch's early 1930s bonbons with Maurice Chevalier and Jeanette MacDonald had long passed. Grable particularly hated *The Beautiful Blonde from Bashful Bend* (1949), a comedy Western that pretty much ended the career of writer-director Preston Sturges. In stories with a show-business background, Grable could still draw; *Wabash Avenue* (1950) was essentially a remake of her own *Coney Island*.

Hollywood's interest in Grable had been revived when she starred in Cole Porter's 1939 *Du Barry Was a Lady* on Broadway. In 1943, M-G-M turned it into a typical wartime hodgepodge with Lucille Ball in the Grable part. The trailer promised "Varga Girls." A comic song "I Love an Esquire Girl" (lyrics by Ralph Freed and Roger Edens, not Porter) was performed by Red Skelton surrounded by women in harem outfits. Twelve models in a variety of outfits from two-piece bathing suits to slinky negligees represented the months of the year. (Future star Marilyn Maxwell was Miss February.) The number culminated with a wordless, unbilled guest appearance by Lana Turner (appropriately, as it was pretty much copied from "You Stepped Out of a Dream"). Vargas created the movie's posters himself.

Not everybody loved an *Esquire* girl. Before *Playboy*, *Esquire* was the most-censored mass-circulation magazine. In 1943, the Postmaster General threatened to withdraw second-class mailing privileges. *Esquire* had run a color gatefold of Jane Russell from the Hurrell session in its issue of January 1943. A ripe Varga Girl was put in the uniform of the Women's Army Corps. Feminism then was in the shaky hands of the suffragist veterans in the National Women's Party, whose big issue was the Equal Rights Amendment. One of their number, Anna Kelton Wiley, the only woman to testify on behalf of the postal ban, faced ridicule as a prude. She acknowledged that she expected that reaction. Critiques of objectification and the "male gaze" were mostly in the future. The pin-up girl, like the flapper of the l920s, symbolized modernity and freedom from convention. *Esquire* provided free subscriptions to servicemen and, in the "something for the boys" ethos of the time, prevailed in court. (The background and legacy of the controversy is discussed by Joanne Meyerowitz in "Women, Cheesecake and Borderline Material: Responses to Girlie Pictures in the Mid-Twentieth Century United States," collected in *Sexual Borderlands: Constructing an American Sexual Past*, edited by Kathleen Kennedy and Sharon Rena Ullman, Ohio State University Press 2003. "The 'Varga Girl' Goes to War," a catalogue essay by Maureen Honey that accompanied an exhibition at the Spencer Museum of Art, University of Kansas, suggests that the heightened secondary sex characteristics of the wartime pin-up served various functions, including a reaffirmation of gender roles at a time when women moved into traditionally male jobs. Military authorities feared that gays and lesbians, removed from the watchful eyes of families and neighbors, were finding each other and forming subcultures. The pin-up also reaffirmed heteronormativity.)

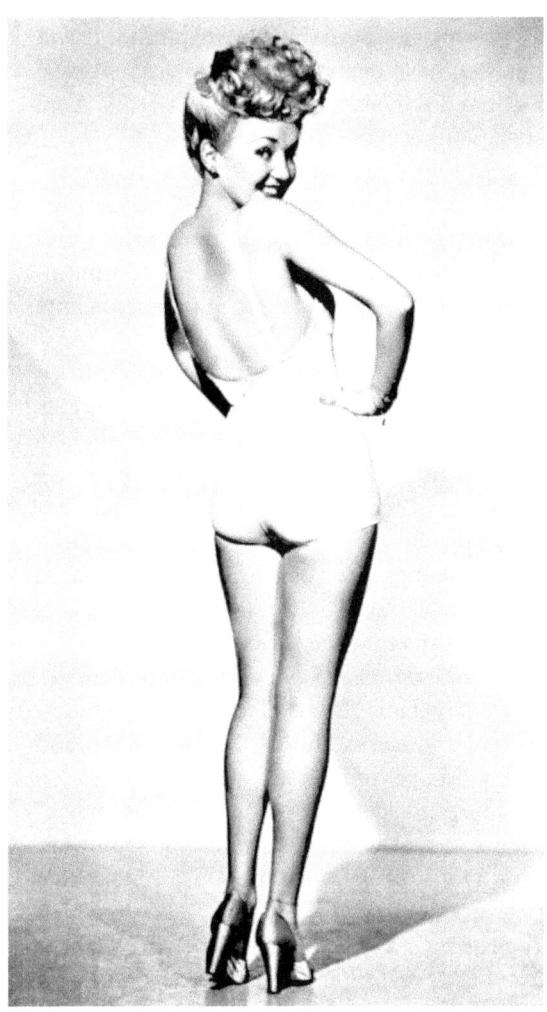

Betty Grable was famed for her legs and Jane Russell had recently shifted emphasis to the breasts, but Grable's iconic pin-up looked ahead to the behind as the focus of erotic interest. Five million copies were struck and distributed to servicemen. 20th Century–Fox.

Even as women moved into male jobs in defense plants, Hollywood reassured men (and women) that sex roles and feminine attractiveness remained intact. Ginger Rogers starred in *Tender Comrade* (1943), while Deanna Durbin brought her Penny Craig character from *Three Smart Girls* (1936) and *Three Smart Girls Grow Up* (1939) to the Lockheed assembly line in *Hers to Hold* (1943). She sang "Begin the Beguine" in coveralls accompanied by an orchestra of male workers. (Lunchtime concerts at defense plants happened in reality.) The finale of *Rosie the Riveter* (1944) depicted the award of the Army-Navy "E" flag, for excellence in war production, to a fictional aircraft company in a ceremony that mixed footage of actual war workers with a Republic Pictures soundstage that doubled as the plant's hangar. Cute females in shorts (it was California after all) wielded rivet guns as they cavorted to the song that gave the film its title.

Low-budget, black-and-white musicals flourished during the war years alongside the Technicolor vehicles for Hayworth and Grable. Universal and Columbia, then second-tier companies, made most of them, but even small studios like Republic and Monogram contributed. Ann Miller tapped furiously in 10 Columbia musicals between 1941 and 1946. Even Simone Simon, star of *Cat People*, was cast in Republic's *Tahiti Honey* (1943) in a costume that exposed her legs and midriff; she also appeared in evening gowns and the inevitable sarong. For Abbott and Costello's *Pardon My Sarong* (1942) at Universal, Katherine Dunham choreographed a "native" number, "Vingo Jingo." Dunham, an African American, knew the dances of Brazil and the Caribbean, but, for director Erle C. Kenton, Tahiti and Haiti might as well have been the same. What mattered was the chance to show improbably white-skinned Polynesians in skimpy outfits, from which Virginia Bruce playfully shielded Robert Paige's eyes.

There is little doubt that mores with regard to premarital and extramarital sex relaxed markedly during the war. The military anti–V.D. campaigns warned servicemen away from prostitutes, but in 1945 military leaders estimated that 40 percent of venereal infections occurred while men were on furlough, usually in their home communities. Instead of organized prostitution, sexual encounters typically began as a pickup, usually in a bar but sometimes at a USO dance.[2]

In Preston Sturges's popular *The Miracle of Morgan's Creek* (1944), a small-town "Victory Girl" with the comic-strip name of Trudy Kockenlocker (Betty Hutton) gets drunk and is impregnated by a soldier possibly named "Private Ratskywatzsky," to whom she vaguely remembers being married. She induces a schnook (Eddie Bracken), whose devotion to her up until now has been unreciprocated, to marry her and save her good name. She becomes a national heroine when she gives birth on Christmas Eve to sextuplets. (This was before fertility drugs.) Critic James Agee of *The Nation* speculated that "the Hays Office has either been hypnotized ... or raped in its sleep."

One of more intriguing minor figures of the war years was Dona Drake. Under the name Rita Rio, she fronted an all-girl orchestra. She danced in New York nightclubs. A number, "The Lady Dances," in the Eddie Cantor vehicle *Strike Me Pink* (1936) might have led to stardom for her but didn't. Her real name was Eunice Westmoreland and she came from mixed black and white ancestry. She passed herself off as a Latina even though she spoke unaccented English. She appeared in music shorts and "soundies" shot in 16mm film and shown in visual jukeboxes that were the music videos of their time. Paramount Pictures gave her the name Dona Drake. Her most prominent role was in the Bob Hope filmization of Irving Berlin's *Louisiana Purchase* (1941), in which she was billed fifth and on-screen for only a little over a minute but got to sing the title song. She tossed off an ermine-trimmed robe to reveal a perfect figure in a sequined bathing suit.

She seemed to have it all: a cute face—a cross between Shirley Temple earlier and Dorothy Malone later—a compact but solid body and a real singing and dancing ability. Stardom never came, perhaps because she had to conceal her background. After an appearance in the Hope-Crosby *Road to Morocco* (1942) and another Hope vehicle *Let's Face It* (1943), Paramount dropped her. She did get top billing in Monogram's *Hot*

Rhythm (1944). When low-budget musicals dried up after the war, she played second leads as a blonde in comedies such as *So This Is New York* (1948), her biggest part, and in *The Girl from Jones Beach* (1949), but then went back to ethnics, most memorably as Bette Davis's insolent Indian maid in *Beyond the Forest* (1949), in which she resembled a younger version of Davis herself with similar black wig.

Racism also inhibited the career of Lena Horne. Although it was not true, she claimed that M-G-M always cut her scenes out of movies distributed in the South, but it did happen in one case. Lloyd Binford, the censor of Memphis, Tennessee, cut the number "Love" from *Ziegfeld Follies* (1946). Despite the stereotypic setting in a low-life bar, the art direction (Lemuel Ayers) and a sensational musical arrangement (Conrad Salinger) created a sensual impact that Mr. Binford must have found too hot for comfort.

The Hollywood view of pin-up culture was perfectly reflected in *Calendar Girl*, a Republic "B" musical of 1947 directed by Allan Dwan. An old-school fire captain (Victor McLaglen) in 1900 New York is outraged after his daughter (Jane Frazee), who posed innocently for her artist boyfriend, finds that he sold a repainted, leggy version to a publisher of calendars. The owner (Irene Rich) of a boardinghouse that is home to artists and theater people tries to mollify McLaglen: "Women have legs and they are very beautiful." Frazee is rewarded with stardom in a Broadway show titled—of course—*Cal-*

Singer Nan Wynn and some improbably tall and light-skinned Polynesians performed in *Pardon My Sarong*, **typical wartime escapist nonsense from Universal.** Universal/MCA.

endar Girl. Screen credit was given to Zoë Mozert for the painting and to her employer, Brown & Bigelow, a leading printer of calendars.

Mozert also did the famous poster for *The Outlaw* that showcased "Mean, Moody, Magnificent" Jane Russell to the near-exclusion of the other stars and the film's Western elements. (She wasn't mean at all and not that moody; her physique may have been magnificent, but her performance was not.)

When *The Outlaw* was released in France in 1948, André Bazin saw a discrepancy between the publicity and the film itself: "The posters for *The Outlaw* show Jane Russell with lifted skirt and generously low-cut dress. In reality it is only her bosom that counts in the film. The fact is that in the past seven or eight years the focus of eroticism in the American film has shifted from the thigh to the bosom, but the public is not sufficiently aware of this change in frontier to allow the publicity departments to dispense with their traditional sources of stimulation." What Bazin did not know was that all the subsequent releases used variations on the original posters from 1943. Sometimes the angle changes or the colors are different; in some versions the pistol she holds is replaced with a whip, but it is still basically what Mozert painted.

A Code Seal for *The Outlaw* had been granted in 1941 only after protracted negotiations. Howard Hughes, who always did things his own way, did not bother to submit a script until after shooting started and then only because Breen requested it. When he saw the actual film, Breen complained to Hays: "Throughout almost half the picture the girl's breasts, which are quite large and prominent, are shockingly emphasized and, in almost every instance, are shockingly uncovered." This was not true. Russell wore a low-cut peasant blouse in only some of her scenes. Otherwise her breasts were covered, unusual only in size and shape. Breen demanded 37 cuts of "breast shots," something that would have made hash of the continuity. Hughes appealed over Breen's head to Will Hays himself. In the end, only about a minute's worth of cuts were made. The final point of contention was a scene in which Billy the Kid (Jack Buetel) watches Russell as she bends over a chest of drawers, her cleavage reflected in a mirror. The image, in long shot, remained in the film.

During a controversial, aborted nine-week run in San Francisco in 1943, the Legion of Decency issued a "Condemned" rating: "The film throughout a very considerable portion of its length is indecent in costuming." Hughes brought it back for broad release in 1946. Hughes took personal charge of publicity and bypassed the nominal distributor, United Artists. In one of his innovations, a skywriting plane drew circles in the air with dots in the center to represent nipples. An ad in the Los Angeles papers asked, "What are the two reasons for Jane Russell's rise to stardom?" The ad answered its own question: "She's daring and exciting." A line drawing of a buxom Russell left no doubt as to the real answer. On opening day in Los Angeles, the mostly male patrons lined the sidewalk and, once inside, made animal noises as the movie unspooled.

The unprecedented vulgarity of the ad campaign caused the Motion Picture Association of America to revoke the Seal its predecessor, the MPPDA, had reluctantly granted. Although the film was played by some major theater circuits before the Code Seal was pulled in April 1946 and during the appeals process, the theaters owned by members of the MPAA and most regional circuits would not play a non–Code picture. For smaller circuits and independents, the picture was a bonanza. *Boxoffice Reports* named Hughes as Producer of the Year for 1946.

By the end of 1946, Hughes could claim that *The Outlaw* had played in 40 of the

4. Something for the Boys

What better way to welcome the New Year than behind a machine gun? Perky Dona Drake makes a patriotic pitch for war bonds. The cute singer-dancer-actress never got beyond supporting parts and leads in "B" pictures, possibly because she had to conceal the fact that she was partly black. MCA.

then 48 states. It was still excluded from many cities, especially those with large Catholic populations. It was literally banned in Boston by a censor who quoted the Legion of Decency verbatim and also in Philadelphia. In the richest market, New York City, the career of *The Outlaw* verged on farce. The New York State Board of Regents had denied the film a certificate when it was submitted in 1942 but reversed itself in 1946. The New York City Commissioner of Licenses then threatened to revoke the operating license of any theater that showed the film and to prosecute the owners. This was a more serious threat than the breach of contract suit brought by United Artists against the three theaters that had booked the film but backed out. The courts upheld the city's position. Finally, in September 1947, amid accusations that Hughes had bribed officials, the film opened at the Broadway Theater ("at popular prices") where it ran continuously until 4 a.m. The newspaper ads shrieked, "2 Years to Make! 2 Million to Produce! Too <u>BIG</u> to Miss!" The numerals were positioned adjacent to the curve of Russell's breast.

The Outlaw had upset an unspoken compact between the studios and the MPAA.

So long as the film itself observed the proprieties, standards for publicity materials, subject to its Advertising Code, were much looser. Like a barker pitching a girlie show to the rubes, movie posters featured voluptuous women in skintight outfits. Taglines promised the forbidden and unspeakable, e.g., "Please don't tell what Mildred Pierce did." The savvy moviegoer knew that even if George Petty himself did the advertising art for *The Petty Girl* (1950), there was no way Joan Caulfield would be seminude on-screen in the fashion of his work for *Esquire*. (The Breen Office did allow some surprisingly risqué art under the credits.)

Some cuts were made to *The Outlaw* that allowed the Code Seal to be restored and the Legion of Decency to re-rate the film from "C" (Condemned) to "B" (Objectionable in part for all). A "B" rating was very desirable; it indicated marketable elements but did not cost bookings. *The Outlaw* went into general release in 1950 under the banner of RKO Radio Pictures, taken over by Hughes in 1948; this gave entrée to the theater chain that RKO still owned. Audiences must have wondered what the fuss was all about.

Jane Russell's photo session for George Hurrell was re-created by painter Zoë Mozert, whose art was used as the basis for the posters. Ads (on facing page) for *The Outlaw* emphasized Jane Russell's body to the detriment of the rest of the cast and the movie's Western elements.

4. Something for the Boys

Duel in the Sun (1946), with Jennifer Jones shrugging and wiggling, had come and gone. The low-cut peasant blouse turned up in *Colorado Territory* (1949) filled by Virginia Mayo and on cantina girls in routine Westerns. Russell had already kidded her sex bomb image in *The Paleface* (1948) with Bob Hope. She was only 19 when *The Outlaw* began production and her big smile at the end of the movie is the most appealing thing in it. Seen today, most of the sexual tension is homoerotic. Thomas Mitchell plays Sheriff Pat Garrett as a blubbering queen, loser to the suave Doc Holliday (Walter Huston) in competition for the young stud, Billy the Kid.

Hayworth, Russell and the Varga/Petty Girl coalesced into an image of the ideal female body that, with some variation, persists to the present. She was everywhere— on the nose of World War II bombers, the back glass of pinball machines, the covers

George Petty's illustrations of star Joan Caulfield for *The Petty Girl* were more risqué than anything in the actual movie. Johnny Mercer's lyric for the title song described the Petty Girl as "shapely, curvaceous, my goodness gracious." For the finale, there was a Petty Girl for each month of the year, something that had already been done with the Varga Girl in *DuBarry Was a Lady*. Columbia Pictures/Sony.

of pulp magazines and paperback novels. Rita Hayworth (36–24–36) and Jane Russell (38–24–36) fell just on either side of an ideal confirmed by academic studies. Devendra Singh at the University of Texas found in a study of *Playboy* Playmates and Miss America contestants from 1955 to 1987 a waist-to-hip ratio within a narrow range of .68 to .71. A 2003 study of *Playboy* Playmates from 1960 to 2000 showed a mean waist-to-hip ratio of .67 and waist-to-bust ratio of .66. This was very close to the proportions of the wartime Betty Grable, at 36-24-34, the ideal of the teenaged Hugh Hefner. A recent study at Newcastle University asked both men and women to design the ideal female figure. For men, the ideal waist-to-bust ratio was at .69, and women picked .67; the women assigned greater importance to large breasts and a slim waist than the men did. Lest anyone claim that this is a "Western" standard, we have the Indian film industry which serves up Old Hollywood escapism with stars to match. How many countries is *Playboy* sold in? (Men's magazines have women on the cover. Women's magazines have women on the cover. Often, they are the same women.)

5

"She came at me in sections"

Women in Postwar Genre Movies

"We got away with murder in those days because it was dance."
—Cyd Charisse

Men did not particularly like it when Christian Dior's 1947 "New Look" lowered hemlines, but otherwise they did not mind a silhouette defined by a "nipped-in waist, high, round bosom" and "narrow shoulders."[1] Dior's dresses flared out from rounded hips to dramatic effect. The "New Look" required new foundation garments. Maidenform in l949 launched its "Chansonette," or "bullet bra," that contained spiral-stitched cups. It was advertised with the famous "I dreamed I went to the opera/joined the circus/etc. in my Maidenform bra" ad campaign. A favorite of Hollywood stars and starlets, it would be the company's best seller into the l960s.

"Liberated Women Cause Increase in Sex Crimes, Say Experts" and "Plunging Necklines, Falsies Get Blame for Rise in Sex Crimes" were two of the headlines given by local papers to the same December 1949 Associated Press story. It quoted a Pittsburgh police official who blamed rape on women who dressed in line with the pressure for curvaceous figures rather than men who, understandably, could not control themselves.

André Bazin predicted in 1946 that, with the war's end, the pin-up girl would lose her social utility and become bifurcated. Her cheerful athleticism be would domesticated in the service of advertising for consumer products. Her sex appeal would be more blatantly expressed.

America's ambivalent attitudes toward sex were in especially sharp relief in the decade after the war. Easy access to women after the liberation of Paris or on occupation duty in Germany or Japan heightened male expectations. Frederick Mellinger founded Frederick's of Hollywood in l946 so that returning G.I.s could dress their wives and girlfriends as pin-up fantasies. With the end of wartime paper rationing, magazines proliferated. *Pageant*, a new digest-format magazine in 1947, featured Hollywood starlets in swimsuits. Newcomer Ruth Roman was seen frolicking in the surf. *Popular Photography* and *U.S. Camera* regularly featured covers by "glamour" photographers, who shared their tips on the inside pages. Books of nude photographs taken on U.S. beaches by André de Dienes, but printed in France for British and French publishers, were hidden in dresser drawers beneath underwear and socks. Playing cards and drinking glasses with images of nude women would be broken out after the children were asleep.

Burlesque, driven out of New York by Mayor Fiorello LaGuardia in 1937, flourished elsewhere and even returned to Manhattan as the Big Band era faded and the 52nd

Street jazz clubs turned to girlie shows. A circuit of about a hundred Skid Row "adults only" theaters showed featurettes that, thanks to the introduction of Eastman Color in 1951, presented burlesque stars in lifelike hues. The *Esquire* calendar was still published and Brown & Bigelow, the leading printer of advertising calendars, had a new star in Gil Elvgren, but illustrators were losing ground to photographers. Full-color nudes turned up in the offices of plumbing supply houses and car repair shops. A new magazine, *Modern Man*, a sort of precursor to *Playboy*, launched in 1951. It joined *Pic* from the 1930s and *See* and *Wink* from the 1940s on newsstands. These consoled the real-life Martys and Angies of Paddy Chayefsky's classic *Marty* on their dateless nights. Little ads in the back pages offered "art photos" or 8 and 16mm films that depicted models undressing or in sexy lingerie, such as those shot by Irving Klaw with Bettie Page. The first issue of *Playboy*, launched in December 1953 (with no date on the magazine because there might not be a second one), featured the iconic Marilyn Monroe calendar. In 1954, "glamour" photographer Peter Gowland published *How to Photograph Women*, the first of his many books on the subject.

It was also a time of moral panic in which drugs, juvenile delinquency (often blamed on working mothers), smut, perversion and Communism were conflated. President Dwight Eisenhower issued an executive order in 1953 that barred gays and lesbians from federal employment on the grounds that they were subject to blackmail and, thus, a "security risk." William H. Mooring, motion-picture editor of *The Tidings*, the newspaper of the Roman Catholic Diocese of Los Angeles, whose column was syndicated to other Catholic papers, wrote in 1954, "There is evidence to connect the infiltration of foreign movie studios by atheists with the upsurge in offensive movies brought to the USA from abroad ... there is a European Communist plan to soften up America by demoralizing and confusing American youth." The police chiefs and social workers who testified at the hearings of Senator Estes Kefauver's Subcommittee on Juvenile Delinquency in 1955 claimed that smut was an even greater threat than Communism, responsible for "sex murders," gang rapes and homosexuality. Even the old Socialist Norman Thomas, a founder of the American Civil Liberties Union, testified in favor of harsher laws.

"Don't underestimate Baghdad," sang Dolores Gray in *Kismet* (1955). If anything, Hollywood overestimated Baghdad, what with *Bagdad* (Maureen O'Hara), *Babes in Bagdad* (Paulette Goddard, Gypsy Rose Lee), *Siren of Baghdad* (Patricia Medina) and *Veils of Bagdad* (Mari Blanchard) just in 1949–53.

Islamic societies, among the most repressive on earth, became for Hollywood an oasis of sexual freedom. It must have been the harem part that got them. The movies' Arabian Nights setting owed more to the Minsky Brothers than to Sir Richard Burton. Former burlesque comedians Abbott and Costello got *Lost in a Harem* (1944), while ecdysiast Ann Corio was *The Sultan's Daughter* (1943).

Apart from the presence of Sabu and some similarity in the sets and costumes, Universal's *Arabian Nights* (1942), with Jon Hall and Maria Montez, had none of the literacy and charm of Alexander Korda's *The Thief of Bagdad* (1940). It was what insiders called a "tit and sand" picture, enlivened by chases and near-beheadings from which characters escaped by hiding in huge urns. *Ali Baba and the Forty Thieves* (1944) was more of the same. Technicolor was only supposed to be used on "A" pictures, but the added cost enabled the Hall-Montez adventures to qualify in a budgetary sense even though they were juvenile "B" pictures at heart.

Hall and Montez made a side trip to Polynesia, Code–era Hollywood's other liberated zone, for *White Savage* (1943) and *Cobra Woman* (1944). (The Code's prohibition against miscegenation applied only to blacks and whites, not to white men and Polynesian women, usually played by white actresses such as Montez and Dorothy Lamour anyway.) Montez was not unusually beautiful and spoke with an unfathomable (actually Dominican) accent, but she wore sarongs and Arabian princess outfits well enough and even inspired a limited vogue of turbans for women. Her rapid rise from small parts to brief stardom is only explicable in a wartime context.

Trade papers reported in mid–1943 that audiences were tiring of war-related films. Arabian fantasies and surrealistic musicals in Technicolor offered escape. Columbia got into the act with 1945's *A Thousand and One Nights* (Cornel Wilde). In Fox's *The Gang's All Here* (1943), a loose remake of *Sunny Side Up*, Busby Berkeley had a platoon of girls wield giant phallic papier-mâché bananas.

After the Hall-Montez series had run its course with *Sudan* (1945), Universal became Universal-International. Escapism was jettisoned for realistic crime dramas (*Brute Force*, *The Naked City*), earnest adaptations of plays by Arthur Miller and Lillian Hellman (*All My Sons*, *Another Part of the Forest*), even Shakespeare with the U.S. distribution of Laurence Olivier's *Hamlet* (1948). After a loss of $3.2 million for 1948, studio manager and company veteran Ed Muhl seized the reins of production and put U-I back in the tit-and-sand business. They had never completely left. Margaret Middleton of Vancouver, British Columbia, took her middle name and mother's maiden name to achieve stardom as Yvonne De Carlo in *Salome, Where She Danced* (1945) and then as the multiethnic, well-traveled sexpot of *Song of Scheherazade*, *Slave Girl* and *Casbah*. *The Desert Hawk* (1950) was a remake of *Arabian Nights*, with De Carlo in the Maria Montez role as Princess Scheherazade. Universal-International's publicity department promoted her as "the most beautiful girl in the world."

U-I's *The Golden Horde* (1951) was unusual for Hollywood Orientalism in that the dancers in the obligatory decadent banquet scene were actual Asians.

At a time when studios were paring contract rosters, Universal-International assembled a harem fit for a sultan: Piper Laurie, who would rebel; Julia, later Julie, Adams; blondes Mamie Van Doren (the studio's "answer" to Marilyn Monroe), Lori Nelson and Leigh Snowden; and the women named Mari (Blanchard) and Mara (Corday). When not pursued by evil wazirs, they had to dodge amatory batrachians or giant tarantulas. Universal-International wrote a "cheesecake clause" into its contracts that required that a new female player "shall, for the first five years of the duration of her contract, display said charms in publicity pictures as well as on the screen."[2]

Allegedly in response to popular demand, Tony Curtis and Piper Laurie, the young stars of *The Prince Who Was a Thief* (1951), were reteamed for *Son of Ali Baba* (1952). Jeff Chandler's prematurely steel-gray hair gave him an air of authority that was denied pretty boy Tony Curtis, but even he had to do *Sign of the Pagan* (1954). As a guest of the Sultan of Morocco in *Yankee Pasha* (1954), he was given Mamie Van Doren as his slave who told him, "Your wish is my command." His mind was really on the rescue of his fiancée Rhonda Fleming, kidnapped by the Barbary Pirates. Based on a novel by popular adventure writer Edison Marshall, it became in the hands of the company's least talented director, Joseph Pevney, just another U-I breast fest. Eight Miss Universe contestants filled out the harem in a repeat of a gimmick the studio used the year before in *Abbott and Costello Go to Mars*.

Maria Montez and Jon Hall starred in *Ali Baba and the Forty Thieves*. Their six Technicolor adventures at Universal between 1942 and 1945 offered mindless diversion from the war. Hall got top billing in their first, *Arabian Nights*, but thereafter it was Montez who was the main star. Universal/MCA.

Sam Katzman, responsible for much of Columbia's low-end product, didn't even pretend to take the genre seriously. After Sylvia Lewis's dance in *Siren of Bagdad* (1953), Hans Conried commented, "I always wanted to play the Palace," a play on the name of the top theater for vaudeville performers. *The Magic Carpet* (1951) had Lucille Ball on the cusp of television stardom, but Katzman's favorite leading lady was British-born, half-Spanish Patricia Medina. She resembled Linda Darnell with even bigger breasts. The tit-and-sand movie and the musical converged in *Here Come the Girls* (1953), one of Bob Hope's weaker vehicles, with a running time of just 78 minutes. Tony Martin, an old hand at this sort of thing, strolled through a harem and serenaded an improbably high quotient of blondes and redheads.

Publicity departments liked to send out pictures of young actresses in swimsuits with their measurements in the captions. The one star legitimately found in or near the water was Esther Williams (at 38–27–34, a little thick in the midriff).

Bazin noted than the two-piece bathing suit was the typical garment of the pin-up girl; Williams's trademark was the one-piece suit. *The One-Piece Suit* was the original title of *Million Dollar Mermaid* (1952). It re-created Annette Kellerman's arrest at Boston's Revere Beach in 1907 over a formfitting, one-piece bathing suit of her own design. This allowed 1950s audiences to feel superior to the prudishness of the olden days, but the laugh was on them. The real Kellerman had swum in the nude on-screen, something Williams could not have done even if she wanted to. *Million Dollar Mermaid* did

Lori Nelson is carried off by the Creature from the Black Lagoon in classic monster fashion in the sequel *Revenge of the Creature*. Amatory batrachians were among the dangers faced by Universal-International's female contract players of the 1950s. Universal/MCA.

re-create the production of a water ballet, probably from 1914's *Neptune's Daughter*, also used as the title of an unrelated Williams film. The flop of *Jupiter's Darling* (1955) ended Williams's M-G-M career, although the swimming scenes were actually integrated into the plot and the script, adapted from Robert E. Sherwood's play *The Road to Rome*, displayed her underutilized comic talent.

After a more than a decade-long detour through Americana (and Canadiana with 1940's *Northwest Mounted Police*), Cecil B. De Mille was back in form with *Samson and*

Delilah, the highest-grossing film of 1949. It was a much-needed hit for top-billed Hedy Lamarr, seen in color for the first time after a string of post–M-G-M independent flops. For *David and Bathsheba* (1951), the Breen Office even allowed a very brief, extreme long shot of Bathsheba nude (from the rear). After all, it was in the Bible! With the Susan Hayward of 1951 as an auburn-haired Bathsheba, David's distraction from his kingly duties was understandable.

As the highly paid screenwriter Ben Hecht wrote, "Immorality, perversion, infi-

A harem-themed musical number in the Bob Hope comedy *Here Come the Girls* was far from the real thing. Tony Martin serenaded an ensemble of blondes and redheads. Paramount.

delity, cannibalism, etc., are unassailable by church and civic league if you dress them up in the togas and talliths of the Good Book." Objectification of women had been more pronounced in "B" and genre movies than in "quality" features. The Holy Bible offered the pretext for a higher class of tit-and-sand movies. Pagan in spirit, the Biblicals let Hollywood have its cake and eat it too. They could fill the screen with semi-naked women in the obligatory decadent banquet scenes and temple dances. The trailer for *Salome* (1953) placed it "in the illustrious tradition of unforgettable motion pictures like *Gone with the Wind*, *Samson and Delilah* and *David and Bathsheba*" (the last two anyway). As it told "the story the world had been waiting 2,000 years to see," the world could wait another 89 minutes into *Salome* to see Rita Hayworth shimmy and writhe. As a priestess of Baal, Lana Turner in *The Prodigal* (1955) wore a costume of little more than strands of pearls.

In flattering the churchgoing *goyim*, Hollywood's mostly Jewish moguls perpetuated an old anti–Semitic trope. The sex and violence in the Old Testament vindicated the civilizing effect of Christianity. Pagan Rome also offered a contrast. The slave market in the early scenes of *The Robe* (1953) offers two voluptuous women in skimpy outfits, "chain mail bikinis" in the words of historian A.E. Larsen,[3] that expose their legs and upper torso. The Christian Diana (Jean Simmons) goes to her death properly covered.

Dance in Hollywood musicals had been mostly tap and ballroom. Berkeley's ensembles hardly required dance ability at all. By the mid–1940s, the impact of Martha Graham could be felt on Hollywood soundstages. Jack Cole combined jazz dance with influences from India and Bali. The leading exponent of balletic dance was Gene Kelly. The Code prohibited "dances that emphasize movements of the breasts, excessive body movements while the feet are stationary." There was no danger of that with Kelly; he pushed himself and his partners to feats of athleticism. For the otherwise expendable *Words and Music* (1948), a pseudo-biography of songwriters Rodgers and Hart, directed by Norman Taurog, Kelly adapted the "Slaughter on 10th Avenue" ballet from their 1936 *On Your Toes*.

The ballet was originally conceived for a film: a never-made vehicle for Fred Astaire and Ginger Rogers. On Broadway, it became one of the first classics of American ballet, choreographed by George Balanchine, who had come to the U.S. three years before from Russia. As a stand-alone piece, it became part of the repertory of the New York City Ballet. It was originally danced by Ray Bolger and Balanchine's then-wife Tamara Geva to Gershwinesque music by Rodgers. (The real George Gershwin wrote the songs and a ballet for an actual Astaire-Rogers vehicle, *Shall We Dance* (1937), that had a similar Broadway-meets-ballet premise.) In the 1937 London production, the female dancer was Vera Zorina, who caught the eye of producer Samuel Goldwyn. She was in two sequences of *The Goldwyn Follies* (1938). During production of the film, she and Balanchine were married. In his water nymph ballet, she rose, dripping wet, from a lily pond in a gold, skintight tunic that showed her slinky, perfectly proportioned body. This made enough of an impression that she was billed by her last name only above the title in Warner Bros.' 1939 film of *On Your Toes*. Balanchine (billed as "Ballanchine" in the credits) trimmed the 14-minute original to 10 but took advantage of the possibilities of cinema with speeded-up action, a shot framed through the legs of the male dancer and an upside-down shot of a menacing figure from the point of view of Zorina bent backward. Kelly's version provided the proper ending that the original never had. The play-within-the-play had the male dancer forced to keep dancing to the point of exhaustion to escape being killed by gangsters. Kelly dispensed with that and condensed the ballet to just seven-and-a-half exciting minutes.

The wholesome Vera-Ellen of Danny Kaye movies was cast as a slut. The Code allowed "dancing costumes cut to allow grace or freedom of movement, provided they remain within the limits of decency." Kelly drove a truck through that loophole. With a skirt slit up her thigh, Vera-Ellen wrapped herself around a lamppost. Kelly was eager to direct and spiked the sequence with daring visual touches: a chair thrown at the camera, a low angle of the dead Vera-Ellen literally tits up on the staircase. (Kelly had to fight for this. The shot was made with a wide-angle—28mm—lens against M-G-M policy that focal lengths shorter than 40mm could not be used. Stars had to be photographed attractively at all times.) With his own character mortally wounded by the same thug, Kelly ended the scene with a high-angle *Liebestod* of the entwined dead lovers similar to then-recent *Duel in the Sun*.

Cyd Charisse had been under contract to M-G-M since 1945. She appeared in straight parts and dance specialties (usually with Ricardo Montalban) but, surprisingly, had never been teamed up with Gene Kelly or Fred Astaire. In *Singin' in the Rain* (1952), she still had no dialogue but was partnered in the Broadway ballet sequence with Kelly's aspiring hoofer. In a bright green flapper-style dress and with a Louise Brooks "black helmet" haircut (short with bangs), she was the girl of a gangster who does George Raft's coin-toss *shtick* from *Scarface*. She initiates a dance with Kelly to "Broadway Rhythm" by wiggling her seductive behind. A jump cut betrays the excision of seven seconds of footage wherein her long legs are wrapped around his body, her crotch brushing against his. She later turns up with long hair as a fantasy object in an abstract interlude where she dances with a plume of billowing silk. She reappears with the black helmet hairstyle at a party where she snubs the now-successful dancer a second time.

The slave market in *The Robe* offered would-be buyers women in what one historian called "chain mail bikinis." 20th Century–Fox.

In *The Band Wagon* (1953), Charisse finally got to be the lead. The big ballet sequence "The Girl Hunt," staged by Michael Kidd, was inspired by the hard-boiled novels of Mickey Spillane.

Spillane's *I, the Jury* was a best seller in 1947. The painter turned novelist Frederic Tuten recalled in his memoir that it spread like wildfire among the young men of his Bronx neighborhood who otherwise never read books. It had too much sex and violence for Hollywood and the private eye cycle was fading anyway. By 1951, as the subject of a spread in *Life* magazine, Spillane was too big to ignore. Director Vincente Minnelli demanded, and got, credit for the ballet's narration on the soundtrack album. It was actually written by librettist and lyricist Alan Jay Lerner. Minnelli stated that there was no attempt to parody Spillane's style, as it was already a parody: "the inevitable blonde and brunette, the vicious kicks in the stomach, the farewell kiss as the good girl—who turns out to be the bad girl—dies." Some lines, like "I hate hard," actually came from *I, the Jury*. Amid "the rats and the hoods and the killers," Astaire was finally in the lowlife milieu that caused him to reject "Slaughter on 10th Avenue" nearly two decades earlier. Charisse has a dual role as a blonde right off the cover of a paperback novel and as a brunette in a red sequined dress. "She came at me in sections, more curves than a scenic railway," says Astaire's cynical "Rod Riley." The blonde, disguised in black hat and overcoat, turns out to be the "Mr. Big" of a shadowy criminal enterprise. "Killers have to die!" declares Astaire and shoots her.

The spoof captures the Spillane flavor better than the straight, cheaply produced adaptation of *I, the Jury* that year. Peggie Castle, usually wasted in low-budget junk, was cool and assured as the blonde psychiatrist Charlotte Manning. In Spillane's novel, she offers her nude body to private eye Mike Hammer in an attempt to save herself. He shoots her in the belly (symbolic impregnation?) and thereby keeps his vow to avenge a friend shot in the same way. Minus the nudity, the movie retained the final dialogue exchange. "How could you?" she asks. His reply: "It was easy."

James Mitchell, an accomplished dancer, played Charisse's choreographer boyfriend in *The Band Wagon* but they didn't perform together. That was rectified in *Deep in My Heart* (1954) with a sensuous dance choreographed by Eugene Loring, another pioneer of American ballet, to composer Hugo Friedhofer's masterly adaptation of Sigmund Romberg's "One Alone." (*The Desert Song* had recently been filmed for the third time by Warner Bros.) As described by Stanley Donen biographer Stephen Silverman, "Mitchell, in his body-tight leotard, and Charisse, in her skirt that parts clear to the waist, all but simulate coitus."[4]

Gene Kelly and Fred Astaire made their last starring musicals for M-G-M in 1957. In a role reminiscent of Clark Gable's in *Idiot's Delight* (1939), Gene Kelly in *Les Girls* was a song-and-dance man who toured Europe with a trio of lovelies: Mitzi Gaynor, Kay Kendall and Taina Elg. Lest anyone pronounce the title as "less girls," the ads helpfully advised that *Les Girls* "rhymes with playgirls." In the title song, Gene Kelly repeatedly vocalized how much he loved "lay girls." The audience was free to imagine that it heard him express a desire *to* lay girls. In addition to the three female leads, the ensemble included Afrogenetic and Asian backup dancers, presumably from the French colonies given the Parisian setting. This bit of racial progressivism would have been unlikely prior to the lifting of the ban on miscegenation in the 1956 revision of the Production Code.

Director George Cukor complained that Gaynor, cast by the studio without his input, was a poor actress and threatened to quit. He obviously favored Kendall in the

Gene Kelly and Vera Ellen were lowlifes in the "Slaughter on 10th Avenue" ballet from *Words and Music*. Kelly had to fight for the low, wide-angle shot of the dead Vera-Ellen over front-office insistence that stars always be photographed attractively. Turner Entertainment.

story scenes, but the picture badly needed Gaynor—and not just because she was a bigger movie name. It was on the skimpy side musically. The five songs of what turned out to be Cole Porter's final score for a movie barely filled one side of the soundtrack LP; none gained popularity. Gaynor and Kelly did a hot mambo in the title number. In "Why Am I So Gone About That Gal?" Kelly and choreographer Jack Cole parodied *The Wild One*, with Kelly as the leader of a motorcycle gang more akin to the Bowery Boys and Gaynor ("Her figure is a poem when she starts to dance...") as a waitress who wiggles her bottom to the jukebox's tune. (Connoisseurs rated Gaynor's behind as the best in Hollywood.)

Cukor did get his way on his visual collaborators, with production designer Gene Allen (hidden in the credits as a "set decorator") and consultant George Hoyningen-Huene, who used color and lighting to striking effect; they also designed the stylish main titles. Instead of front-office favorite Helen Rose, Cukor was able to engage Orry-Kelly, whose flamboyant costumes won an Academy Award. (Cukor, Cole Porter, screenwriter John Patrick, Jack Cole, Gene Allen, Hoyningen-Huene and Orry-Kelly were all gay; this encomium to the fairer sex, like a lot of Hollywood's ostensibly heterosexual fantasies, drew on the talents of gay men.)

Even as they poisoned America with pornography, Communists themselves were sexually repressed, at least according to Hollywood. In *Silk Stockings*, three Russians on a trade mission to Paris were led astray by a trio of French beauties, among them Barrie

Chase, Fred Astaire's future (and last) dance partner. Janis Paige, as an Esther Williams–like aquatic movie star, extolled fancy capitalist lingerie ("Satin and Silk"). Cyd Charisse, in the old Garbo part as Ninotchka, stretched the silk stockings of the title song over her long legs and danced in her teddy to an instrumental version. Femininity meant submission to gender roles. Cole Porter's lyrics to the song "Without Love" claimed "a woman to a man is just a woman, but a man to a woman is her life." After Joe Breen retired as head of the Production Code in 1954, there was less need to bowdlerize Porter's lyrics, as happened with the film version of *Kiss Me Kate* (1953). The song "Stereophonic Sound" lost a reference to "Marilyn's behind," but in "All of You," Astaire was able to tell Charisse, "I'd love to make a tour of you," that included "the East, West, North and the South of you."

Charisse had two solos in *Party Girl* (1958), but without a partner it wasn't the same.

In the early 1950s, M-G-M's main rival in the musical field was Warner Bros. Dull or over-the-hill directors, hackneyed backstage storylines, sometimes rehashed from 20 years earlier, and the uninspired dance numbers staged by LeRoy Prinz gave Warner musicals a shopworn quality that even the lively arrangements of musical director Ray Heindorf could not overcome. Warner Bros.' purchase of five major music publishers in the early sound era gave it access to the catalogue of almost every major songwriter, save Irving Berlin, so there was less incentive to commission new songs.

Virginia Mayo was the ripest tomato at Warner Bros. For Raoul Walsh, she did Westerns and was the prize that awaited adventurers such as Captain Horatio Hornblower at the end of their heroics. In her best-known film with Walsh, she was the slutty, gum-chewing wife of gangster James Cagney in *White Heat* (1949).

That same year, *The Girl from Jones Beach* afforded a partial break from typecasting. A press agent (Eddie Bracken) sells a sponsor on the idea of a television show that would include pin-up artist Bob Bradford and his "Bradford Girl." Unlike the prolific real-life illustrators Alberto Vargas and George Petty, Bradford has only one "Bradford Girl." The film's gimmick is that there is no "Bradford Girl." Bracken discovers that the artist has created a composite from the attributes of 12 different women: legs, arms, etc. In an innuendo that got past the Breen Office, Bracken asks one large-breasted model, "Have you ever been to the Pyramids?" Initially reluctant, Bradford (Ronald Reagan in the sort of part soon to be associated with Robert Cummings) agrees to the television show because his gifts of jewelry to 12 women have left him cash-strapped. But how to find a real "Bradford Girl"? About to drown himself off of Jones Beach, Bracken looks through his binoculars to see Virginia Mayo in a white bathing suit: a freeze-frame emphasizes a "Eureka" moment. When she walks out of the locker room right past him, now fully dressed, he doesn't recognize her. Mayo is a teacher and wants to be appreciated for her mind, but the audience for a Hollywood film of 1949 knew that physical attraction must eventually prevail. Reagan enrolls in her citizenship class by pretending to be a Czech immigrant. He undresses her with his eyes and imagines her in a white bathing suit that he sketches on his test paper. Her claim that she wants only intellectual companionship yields an exchange of quotations from Shakespeare, Molière and Oscar Wilde.

Ultimately, Mayo appears publicly in a swimsuit as the "Bradford Girl" but loses her job. She sues for reinstatement in an improbable court proceeding with a judge and no jury. It's not just Mayo but Hollywood itself that is on trial. Of course, Mayo must wear the bathing suit in the courtroom, with a camera aimed admiringly upward to emphasize her statuesque proportions. The plaintiff's case is bolstered by a film compilation narrated by Reagan that traced the history of the swimsuit in reverse chronological order that began with racy two-piece suits on the French Riviera, modified to conceal the navel. (Real bikinis would have run afoul of the Production Code.) An Annette Kellerman look-alike is in the famous one-piece suit that was then considered indecent exposure. Mayo wins reinstatement, of course. In illustration of the dictum that men seek sex and find love while women seek love and find sex, Reagan looks at Mayo in her bathing suit and imagines her fully dressed; Mayo looks at Reagan and sees him in swim trunks.

Cyd Charisse, long-legged dancing star of M-G-M musicals, appeared with Gene Kelly in *Singin' in the Rain* **(above), with Fred Astaire in** *The Band Wagon* **(top, facing page) and with James Mitchell in** *Deep in My Heart* **(bottom facing page). Turner Entertainment.**

5. "She came at me in sections"

Although Warner Bros. employed their contract stars to the limit of their obligations, Mayo couldn't be in all their movies. For *Kiss Tomorrow Goodbye*, a 1950 crime film with James Cagney, much inferior to the now-classic *White Heat*, blonde Barbara Payton was costumed similarly to Mayo in the earlier film. Newcomer Mari Aldon took the Mayo part in Walsh's *Distant Drums* (1951). Her sole costume featured a low-cut blouse that she filled impressively.

Mayo herself was reunited with Cagney, a year after their association in *White Heat*, more happily in a Brooklyn-themed number in *The West Point Story*. Mayo and the movie's other stars, Doris Day, Gordon MacRae and Gene Nelson, would become, in various combinations, the Warner musical stock company. Day didn't get to be sexy and tough until she herself was teamed with Cagney in *Love Me or Leave Me* at M-G-M in 1955. In the early 1950s, Warner Bros. sometimes cast Day as a tomboy. In *Calamity Jane* (1953), it was not at all clear at first that she was female.

There were no doubts about Mayo, their second-string musical star, in *Painting the Clouds with Sunshine* (1951). In a skintight dress with a laced-together neckline that plunged between her breasts (the cleavage was actually covered by flesh-colored fabric), she and Nelson danced to "The Birth of the Blues" bathed in blue light on an illuminated floor. In *She's Working Her Way Through College* (1952), she was an improbably mature student with a secret life as a stripper. The script was a Hollywood blacklist–era remake of *The Male Animal* (1942). Henry Fonda's role as a liberal college professor who defies the administration to read anarchist Bartolomeo Vanzetti's speech to the court that sentenced him to execution in his class was assumed by House Un-American Activities Committee fink Ronald Reagan. His courageous stand was to defend Mayo's right to remain in school despite her sexy past. Her Code–regulated burlesque number was necessarily all tease and no strip. As compensation, Mayo was better-looking and a better dancer than real burlesque queens. A follow-up, *She's Back on Broadway* (1953), hit uncomfortably close to home. Mayo played a movie star whose career was drying up at the age of 27. (Mayo was 32 at the time.)

Crime Does Not Pay was the title and thesis of an M-G-M series that started in 1935, soon after the implementation of the Code, and ran until 1947. Before they met their Code–dictated demise, movie criminals enjoyed the company of exciting women such as the nightclub singers played by Ava Gardner in *The Killers* (1946) or Lizabeth Scott in anything. In *Armored Car Robbery* (1950), the mastermind of the robbery (William Talman) gets chopped up by a propeller before he can fly to Mexico with a burlesque queen, the trashy/elegant Adele Jergens. He does get to enjoy her mild Code–approved striptease, performed with a white feather boa in which she does not actually take anything off. Peggy Cummins made her entrance in *Gun Crazy* (1950) in an orgasmic burst of gunfire. A slavering John Dall admired her marksmanship and skintight breeches as she put a phallic pistol between her thighs and fired.

Film historian William K. Everson devoted one chapter in his book *The Bad Guys* to "The Bad Girls." Male villains could be suave or ugly, tall or squat, gaunt or literal "heavies." Except for a few older character actresses, all of his bad girls were temptresses. *Movies: A Psychological Study* by Martha Wolfenstein and Nathan Leites in 1950 identified a character type prevalent in Hollywood movies after 1945: the Good Bad Girl. She was beautiful, with a past shady enough to be interesting yet not so steeped in crime to preclude what the producer character in *The Bad and the Beautiful* called "a picture that ends with a kiss and black ink on the books." Rita Hayworth in *Gilda* and

5. "She came at me in sections" 93

Top and bottom: Marie Windsor wasn't always a Bad Girl but those were her most memorable roles. She tormented perennial fall guy Elisha Cook, Jr., one time too many in Stanley Kubrick's early feature *The Killing* and he shot her. United Artists.

Ava Gardner in *The Bribe* (1949) are classic examples. Soon after the Wolfenstein-Leites book was published, the Good Bad Girl gave way to the Really Bad Girl.

From her experience as an usherette, the teenage Lily Tomlin concluded that the bad girls were the only women in movies who had any fun. She may have had in mind the likes of Phyllis Thaxter and Dorothy McGuire, prematurely desexualized as loyal wives and dutiful mothers. One of Tomlin's favorites was Beverly Michaels. The first important entry in Michaels's short, lurid filmography was Hugo Haas's *Pickup* (1951). Her best-known film is *Wicked Woman* (1954), a gender-reversed variation on *The Postman Always Ring Twice* from 1946. Dressed all in white like Lana Turner, she comes into town on a Trailways bus. She gets a job in a café run by Richard Egan and his shrewish wife. A murder plan is hatched, but never implemented, after Egan finds Michaels in a compromising position with the bald, sweaty and hissy-voiced Percy Helton. Instead of the usual death or imprisonment, Michaels gets to go back on the bus, where she casts her eyes on a new victim.

Marie Windsor could barely make it to the end of a movie without getting shot. She was the innocent victim of sexually frustrated Arthur Franz in *The Sniper* (1952) and, in a twist, was the policewoman decoy who took the bullet meant for a gangster's real wife in *The Narrow Margin* (1952). More usually, she was complicit in her own demise. Her big eyes, sensuous mouth and honeyed voice left rich and not-so-rich men considerably poorer and snared husbands who were quickly cuckolded. As the mink-clad adulterous wife of big-shot lawyer Edward Arnold in *City That Never Sleeps* (1953), she was shot by her sleazy lover (William Talman) after she fingered him for the shooting of her husband; she staggered and fell dead on a Chicago street. In the all-too-perfectly titled *No Man's Woman* (1955), she was shot upon emergence from the living quarters above the art gallery she owned and tumbled (via stuntwoman) down the stairs. Her best role was in Stanley Kubrick's *The Killing* (1956) and had her in blonde hair and Frederick's of Hollywood–style loungewear. She tormented husband Elisha Cook, Jr., until the worm turned, to her surprise if no one else's, and got shot again.

6

"Looking for trouble"

Howard Hughes vs. the Production Code (Again)

> "I want her tits bouncing off the screen, hitting them in the eye, and bouncing back onto the screen."
> —Howard Hughes

Former New York couturier Michael Woulfe was brought to RKO by Laraine Day, for whom he designed in *The Locket* (1946). Promoted to head designer in 1949 by new owner Howard Hughes, he had overall responsibility for costume but soon found that his main job was to display female stars as the boss liked to see them. Terry Moore's wardrobe as a social worker with a refugee release agency in *Gambling House* (1950) included a neckline that plunged almost to the waist. In a renewed bid for Western stardom in *The Half-Breed* (1952), *The Outlaw*'s Jack Buetel was again outshone by breasts, this time Janis Carter's as a saloon singer.

When 3-D came along, Hughes immediately grasped its potential for his favorite subject. One historian of 3-D cinema has written that RKO did not contribute significantly to the 3-D craze of 1953–54. That was because RKO produced so few movies of any kind. Production was shut down in April 1952, ostensibly to root out Communists. It was restarted in May to let Jean Simmons settle her hated contract with three films made back-to-back. By summer, the last of these was completed and Hughes put the company up for sale. The sale boomeranged when the buyers were revealed to have gangland ties and Hughes came back in full charge. Amid the chaos, only one picture (*Split Second*, directed by Dick Powell) was made. The six 3-D productions planned for 1953, of which five were made and four released in 3-D, were central to the studio's revival. All would be in Technicolor, a departure for *noir*ish RKO.

The aptly titled *Second Chance* was put into production in February of 1953, the first activity at the studio in four months. The script was an old one. To avoid testimony in a Senate investigation, a woman flees to an unnamed South American country (actually Mexico), to which her gangster ex-boyfriend sends a hit man to kill her. Linda Darnell's body is showcased as she wanders around the streets of the village, where she meets a broken-down American boxer played by Robert Mitchum. The one novel angle had the hit man (Jack Palance) fall in love with his intended victim and decide to kill his rival instead.

It wasn't much, but Hughes evidently liked the story as he all but remade it a few months later as *Dangerous Mission*. This time, Piper Laurie, borrowed from Universal-International, was a witness to a gangland murder, her refuge was Glacier National

Park and park ranger Victor Mature was the beefy protector. The climactic fight on a very fake studio-built glacier had Vincent Price buried in an avalanche in place of Palance thrown from a funicular car. Supplemental eye candy was provided by Betta St. John as an Indian, and a tribal ceremony furnished the local color represented by a Latin dance team in the earlier film.

Devil's Canyon was a dull Western, much of it set inside a prison; "500 men and one woman" read the leering ad copy. Virginia Mayo, named "Miss 3-D" in 1951 by the makers of Stereo Realist cameras, was resplendent in a tight-fitting blouse and jeans.

Hughes then deployed his ultimate weapon: "J.R. In 3D. Need We Say More?" No longer the *naïf* of *The Outlaw*, the Jane Russell of the early 1950s was a lacquered sex bomb, perfectly made up and coiffed, in RKO potboilers. In *His Kind of Woman* (1951), she was dressed by Howard Greer, an old favorite of Hughes from *Hell's Angels*. For *Macao* (1952), she wore a Michael Woulfe gold lamé gown that weighed 21 pounds.

Her greatest success came away from her home studio in *Son of Paleface* with Bob Hope and, especially, in *Gentlemen Prefer Blondes*. Critic Andrew Sarris claimed that his fellow G.I.s at Fort Devens preferred Russell to Marilyn Monroe. Her big number, "Is There Anyone Here for Love?" choreographed by Jack Cole, mixed her up with Olympians in flesh-colored trunks, too involved with their physiques to notice her.

For *The French Line*, Hughes had planned to have Jane Russell wear what would have been the first bikini in a Hollywood movie. Introduced in France in 1946, the bikini was named for the atoll where the United States conducted its first postwar A-Bomb test four days earlier. (It was named *Gilda* with a picture of Rita Hayworth slapped on it.) No established model would wear it, so the designer had to hire a dancer from the Folies Bergère for the public showing. The bikini was still controversial in 1951, when American "B" actress Jean Parker was arrested for indecent exposure at Australia's Bondi Beach. It was banned in Spain, Italy, Portugal, Belgium and towns on France's Atlantic coast but not at Cannes, where the then-unknown Brigitte Bardot was famously photographed in one at the 1953 film festival even though she had no film showing. Esther Williams, on-screen, pointedly rejected a bikini in favor of her trademark one-piece suit.

The French Line was a loose remake of *The Richest Girl in the World* (1934), but more directly copied from *Gentlemen Prefer Blondes*. It started shooting in July 1953 just as *Blondes* went into release. Russell played a Texas oil heiress, a sort of female Howard Hughes. Afraid that men are only interested in her for her money—a cynical reviewer noted that there were at least two other reasons—or intimidated by it, she pretends to be an impoverished model who goes by ship to a fashion show in Paris. Per Hollywood convention, "models" were not the emaciated creatures of *Vogue* or *Harper's Bazaar* but voluptuous showgirl types. The picture was a pretext for Russell's big number, "Looking for Trouble." The number actually started shooting with a two-piece costume that exposed her midriff but still covered the navel. (The original costume is shown in "Howard's Way," part six of the BBC series *The RKO Story: Tales from Hollywood*. The censorship issues surrounding *The French Line* figure prominently in the episode.) The Production Code did not explicitly prohibit navels. In practice, they were always covered. Perhaps an orifice in a female's midsection caused the male mind to wander further down. Movie Tarzans were also covered.

Russell was not comfortable in something she associated with "naughty girls in the South of France" and the crew sided with her. She refused to continue until the studio came up with a one-piece costume. Woulfe created a skintight catsuit that weighed only five ounces. Concealed wires pushed up the breasts. Russell herself suggested that there be three scalloped cutouts in the torso. The navel was still covered but one of the cutouts exposed flesh below the waist, daring for the time. The openings were outlined with silver rhinestones. The costume was made of black satin silk that Woulfe thought went well with her dark hair, perhaps thinking of the black jumpsuit in the pool number from *Gentlemen Prefer Blondes*.

At 32, Russell was still physically impressive. While *The French Line* had the usual "breast shots," notably in a bubble bath, her entire body was eroticized. In the most brazen come-on since Mae West's first two starring features, Russell, sprawled on a white satin pouffe, declares her desire for a man, any man "from 17 to 70." In 3-D, this must have seemed to men in the audience like 1985's *The Purple Rose of Cairo* in reverse. In that Woody Allen film, a character descended out of the screen and into the audience. Russell invited men to leave their seats and enter the screen.

Once again, Hughes had upset the unspoken compact. Because musicals were seen as frivolous entertainment and everything operated on a stylized level, the *pas de deux* that culminated in implied intercourse and the ensemble numbers that hinted at multiple-partner sex passed unnoticed.

Virginia Mayo was the busiest star at Warner Bros. In *The Girl from Jones Beach*, she had to go to court to get her teaching job back after she posed as the "Bradford Girl." She also danced with Gene Nelson in the "Birth of the Blues" number in *Painting the Clouds with Sunshine* and was a burlesque star in *She's Working Her Way through College*. Warner Bros.

Joseph Breen, near the end of his run as Production Code Administrator, had warned RKO that there would be no Code Seal unless cuts were made. Hughes was determined to thrust his fantasy woman on the public. He didn't even bother with an appeal. The picture would open without a Code Seal.

St. Louis, not usually known for film premieres, was chosen presumably for its 65 percent Catholic population. One week before Christmas 1953, a two-column teaser ad appeared in Friday's *St. Louis Post-Dispatch*. It had the tagline "Jane Russell in 3D. It'll knock both your eyes out." The Sunday paper had a three-column ad: "Jane Russell in 3-Dimension—and what dimensions." The following Sunday, two days before the premiere, there was a four-column ad: "J.R. in 3D. That's All Brother!" With an 80-foot-high poster of Russell above the marquee, the 5,000-seat Fox Theatre was standing room only at noon on opening day, December 29, 1953, the first matinee there in four years. Officers of the morals squad were among the first to be admitted, but the film was not seized and there was no prosecution.

The Archdiocesan Council of Catholic Men drafted a statement to be read by parish priests that urged a boycott of the film. They tried to enlist Protestant and Jewish figures without success. One of the authors of the document was Breen's deputy Jack Vizzard dispatched from Hollywood, so closely were the PCA and the Church entwined.

As if the calls for boycott were not enough, Archbishop Joseph Ritter took to the pulpit on the first Sunday after the premiere to pronounce it a mortal sin to see the picture. The theater put a signboard out in front to warn Catholics (and garner news coverage).

With a few cuts, the film was resubmitted to the Code Administration in January 1954, but they still did not grant a Seal. This was something of a crisis, as no MPAA member company had ever released a film without a Code Seal. The one penalty they could impose was a $25,000 fine, unchanged since 1934. RKO simply withdrew from the MPAA. Hughes claimed the controversy had been good for business but, by February, bookings had been secured in only three cities. Deals were made with state censors for cuts, in some cases deeper than what the PCA had called for. In Chicago, RKO had to sue the local censor board. RKO caught a break in Ohio when the U.S. Supreme Court invalidated the censorship statute in an action brought by the producers of the American remake of *M*. Eventually, 200 play dates were secured, but a Technicolor musical needed thousands to recoup.

Except for Loew's, which wouldn't be disentangled from M-G-M until 1958, the former producer-owned theater chains were no longer obligated to show only Code–approved films. Even so, only Fox West Coast Theaters (National Theaters) booked the film. Paramount Theaters, Stanley Warner and even RKO passed. The possibility that their managers might be prosecuted was real. In Indianapolis, the RKO branch office and four theaters were charged with obscenity. Mostly, the picture played without incident, although there were scattered protests. In Greenwich, Connecticut, Catholic priests and their lay supporters complained of "moral filth" and "spiritual polio." Despite pickets in front of the theater, the film was not pulled. The Kansas Board of Review called Russell's dance "obscene as it emphasizes lewd and indecent movements tending to stimulate impure sexual desire and lascivious thoughts."

In 1958, literary critic Lionel Trilling wrote of the newly legalized *Lolita*, "I see no reason in morality (or aesthetic theory) why literature should not have as one of intentions the arousing of thoughts of lust…. I can discover no ground for saying that sexual pleasure should not be among the objects of desire which literature presents to us."

Professor Trilling did not speak up on behalf of lust in *The French Line*. No one did. The increasingly frequent censorship controversies of the l950s involved subject matter more than imagery: an unpunished rape in *A Streetcar Named Desire*, a past abortion in *Detective Story*, the word "virginity" in *The Moon Is Blue*. Their respective directors, Elia Kazan, William Wyler and Otto Preminger, had argued for the liberalization of the Code to enable "mature" themes, but did not defend Hughes. *New York Times* film critic Bosley Crowther blamed him for trivializing the fight against censorship. The Code had seemed to be on the way out. *The French Line* reminded everyone why it had been imposed in the first place. The studio heads reaffirmed support for the PCA; some theater circuits pledged to show only Code–approved films even though they had no obligation to do so. The Code even acquired a sibling in the Code of the Comics Magazine Association that generally followed the movies' version but with a timely provision: "Females shall be drawn realistically without any exaggeration of physical qualities."

In May 1954, *The French Line* somehow got past the New York State censors. The Criterion Theater in Times Square did $73,000 in two weeks, the best business there in months. John McCarten in *The New Yorker* expressed relief that this would probably be the last 3-D film he would have to endure.

In April 1955, Hughes quietly capitulated. A cut version got a Code Seal; the fine was lifted but the new prints would not go into release until June. Now only in 2-D, the Code–approved version was announced with a misleading ad campaign that touted "That Film, That Dance You've Heard So Much About." It was (mostly) "that dance," albeit only in long shot, but what really had caused the trouble was what happened when Russell stopped dancing. Cuts eliminated the closer shots with the provocative monologue and Russell's undulating breasts. Audiences must have wondered what the fuss was all about. When the movie was finally approved in Kansas in December, a defensive censor board demanded, and paid for, a notice on the movie page of the *Topeka Capital-Journal* advising that what was exhibited was the revised version. The paper buried it in another section.

With 4,000 bookings in the U.S. and Canada, *The French Line* grossed over $2 million with a profit of about $300,000 to $400,000, enough for a modest success and about what it would have made had it been released normally. The Legion of Decency maintained its "Condemned" rating, called the film "grossly obscene" and complained of "suggestive, indecent action and dialogue gravely offensive to Christian and traditional standards of morality and decency and capable of grave, evil influence upon those who patronize it, especially youth." The cut version of *The French Line* would be sold to television in 1956 along with the rest of the RKO library, but, as late as l958, the Legion forced a San Antonio station to cancel a scheduled showing.

Russell, who was very religious, resented being dragged into another manufactured controversy and extracted a private promise from Hughes never to do that to her again. He kept his word, so much so that her next and last RKO feature *Underwater!* was quite dull. She was given a fake Cuban accent and an underwater swimming scene. A bigger splash was made by Jayne Mansfield at the press junket in Florida when a strap broke on her bathing suit and exposed her breasts to the assembled photographers.

The title *Son of Sinbad* suggested a sequel to the 1947 Douglas Fairbanks, Jr., Technicolor adventure *Sinbad the Sailor*. Although it used some of the sets from that film, it was a vehicle for the mainstream debut of Lili St. Cyr, fresh from her triumph in *Striporama* (1953). The script, such as it was, was rewritten during shooting. Vincent Price and Dale Robertson amused themselves in water fights while waiting to be handed their lines. Some of the sets were obviously assembled on short notice, e.g., an oasis with cardboard palm trees and a painted backdrop. There were parts for 137 women, including girls that Hughes had under personal contract and stashed in Hollywood apartments. Piper Laurie, the original female lead, became ill and her role was reshaped for Sally Forrest.

Forrest, championed by Ida Lupino as a younger version of Lupino herself, had gotten to dance in a few films, one of which was *Excuse My Dust* (1951). Set in the horseless-carriage era, the Red Skelton comedy takes a bizarre turn as Macdonald Carey imagines what women might be like 50 years hence, freed from bustles and corsets. In anticipation of Hubert Selby, Jr.'s 1964 low-life classic *Last Exit to Brooklyn*, a waterfront number choreographed by Hermes Pan has Forrest, possibly a prostitute, flirt with a group of dockworkers and sailors. She initiates a consensual gang bang from which she emerges satisfied and the men exhausted.

Already stuffed with specialties by Lili St. Cyr, Kalantan (an exotic dancer from New Orleans' Bourbon Street) and belly dancer Nejla Ates (from Broadway's *Kismet*), the film had Forrest cure Sinbad of his roving ways with a demonstration that she was

Above and facing page: Jane Russell contributed to the design of her costume in the "Looking for Trouble" number in *The French Line*. The closer shots that displayed Russell's bosom and her provocative monologue had to be eliminated before the Production Code Administration would grant a Seal. RKO.

all the woman he needed. She does a pole dance at the end of which Dale Robertson grabs her to himself in as close an approximation of intercourse as was possible in the Hollywood of 1953. Forrest would recall that her costume got smaller and smaller as shooting approached. The final version was a gold drapery cord taped to her body and a flesh-colored G-string. An emerald was glued to her navel.[1]

Sinbad's release had been held up by disputes with the Code over St. Cyr's numbers and a montage of gyrating women under the opening credits that would be replaced by conventional title art. The Legion of Decency condemned the film's "blatant, continuous violation of the virtue of purity, grossly salacious dancing and indecent costumeing [sic]." Their judgment: "This picture is a challenge to decent standards of entertainment and, as an invitation to juvenile delinquency, it is especially dangerous to the moral welfare of youth."

Originally produced in 3-D, *Son of Sinbad* was converted to the wide-screen Superscope process. The image was cropped at the top and bottom to a 2:1 aspect ratio that didn't do the dances any good. The only evidence of the 3-D version was a View-Master preview reel issued in 1953. Because of the delay, it was not St. Cyr's first Hollywood film, but it did benefit from the intense coverage of her 1954 trial for indecent exposure during her act at Ciro's, a nightclub/restaurant in Hollywood. (She waged a vigorous defense and was acquitted.)

There was a half-hearted attempt to release *Sinbad* without a Code Seal, but it ran up against the usual obstacles from state censor boards. The Kansas Board of Review cited "reel 4 where dancer is nearly nude and the swinging of her callipygian charms as she arises." RKO sued but, without a marquee name like Jane Russell for theater owners, it wasn't worth a fight.

Dance sequences allowed for sexual scenarios not permissible in realistic settings. Sally Forrest took on multiple male partners in the waterfront number of *Excuse My Dust* and emerged triumphant. A dancer from childhood, she had a unique style seen in too few movies. Turner Entertainment.

By 1955, enough cuts were made that a Code Seal was granted, but the Legion still gave it a "Condemned" rating. The premiere was again at the Fox Theatre in St. Louis on May 31, with a broad release the next day. RKO promoted it as the greatest array of female beauty since the Ziegfeld Follies and four "Sinbadettes" were sent on a promotional tour. It opened in New York in July, one week after the announcement of the sale of RKO to the General Tire and Rubber Company. William K. Zinsser in the *New York Herald Tribune* expressed mock regret—prematurely—that there would be no more Howard Hughes productions. RKO's new owners, the Catholic O'Neil family, had no use for the picture and withdrew it from distribution in August. It subsequently fell into the hands of Excelsior Pictures, victors in a court fight to exhibit the 1954 nudist film *Garden of Eden*. (*Garden of Eden* was a landmark nudist film from both a production and legal standpoint. Made in color with a budget of $300,000, the film was directed by Max Nosseck, who had a hit with *Dillinger* [1945]. The cinematographer was Boris Kaufman, winner of 1954's Oscar for Best Cinematography for *On the Waterfront*. It had an actual story. A pert young Korean War widow with a six-year-old daughter escapes the tyranny of her father-in-law. With her erect breasts, round but compact buttocks and long legs, Jamie O'Hara impressed in the inevitable nude swimming scenes. In his professional film debut was R.G. Armstrong [not nude on-screen], later a familiar face in TV Westerns as a backwoods paterfamilias.) Also known as *A Night in A Harem*, *Son of Sinbad* was still playing the nudie circuit into the l960s.

Hughes bequeathed two unexploded bombs in the form of his costliest personal productions. Both starred John Wayne, then at his box-office peak. *Jet Pilot*, started in l949 and announced for release in 1952, would finally be seen in 1957. The zany anti–Communist romp has a Soviet aviatrix land at an Alaskan airbase and pretend to defect. A very young Janet Leigh submits eagerly to being strip-searched as jets whoosh by in approving comment. On a trip to Palm Springs, Wayne buys her a wardrobe that includes a polka-dot sunsuit and a rather dated (by 1957) ensemble of gold lamé top and plush maroon harem pants. His-and-hers F-86 Sabre Jets, flown in close formation, suggest copulation.

Then there was *The Conqueror* (1956). Contrary to reputation, *The Conqueror* is not one of the worst movies ever made; it's not even the worst Genghis Khan movie ever made. (That would be *Genghis Khan* with Omar Sharif in 1965.) A solidly professional supporting cast includes Agnes Moorehead, Thomas Gomez, William Conrad and Ted de Corsia. The rhapsodic score is by Victor Young, a master of Hollywood Orientalism (*Samson and Delilah* and, yes, *Son of Sinbad*). The large-scale horse action staged by Cliff Lyons is as exciting as his work on *The Searchers* (1956). *The Conqueror* is essentially *The Searchers* from Chief Scar's point of view. The spirit of the savage and brutal Comanche warrior hunted down for years by Wayne in John Ford's classic Western informs the hero of *The Conqueror*, played by Wayne himself. *Life* magazine

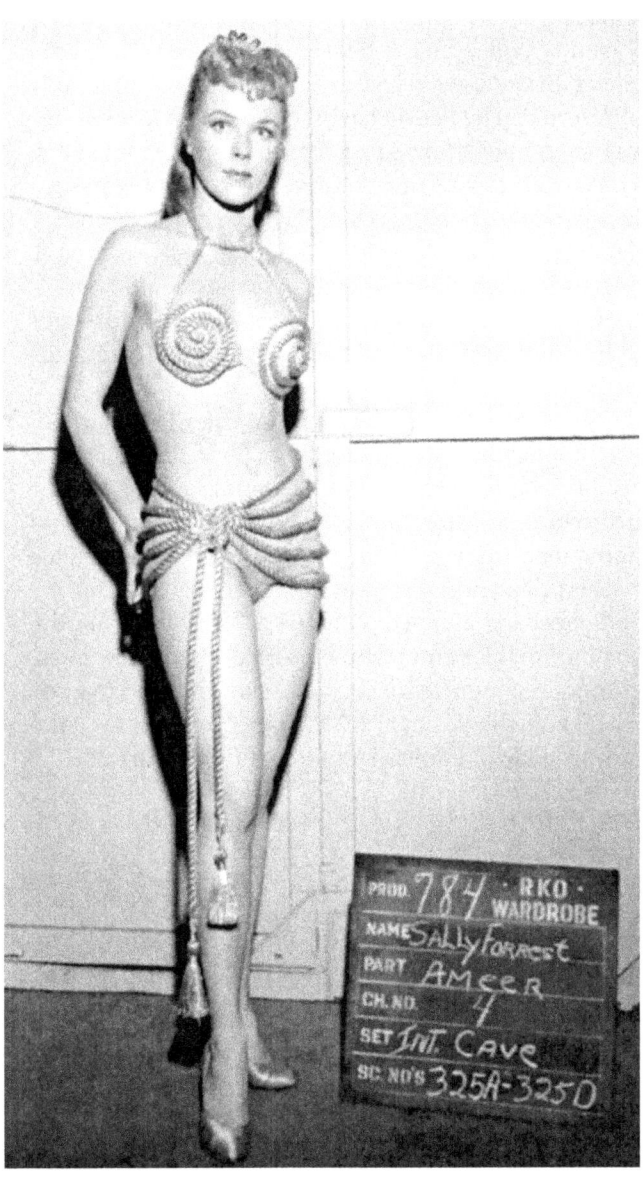

Sally Forrest's costume in *Son of Sinbad* was just a strand of drapery cord. Executive producer Howard Hughes specified "maximum nudity" to set her climactic dance apart. Designer Michael Woulfe thought her body "perfect" and was happy to expose nearly all of it. Her pole dance was to Woulfe "an erotic symphony" but her "callipygian charms" were too much for the Kansas censors. RKO.

yoked the two movies in a feature, "John Wayne—East and West." Wayne's line readings ("Yer beyootiful in yer wrath") are as truly terrible as everyone says, but the role allows him a raw sexuality unconstrained by his customary chivalry. At his first sight of Susan Hayward, the camera pans slowly up her body to her face. He pulls her dress off in front of his men and her husband-to-be. Later, he forces himself on her in a ditch and slaps her face when she expresses contempt for him.

At the obligatory decadent feast in Wayne's honor, he is treated to a dance by "the woman from Samarkand." The dancer, Sylvia Lewis, had to stand for hours in a body stocking to which strips of red satin were stitched—Michael Woulfe's most bizarre creation yet. The illusion of nudity was so complete that some censor boards removed the scene. Having watched sullenly, Hayward sees a chance for revenge when two masked dancers wield swords that they place in a pit of flaming coals. Hayward surprises everyone by taking the floor herself. Hayward was self-conscious about her legs, so Woulfe came up with a floor-length skirt—in white, which he thought best showed off her coloration. In a sensuous dance that Hughes screened over and over for himself in later years, she pulls a red scarf through her hand as if stroking a penis. At the end, she grabs the heated swords and hurls one at Wayne.

This sort of thing was usually done by stars of lesser stature than Hayward, an Academy Award nominee for *I'll Cry Tomorrow* (1955), made after, but released before, *The Conqueror*. According to one of his biographers, Charles Higham, Hughes's lust for Hayward was rekindled by her performance as Messalina in 20th Century–Fox's *Demetrius and the Gladiators* (1954) and a loan-out was arranged with an under-the-table payment to Fox production chief Darryl Zanuck.

The Conqueror obtained a Code Seal and escaped with just a "B" rating from the Legion, even though it was the most immoral, or amoral, of the all the Hughes pictures. Its protagonist was a rapist. He gloried in conquest for its own sake with no larger or nobler purpose. "The World? I Will Take It! The Woman? I Will Tame Her," bellowed the ads. Ruthlessness and guile were rewarded with empire and a beautiful consort.

7

Hollywood or Bust

Fifties Blondes and "Mammary Madness"

"There is the absurd idea, that in order to be beautiful, a woman's bust must look like a set of toy balloons."
—*Physical Culture*, Vol. 23 (1903)

"If a girl has tits, she can go far in this business."
—Louis B. Mayer

Marilyn Monroe was everywhere in 1952 with five features in release. The poster for *Don't Bother to Knock* showed her in a bathing suit that she never wore in the film. Her performance in the film as a mentally disturbed babysitter showed that she was a limited actress; *Monkey Business* demonstrated that it didn't matter. As the secretary to old lecher Charles Coburn ("Anybody can type"), she was described by Cary Grant as "half-child," to which his wife (Ginger Rogers) replied "not the half that's visible." Howard Hawks, like Billy Wilder later, understood that Monroe could really play only versions of her public self.

For 1953, Monroe had *Niagara*, in which she got top billing for the first time, *Gentlemen Prefer Blondes* and, in the new CinemaScope process, *How to Marry a Millionaire*. All were in Technicolor. Monroe was now arguably the most famous person in the world. The trailer for *Niagara* promised "Niagara and Marilyn Monroe, the two most electrifying sights in the world!" Other stars had posed for cheesecake pictures, but Monroe could turn a whole movie into cheesecake or at least the scenes she was in. In *Niagara*, she was showcased walking. As she crossed a cobblestone street, she walked away from the camera for about 15 seconds (it seemed longer). She walked across the patio of a tourist lodge in a tight red dress. "Get out the firehose," says an admiring male (Casey Adams a.k.a. Max Showalter), who asks his wife why she never wears a dress like that. Her reply: "For a dress like that you have to start making plans when you're about 13."

A myth has grown up that Monroe was fat by modern standards. This a misunderstanding caused by the fact that dress sizes have changed as women have gotten heavier. It is a matter of record that her measurements were 35-22-35 and that she wore a 36D bra. When she died at age 36, the coroner's report gave her weight as 117 pounds. When a number of her extant costumes were put on display, they were a tight fit on a Size 2 mannequin. In other words, her proportions were enviable then and still are.

The pink gown and matching gloves she wore in "Diamonds Are a Girl's Best Friend" were not designer Billy Travilla's initial effort. He first put Monroe in strands of jewels beneath which she appeared to be nude. When that was rejected, he hastily came up with a replacement made from drapery material. In *There's No Business Like Show Business*, she did box-office duty with "Heat Wave," letting her seat wave as per the lyric, and performed two other numbers in that tired backstage chronicle. Increasingly and publicly at odds with 20th Century–Fox, she inspired imitators and possible successors.

Columbia touted Cleo Moore as the blonde Rita Hayworth, and when Hayworth returned, as the studio's "answer" to Marilyn Monroe. She replaced Beverly Michaels in the works of low-budget *auteur* Hugo Haas, who typically cast himself as a middle-aged European immigrant beguiled—and betrayed—by a much younger blonde woman. Moore was not all that interesting a screen personality and Columbia never gave her the kind of part that would make a star. Her last picture at Columbia, a second feature with the double-*entendre* title *Over-Exposed* (1956), finally gave her a good role. She went from "B" girl to swimsuit model to photographer, and when excluded from serious jobs by sexism, to "the camera cutie of the nightclubs." A typically misleading poster screamed, "CONFIDENTIAL story behind the blackmail photo racket!" (In the actual movie, one of her pictures was stolen and sold to a scandal magazine.) Another tagline touted, "CLEO MOORE the most EXCITING FIGURE SINCE MARILYN MONROE. NUFF SAID." Actually, she was heavier than Marilyn, with a larger waist and a bigger rear end.

By then, Columbia had a Marilyn fighter actually named Marilyn. She made her official debut with a new first name in *Pushover* (1954) as Kim Novak. (Previously, she was one among other anonymous young women in both *Son of Sinbad* and *The French Line*.)

There were the obligatory gangster girlfriend and dumb blonde parts. In *Phffft!* (1954), Novak performed an uncanny imitation of Monroe in *The Seven Year Itch*, quite a feat as that film hadn't been made yet. (George Axelrod wrote both.) Her career unfolded in reverse. She largely skipped the cheesecake phase and had her best opportunities, including *Picnic* (1956) and a dual role in *Vertigo* (1958), by the age of 25. The photographer who shot her publicity photos said that it was impossible to take a bad picture of her. Columbia boss Harry Cohn called her a "fat Polack." Her movies therefore emphasized her face rather that her body, although

Above and facing page: Susan Hayward in costume for the dance that Howard Hughes so loved in *The Conqueror*. She threw a sword at John Wayne but ended up by his side. "For a hundred years, the fruit of their loins ruled half the world." Universal.

Jeanne Eagels (1957) contrived to have the young Jeanne, part of a girlie show, do a dance that gets her arrested. In *Pal Joey* (1957), a tentative striptease was stopped short by a possessive Frank Sinatra. In her thirties, her parts increasingly stressed her body. In *Kiss Me, Stupid*, she wiggled her rear as Polly the Pistol, a part originally planned for Marilyn Monroe. That movie and *Of Human Bondage* got her on the Legion of Decency's condemned list twice in 1964. In *The Legend of Lylah Clare* (1968), she went around with an exposed bra and did a Lady Godiva act in *The Great Bank Robbery* (1969).

Alfred Hitchcock unconvincingly blamed the disappointing returns of *Vertigo* on the age gap between James Stewart (49) and Kim Novak (24). Such pairings were the norm, e.g., Audrey Hepburn with Fred Astaire in *Funny Face* (1957), Cary Grant with Jayne Mansfield and Suzy Parker, the model Fox tried unsuccessfully to make a star, in *Kiss Them for Me* (1958). Howard Hawks cast John Wayne with the much younger Angie Dickinson in *Rio Bravo* (1959) and Elsa Martinelli in *Hatari!* (1962), possibly a reflection of the director's own appetites in his late sixties. That Stewart, Ray Milland and Grant were older than Grace Kelly in the three films Hitchcock made with her did not seem to hurt, nor did her pairings with Gary Cooper, Clark Gable and Bing Crosby. When Kelly defected to become Princess Grace of Monaco, it was a storybook tale come true for young women, but a loss Hollywood could ill afford. One of the few female stars with box-office clout, she was what men wanted and women wanted to be. No one wore the clothes of the 1950s better.

Although Kelly represented the ideal of urbane men like Hitchcock and Prince Rainier, a minor character in *Rear Window* was the generic male fantasy circa 1954: "Miss Torso," played by 17-year-old Georgine Darcy. Stewart's voyeurism is accidental and, due to his incapacitation, innocuous. His nurse (Thelma Ritter) calls him a Peeping Tom, but he is asleep in his wheelchair for the first appearance of Miss Torso after the opening credits and misses a glimpse of her nude back as she affixes her bra. In an image out of a Gil Elvgren pin-up, she hangs her undies out the window. Miss Torso is revealed as a dancer. She gyrates in a leotard to the musi-

Marilyn Monroe's rejected costume from *Gentlemen Prefer Blondes* was Billy Travilla's first effort before he came up with the pink gown and matching gloves for the "Diamonds Are a Girl's Best Friend" number. 20th Century–Fox.

cal cue titled "Farewell and Frenzy" from *A Place in the Sun*, a bit of self-quotation from composer Franz Waxman. Unlike the sinister ogling of Janet Leigh by Anthony Perkins in *Psycho*, Miss Torso serves as a playful counterpoint to the dismembered wife (Mrs. Torso?) of the salesman played by Raymond Burr. Her irrelevance to the main story is demonstrated when her soldier husband/boyfriend turns out be a short, ethnic-looking schlub.

In the first year of the 1950s, Gloria Swanson's Norma Desmond in *Sunset Boulevard* was portrayed as insane to imagine that she could still play leads at the age of 50. In the decade's last year, Clark Gable, nearly 60, was paid a million dollars to star opposite the much-younger Marilyn Monroe. The decade was unkind to established female stars. Bette Davis, after the triumph of *All About Eve* (1950), played a has-been forced to sell her possessions at auction in *The Star* (1952). Journalists on the set of *Clash by Night* (1952) clustered around Marilyn Monroe but ignored forty-something Barbara Stanwyck. An actress who once played madcap heiresses, card sharps, burlesque stars, missionaries and murderesses would increasingly be relegated to Westerns, cast as a cattle queen. Joan Crawford held on by sheer force of will. She, too, did a Western, *Johnny Guitar* (1954), with a gender reversal on the classic shootout as she and Mercedes McCambridge faced off against each other with their male costars on the sidelines. Clark Gable frolicked with a quartet of well-upholstered lovelies in *The King and Four Queens* (1956), even though he was a decade older than their stepmother (Jo Van Fleet). It couldn't all be blamed on industry sexism. Audiences reportedly laughed out loud when 50-year-old Claudette Colbert played opposite a younger Barry Sullivan in *Texas Lady* (1955).

Sexual glamour has a limited shelf life. According to Christian Rudder, cofounder of the online dating site OkCupid, women up to the age of 30 prefer men who are a few years older. After 45, they prefer men a few years younger. Men of every age prefer 20-year-olds! Another study of online dating published in *Science Advances* found that men's desirability peaks at 50 and women's at 18.[1] Miss America contestants can be no older than 24, Miss USA/Miss Universe 26.

The usual apprenticeship in low-budget pictures and supporting parts meant that career-defining roles for female stars came in their late twenties, e.g., Rita Hayworth in *Gilda* (28) and Marilyn Monroe in *Gentlemen Prefer Blondes* (27). Sex appeal was thought to fade after 30 and be largely gone by 35.

By the mid-to-late 1950s, the opulent beauties of the decade's early years were fading. The titles were hot even if the stars were not. *The Fuzzy Pink Nightgown* (1957) ended Jane Russell's stardom. *Fire Down Below* (1957) referred to the nether regions of an aging Rita Hayworth as well as the shipboard setting. Anyone naïve enough to think Maureen O'Hara would be nude in *Lady Godiva (of Coventry)* (1955) got a glimpse of body stocking covered by a mane of hair. An overripe Ava Gardner lent marquee weight to *The Naked Maja* (1958), a dubbed coproduction for which Goya's famous proto-centerfold was only seen in the trailer.

In hindsight, the years 1952–56 were the Golden Age of female beauty on the screen. If sensuality was wine, 1956 was a vintage year. Dorothy Malone, around since the 1940s, burned up the screen in *Written on the Wind* and won the Academy Award for Best Supporting Actress in 1956. She danced the mambo with Rock Hudson at a party and performed a modified strip to a raucous version of "Temptation" as her father died on the stairs. Left alone at the end, she stroked the phallic model of an oil well in consolation.

Slightly Scarlet (1956) was the

Dorothy Malone won an Academy Award (Best Supporting Actress, 1956) for her performance as the trampy oil heiress Marylee Hadley in *Written on the Wind*. The visual boldness, unrestrained emotionalism and operatic excesses of Douglas Sirk's direction took the overripe melodrama to the verge of self-parody but also lifted it to art. Universal/MCA.

sort of movie that would have been made in black and white a few years earlier. The script, based on a novel by James M. Cain, had something to do with crime and political corruption, but nobody cared about that when redheads Rhonda Fleming (in shorts) and her nymphomaniac sister Arlene Dahl (in Capri pants) were on-screen. Capri pants, designed in 1948 by Sonja de Lennart, were usually an indicator of sexual abandon, although Audrey Hepburn and Doris Day wore them too.

Marilyn Monroe did not think *How to Be Very, Very Popular* (1955), in which she would costar with Betty Grable, worthy of her status. It was adapted by Nunnally Johnson from a 1930s property. A pair of showgirls witness a gangland murder and flee to a college campus, where they pretend to be students and hide out in a fraternity house. (A few years later, Monroe would do much the same story, with the genders reversed, as *Some Like It Hot*.) Her replacement, Sheree North, was known for frantic dance routines, such as her guest shot in *Living It Up* (1954). During her Fox buildup, it came out that she had done risqué dance films for the mail-order market. This did not hurt her any more than the nude calendar hurt Monroe. In *The Best Things in Life Are Free* (1956), her "Black Bottom" was predictably frenetic but "The Birth of the Blues," danced with Jacques d'Amboise, was an erotic narrative poem in the M-G-M style. The song had become something of a chestnut in movies and on television variety shows, but this last of the pseudo-biographical songwriter cavalcades reconnected it with its actual writers (Buddy DeSylva, Lew Brown and Ray Henderson). The sequence somewhat resembled the Sally Forrest waterfront number. North, probably a streetwalker, passes by the window of a Southern jail and flirts with the prisoners. They are all white,

With redheads Rhonda Fleming (right, in shorts) and Arlene Dahl (in Capri pants), it was easy to forget that John Payne was the first-billed star of *Slightly Scarlet*. RKO.

even though some black men were seen earlier as they mimed the playing of musical instruments. The black men disappeared once North's legs were seen through the window. D'Amboise escapes with improbable ease and he and North all but consummate intercourse before a sheriff wearing a cartoonishly large star spoils their fun and takes d'Amboise back to the pokey.

The real Marilyn returned to Fox for *Bus Stop* (1956). Her self-described "chantooze" character was epitomized by a Billy Travilla costume that featured fishnet stockings with a hole in them.

Her would-be successor Jayne Mansfield was also at the studio. The back canvas on

Ballet star Jacques d'Amboise and sexy Sheree North danced to "The Birth of the Blues" until the sheriff intervened in *The Best Things in Life Are Free.* **20th Century–Fox.**

her folding chair did not need a name, just "40–21–35." Her Broadway hit *Will Success Spoil Rock Hunter?* (George Axelrod again), in which she was onstage in a towel, would become her second starring film. Director Frank Tashlin filled her first, *The Girl Can't Help It* (1956), with visual puns, e.g., Mansfield holding milk bottles to her chest. In his most cartoonish scene, she is so hot that she causes a cake of ice to melt in the iceman's tongs. The milkman's bottles boil over. John Waters called the latter a "cum shot." Jayne Mansfield in a red tail-finned 1957 Lincoln convertible offered a quintessential '50s version of paradise. Like the 1959 Cadillac, the design work for which began around the same time, Mansfield represented the apogee of excess.

A director (George Sidney) and a veteran press agent assessed the trinity of mid–'50s blondes for *Time* magazine's Hollywood correspondent, Ezra Goodman. "Monroe is a kept women for old men," declared Sidney. The press agent chimed in, "Mansfield is whorey. With Mansfield you cheat on your wife. With Kim Novak, you leave your wife to marry her."[2]

7. Hollywood or Bust

Julie London made a guest appearance in *The Girl Can't Help It*. London, occasionally seen in movies since 1944, was best-known for her Liberty Records albums. A joke at the time claimed that men who bought them threw the record away and played the cover. Tom Ewell, as London's alcoholic former agent, picks up "Julie Is Her Name" from a stack of albums and slips the disc from the jacket. As her 1955 hit "Cry Me a River" plays, her apparition fills various rooms in his house in a different sexy outfit each time. A few leading roles followed, notably in *Man of the West* (1958). With a knife held to Gary Cooper's throat, she is forced by Jack Lord to strip. She goes through multiple layers but only gets as far as her corset, to the disappointment of the planet's male population.

Anita Ekberg, also known as Anita Iceberg (for her acting) or Anita Sexberg (for her 40-inch bust), was a former Miss Sweden. *Hollywood or Bust* (1956), another Frank Tashlin effort, made her the fantasy object of Jerry Lewis, a star-addled, drooling fan

Director Frank Tashlin got away with a visual pun in *The Girl Can't Help It* as Jayne Mansfield clutched two milk bottles to her own jugs. The real object of Tom Ewell's fantasies was guest star Julie London, the sultry-voiced singer who was to men of the 1950's possibly the hottest woman on the planet. 20th Century–Fox.

who hugs popcorn and soda cups in the largest sizes, i.e., Hollywood's ideal moviegoer. In their next-to-last film together, Lewis and Dean Martin make a cross-country journey to Hollywood where Lewis, after the usual mishaps, literally falls into bed with his dream girl after he drops from the rafters of the soundstage. In *Zarak* (1956), she danced as a blonde Afghan opposite Victor Mature, without whom no film of this type was quite complete. A bearded Mature forsook his usual loincloth for a warlord's uniform.

Greta Thyssen, a former Miss Denmark, never got beyond television and low-budget movies, even a "Three Stooges" short. Among homegrown blondes, *zaftig* Barbara Nichols had a Queens accent that limited her to secondary parts. Joi Lansing became a popular pin-up on the strength of a recurring role on *The Bob Cummings Show* as his favorite photographer's model, to whom producer Paul Henning cruelly juxtaposed flat-chested Nancy Kulp. One of her few "A" pictures was *A Hole in the Head* (1959), with her shown as arm candy to the nasty *macher* played by Keenan Wynn.

A beautiful blonde who didn't seek or get much publicity, Karen Steele mainly appeared in Budd Boetticher's Randolph Scott Westerns. In *Westbound* (1958), she fought with a fading Virginia Mayo, who was at the end of her contract. She was also in Boetticher's *The Rise and Fall of Legs Diamond* (1960), incongruously protuberant in fashions designed for flapper-era boyish figures. Unable to compete with what critic Molly Haskell called "mammary madness," one Vikki Dougan styled herself as "The Back" in gowns that plunged to expose butt cleavage. She got more attention from newspaper columnists and photographers than from producers.

RKO was on its last legs in 1956, even if the legs belonged to shapely Diana Dors, brought over from England for three pictures of which two were made. British Joan Collins, a graduate of the Rank Organisation "charm school," came to Hollywood for a jewel-in-the-navel part in *Land of the Pharaohs* and was Evelyn Nesbit in *The Girl in the Red Velvet Swing* (both in 1955). The surviving fragments of Rouben Mamoulian's aborted *Cleopatra* suggest

Swedish Anita Ekberg was an improbably blonde Afghan in a dance sequence from *Zarak*. Columbia Pictures/Sony.

that 20th Century–Fox could have saved itself a lot of money and trouble if they had gone ahead with Collins in the title role, Peter Finch as Caesar and Stephen Boyd as Antony. Like Julie London, Angie Dickinson and Sheree North, she would have a late career revival in series television.

British, German and Scandinavian actresses fit easily into Hollywood's standards of beauty. A touch of exotic spice was piquant but, Hollywood being Hollywood, the artificial was better than the real. Hence, Jennifer Jones, née Phylis Isley of Tulsa, Oklahoma, was "Pearl Chavez" in *Duel in the Sun*. Jean Peters of Canton, Ohio, was "Catana, the peasant girl" in *Captain from Castille* (1947) and even played the wife of Zapata. The half-Spanish Margarita Cansino had to be de-ethnicized and remade as all-American Rita Hayworth before she could partially revert to play hot-blooded temptresses in *Blood and Sand* (1941) and *The Loves of Carmen* (1948). Real Latinas were stereotyped as the "Mexican Spitfire" (Lupe Velez) or the "Cuban Fireball" (Estelita Rodriguez).

Foreign travel and the large number of servicemen stationed overseas made American culture more cosmopolitan in the 1950s. Foreign markets accounted for as much as 50 percent of box-office receipts. This meant greater acceptance of ethnic variety, e.g., Katy Jurado (Mexico) and Sarita Montiel (Spain). Italy's Gina Lollobrigida impressively wore an aerialist costume in *Trapeze* (1956). Sophia Loren had a greater impact through the poster for her first U.S. film, *Boy on a Dolphin* (1957), than her actual performance. Loren's flamenco dance enlivened a turgid *The Pride and the Passion* (1957). Her longevity compared with the limited careers of Jayne Mansfield and Anita Ekberg suggests that a 38-inch bust was the upper limit of sexual/aesthetic attractiveness before cartoonishness took over.

The plenitude of pulchritude created openings for unconventional types, e.g., Joanne Woodward, wearing no makeup and all seriousness in television dramas and as an Oscar winner for *The Three Faces of Eve* (1957), the half-Cherokee Keely Smith with straight black hair in *Thunder Road* (1958) and Carolyn Jones, specialist in free spirits and sad weirdos.

8

"Banned by Cardinal Spellman"
Baby Doll *and Southern Decadence*

Overshadowed by the upheavals of the 1960s, the years between 1954 and 1957 saw a shift in the cultural winds. The addition of "Under God" to the Pledge of Allegiance in 1954 and the adoption of "In God We Trust" as the national motto in 1956 were the last triumphs of the moral guardians. Even the Comic Book Code was a Pyrrhic victory. William Gaines, publisher of the most notorious horror and crime comics, relaunched *Mad* magazine in 1955 with a derisive view of American commercial culture. That same year, in the first issue of *National Review*, William F. Buckley declared of his new conservative magazine that it "stands athwart history yelling 'Stop!'" Buckley and his cohorts were unable to stop much of anything. Authority figures of the older generation were losing control of the culture.

Do movies shape society or do they reflect it? In 1955, seventh graders were yelling "Hey, Teach!" in imitation of the delinquents in *Blackboard Jungle*. Stores ran out of the red jacket with red zipper worn by James Dean in *Rebel Without a Cause* and there was a fad for the "Black Leather Jacket and Motorcycle Boots" referred to in a Top 10 hit record obviously inspired by *The Wild One*. Did Marlon Brando and James Dean foster alienation in adolescents or did their popularity capture something in the air? Most likely, movies pick up on changes that are already at work and then repackage them to the broader public.

Cracks appeared in what social critics dubbed the Eisenhower Ice Age. Elvis Presley had four gold records in 1956. Grace Metalious's sexy *Peyton Place* sold 60,000 copies in 10 days. Patricia Bosworth has characterized the era as one "which on the surface was dark and puritanical, but underneath was a seething ferment of creativity, with painters, poets, photographers, writers, and actors all clamoring to be heard."[1]

Tom Lehrer's records built an underground following. Robert Frank was taking the photographs that would become his 1959 book *The Americans*. Mother-in-law jokes gave way to Lenny Bruce, Mort Sahl and the team of Mike Nichols and Elaine May. A 1952 article in the *New York Times Magazine* by John Clellon Holmes, revealed, or invented, the Beat Generation. There were no more than a dozen or so actual beats. After the obscenity trial of Allen Ginsberg's "Howl" in 1956 and the publication of Jack Kerouac's *On the Road* in 1957, the "beatnik" entered popular culture, personified by Bob Denver as the goateed "Maynard G. Krebs" of television's *The Many Loves of Dobie Gillis*.

Political repression eased after the 1954 Senate censure of Joe McCarthy, the publication in 1956 of John Cogley's *Report on Blacklisting* and the embarrassment of a Best Screenplay Oscar awarded to the blacklisted Dalton Trumbo under a pseudonym. In

1957, the Supreme Court reversed the 1951 conviction of the leaders of the U.S. Communist Party under the Smith Act that made advocacy of the violent overthrow of the U.S. Government a crime.

Hollywood reflected the changing times with more "adult" subject matter, but also in the way the industry was structured. Dore Schary, ousted as M-G-M production chief along with Loew's chairman Nick Schenck in 1956, would later identify 1953 as the last year of the classic studio system. Traditionally, movies had been marketed with familiar combinations of star and genre: Errol Flynn swashbucklers, Betty Grable musicals, Abbott and Costello comedies, etc. As habitual moviegoing dried up, the coming attractions stressed the uniqueness of an individual production in an effort to convince audiences that they hadn't seen it all before. James Mason, star and producer of *Bigger than Life* (1956), appeared on-screen in the trailer to make a personal appeal to the audience on behalf of his drama about a teacher whose personality is transformed by addiction to cortisone. In the trailer for *The Wrong Man* (1956), Alfred Hitchcock claimed that the true story of an ordinary man falsely imprisoned represented a complete departure from the murderers he had previously put on-screen. To sell the interracial drama *Edge of the City* (1957), M-G-M went so far as to have the script girl testify that the story was unlike any she had ever worked on.

Elia Kazan was arguably the most influential cultural figure in the America of the mid–1950s. The director of plays by Tennessee Williams and Arthur Miller in their original productions also guided Marlon Brando to an Oscar in 1954's *On the Waterfront* (with a Best Director award for himself) and made a star of James Dean in *East of Eden* (1955). Kazan's commercial and critical stature enabled him to deal on an equal footing with studio heads, even one who boasted that his name was on the water tower. In a letter to Jack L. Warner, he wrote, "We are now obliged as a matter of preservation to put on the screen of motion picture theaters only that which they cannot see and never will see at home." In October 1956, a billboard for Kazan's *Baby Doll* dominated an entire block of Times Square. It bore an iconic image of Carroll Baker as the still-virginal 19-year-old bride inside a crib sucking her thumb. At 135 feet from head to toe, it dwarfed the billboard of an aquatic Jane Russell in *Underwater!* the previous year. It was not the work of a crass publicity department. Kazan, the self-described "Greek Barnum," himself chose to follow in the footsteps of industry pariah Howard Hughes.

The film's premiere was scheduled for December 18, just a week before Christmas. The previous Sunday, Francis Cardinal Spellman took to the pulpit of St. Patrick's Cathedral in New York City as crowds of holiday shoppers and tourists passed by outside on Fifth Avenue. He attacked the film as evil and corrupt. He also denounced the MPAA for its award of a Code Seal. After the loyal Catholic Joe Breen retired in 1954, he was replaced by the urbane Geoffrey Shurlock. Shurlock allowed "hell" and "damn" in dialogue. (David O. Selznick famously had to go over Breen's head to Will Hays for a one-time dispensation to let Clark Gable utter the line "Frankly, my dear, I don't give a damn" in *Gone with the Wind* in 1939.) The Code Administration could no longer be counted on to follow in lockstep with the Legion of Decency. The Church would have to mobilize pickets from the Knights of Columbus and Catholic War Veterans, a potent threat in the past.

Kazan had Warner Bros. add "Banned by Cardinal Spellman" to the newspaper ads. At first, the controversy boosted attendance but in the second week business dropped off. Kazan blamed the presence of priests in the lobby, who warned away patrons and

even took the names of parishioners they recognized. It was more likely poor word of mouth. Kazan thought of the film as a dark comedy, but audiences didn't get the joke. Moviegoers primed for what *Time* called "possibly the dirtiest American-made motion picture that has ever been legally exhibited" got a black-and-white "art house" film with no stars, no characters to root for and, worst of all, no sex.

The most erotic scene, Carroll Baker's seduction by Eli Wallach in a porch swing, owed its power to Tennessee Williams's dialogue, the actors' reading of it and their facial expressions. In an unintended tribute to Kazan's direction, the film's attackers imagined they saw Wallach's unseen hands roam across Baker's body. Several critics pointed out that the Church had not condemned *From*

The billboard that Howard Hughes put up for *Underwater!* in Times Square was dwarfed by the one for Elia Kazan's *Baby Doll* that took up a whole city block.

Here to Eternity (1953), even though adultery was glamorized in a surfside embrace. *Baby Doll* never went beyond flirtation, although an ambiguous ending left open future possibilities. Carroll Baker spent much of her screen time in a slip or in the sleepwear henceforth known as "baby dolls." Some noted that there were scantier costumes in *The Ten Commandments*, released around the same time, but the Bible rendered DeMille unassailable, as always.

It came out that the driving force behind the Spellman attack was Martin Quigley, consultant, for a fee, on censorship matters. In that capacity, he had cut four minutes from *A Streetcar Named Desire* (1951) over Kazan's public objection.

The Legion of Decency's campaign against it certainly hurt *Baby Doll*. It got only 4,000 bookings instead of the 10,000 to 20,000 expected and did not show a profit until it was rereleased in the 1960s. The Legion hurt itself more. When it was formed, the Legion was the most aggressive of a broad spectrum of groups that wanted the movies cleaned up. The Legion had gotten the Protestant Federal Council of Churches and even some Jewish groups to support their campaign. Eleanor Roosevelt praised the establishment of the Production Code on her twice-weekly afternoon radio program.

By 1957, the Legion was increasingly isolated. In 1952, the U.S. Supreme Court heard *Joseph Burstyn, Inc. v. Wilson*, which came to be known as "the *Miracle* case." *The Miracle* was one part of a two-segment film collectively titled *The Ways of Love* that played at The Paris Theatre in New York City in 1950. Directed by Roberto Rossellini, it had Anna Magnani as a mentally disturbed peasant woman who imagines herself to be the Virgin Mary after being impregnated by "Saint Joseph" (Federico Fellini). Catholic groups denounced the film as blasphemous and picketed the theater. Political pressure

Trapped in a stagnant Southern mill town, Aldo Ray carried on an affair with his sister-in-law, played by the voluptuous Tina Louise. *God's Little Acre* was the first major company release advertised as restricted to age 18 and over. United Artists.

120   Hollywood and the Female Body

forced the State Board of Regents to withdraw the license to exhibit the film. In finding for the distributor, the Court extended First Amendment protection to the movies. This did not immediately put an end to state and local censor boards but made it increasingly hard for them to prevail against a determined litigant.

With television on five hours a day in the typical home, the protectors of children

Julie Newmar as Stupefyin' Jones stupefies unbilled guest star Jerry Lewis, while Daisy Mae (Leslie Parrish) tries to shield the eyes of *Li'l Abner* (Peter Palmer). This was the comic version of the decadent South portrayed by Tennessee Williams and Erskine Caldwell. Paramount.

turned their attention to the newer medium. That attendance at a movie could be a "Mortal Sin" struck even Catholics as absurd. Non-Catholics resented limitations on their entertainment choices. Protestant clergy had seethed quietly for years over Hollywood's fawning relationship with Catholicism, typified by all the priests played by Bing Crosby, Spencer Tracy and Pat O'Brien.

Over the next few years, the Legion would condemn *Some Like It Hot*, *Breathless*, *Never on Sunday*, *Psycho* and *Spartacus*, to no apparent effect at the box office.

The big winner in the *Baby Doll* brouhaha was Tennessee Williams, even though he never actually finished the script, based on a pair of his one-act plays. *Cat on a Hot Tin Roof*, from his 1955 play, was one of 1958's top-grossing movies. As Maggie the Cat, Elizabeth Taylor, the last big contract star at M-G-M, slinked around in a slip designed by Helen Rose. Between 1958 and 1964, there would be eight feature films based on source material from Williams. Members of The Actors Studio would have ample opportunity to work on their Southern accents.

Kazan protégé Lee Remick made her debut as a nubile baton twirler ogled by Andy Griffith in *A Face in the Crowd* (1957). She became the screen avatar of William Faulkner, rediscovered amid the vogue for Southern decadence. As Temple Drake in *Sanctuary* (1961), Remick was a governor's daughter who received her sexual education in a brothel before being raped in a corn crib. As in *Baby Doll*, a young blonde yoked to an ineffectual husband (Bradford Dillman, a personification of the declining aristocracy more interested in his bottle than her) was drawn to the superior virility of a swarthy Latin (Frenchman Yves Montand playing an Italian).

Some critics thought *Baby Doll* an offshoot of *Tobacco Road*, the 1932 Erskine Caldwell novel made into one of Broadway's longest-running plays. Caldwell's novel *God's Little Acre* had been a steady seller but was considered too raw for the screen until l958, when it was the first major company release marketed with a notice that restricted admission to age 18 or older.

In *God's Little Acre*, the farm of the title lies fallow, pockmarked with holes dug by the patriarch (Robert Ryan) in a demented search for buried gold. The mill in town has shut down. With nothing else going on, the Aldo Ray character seduces his gorgeous sister-in-law (Tina Louise, in her film debut). With his own vitality recharged, he turns on the power at the mill, only to be killed by a guard. Ryan goes on digging holes.

Baby Doll associated the economic stagnation of the South with the probable impotence of the Karl Malden character. In reality, Southern economic growth outpaced the rest of the nation in the 1950s, due in part to right-to-work laws that stymied organized labor as jobs were drawn from the unionized North. This was not reflected in the movies' South, a place of decaying mansions inhabited by vibrant, unfulfilled women and weak, often alcoholic, men.

The comic version of the decadent South was *Li'l Abner*, Paramount's 1959 version of a successful stage musical based on cartoonist Al Capp's characters. The strip originated in 1934 and was itself influenced by *Tobacco Road*. Caldwell had an Ellie May and Capp a Daisy Mae. As Daisy Mae, Leslie Parrish was less voluptuous than her drawn counterpart, but nobody complained about Julie Newmar as Stupefyin' Jones.

9

Bikini Beach

From the Fifties to the Sixties

A wave of technological innovation in the 1953–55 period—3-D, stereophonic sound, CinemaScope, VistaVision, Todd-AO—helped movies retake ground from television. The "CinemaScope rebound" faded by 1957 and attendance began to fall again. The "product shortage" of which exhibitors perennially complained became real. RKO and Republic were gone and Universal-International shut down for most of 1958 to regroup. A new company, American International Pictures, moved into the breach with cheaply produced films whose main selling point was their titles, e.g., *I Was a Teenage Werewolf* (1957) and *Dragstrip Riot* (1958). The former theater-owning "majors" M-G-M and Paramount cut back production from some 50 pictures a year at the start of the decade to just over 20 at the end. Their sales departments could set stiff terms for popular titles. As older, more conservative audiences deserted the cinema for television, theater owners were more willing to take risks.

Exploitation pictures, previously the realm of fringe producers, showed up on the release schedules of major companies. Warner Bros. distributed 1957's *Untamed Youth* ("Youth turned rock n' roll wild"), starring Mamie Van Doren and fellow U-I alumna Lori Nelson. It was the second Warner film that year after *Baby Doll* to be condemned by the Legion.

Only a publicity campaign that referenced *Blackboard Jungle* and the reuse of the school set from *Tea and Sympathy* marked *High School Confidential* (1958) as an M-G-M product. Producer Albert Zugsmith served up sex, drugs and rock n' roll—even a beatnik poetess for topicality. Zugsmith, who gave Van Doren her only prominent role at Universal-International (*Star in the Dust*), billed her as a "guest star." Her Capri pants were so tight that her *mons pubis* was outlined by creases, but the high school chicks at a pool party were still in one-piece suits with no bikinis in sight. Zugsmith cast Van Doren against type as a dutiful wife and mother in *The Big Operator* (1959), with a snarling Mickey Rooney as a Jimmy Hoffa–like labor leader. The film flopped. Van Doren's role in Zugsmith's *The Beat Generation* (1959) was also secondary; essentially it was a *policier* about a serial rapist (Ray Danton) and justified its title by having him spout sub-Nietzschean philosophy in a boho hangout. Zugsmith liked to push boundaries and Van Doren was willing to help. Playing a 16-year-old (she was 27) in *Girls Town* (1959), she was nude behind a frosted shower door. The scene was cut from the film. She was so much a part of Zugsmith's world that in *College Confidential* (1960), her 29-year-old coed was described as "a Mamie Van Doren type."

For a time, Van Doren seemed a genre unto herself. In *Girls, Guns and Gang-*

Cheap movies with exploitable elements partly filled the product gap after the major studios retrenched in the 1950s. A selling point of *The Unearthly* (1957) was the body of *Playboy* Playmate Sally Todd and things that might happen to it. "AB-PT Pictures" was a venture of American Broadcasting-Paramount Theatres. With fewer movies to book, the theater chain went into production itself. Another AB-PT production had the provocative title *Eighteen and Anxious*.

sters (1959), she got to make like Rita Hayworth in a nightclub number. *Vice Raid* (1960) had her in "the V-Girl racket." Neither was produced by Zugsmith and were not successful.

Platinum blondes in sequined dresses and dangling earrings were pretty much last year's model by 1960, but Zugsmith cast Van Doren in *Sex Kittens Go to College* anyway. Second lead Tuesday Weld was more plausibly a sex kitten and Brigitte Bardot's sister, Mijanou, indisputably one.

Zugsmith was one of the first producers to circumvent the Code with different versions for the domestic and foreign markets. For the European version of *High School Confidential*, the breasts of Mamie Van Doren and Jan Sterling were partially exposed. *Sex Kittens Go to College* gained an extended striptease sequence.

It was Brigitte Bardot for whom the term "sex kitten" was coined. Roger Vadim's ... *And God Created Woman* opened in October 1957 at New York's Paris Theatre and set the house record. An English-dubbed version became the most successful foreign film in the U.S. to that time. The distributor, Kingsley International, was actually owned by Columbia Pictures. As an MPAA member, Columbia itself could not distribute it because of the nudity. There was just one nude shot of Bardot lying facedown. It was easily excised, and the film even played local television in New York within a few years. The old picture *Ecstasy*, still in circulation, showed much more.

Showman Kroger Babb, who made millions from an exploitation movie called *Mom and Dad* (1945), notorious for its then-shocking footage of female anatomy and actual childbirth, acquired U.S. rights to Ingmar Bergman's *Summer with Monika*, made in Sweden in 1953. Retitled simply *Monika*, it was released in 1955 with ads that touted "The story of a very bad girl" and blared "Naughty and nineteen! The Devil controls her by radar!" Butchered to a 62-minute running time from the original 95, the Babb version eliminated most of the later downward spiral of the young lovers' fortunes after the girl becomes pregnant but, of course, retained the full-length rear view of young Harriet Andersson walking down to the beach to skinny-dip. (In a review of Bergman's autobiography in *The New York Times Book Review*, Woody Allen recalled that as a youth he was lured to the Jewel Theater in Brooklyn by the prospect of a nude woman on-screen; it took two more Bergman films before he fully appreciated the director for himself.)

...And God Created Woman was in color and had an offhandedness about it. In a contemporaneous Hollywood film, *Lisbon* (1956), a leering Ray Milland found Yvonne Furneaux reclining outdoors, her torso covered by a sombrero. "Like to sell that hat?" he taunts. After he leaves, she turns over to reveal that she was not nude but in a bathing suit. When a middle-aged Curd Jürgens came upon Bardot sunning herself in the nude, neither he nor she made much of it.

In the words of Thibaut Schilt, associate professor of French at Holy Cross College, "The originality of Bardot's character lies in her making no apology for her nakedness and sexual exuberance." Although Americans associated France with hedonism and sexual sophistication, Bardot was something radically new even there. She fascinated the critics of *Cahiers du Cinéma* as "the ultimate modern woman of the cinema," said Schilt. The magazine's editor, André Bazin, detested *...And God Created Woman* for its "documentary" approach to sex. (Unfortunately, or perhaps fortunately, Bazin died in 1958 and never had to address the proliferation of nudity and sex scenes in the next decade.)

Although France did not have anything like the Production Code, censorship there was fairly strict. Nonetheless, they had a realistic acceptance of sex between unmarried people and allowed an occasional exposed breast, as in *Rififi* (1955), directed by American expatriate Jules Dassin, and in vehicles for Martine Carol, best known in the U.S. for *Lola Montes* (1955). Until Bardot, the French were greater appreciators of the erotic than creators of it. Even as they ridiculed American Puritanism, critics Ado Kyrou and Joseph Lo Duca drew mostly on Hollywood for their tomes on sex in cinema.

The success of the Bardot picture was probably responsible for the importation of *Liane, Jungle Goddess*, produced in West Germany in 1956. Briefly nude in title role was a cute blonde, Marion Michael, only 15 at the time. To the chagrin of librarians, stills of Michael in Daniel Blum's 1959 *Screen World* fell victim to razor blades. Distributors Corporation of America released the English-dubbed version on a double bill with Ed Wood's *Plan 9 from Outer Space*, since proclaimed the worst movie ever made. The company promptly went out of business.

Facing page: **Mamie Van Doren was a flashy, and fleshy, presence in** *Untamed Youth* **(top) at Warner Bros. and in Albert Zugsmith's** *High School Confidential* **with Russ Tamblyn (left) and Jan Sterling (center) at M-G-M. Even the major studios turned to exploitation pictures in the 1950s. Warner Bros./Turner Entertainment.**

9. *Bikini Beach*   125

Debra Paget's sizzling dance in Fritz Lang's two-part Indian epic got cut when it was released in the U.S. as *Journey to the Lost City*.

Debra Paget's name in the titles promised a hot dance number, even in a family entertainment like *Stars and Stripes Forever* (1952). Her dance in *Princess of the Nile* (1954) initially caused the film to be denied a Code Seal, even though it copied Jack Cole's choreography for Gwen Verdon in *David and Bathsheba*. (The Bible could always get a pass, but the Breen Office was still smarting from *The French Line*.) Producer Leonard Goldstein made a dozen cuts and lengthened reaction shots to keep the music in sync. Paget performed the unexpurgated version in her Las Vegas act in 1957. With her Hollywood career mostly over and Fritz Lang's definitively over, they were united in a German production, the two-part Indian epic *Der Tiger von Eschnapur/Das indische Grabmal* (1959). In his next-to-last American film, Lang had served up a leggy Rhonda Fleming. Now he would outdo himself. Paget's sensuality had always seemed too intense for conventional parts. Here, in a temple dance, she bursts her wraps to reveal a nearly nude body. Although the sequence was partly undercut by the obvious artifice of a serpent suspended by a wire and German actors dyed nut-brown, the dance may be the most erotic ever seen on film. Originally intended to be shown on successive nights, the two-part film was condensed into a 94-minute version released in the U.S. by American International as *Journey to the Lost City* (1960).

In 1959, Russ Meyer made *The Immoral Mr. Teas*, a nudie without the pretext of health, sunshine and volleyball. Filmed in short takes without dialogue, but with a comically irrelevant narration, it follows the, so to speak, titular protagonist as he undresses women with his eyes. He watches a glamour photographer, likely based on Meyer himself, stage a photo shoot with a blonde in a bikini who frolics in the surf; the film is at once a parody and the thing being parodied. Mr. Teas also gets to see three women bathing fully nude in a lake.

Doris Wishman entered the movie business in 1961 with *Diary of a Nudist*. Although her later films were increasingly violent, she played it fairly safe in her first feature. Unlike *Garden of Eden*, there was no imprimatur from naturist organizations. Instead of the varied body types that would be seen at a real nudist colony, the emphasis was entirely on young women.

Although New York City was the premiere market for "art" films, it was still subject to laws that required every feature film to display a certificate from the Motion Picture Division of the State Board of Regents (Education). Shirley Clarke's film of Jack Gelber's drug play *The Connection* was denied a certificate because of the repeated use of the word "shit." The initial run was shut down by police in 1961. A second attempt in 1962 resulted in the arrest of the projectionist.

The professional sleaze merchants knew how to game the system. Jerald Intrator's *Satan in High Heels* (1962) starred Meg Myles, who had attracted attention in Phil Karlson's *The Phenix City Story* (1955) with her performance of "Phenix City Blues" in a G.I. joint. (Publicity at the time claimed her measurements as 44-24-36, although she later

Nude on the Moon was an early effort from cult producer-director Doris Wishman, whose films became increasingly violent as the 1960s unfolded. American Genre Film Archive.

ridiculed that.) She recorded several albums including one for Liberty, home to Julie London. In *Satan*, Myles plays a burlesque stripper who flees the carnival midway to sing in New York nightclubs. Although dull, the film was surprisingly competent for a marginal production with very professional black-and-white cinematography and a supporting cast of New York theater and television pros that included Grayson Hall as a butch club owner who smokes through a cigarette holder. The score by jazz guitarist Mundell Lowe became a collector's item on LP. The raciest element in the picture was an extreme long shot of Myles going for a nude swim. Her big number, "The Female Is the Deadliest of the Species," was delivered in a leather outfit for the fetishist trade, riding crop in hand.

In 1963, Intrator was hired by William Mishkin to direct a landmark of cinema trash. Mishkin's *modus operandi* had been to buy foreign, usually French, films for a song, cut them just enough to satisfy the censors, affix a sexy title and then spend aggressively on promotion. He then produced on his own *The Orgy at Lil's Place* (1963). The film's impact came from its title. The word "orgy" had not been used in the title of a film since Lubin's *The Orgy* in 1915. The film was passed by the New York State censors with no cuts. (By contrast, *The Immoral Mr. Teas*, distributed by Mishkin in New York, was cut to a mere 47 minutes, 16 short of its intended running time.) There were no constraints on marketing other than the reluctance of newspapers to accept the ads. Mishkin developed an alternate set of press materials in which the title was simply *At Lil's Place*.

The story was a familiar one: a girl comes to the big city to seek fame and fortune as a model or actress, only to be victimized and exploited. In this case, it was two girls, sisters Ann and Sally. Ann, who narrates the story, was played by Kari Knudsen, later *Playboy* Playmate of the Month for February 1962. The advertising used the well-worn SEE trope: "SEE The Attempted Assault!" "SEE The 'ART' Class!" "SEE The Whipping Scene!" "SEE The Vice Raid!" "SEE Beautiful Girls Wrestling!" "SEE Passions Run Riot!" In reality, the scenes occur as part of the increasingly explicit photo shoots in which the girls participate. Her agent gets Ann to go to a party to meet the famed Lil who can boost her career. At the party, there's a game called "strip dice." "With a roll of the dice, off comes a dress," explains Ann. She laments, "It wasn't a party, it was a full-scale orgy!" Ultimately, Sally and Ann both get marriage proposals and quit the business. The film was still in black and white, but with the closing scenes "in blushing color," as the ads put it.

The Orgy at Lil's Place is considered by some the first "roughie," a trade term for cheap sex-and-violence pictures. Another plausible candidate was *Scum of the Earth* (1963), produced in Florida for $11,000 and directed by Herschell Gordon Lewis (as Lewis G. Gordon). A high school girl who needs money for college is induced to pose for a photographer. At first, it's only swimsuit stuff but escalates to toplessness. A threat to send the pictures to her father is used to blackmail her into posing nude. Even though Gordon Lewis had previously made a "nudie cutie," *The Adventures of Lucky Pierre* (1961), there is no real nudity in the film. The *Excelsior v. New York Board of Regents* decision made it possible to film nudity, but the combination of sex and violence, especially in gritty black and white, was still touchy. Violence in the film was minimal compared to what came later. In an episode unrelated to the main story, a woman is abducted on the street, taken to a motel and whipped with a belt. Her exposed back reveals welts. The film's ludicrous climax had the head of the pornography ring, chased on foot by cops, run into the ocean. He put a gun (a starter pistol) into his mouth and fired. In a trick lifted from Hitchcock's *Spellbound* (1945), there was a flash frame of red. The voice-over narration called pornographers "the scum of the earth." Intentionally or otherwise, the parallel between the pornography racket and exploitation film production was inescapable.

As the fifties turned into the sixties, nudity in full color was readily available in "skin" magazines. Black-and-white exposés of reform schools and nightclubs were passé and gave way to spoofs. Zugsmith changed with the times and cast his favorite star, Mamie Van Doren, in *The Private Lives of Adam and Eve* (1960). Seven years after Jane Russell rejected her costume for *The French Line*, the bikini finally came to the American screen. Van Doren as Eve and Fay Spain as Lilith wore skimpy outfits credited to Frederick's of Hollywood. Van Doren wore only the bottom with her breasts covered by long blonde tresses. Her navel still had to be covered by a leaf-shaped protrusion. Martin Milner, showing off his fine physique in a loincloth as Adam, also had his navel obscured but displayed the scar where his rib was taken out. This odd, dreadful film started off in black and white with a modern story set in Paradise, Nevada, then turned to color for a dream sequence in the Garden of Eden. When Eve eats the forbidden apple, it reverts to black and white.

"Itsy Bitsy Teenie Weenie Yellow Polka Dot Bikini," a pop hit in 1960, helped to legitimize the bikini. American International shifted from drag-strip riots and teenage werewolves to *Bikini Beach*, *How to Stuff a Wild Bikini*, *Dr. Goldfoot and the Bikini Machine* and *The Ghost in the Invisible Bikini*. *It's a Bikini World* declared a late (1967) entry in the beach-party cycle and so it was.

The beach hadn't played much of a part in Hollywood movies since the Mack Sennett era. Thanks to occasional titles like *Woman on the Beach* (1947) and *Female on the Beach* (1955) or the opening scenes of *Mildred Pierce* (1945), where lounge lizard Monte Baragon (Zachary Scott) is shot by his stepdaughter in a lavish beach house, the beach was somewhat sinister.

The movie that started the modern beach cycle was *Gidget* (1959). Instead of one of the usual hacks, the director was Paul Wendkos. Wendkos was known for the low-budget crime film *The Burglar*, shot in Philadelphia and Atlantic City and acquired for release by Columbia who brought him to Hollywood for *The Case Against Brooklyn* (1958). That background didn't keep him from shooting it in the style of the TV sitcom it later became. "Gidget," a combination of "girl" and "midget," was a real person, the daughter of Frederick Kohner, author of the novel on which the movie was based. The movie Gidget (Sandra Dee) is condescended to by the surfer fraternity because she is only 16, short and has small breasts. (She does exercises to make her chest bigger.) The title song is conveniently played on the radio so that James Darren, a pop star on Columbia's new Colpix record label, can sing to it. Other musical numbers are performed by the Four Preps, one of those then-ubiquitous crew-cut quartets. Gidget aspires to join the luau at the beach, even if she has pay someone to take her. In her effort to make Darren jealous, Gidget agrees to go with a thirtyish "surf bum" (Cliff Robertson) to his friend's beach house. She rejects coffee in favor of beer. He puts romantic music on the radio that just happens to be the song "From Here to Eternity," an allusion to an earlier Columbia picture with a famed beach scene. Dee gets cold feet and Robertson thinks better of it and sends her away before her parents can show up to save her honor. In the end, Darren gives Gidget his fraternity pin.

Yvette Mimieux in *Where the Boys Are* (1960) was not so fortunate. This popular movie depicted four young women on spring break in Fort Lauderdale, Florida. One of the women (Dolores Hart) became somewhat notorious at her college for her defense of "making out." She rejects the opportunity to put her ideas into practice when a wealthy Ivy Leaguer (George Hamilton) tells her that "morality went out with the raccoon coat." She remains a virgin, holds out for love and is rewarded at the end when Hamilton proposes to make things permanent. (In reality, Dolores Hart became a nun and the subject of the documentary *God Is the Bigger Elvis*.) By contrast, Mimieux's character loses her virginity while drunk and is subsequently raped. She is seen walking dazedly into traffic. The double standard was still very much in effect; the males in the movie were not virgins and suffered no guilt. Connie Francis, the top star on M-G-M's record label, was in the movie and sang the title song, a big hit for her.

Beach Party (1963) represented an attempt by American International Pictures to broaden its market. Low-budget, black-and-white movies weren't selling anymore even with provocative titles. With a budget of $300,000, tiny by major company standards but top of the line for AIP, and in Pathé Color and widescreen, *Beach Party* represented a bid for the mainstream. It owed something to the Gidget movies and *Where the Boys Are*. "When 10,000 kids meet 5,000 beach blankets, something's bound to happen," promised the trailer.

Everyone remembers *Beach Party* as a Frankie Avalon and Annette Funicello movie, but the top-billed names were actually Bob Cummings and Dorothy Malone. Cummings's character, Dr. Robert Sutwell, is an anthropologist who made his name studying puberty rites in the South Pacific. This is obviously a reference to the work of Margaret Mead (*Coming of Age in Samoa*), who discovered that puberty rites did not necessarily require marriage, a finding that has since been come under attack. For his current project, Sutwell decides to study the puberty rites of Malibu surfers: "A true subculture. They live in a society as primitive as that of New Guinea." Annette becomes Sutwell's "first contact" after he rescues her from a motorcycle gang and she serves as his native guide and interpreter. Annette's romance with Frankie has stalled because she wants to remain a virgin until marriage and he wants them to share a beach cottage "all alone, just like we're married." Frankie has turned his attention to a more receptive blonde.

We learn that Sutwell missed out on his own adolescence in pursuit of academic success. By the film's end, with the help of the kids, he rediscovers the youth he never had and belatedly notices his assistant, the still-radiant Dorothy Malone. She suggests that his monograph titled "Behavior Patterns of Young Adults and their Relationship to Primitive Tribes" be given a shorter title: "Teenage Sex." In the end, Sutwell revises his view and concludes that adolescents are not an alien culture after all but are passing through a necessary phase on their way to maturity.

As Gary Morris has pointed out, the beach in these movies was America's backyard and the Pacific Ocean its swimming pool. Annette Funicello, still under contract to Disney, was required not to wear a bikini. Like Connie Francis in *Where the Boys Are*, Annette was somewhat pudgy and ethnic-looking compared to the conventional beauties that surrounded her. Annette's song "Treat Him Nicely" echoed the melody of "Where the Boys Are." Plenty of other women did wear bikinis. Quinn O'Hara in *Ghost in the Invisible Bikini* showed the 38-23-36 measurements that landed her in ads for a dietary supplement called Wate-On.

George Axelrod's 1966 satire *Lord Love a Duck,* in which beach movie producer Martin Gabel comes up with *I Married a Teenage Bikini Vampire,* was actually behind the curve. AIP had already begun to cross-pollinate the beach-party series with performers (Vincent Price, Boris Karloff and Basil Rathbone) from their other major series, the Roger Corman horror movies. The end credits of *Beach Party* conclude with a crossplug for Corman's *The Haunted Palace* starring Price, seen as "Big Daddy" in *Beach Party.* AIP cofounder Samuel Z. Arkoff told an interviewer in 1974, "Nobody was able to compete with us on the beach pictures. The other companies saw that they were successful, that they should make some but they didn't understand the fundamentals. We had no parents or serious adults in any of our beach pictures. The adults were comic."

After the Berkeley riots of 1964 and the Watts uprising in 1965, California, home of the post–World War II suburban dream, came to occupy a more complicated place in the American imagination. The last two AIP beach movies actually lost money.

In November 1966, there was a disturbance at a club called Pandora Box's where teenagers massed to hear new music. Police imposed a 10 p.m. curfew. Police Captain Charlie Crumly blamed what became known as the Riot on the Sunset Strip on left-wing groups and "outside agitators … advocating free love, legalized marijuana and abortion." (There was no riot, only protest marches.) The police crackdown was immortalized in Buffalo Springfield's "For What It's Worth," written by Stephen Stills. ("There is something happening here, what it is ain't exactly clear.")

Within four months, a movie called *Riot on the Sunset Strip* (1967), with actual footage of the protests, appeared in theaters. Not surprisingly, it was released by American International; it was not produced by AIP mainstay Roger Corman but "B" movie veteran Sam Katzman. It was directed by 60-year-old Arthur Dreifuss, who managed one "quality" project, a film of Brendan Behan's *The Quare Fellow* (1962), in a long list of credits that went back to Monogram and PRC in the 1940s. A sort of updated *Reefer Madness,* it is as artificial and out of touch as one might expect from this duo. Aside from a few long shots of the actual Sunset Strip, it all takes place on soundstage sets and the back lot, where the entrance to Pandora's Box was re-created. (When the real Pandora's Box was slated for demolition, the protesters included Jack Nicholson, Peter Fonda and Dennis Hopper, who would soon be involved in more persuasive youth revolt movies of their own.)

Unlike Captain Crumly, the movie's cop (Aldo Ray) is a voice of restraint and stands up to the upscale business owners who want him to bust the heads of the "kooks." Things hit home when Ray's estranged daughter (Mimsy Farmer) gets caught up in the Sunset Strip scene. When some of her friends break into a house for an impromptu wild party, she is given an LSD-laced cocktail. To the accompaniment of some early psychedelic rock, she gyrates like Ann-Margret doing her Las Vegas act before she is led upstairs. She isn't raped exactly. She is aware enough to resist but doesn't. When the police raid the house, her father calls an ambulance for her. In her hospital room, where she is up and about, she tells her father that she had sex with five men. She projects indifference to the experience, but he tracks down and punches out two of the assailants. In the end, there is no riot and father and daughter are reconciled. Over shots of actual protests, the narrator tells us, "Soon half the world's population will be under 25 years of age…. What will they do?" Over the next few years, the movies would answer that question.

The same production team was responsible for *The Love-Ins* (1967). How little studio affiliations meant by the mid–1960s is evidenced by the fact that *Riot on the Sunset*

Strip was released by American International and *The Love-Ins* by Katzman's former home studio, Columbia. Both were actually made at M-G-M, Katzman's current home base, betrayed by the reappearance of the school set from *Tea and Sympathy*. (*Riot on the Sunset Strip* was originally planned for an M-G-M release. For M-G-M, Katzman produced *Hot Rods to Hell*, a throwback to the juvenile delinquent cycle of the 1950s, initially developed 10 years earlier as a follow-up to *Blackboard Jungle*.)

Part of the appeal of the youth revolt movies was the possibility that a strung-out hippie chick might get naked. *The Love-Ins* didn't actually deliver in that regard, but it didn't entirely disappoint either. In a truly bizarre sequence, Susan Oliver takes an LSD trip in which she imagines herself as Alice in Wonderland surrounded by Lewis Carroll's characters. This was probably inspired by Grace Slick's "White Rabbit" (not heard in the film), written after an acid trip. Amid a lot of stroboscopic flashes, Oliver lies on her back on the floor as if ready for sex.

LSD-induced fantasies accounted for much of the running time of Roger Corman's *The Trip* (1967), written by Jack Nicholson. A director of television commercials (Peter Fonda) drops acid multiple times. The sequences combined 1920s German stage expressionism and op-art with the flash frames and intentional overexposure of "underground" filmmaking. One of these sequences had what may be the first threesome in a Hollywood movie, albeit dark and with the details obscured by graphics, as Fonda has sex with his estranged brunette wife and his new blonde girlfriend.

A relatively benign motorcycle gang headed by Eric von Zipper (Harvey Lembeck) was a fixture of the AIP beach movies. With Corman's *The Wild Angels* (1966), things took a darker turn. In the film's most notorious sequence, the funeral of a dead biker (Bruce Dern) becomes a party-cum-orgy as a rural church is trashed. The bikers place a pair of shades on Dern's corpse and plant a joint in his mouth. His "old lady" (Dern's real-life wife Diane Ladd) is raped by four men behind the altar. Gang leader Peter Fonda temporarily abandons his "old lady" (Nancy Sinatra) for sex with the buxom Mama (Joan Shawlee), who previously offered herself as the prize in a motorcycle race. Elsewhere in the movie, the biker chicks (though not top-billed Sinatra) strip down to bra and panties.

More biker movies quickly followed. In Richard Rush's *Hell's Angels on Wheels* (1967), Jack Nicholson, newly initiated into the subculture, is taken aback when offered sex by a biker chick (AIP regular Salli Sachse) in front of her roommate. She accuses him of "middle-class morality." In *Devil's Angels* (1967), directed by Daniel Haller, the art director on the AIP Poe series, Mimsy Farmer got high again, this time on marijuana. She wasn't raped but the rumor of a rape touches off a war between the bikers and the townies.

Even Annette Funicello got caught in AIP's turn toward harder material with *Thunder Alley* (1967). Director Richard Rush incorporated real footage of a fatal crash at Darlington Speedway and featured a party/orgy with stock car drivers and their girlfriends. Rush, who went on to direct the cult film *The Stunt Man* (1980), brought a realistic, almost documentary, edge to his hippie and biker flicks, with extensive use of handheld cameras for immediacy. *Psych-Out* (1968) was shot on location in San Francisco's Haight-Ashbury neighborhood.

The hippie and biker movies overlapped and not just in terms of personnel. The bikers smoked dope and the hippies were not all peace-and-love flower children. They got into fistfights with local straights who taunted them for their long hair and effeminate clothing.

A bikini, or a very skimpy sunsuit, played a role in Stanley Kubrick's *Lolita* (1962). When Humbert Humbert (James Mason) first spies the nymphet who goes on to be his downfall, she is playing the "Lolita ya-ya" theme on her portable radio. "How did they ever make a movie of Lolita?" cooed the seductive female voice in the radio spots. The cynical reply was that they didn't. Martin Quigley, of all people, helped the producers navigate the objections from the Legion of Decency and the Production Code. It wasn't that difficult. Lolita's reputation as a dirty book derives mostly from the age gap between Lolita and Humbert. Only one paragraph confirms their physical relationship and even that is circumspect.

With a screenplay by Vladimir Nabokov himself, the movie was better than might have been expected. In the novel, both Lolita and Humbert are dead when the story begins, and it is explained that the ridiculous name "Humbert Humbert" is a pseudonym for the subject of a case study. This is omitted from the film, but the movie improves on the novel in one respect. Aided by Peter Sellers's gift for mimicry, Humbert's more successful rival, Claire Quilty, a minor presence in the novel, becomes in the movie his *doppelgänger*, mocking and thwarting him at every turn. He shows up at a police convention held at the hotel to which Humbert takes Lolita and as the guidance counselor at her high school (a woman in the novel) who encourages her to try out for the school play over Humbert's objections. Some critics thought that 15-year-old Sue Lyon was too mature for the part. (When Humbert sees first sees her, she is 12 years old in the novel, but that was changed to 14 for the film.) By the story's end, she is 17 and the mother of a child.

Even when not in bikinis, the new female stars were mostly beach bunnies. A generation earlier, in 1932, the *Three on a Match* trio of Bette Davis, Joan Blondell and Ann Dvorak was worldly wise in its twenties. Sandra Dee, Connie Stevens, Ann-Margret, Yvette Mimieux and Carol Lynley were stuck in prolonged adolescence.

The industry calculated that "the kids" were now the core audience and wanted to see themselves on the screen. Young love did have its hazards, chiefly unwanted pregnancy. Carol Lynley was made pregnant by Brandon deWilde, of *Shane* fame, in *Blue Denim* (1959). Unlike the stage play on which it was based, the girl did not have an abortion but went to another town until the baby was born. Troy Donahue impregnated Sandra Dee in *A Summer Place* (1959), to which teenage girls flocked in sufficient numbers that writer-producer-director Delmer Daves had him embrace the women of the Warner Bros. contract list in *Parrish* (1961), *Susan Slade* (1961) and *Rome Adventure* (1962), all awash in music by Max Steiner. In *Susan Slade*, Connie Stevens is made pregnant not by Donahue but by a mountain climber killed off early in the film. She tries to abort the baby and/or kill herself by charging her horse into the ocean. Her parents then pretend the baby is their own. While she is talking to Donahue, the baby picks up a cigarette lighter and bursts into flames! At the hospital, she admits the baby is hers. Donahue offers to help raise the child.

The trailer for *Susan Slade* proclaimed the story as that "of a girl of today, living at today's upbeat tempo, playing at today's jet-age speed." The one for *Parrish* extolled young people for "fighting the old morals." Suzanne Pleshette, in her first film, came up against the old morals in the opening scene of *Rome Adventure* (1962). As the assistant librarian in a women's college, she is forced to resign by a faculty committee because she gave a senior girl her personal copy of a sexy book called *Lovers Must Learn* by "Irving Fineman." (Irving Fineman was the author of the 1932 novel *Lovers Must Learn* on which the movie was based; it took place in Paris, not Rome. *Rome Adventure* was titled *Lovers Must Learn* in the UK.)

One way to establish maturity was to play a prostitute. To judge by the Academy Award nominations, 1960 was The Year of the Whore. Former Rodgers and Hammerstein ingénue Shirley Jones went against type in *Elmer Gantry* and was rewarded with the Best Supporting Actress Oscar. Melina Mercouri in *Never on Sunday* lost out as Best Actress to Elizabeth Taylor in *BUtterfield 8*. The 1935 John O'Hara novel was updated to the then-present. Taylor was not technically a prostitute. She wrote "No Sale" in lipstick on the bedroom mirror of a man with whom she spent the night after he left $200 on the dresser to pay for the dress he tore off. Like Holly Golightly in *Breakfast at Tiffany's*

Troy Donahue and Connie Stevens were groomed for big-screen stardom in the Warner Bros. television series *Surfside 6* and *Hawaiian Eye*, respectively. It was hoped they would bring the youth audience to the Delmer Daves-directed soap operas *Parrish* and *Susan Slade*. They were reteamed in *Palm Springs Weekend,* a less popular knockoff of M-G-M's *Where the Boys Are*. Warner Bros.

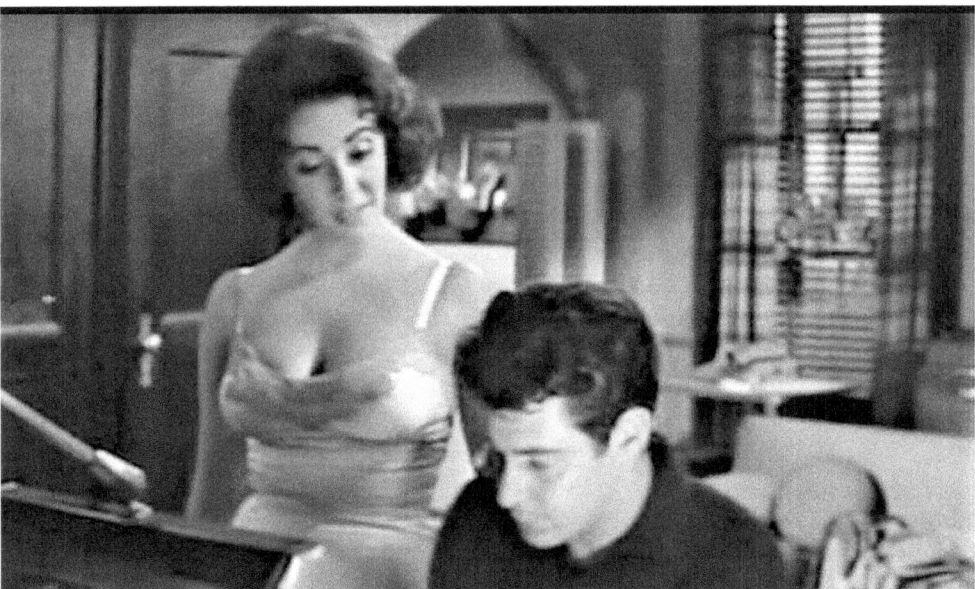

Playgirl Elizabeth Taylor in *BUtterfield 8* seems about to burst out of her Helen Rose-designed slip as songwriter Eddie Fisher (her then-husband in real life) plays the piano. Turner Entertainment.

the following year, she glided through Manhattan social circles with no visible means of support. Taylor stipulated that Helen Rose do her wardrobe, but the most memorable costume was again a slip that Elia Kazan described as "several sizes too small into which she seemed to have been sewn." With her breasts flowing over the top, she stood next to songwriter Eddie Fisher seated at his piano and purred, "Can I help you with anything?" to scattered snickers from the audience.

With prostitution in decline in 1960s America from amateur competition as premarital sex gained acceptance, most stories took place in the bad old days of the 1920s and '30s or in foreign locales. Shelley Winters played New York's celebrity madam, Polly Adler, in *A House Is Not a Home* (1964), with Cesar Romero as vice king "Lucky" Luciano and the then-unknown Raquel Welch among Polly's girls. *The World of Suzie Wong* (1960), filmed in Hong Kong, had the delightful Nancy Kwan in tight-fitting dresses slit to the hip. There had been Anna May Wong in the distant past and Shirley Yamaguchi in a couple of 1950s movies, but Kwan was the first real Asian star. In her next film, *Flower Drum Song* (1961), she sang (dubbed) "I Enjoy Being a Girl" and danced to multiple mirror images of herself.

In 1959, Dorothy Dandridge, the only glamorous African American female star in movies at the time, played a cocaine-addicted hooker in *Porgy and Bess*. Like Lena Horne earlier, she could at first only play the lead in black-cast films, e.g., *Bright Road* (1953) and her big hit *Carmen Jones* (1954), both opposite Harry Belafonte. The Code ban on miscegenation was lifted as part of the 1956 revision. For his first personal production after stepping down as production chief at Fox, Darryl F. Zanuck, who styled himself as "the man who has made a tradition of breaking tradition," put Dandridge in *Island in the Sun* (1957). With his usual mix of mild controversy couched in commercial calculation, Zanuck offered two interracial romances to demonstrate progressivism with the tang of forbidden fruit. Dandridge's character was designed to have Indian ancestry to make her romance with a white scion of the planter class more acceptable. Harry Belafonte, as a labor leader, was given an older white woman to embrace, faded star Joan Fontaine who had little to lose. Neither couple kissed. Dandridge did kiss James Mason in *The Decks Ran Red* (1958). *Tamango* (1959), made earlier but released in the U.S. later, went much further. Made in Europe by the blacklisted director John Berry, it had Dandridge as the mistress of a slave ship captain played by Curd Jürgens. Controversy over miscegenation held up the film's release but the distributors turned interracial sex to their advantage in sensationalistic television spots.

Paris still connoted sexual naughtiness when Billy Wilder filmed *Irma La Douce* (1963) with Shirley MacLaine as a "poule" (prostitute) and Jack Lemmon as a gendarme turned her "mec" (pimp). Wilder used the characters from a David Merrick Broadway musical but ditched the songs, although the melody of the best-known one, "Our Language of Love," figured prominently in Andre Previn's background score. MacLaine's bare back and a glimpse of breast made it clear that she was nude under the covers of the bed she shared with Lemmon. Although veteran producer Hal Wallis called it, "the filthiest thing I have ever seen on screen," Wilder's skill in fashioning popular entertainment from potentially distasteful material had not deserted him. It became his most profitable film with a then-huge gross of $20 million, even though it was marketed as "adults only."[1]

After an indifferent debut in *Tall Story* (1960), Jane Fonda played a 1930s prostitute in *Walk on the Wild Side* (1962) from a Nelson Algren novel. Almost a dozen years before Fonda's Oscar-winning performance in *Klute* (1971), Anne Francis was a prostitute in therapy in the low-budget *Girl of the Night* (1960), one of the few set in the contemporary U.S.

Before the Minsky Brothers were banished from Broadway in the late 1930s as part of Mayor LaGuardia's moral crackdown, burlesque enjoyed a reverse-snob glamour with Gypsy Rose Lee taken up by the smart set. Dorothy Arzner's *Dance, Girl, Dance* (1940) offered a proto-feminist critique, with Maureen O'Hara tongue-lashing the audience from the stage. For the most part, Hollywood regarded burlesque with amusement, e.g., Barbara Stanwyck in *Ball of Fire* (1941) and *Lady of Burlesque* (1943) and Ginger Rogers in 1942's *Once Upon a Honeymoon* (with songwriter Johnny Mercer's 1940 novelty hit "Strip Polka" quoted in the score).

By the time Ann Corio's 1962 revue *This Was Burlesque* treated it as history and nostalgia, Hollywood had grown disenchanted. In the film version of *Gypsy* (1962), Natalie Wood became a star in a field she was forced to enter by a grotesque stage mother. The complex dynamic of their relationship made *Gypsy* the rare musical, not adapted from a straight play, where the book is strong enough to stand on its own even without songs (not that one would want that). Gypsy Rose Lee herself was in *The Stripper* (1963) at 20th Century–Fox, where she had been briefly under contract in 1937 under her real name, Louise Hovick, to deflect controversy. Based on William Inge's play *A Loss of Roses*, the title was changed to the much more commercial *The Stripper*, possibly to piggyback on David Rose's 1962 instrumental hit (not heard in the film). It would have been more commercial still if producer Jerry Wald, who died before release, had been able to engage his first choice, Marilyn Monroe. Joanne Woodward, in a blonde wig, was not especially sexy but perhaps better suited to portray the sad dregs of show business.

The low-budget *A Cold Wind in August* (1961), released independently without a Code Seal, offered Lola Albright as a 35-year-old stripper involved with a 17-year-old boy. It depicted a mature woman at once desirable and desiring but also mentally unbalanced. It was rereleased as *The Undergraduate* to capitalize on the more famous "cougar" played by Anne Bancroft in *The Graduate* (1967).

Samuel Fuller retained a fondness for burlesque. In *The Crimson Kimono*, "Sugar Torch" (Gloria Pall) was murdered while running through the street after witnessing a murder in her dressing room (though not before doing her act). *Shock Corridor* (1963) gave Constance Towers an original song, "I Want Someone to Love," performed through feathers. (Marlene Dietrich in *Blonde Venus* at least took off the ape head to render the lyrics of "Hot Voodoo.") As she strips, she leans forward to jiggle her breasts. This was a violation of the previous unwritten rules as explained in 1954 by Kenny Williams, who staged Gloria Grahame's dance in *Naked Alibi*. A dancer could do a "bump" (a rapid movement of the hips to the side) but not forward. A "grind" (circular movement of the torso) would not get by. Towers's character contends she does it for the money: "Do you think I like singing in a sewer with a hot light on my navel?" (Her navel is actually covered.) The film's trailer contradicts her: "Diagnosis: Manic Sensualist."

In *The Oscar* (1966), Frankie Fane (Stephen Boyd), a heel who has stepped on everybody on his way up, is about to receive the Best Actor award when a flashback shows his years as master of ceremonies in a strip joint. As Jill St. John takes to the stage, she is pawed by the customers. She strips down to bra and panties and, shot from the rear, takes off her bra.

By the early 1960s, the studios and the television networks were no longer rivals but existed in a symbiotic relationship. Features that flopped in theaters often drew higher ratings than the networks' filmed series, produced by the same companies. This posed a dilemma. How could Hollywood offer moviegoers something that they could not—pace Kazan—get at home without jeopardizing the television sales that made up the losses from theatrical distribution? One solution was the "clean dirty" movie. The leading practitioner was Stanley Shapiro, scenarist of *Pillow Talk*, *Lover Come Back* and *That Touch of Mink*, all with Doris Day. Oscar Levant cracked, "I knew Doris Day before she was a virgin." (Actually, in *Pillow Talk*, it was Day who proposed to Rock Hudson that they go away for the weekend.)

Hollywood sex comedies—*Boys' Night Out*, *Bachelor in Paradise*, *Under the Yum Yum Tree*, *Sex and the Single Girl*, et al.—were all talk and no action. Some of the talk was admittedly clever. In *Wives and Lovers* (1963), Jeremy Slate said of former bedmate Shelley Winters, "I knew her intimately but not well." However, Hollywood by then had to compete with the likes of *Boccaccio 70*, imported by Joseph E. Levine with no Code Seal and a "Condemned" rating. It had Loren and Ekberg for the ads, renowned directors Vittorio De Sica, Federico Fellini and Luchino Visconti for the critics. Levine was less successful with Jean-Luc Godard's *Contempt* (1963). Pressured by producer Carlo Ponti to include a nude scene for Brigitte Bardot, Godard retaliated. Protracted shots of Bardot nude rendered the film uncommercial, more a critique of sex in cinema than an example of it. Levine tried to salvage it with a lurid ad campaign.

The Chapman Report (1962), seen today, is milder than a television soap opera. At the time, like *Irma La Douce* the following year, it tested the limits of acceptability. George Cukor was hired to bring class to a script that six writers extracted from a trashy best seller by Irving Wallace. Dr. Chapman (read Kinsey) gives a presentation to a women's club in the wealthy Southern California suburb of Pacific Palisades. He seeks volunteers who will answer questions about their sexual histories.

138   Hollywood and the Female Body

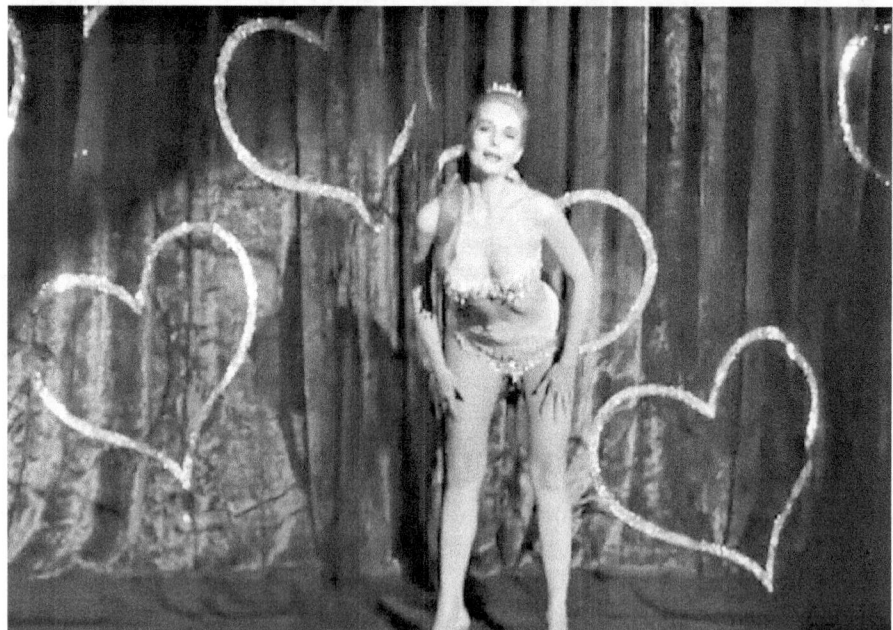

In Samuel Fuller's *Shock Corridor,* Constance Towers was the stripper girlfriend of a reporter who got himself committed to a lunatic asylum to write an exposé but then went crazy for real. ("What a tragedy! An insane mute will win the Pulitzer Prize!") Fuller had her do her act and bend forward to show her breasts. Allied Artists.

The women's parts were crucial, and a quartet of interesting actresses was assembled for the main roles: Claire Bloom, Glynis Johns, Jane Fonda and Shelley Winters. Darryl Zanuck, the once and future king of 20th Century–Fox, had set up the project there but ran into the chaos of *Cleopatra* and, perhaps, the prudery of chairman Spyros Skouras. A phone call to Jack L. Warner got the package moved to Warner Bros., where Zanuck had been production chief three decades earlier. The male roles were cast from the Warner television stable, who were paid their usual salaries.

The Claire Bloom character was an alcoholic nymphomaniac. Cukor let the audience know that she was doomed by photographing her in shadow. She tries to seduce the bottled-water deliveryman (Chad Everett) but turns on him in a fit of self-loathing. An abusive relationship with a jazz musician (Corey Allen) culminates in an implied gang rape at his apartment and her subsequent suicide. At the other extreme was Glynis Johns, a culture-vulture who makes spoken word recordings and is also an artist. She spies hunky Ty Hardin playing football on the beach with his male friends and proposes that he model for her. He is embarrassed when she wants him to pose nude. Cukor may have been a "woman's director" but he took an avid interest in Hardin's physique. Their scenes are played for comedy. Falling somewhere in between were the trials of Shelley Winters, who almost leaves her businessman husband for the director of her little theater group, and Jane Fonda as a young widow, supposedly frigid in contrast to the sensuality she radiated on-screen. The women spoke to their interviewer from the other side of a partition as if in the Catholic confessional. In a breach of professional decorum, one of Chapman's researchers (Efrem Zimbalist, Jr.) starts a relationship with Fonda, who turns out not to be so frigid after all.

The Legion of Decency was a shadow of its former self by 1962 but Warner and Zanuck had tangled with it in its heyday and came up with a revised ending that upheld conventional mores. A new line was given to Andrew Duggan as Chapman to say in summation: "We lose sight of the fact the vast majority fall right into this column: happily married women. And men."

A subgenre of the "clean dirty" movie was the Southern California adultery comedy. The template was 1960's *The Facts of Life* with Bob Hope and Lucille Ball. Frequent Hope screenwriters Norman Panama and Melvin Frank had written the script some years earlier as an Americanized *Brief Encounter* with James Stewart and Olivia de Havilland but reworked it for comedy. At first, Hope and Ball don't like each other. When he plays emcee at a country club dinner, she finishes his tired jokes before he can get the words out. The carefully crafted screenplay, which won an Academy Award, brought them together and then found ways to keep them apart. Hope leaves Ball in their motel room while he gets coffee; on his way back, he can't find the motel because they all look alike. Ball gets tired of waiting and takes a cab home. Ultimately, they return to their respective spouses. Hope was Hope but Ball attempted a characterization beyond her "Lucy" role. Both were too old and too protective of their images to strike any erotic sparks.

By the time of *A Guide for the Married Man* (1967), we were deep into the Swinging Sixties. Walter Matthau leaves his house for work at the same time as his neighbor (Sue Ann Langdon) leaves hers. He watches her swaying walk that director Gene Kelly emphasizes with a zoom into a close-up of her bottom. The bottom becomes a freeze-frame over which the movie's title is superimposed; this leaves no doubt as to where things are headed. As he drives to work, Matthau stops at a light and sees a quintet of babes wearing short skirts in mod colors and he stares long enough to get a horn. The film's joke is that Matthau already has the perfect woman in his wife (Inger Stevens). She makes him gourmet meals from inexpensive ingredients, brings him beer on the patio and bends forward to reveal some impressive cleavage. The deadening effect of marriage on sexual desire is illustrated by the fact that Matthau has his nose in a book as his wife, in a separate bed, exercises her beautiful body. She shakes her perfect behind in a skintight white leotard that she unzips to expose her breasts to him before going to bed. (In the American version, she was photographed from behind. In the European version, the audience also got to see her breasts.)

Matthau's friend (Robert Morse) tells him that even if you have steak every night, you miss the taste of fish. His reason for the pursuit of women is pretty much the same that Edmund Hillary gave to climb Everest: because they are there. Morse is an expert philanderer and offers Matthau pointers on how to carry off an extramarital affair and avoid the pitfalls that may get him caught. These are illustrated in vignettes enacted by 14 guest stars, mostly from television, enlisted as "technical experts." To illustrate the principle of "deny, deny, deny," Joey Bishop, when caught in bed by his wife with another woman, responds "What woman?" Movie star Carl Reiner is captivated by "a new kid the studio just put under contract" (Linda Harrison, real-life 20th Century–Fox contractee, soon to become semi-famous in *Planet of the Apes*, in big sunglasses and an unbecoming blonde wig). He journeys halfway around the world, with the help of back projection, for a rendezvous with "Miss Stardust" at a ski chalet in the Swiss Alps, only to be surprised by his wife and her detectives. Matthau finally gets his chance with a wealthy widow for whom he acts as an investment advisor, played by the busty, butty Elaine Devry. In their motel room, she strips down to a black lace teddy as he stammers and stalls. He imagines his wife in tears and chickens out. Monogamy is upheld.

A Guide for the Married Man was also the last film made by Jayne Mansfield, brought back to Fox, her former home studio, for a guest shot as one of the "experts." Her three-minute bit with Terry-Thomas involved the search for her missing bra, telltale evidence of an affair. (Mansfield died in a car crash in June 1967, a month after the film's release.)

Mansfield's last important film for 20th Century–Fox was the Western comedy *The Sheriff of Fractured Jaw* (1958) directed by Raoul Walsh. Her body was shown to advantage in corsets and dance-hall outfits. *It Happened in Athens*, set during the first modern Olympics in 1896 Greece, was planned for release in conjunction with the 1960 Olympics but was considered so weak that it was not released until 1962, by which time Mansfield's contract had expired. In the interim, she was loaned out for low-budget pictures that included *The George Raft Story* (1961) at Allied Artists, home of black-and-white crime films.

Mansfield played a character called in the trailer "The Movie Star," a possible composite of Carole Lombard and Betty Grable (with whom Raft had had an affair in the early 1940s). Additional stimulation was provided by Julie London ("The Torch Singer") and Barrie Chase ("The Bolero Dancer"). The supposedly Swinging Sixties had not yet caught up to the pre–Code era. In 1934's *Bolero*, made by Paramount just before the Code crackdown, the real George Raft and a braless Carole Lombard danced to Ravel's sexy showpiece in an elaborate number shot from multiple angles. It climaxed with him on top of her. The biopic, in a scene designed to show Raft's desire to break away from gangster parts with a musical, had Ray Danton as Raft dance with Barrie Chase, implau-

Walter Matthau fails to appreciate the efforts of his wife, Inger Stevens, to keep her body in shape for him in *A Guide for the Married Man*. Typical of Hollywood comedies in the 1960s, it portrayed infidelity as light-hearted fun, only to reaffirm conventional morality at the end. 20th Century–Fox.

sibly, to "Temptation" (from a 1933 M-G-M film) in a bare-bones set with minimalist camerawork.

David Thomson called Jayne Mansfield "the swan song of pre-nude sexuality in films," but it was Mansfield who would lead the transition to the nude era. *Promises! Promises!*, a cheap black-and-white sex comedy, was among top grossers in 1963. It had some slim Hollywood bona fides. Tommy Noonan, its producer, cowriter and male lead, had been in *Gentlemen Prefer Blondes* and *A Star Is Born*. King Donovan, a character actor familiar from *Invasion of the Body Snatchers* (1956), directed. Marie "The Body" McDonald, a minor star of the 1940s, was the second female lead, a last-minute replacement for Mamie Van Doren. (Van Doren later appeared in a similar Noonan effort, 1964's *3 Nuts in Search of a Bolt*, in which she bared her behind to stay current.) The plot had two couples meet on a ship and get drunk together. Both women end up pregnant, not necessarily by their husbands. So much for the sanctity of marriage!

It was one thing to know that Mansfield's large breasts must have had nipples; it was another thing to see them. The release was keyed to a pictorial in *Playboy*, referenced in the film's trailer and posters. "This is the first time I've ever appeared COMPLETELY

NUDE!" she was quoted as saying. The *Playboy* spread got Hugh Hefner arrested for obscenity by the Chicago police.

What *Esquire* was to the early 1940s, *Playboy* was to the early 1960s. *Playboy* was a frequent stop for actresses on the way up (Stella Stevens in 1960) or down (Elaine Stewart in 1959). Movies were part of the larger cultural universe and belonged to a visual galaxy that included magazine photography, advertising, comic books and cartoons. The disparity between what was seen in print but not on-screen could not be maintained forever.

As members of the MPAA, the major studios had to uphold the Code's provision that "complete nudity in fact or in silhouette is never permitted.... Nudity can never be permitted as essential to the plot."

With skills perfected over more than 30 years, Alfred Hitchcock was able to suggest nudity within the provisions of the Code in his phenomenally successful *Psycho* (1960). Marion Crane (Janet Leigh) is spied on by motel manager Norman Bates (Anthony Perkins) through a hole in the wall. (Gus Van Sant's remake, which mostly follows the original, "improves" on it in that it has Norman Bates masturbate during this scene.) Janet Leigh erroneously claimed that she alone did the shower scene. The nude shots were made with a model, Marli Renfro, who later appeared in *Playboy*. Fifty-two pieces of film comprised the scene. A prosthetic torso that showed the navel but cut off above the pubic area was employed to depict the knife entering the abdomen; in reality, the knife was withdrawn and the shot printed in reverse.

After *Psycho*, a specter haunted Hollywood. When would there be a real nude scene and who would do it?

There were some near misses. Natalie Wood was an on-screen surrogate for the postwar generation as a child (*Miracle on 34th Street*), a teenager (*Rebel Without a Cause*) and a young woman (*Marjorie Morningstar*). She would go on to get an illegal abortion in *Love with the Proper Stranger* (1963) and flirt with group sex in *Bob & Carol & Ted & Alice* (1969). For *Splendor in the Grass* (1961), Kazan filmed a scene in which Wood jumped from the bathtub and ran naked down the hall. Even a director with the right of final cut was still contractually obligated to deliver a Code–acceptable release, so the scene got trimmed. Marilyn Monroe was playfully nude as she paddled around a pool in the surviving footage from *Something's Got to Give* (1962). Carroll Baker still possessed a racy image from *Baby Doll* and was poised to break the barrier in Joseph E. Levine's first studio production, *The Carpetbaggers* (1964). The highly anticipated nude scene was but a single shot of her seated with her upper body reflected in a mirror. Preview audiences saw it, but it was cut for general release.

Cleopatra (1963) showed more of Elizabeth Taylor than usual. She received a massage facedown, naked except for a towel over her backside. Part of her butt cheek and some side boob were visible. A dancer in Cleopatra's entrance into Rome was topless except for rosettes that covered her nipples. With $40 million and the survival of 20th Century–Fox at stake, the PCA was inclined to be lenient. Taylor was indirectly nude in *The Sandpiper* (1965) via the statue for which she posed for sculptor Charles Bronson. She covered her actual breasts with her hands when clergyman Richard Burton visited the studio.

One common dodge was to make different foreign and domestic versions. Overseas audiences got Elke Sommer nude in *The Victors* (1963); the U.S. did not.

The Code Administration did make one exception. *The Pawnbroker* (1964) had a scene in which a black prostitute exposed her breasts to an emotionally dead concentration-camp survivor. It was hardly erotic, just sad and embarrassing for both. Like the U.S. Supreme Court's ruling in *Bush v. Gore*, it was a one-shot, not intended as precedent. The Legion of Decency warned that even one exception would open the floodgates. This would turn out to be true, although not immediately.

Howard Hawks's *Man's Favorite Sport?* (1964) was more typical of the era, with a montage of Peter Gowland "glamour" shots under the credits to clarify that the sport wasn't fishing.

Mainstream Hollywood edged closer to nudity when veteran George Sidney, who had directed Ann-Margret in *Bye Bye Birdie* (1963) and *Viva Las Vegas* (1964), put her in *The Swinger* (1966). She wasn't really that much of a swinger but pretended to be to get her stories published by a *Playboy*-type men's magazine. Sidney used "with it" stylistic touches—jump cuts, freeze-frames, speeded-up action—lifted from Richard Lester's Beatles films to enliven a retarded script. In a reference to the vogue act of body painting, Ann-Margret turned herself into a human paintbrush rolling around in a wet swirl of colors on the floor. She was actually wearing a bikini. In the next decade, she would really be nude in *Carnal Knowledge* (1971) but would writhe, clothed, again in messy liquids (bubble bath, baked beans, chocolate) in *Tommy* (1975).

Hollywood was caught napping by the international success of the British-made James Bond films. In *Dr. No* (1962), Ursula Andress, a.k.a. "Arseula Undressed," emerged from the ocean in a white bikini, her navel proudly displayed. The taboo had actually been shattered by German actress Christine Kaufmann as a *fraülein* raped by four Ameri-

Ann-Margret was never actually nude in *The Swinger*, but she did display more of the body that made her the stuff of young men's dreams in the 1960s. Paramount.

can G.I.s in *Town Without Pity* (1961). The glimpses of her navel were brief and oblique and, in the most frontal shot, blurred in printing. The PCA conceded that the bikini, important to the story and entered as evidence at trial, had become acceptable beachwear. Rosanna Schiaffino exposed her navel in long shot in the film-within-the-film of *Two Weeks in Another Town* (1962). In a few years, navels would even been seen on television, at least in grown-up shows like *Burke's Law* when Nancy Kovack guest starred. (Barbara Eden on *I Dream of Jeannie* and Dawn Wells of *Gilligan's Island* remained covered up.)

Proclaimed the sexiest woman on earth by Hugh Hefner, Andress was promptly put in Hollywood movies. Again in a bikini, she had *Fun in Acapulco* (1963) with Elvis Presley. In *4 for Texas* (1963), which also brought back Anita Ekberg, she was silhouetted seminude in a filmy negligee as she stood framed by a doorway, to the delight of Dean Martin.

Dean Martin was nobody's idea of a secret agent, but his booze-and-broads persona made the Matt Helm series a viable Bond knockoff. A recurring character in all four was an assistant with the jokey name of Lovey Kravezit (Beverly Adams). In one-off appearances were Stella Stevens, Ann-Margret, Nancy Kovack, Tina Louise and even Cyd Charisse. There was also newcomer Sharon Tate.

Tate, as a bikini-clad skydiver in *Don't Make Waves* (1967), was ogled by another aging roué, Tony Curtis, whom she rescued from a surfing accident. M-G-M furnished

The Navel Academy, Part II: Ursula Andress, the first "Bond girl" in *Dr. No*, made an indelible impression in her white bikini. The taboo on belly buttons had actually been broached the previous year by Christine Kaufmann in *Town without Pity*, but Andress rendered it definitively dead. United Artists.

Sharon Tate in *Don't Make Waves* was a skydiver and surfer named Malibu who rescued Tony Curtis from a surfing accident. Tate seemed headed for stardom after *Valley of the Dolls* in 1968 but was murdered in 1969. Turner Entertainment.

life-size standees of Tate to theater lobbies. Raquel Welch, an old-style sex goddess in the Rita Hayworth/Jane Russell mode, decorated dorm rooms and Vietnam hootches in the poster for *One Million Years B.C.* (1966). Of the younger actresses, Jane Fonda was the most audaciously sexualized, sometimes against her will. She sued Walter Reade Theatres over an 80-foot billboard above Times Square for Roger Vadim's *Circle of Love* that featured her nude backside. It was hastily draped with a sheet, then painted over. She also sued *Playboy* over nude pictures taken on the set of Vadim's *La Curée*. In Vadim's *Barbarella* (1968), she was put into the Excessive Machine to be executed by sexual pleasure. Her multiple orgasms melted its circuits. (Masters and Johnson's *Human Sexual Response*, published in 1966, was still fresh in people's minds.) In *Hurry Sundown* (1967), a late entry in the Southern decadent cycle, her husband (Michael Caine) was more interested in his saxophone than her. She picked up the sax herself and fellated the mouthpiece, giving off beckoning little toots.

For the scene in *The Graduate* (1967) when Dustin Hoffman sees Mrs. Robinson nude, his head spins around as if on a swivel. This was accomplished by making four brief shots, in which the camera was moved 90 degrees and the actor turned toward the new placement. Anne Bancroft was photographed in a simple head and shoulder shot.

A body double was used for the midriff and breasts. Subliminal flashes of the double were edited into Hoffman's reaction as shot from behind Bancroft's back. Cinematographer Robert Surtees wrote that "the audience believed it had seen a nude woman."[2]

The barrier against actual nudity fell like the backdrop pulled from its roller by two silly girls or "birds" who ran amok in the studio of photographer David Hemmings in *Blow-Up* (1966). He pulled off their pantyhose and they took off his shirt as they rolled around on the crumpled paper. A good time was had by all. The nude young women showed glimpses of pubic hair. Director Michelangelo Antonioni refused to cut the scene, so M-G-M created a fake subsidiary, Premier Productions, to release its first non–Code film. United Artists had previously put out *Kiss Me, Stupid* through its "art" division, Lopert Films, even though it had a Code Seal. Such subterfuge would soon be unnecessary. MPAA's new president, Jack Valenti, decided to ditch the Production Code in favor of a ratings system to be implemented by 1968. In the interim, the phrase "Suggested for Mature Audiences" turned up on movie ads and accounted for 60 percent of all Code–approved films.

The birth control pill, introduced in 1960, was first prescribed only to married women. By the mid–1960s, doctors offered it to single women. Once premarital sex was acknowledged as the norm, the rationale for censorship, at least for adults, pretty much evaporated. The censors themselves saw the futility of their project and were ready to throw in the towel. In his book *See No Evil*, an insider's account of the workings of the Production Code Administration, Jack Vizzard quoted his boss Geoffrey Shurlock as saying, "This deification of the female waterworks is too much."

At the 1968 Academy Awards, emcee Bob Hope said, "Last year we gave you the dirty words. This year we gave you the pictures to go with them."

In the last year before the ratings system was to go into effect, directors tested the limits of what they could get away with. Joy Harmon made movie history in *Cool Hand Luke* (1967) in a small part in which she did not say a word. As a road gang of convicts digs a ditch, she comes out of her house and washes her car. The spray from the hose represents ejaculation, while the suds all over the front of her dress suggest semen from multiple men. In a shot from inside the car, she presses her breasts to the side window. (In reality, Harmon's actions and the men's heated reactions were filmed separately, and the three-minute sequence was created in the editing room.)

In *The Night of the Generals* (1967), there was a "now you see it, now you don't" intimation of cunnilingus. In long shot, a man can be seen kissing his way up the body of a woman on her back in bed. In a two-shot, we see Tom Courtenay and Joanna Pettet, who have obviously just shared an intimate moment. Because nothing was actually shown, the film got a Seal. *Charlie Bubbles* (1968), directed by Albert Finney, was not treated so lightly. Liza Minnelli, in her first film, takes off her bra and panties as seen from the rear. In the next shot, her head moves out of the frame (leaving her wig behind) and she performs oral sex on Finney. *Charlie Bubbles* did not get a Code Seal and was released by an ad hoc art subsidiary, Regional Films.[3] The Regional Films label was also used for *I'll Never Forget What's 'Isname* (1967), in which there was a suggestion of cunnilingus performed by Oliver Reed on Carol White.

The Sweet Ride (1968) had a long shot of Jacqueline Bisset topless in the surf. Leering males Anthony Franciosa and Bob Denver share binoculars to gawk.

Lee Marvin in *Point Blank* (1967) used Angie Dickinson as bait to get access to John Vernon in his penthouse apartment. Vernon unbuttons her dress, exposing her bra. In bed, her behind faces the camera and his hand reaches to pull down her panties. There is a cut before anything is shown. Afterward, Angie in long shot and out of focus can be seen getting dressed, obviously after sex.

Age classification as an alternative to the Code had been suggested for decades. Neither the industry nor its critics were interested. Producers and theater owners wanted the largest possible audience. The Legion and the censor boards, for all their professed concern for impressionable youth, didn't want adults exposed to sexual material either. In 1966, the Legion of Decency became the less fearsome National Catholic Office for Motion Pictures, or NCOMP, mocked by critic John Simon as "non compos mentis" or "nincompoop." Prior restraint largely ended, as the most of the remaining state censor boards folded—New York in 1965, and Kansas and Virginia in 1966. (The Maryland Board lasted until 1981. Its last action was to review *The Muppet Movie*. It passed.)

The new ratings system went into effect on November 1, 1968. It had four categories. "G" was for general audiences. "M" was for Mature (later changed to "PG" for Parental Guidance as producers thought that the "Mature" label might cost them viewers). "R" meant Restricted; persons under 16 not admitted except with a parent or guardian, raised to 17 in 1970. "X" meant no one 16 or under admitted, raised to 17 in 1970. The latter was lifted from the British Board of Film Censors classification system. The "X Certificate," created in 1950, meant no one under 16 admitted; it was raised to 18 in 1963. Americans knew it from the 1967 song "Lady Godiva" by Peter and Gordon: "He directs Certificate X."

In a 2018 report that commemorated 50 years of the ratings system, the MPAA calculated that about 57 percent of the more than 30,000 films submitted to the ratings process carried the "R" rating.

10

The Nude Scene
Children Under 17 Not Admitted

The Associated Press rated 1968 as the most event-filled year in its history. Away from the headlines—Vietnam, assassinations, urban and campus riots, a presidential election—the first crop of X-rated titles showed up on the movie pages. The first to receive the new "X" rating was Brian De Palma's low budget comedy *Greetings*, in which a filmmaker portrayed by the then-unknown Robert De Niro persuades a young actress to strip down to her panties. Some of the other early "X" movies were countercultural, such as Ralph Bakshi's *Fritz the Cat* and Andy Warhol's *Lonesome Cowboys*.

In 1969, the R-rated *Bob & Carol & Ted & Alice* flirted with wife-swapping ("First, we'll have an orgy and then we'll go see Tony Bennett"). The sight of Natalie Wood and Dyan Cannon stripped to bras and panties overcame male misgivings. The two couples end up nude in bed—under the covers—but stop short and stay with their spouses. Friendship and fidelity win out over transient sexual excitement. A low-budget, independent release, *All the Loving Couples*, written by tough-guy actor Leo Gordon, took things further for an "X" rating. Four couples have a Friday night swingers' party in a Southern California home. One couple is new to the scene; the others are experienced. One of the women is shown fully nude from the rear. There are some exposed breasts. Polaroid pictures of couples naked in bed are passed around. To fill the time leading up to the main event, there is political bickering between a Jewish Democrat and a right-wing former Marine. To get the guests in a horny mood, the host projects a Bonnie and Clyde–themed black-and-white, silent stag film from the 1930s (actually a re-creation/parody). When the bed-hopping finally came, the direction was so inept that it was not clear who ended up with whom.

Some "X" movies came from established directors. One of the most influential was Robert Aldrich's *The Killing of Sister George* (1968) from a witty play. The central relationship is a classic butch/femme lesbian couple, the heavyset Beryl Reid and the younger, conventionally pretty Susannah York. Scenes in a gay club where men danced with men and women with women were fairly daring for the time. What really earned the "X" was a scene in which an ostensibly straight woman (Coral Browne) approaches the Susannah York character, who exposes her breast to be touched and kissed. York is also (presumably) stimulated manually to climax as only her face, in the throes of orgasm, is shown. Another X-rated film, *Midnight Cowboy*, actually went on to win the Academy Award for Best Picture in 1969. United Artists actually requested the rating. *The Killing of Sister George* and *Midnight Cowboy* were re-rated to "R" in 1972. The movies had not changed; the context had. Profanity, nudity and sex scenes had become commonplace.

The name of D.H. Lawrence was associated in the public's mind with sex because of *Lady Chatterley's Lover*, but also carried literary prestige as he was by then taught in college classes. Made before the creation of the ratings system, *The Fox* (1967) was mildly scandalous for its scenes of two women (Anne Heywood and Sandy Dennis) kissing. The X-rated *Women in Love* (1969) went much further. Set in 1920, it had two sisters who represented "modern" women of the post–World War I era. Glenda Jackson, who would win the Academy Award, was nude from the waist up. Jennie Linden showed a glimpse of her breasts in a lyrical, slow-motion outdoor sex scene with Alan Bates. Director Ken Russell and scenarist Larry Kramer were both gay and took more interest in a nude wrestling match between Bates and Oliver Reed, illuminated by the light from a fireplace, in which Reed's penis could be seen in long shot. This was supposed to further male bonding. *Women in Love* had first-rate art direction, costume design and cinematography (although Ken Russell overused the zoom lens, already a visual cliché of the era) and was a critical and popular success.

Even R-rated movies included things previously unimaginable. Antonioni's *Zabriskie Point* (1970) reflected the director's fascination with the counterculture. The young leads (Daria Halprin and Mark Frechette) take their clothes off in Death Valley. As they make love, the hills are populated with naked or partially clad couples (from Joe Chaikin's Open Theatre) who writhe and cavort. There is one briefly glimpsed threesome. The scene ends with a clear indication of fellatio. Daria raises her head, previously buried in Mark's crotch, smiles and kisses him on the mouth.

A 1970 episode of the 20th Century–Fox–produced television series *Bracken's World* set in the thinly disguised Century Studios was entitled "The Nude Scene." An actress (Lois Nettleton) is asked by a director to be nude on camera. She is promised a closed set but the crew of six "is still more than the one person I'm used to being nude in front of." Her "civilian" husband, a doctor, leaves the decision up to her but is obviously uncomfortable. He mourns the old movies, "where they cut away just before the big moment," and adds, "Maybe it was the best way." The film within the show is called *A Time for Love*. The story tells of a woman who lost her husband and child in a car crash. When she remarries, she doesn't want another child. Her new husband wants a child. The impasse nearly produces a divorce. In the "nude scene," she gives herself to him to conceive a child. The final scene is described as "explicit," though it obviously isn't as how that term came to be used.

The nude scene provokes a confrontation between studio head John Bracken (Leslie Nielsen) and the woman charged with the development of new talent for the studio (Elizabeth Allen). She asks, "What do I tell them? Forget the talent honey, just take off your clothes." Unknown to her, one of her protégés (Karen Jensen) has already declared her willingness to do a nude scene "in a second." In a reference to the practice of using phony subsidiaries, Allen suggests that movie be released under the banner of "Peepshow Films." Bracken defends the integrity of the project; he backs the director's vision but also acknowledges nonartistic realities: "The motion picture industry is a disaster area. Every studio in town is in deep, deep trouble. Forty-six percent of the labor force is unemployed…. They no longer come to us; we have got to go to them."

Convinced by the director that the nude scene is the only valid way to do it, Nettleton drops her nightgown to reveal only her shoulders and the scene unfolds off camera. Everybody, including the contrite talent coach, agrees that the picture is an artistic triumph, although it seems more like a made-for-TV soap opera than anything movie audiences would have paid for in 1970.

To show that Bracken has not been won over by rank commercialism, the episode includes a sleazy director who is excited by the prospect of "a whole lot of skin going on" and praises Bracken for "getting behind sex in big way." He opines, "Images on the screen are what matters—movement, color. We're leaving story behind." When he runs a scene for Bracken in the screening room, some seductive dialogue is heard from the unseen actors. The director beams as Bracken winces. Bracken informs him that Century is not in the business of pornography but makes only quality pictures. "You're off the picture," he decrees.

Bracken's real-life counterpart, Fox production chief Richard Zanuck, was not so judicious. After the disappointing returns from *Hello, Dolly!* (1969) and the big-budget disasters of *Star!* (1968) and *Tora! Tora! Tora!* (1970), the cost-to-profit ratio of Russ Meyer's *Vixen!* (1968) must have seemed very tempting.

The foreword to Fox's first X-rated production informed us that it was not a sequel to *Valley of the Dolls*, the profitable 1967 film version of Jacqueline Susann's best seller. Coscripted by film critic Roger Ebert, Russ Meyer's *Beyond the Valley of the Dolls* (1970) was almost a parody of the earlier film.

Three Midwestern girls bring their rock band to Hollywood, where they are taken up by a music producer known as Z-Man (John Lazar), who presides like Caligula over sex-and-drug orgies. Three newcomers were the leads, but Meyer was able to populate the supporting cast with his favorites: lantern-jawed Charles Napier, Erica Gavin from *Vixen!* and Henry Rowland, who would become a fixture as "Martin Bormann." The voluptuous Edy Williams, whom Meyer married during production, played a "nudie" star and provided most of the near-nudity and simulated intercourse.

If *Beyond the Valley of the Dolls* was not Meyer's best film, it was his best-looking. The budget of $900,000, small by major studio standards, was the most generous that he ever had. Whatever their problems at the box office, the Zanucks, father and son, had rebuilt Fox's technical standards. Their art department was Hollywood's best and Meyer had a name cinematographer (Fred Koenekamp) to spell him on camera duty.

In the film's violent climax, Z-Man is revealed to be a woman, or transsexual, after the exposure of his/her breasts, and goes on a murderous rampage. He/she sticks a gun into the mouth of the Erica Gavin character and pulls the trigger. (A replica was made of Gavin's head.) Wielding a sword, he/she beheads a blonde beach-boy actor and chases his/her Nazi manservant into the ocean, where the surf turns red with blood.

Things turn upbeat for a pseudo-inspirational finale. The trio's original manager, a paraplegic who was paralyzed in a suicide attempt after being displaced by Z-Man, recovers the ability to walk. There is a triple wedding. It was trash but, as intended, grossed 10 times its cost.

Fox's other big X-rated production, *Myra Breckinridge* (1970), was not so successful. It was based on a Gore Vidal novel about a New York film critic, Myron Breckinridge, who adores American movies of the 1940s and undergoes a sex change operation to become his ostensible widow, Myra Breckenridge, in order to claim an estate in Los Angeles. The real-life critic and Old Hollywood buff Rex Reed played the pre-op Myron. The doctor was cadaverous horror-movie veteran John Carradine who warned, "If we cut it off, it won't grow back." Raquel Welch was Myra. British director Mike Sarne, whose only previous film was the swinging London, low-budget *Joanna*, imported by

Edy Williams was not the star of *Beyond the Valley of the Dolls* but provided most of the nudity and simulated intercourse. She married director Russ Meyer during production. 20th Century–Fox.

Fox in 1968, stated Welch's value to the film was that "she was a little bit of a joke." It was nevertheless a step up for Welch, who had previously been utilized mostly for her body. She looked stylish in a neo–1940s wardrobe by Theadora Van Runkle and gave a droll performance.

In a scene that must have left audiences in disbelief that they had really seen what they thought they saw, Myra straps on an unseen dildo and sodomizes a male chauvinist beach boy-type actor (Roger Herren.) This is followed by images of a dam breaking, a roller coaster and an atomic bomb. (Stock footage, mostly from the Fox library, was employed as ironic counterpoint throughout.) Myra also seduces the actor's girlfriend, a blonde ingénue (the young Farrah Fawcett) who unexpectedly finds that she can have sexual feelings for another woman but wishes Myra were a man. Mae West, in her first movie since 1943, made a comeback as a predatory agent with a taste for young muscle-men.

An R-rated Fox film of 1970, *MASH*, had a nude scene far less delicate than the fictional one Bracken approved. Major Frank Burns (Robert Duvall) and Major Margaret Houlihan (Sally Kellerman) have both affected rigid by-the-book personas. After their lovemaking is broadcast from a hidden microphone over the camp's P.A. system, Houlihan becomes known as "Hot Lips," after Burns's pet name for her. To settle a bet whether "Hot Lips" is a natural blonde, a shower tent is rigged with sandbags so that the walls lift up, leaving her fully naked in front of an audience and humiliated.

In the early 1970s, two books from writers influenced by the feminist movement looked at women's roles in American movies from the silent era to the then-present. Molly Haskell's *From Reverence to Rape* was the more intellectual, while Marjorie Ros-

As *Myra Breckinridge*, Raquel Welch shows her vaginoplasty scars to skeptical males, including John Huston (left), to prove that she is really the former Myron Breckinridge. 20th Century–Fox.

en's *Popcorn Venus* was the more comprehensive. Haskell, the wife of *auteuri*st film critic Andrew Sarris, concentrated on a few directors. Rosen dealt with the whole range of commercial filmmaking in the context of larger social trends, such as the increased presence of women in the workforce.

The most influential work of feminist criticism was a 1974 essay by Laura Mulvey in the British magazine *Screen* that claimed that in commercial cinema "the unconscious of patriarchal society has structured film form." Mulvey introduced the idea of "the male gaze." The camera is active and male; the object of its gaze is passive and female. Men take erotic pleasure in looking at women. From the perspective of 40 years on, Mulvey was surprised at the impact of her article. It had appeared in a small-circulation specialized magazine and was only intended to be exploratory. Instead, it took on a canonical significance, with the phrase "the male gaze" entering the general discourse.

Haskell argued that women had actually lost ground over the previous few decades as the career women played by the likes of Katharine Hepburn and Rosalind Russell had given way to sexual playthings. She deplored the extreme misogyny in the then-recent *A Clockwork Orange* and *Straw Dogs*.

A Clockwork Orange (1971) was Stanley Kubrick's first film since the landmark *2001: A Space Odyssey* (1968). Alex (Malcolm McDowell) and his "droogs" (friends) relish "ultraviolence." In the film's most notorious scene, the gang invades the home of an old writer. As Alex sings and dances to "Singin' in the Rain," he kicks the man repeatedly in rhythm to the music. The man is made to watch as his younger wife has her clothes cut away at knifepoint. Initially, her breasts are exposed but she is soon fully naked. With her mouth taped over, she is raped by the young men, who wear penis-shaped false noses.

Kubrick was already famous when Sam Peckinpah was a cult figure, best known for a modest Western *Ride the High Country* (1962) that brought together Joel McCrea and Randolph Scott at the end of their careers. *The Wild Bunch* (1969) made Peckinpah's name synonymous with violence. The equation of slow motion with death at the end of *Bonnie and Clyde* (1967) was taken to a new level. The four-minute climactic massacre was fashioned by Peckinpah and his editor, Roger Spottiswoode, from over a hundred pieces of film, many in slow motion, others only a few frames long. One image showed a Mexican prostitute bleeding from her breasts and belly after a shotgun blast.

The violence in *Straw Dogs* (1971) was on a smaller scale but even more disturbing. David Sumner (Dustin Hoffman), an American mathematician, comes with his wife Amy (Susan George) to a village on the Cornish coast of England that was formerly her home. The first glimpse of Susan George shows her in a white sweater with her nipples protruding as the townsfolk stare. Although David hoped to get away from the violence of America, depravity stirs just below the surface of the quaint village. A teenaged girl, possibly in an incestuous relationship with her brother, flirts with the town pariah, a suspected sex offender (an unbilled David Warner).

David claims to be apolitical but the home has the popular anti–Vietnam War poster "War Is Not Healthy for Children and Other Living Things" to suggest his pacifist leanings. He listens to classical music and spends most his time at a blackboard covered with equations. His wife feels neglected and resents his imputation of her intellectual inferiority.

In a misguided attempt to fit in with the local men, David hires Amy's ex-boyfriend Charlie and his pub mates to reroof the garage. They drag out the job and pad their time.

Susan George stirred up the locals in Sam Peckinpah's *Straw Dogs* as she walked through town with her nipples visible through a white sweater. Cinerama Releasing.

Even worse, they have access to the house. One steals a pair of Amy's panties from her drawer as a trophy. Amy complains to David that the workmen were "practically licking my body" as she got out of the car, although she hiked up her skirt and revealed her white lace panties, aware that they were looking. David criticizes her for going around without a bra. She takes off her top and lets the men see her exposed breasts.

Dustin Hoffman criticized the casting of Susan George on the grounds that an intellectual would not have married "a Lolita type." Peckinpah was adamant; he wanted a "cocktease." George's sensuality is crucial to the film.

David and Amy find their cat hanged in the bedroom closet. Amy wants David to confront the men, but he wants to "catch them off guard." She becomes even more disgusted with his inaction when she hears them laughing and writes "Did I catch you off guard?" on his precious blackboard.

To gain the confidence of the men, David agrees to go duck hunting. They send him off alone. The hunting trip is just a ruse to get him out of the way. Charlie comes to the house, where Amy is alone. She offers him a drink in an attempt to find out about the cat, but he interprets it as a sexual overture. She slaps him. He hits her, she slaps him again. He pulls her across the room. He kisses her on the mouth. She struggles. He raises his hand to strike her. He undoes her blouse, exposing her breasts, and kisses her on the mouth. He pulls off her panties. The scene takes a controversial turn. There is a shot of the fireplace with a flickering flame, a metaphor for Amy's rekindled passion for her old flame. Amy kisses Charlie appreciatively. He kisses her gently on the lips. He says, "Sorry." She says, "Hold me." Feminist critics pounced on the suggestion that

10. The Nude Scene

women enjoy rape. Peckinpah's defenders argued that this particular woman, in an encounter with someone with whom she was previously involved and after a fight with her husband in which she challenged his manliness, might well be up for rough sex. Hoffman downs a duck. He throws it back into the grass and wipes his hands on his sweater, squeamish over even a small act of violence.

We then see the muzzle of a shotgun. Charlie's buddy Norman appears. Even though Charlie shakes his head "No," Norman rapes Amy facedown. (Producer Daniel Melnick tried to persuade the British censors that this was rear-entry intercourse, but Peckinpah told Susan George that she would be "buggered," a term with which the 21-year-old actress was not familiar.) She screams, "No! No!" This second rape is confusingly presented partly because some footage was trimmed to avoid an "X" rating. Susan George refused to be photographed in what she called a "gang bang" and insisted that only her face be shown. There is a brief shot, just few frames long, in which Charlie, instead of defending Amy, helps Norman hold her down. (So much for the argument that she is attracted to the alpha male who can protect her.) The movie's original editor quit with a complaint that Peckinpah's footage wouldn't cut. The replacement editor, Roger Spottiswoode again, intercut the rape with shots of David as he leaves the scene of the failed hunt. The crosscutting serves to render the rape almost abstract.

At a church social, Amy has to see her attackers. The rape is replayed in her mind in flashbacks. The teenage girl leaves the social in the company of the David Warner character. Driving home, David and Amy hit the David Warner character, unaware that the villagers are after him for the strangulation of the young woman. David takes him into their home.

In defense of his home, the mild-mannered intellectual proves to be surprisingly adept at violence, in a sequence that goes on for 21 minutes and in which more windows are broken than the house seemingly has. Amy wants David to give the man up and even

Susan George suffers a rape at the hands of an ex-lover, or was it? Cinerama Releasing.

opens the door for the attackers. He kills all five intruders. David crowns Charlie with an antique trap, used to snare poachers, and snaps it shut, breaking his neck. Amy looks on David, not with admiration, but fear. He has violated his principles but can derive satisfaction from the fact that she can no longer call him a coward. His violent rampage comes not to avenge his wife's rape, of which he is unaware, but to assure due process for an accused molester and murderer who is, in fact, guilty.

Even before *Straw Dogs* and *A Clockwork Orange*, violence against women on-screen had escalated. The worst examples were not likely to be the basis of "think" pieces in the Sunday *New York Times*. After New York abolished its censor board in 1965, the "roughies" got rougher. In titles like *The Sin Syndicate* (1965) and *A Taste of Flesh* (1967), women were stripped naked, kicked and beaten.

An unlikely hit of 1971 was *Ginger*, produced by a New Jersey Oldsmobile dealer and written and directed by a neophyte (Don Schain) with one soft-core feature to his credit and with his then-wife (Cheri Caffaro) in her first important role as the title character. Atrociously acted, sluggishly paced, with audio, camerawork and production values that would have disgraced a syndicated television show, it was nevertheless savvy in its marketing. The television ads played up Caffaro's body and necessarily downplayed the violence. Caffaro herself appeared in theater lobbies to sign autographs.

Caffaro as Ginger was a female counterpart to James Bond and Mike Hammer, introduced driving a yellow Corvette. A private detective agency hires Ginger to infiltrate a gang that blackmails wealthy male residents of a Jersey Shore town, luring them to motels where they are filmed and recorded having sex with prostitutes. Her two predecessors have been killed. Ginger is offered $50,000 but, as it has been established that she is independently wealthy, she has other motives. "Her body is a weapon," declared the ads. While she did display some martial arts skills, she was not above using sex to extract information.

One of the gang awakens to find himself naked and tied to a bed as Ginger reveals that she drugged his drink. This may be the first non-pornographic American film in which male genitalia is clearly displayed. (The genitals belong to gay porn star Casey Donovan.) Ginger threatens the man with castration if he does not reveal the details of the blackmail operation and the name of the gang's drug supplier. She torments him by stripping naked. Caffaro was not all that beautiful and her breasts were small by the standards of exploitation films, but she was willing to appear totally nude. In the unlikely event that anyone thought she was a natural blonde, a dark thatch of pubic hair proved otherwise. She displays herself front and back to show the man what he will be missing. Even though he tells her everything she wants to know, the scene ends with the glint of a knife blade and a scream. In the next scene, we learn he was taken to the hospital with his balls cut off. In flashbacks, it is revealed that Ginger was gang-raped at 16 and was tricked into sex as an adult by a cad who promised marriage but reneged.

A subplot involves a white college girl who is hooked on drugs. When her black drug dealer demands a higher price than she can pay, she reluctantly gives him her body. Ginger shoots the drug dealer, whose death no one mourns, and gets away with it.

The leader of the gang surprises Ginger in her motel room and tells her that she will be raped and hooked on heroin. He punches her in the gut and crotch. He strips her naked except for her panties and ties her hands behind her back. He peels off her panties and turns her over to display her pubic hair yet again. He kisses her on the nipples for over a minute. She gives a little grunt to indicate forcible penetration. The camera lovingly chronicles the rape for another minute. He then injects her with a hypodermic needle. When he is finished, he goes out the door and we hear a burst of off-screen gunshots. This may be an homage to *The Big Sleep* (1946), in which gambler Eddie Mars was shot by his own men who mistook him for Humphrey Bogart. (More likely it was an economy move to avoid the expense of a fully staged scene.) At the film's end, Ginger is fully recovered. She has gotten over her hatred of men, with her most recent rape taken in stride as an occupational hazard. She climbs into her private plane and flies off, primed for new adventures. There were two sequels, with the profits of the first film invested in better production values.

The irony and relative complexity of *Straw Dogs* were missing from later rape-and-revenge movies. Rape scenes are problematic in movies. It is much easier, at least for male directors, to depict the arousal of the attacker than the psychological violation of the victim. Rape is commonly described as a crime of violence rather than sex but, in movies, the victim is almost always young and good-looking. Rape affords the audience, or more precisely the men in audience, the vicarious thrill of sex with an attractive woman.

Ida Lupino, the only female director at the time, avoided this in her 1950 film *Outrage*, made under the watchful eye of Joseph Breen. He decreed that the word "rape" not be used in favor of euphemisms such as "assault." For reasons best known to himself, he also required that the rapist not be a stranger but be known to the victim. The counterman at a lunch wagon near where the young female victim (Mala Powers) works has previously engaged in crude flirtation. His stalking of her and her mistake-prone efforts to evade him were depicted expertly in the style of Hitchcock or Fritz Lang, the suspense heightened with high and low angles and dramatic shadows. Lupino eschews the cliché music that disfigures so many movies of the era in favor of natural sound. Powers slips into the cab of a parked truck and blows the horn to signal for help. This only allows the rapist to locate her. The rape itself was not shown. Powers blacks out and the screen grows blurred. The camera pulls back with the actual rape scene obscured by the corner of a building. An old man looks out the window but does nothing. He closes the window as the girl's innocence is brought to an end. The police are of little help and she is unable to pick out the rapist in a lineup. Her family, coworkers and boyfriend regard her as soiled. She runs away and the rest of the film shows her attempts to regain trust in the world.

In the rape-revenge movies of the 1970s, the audience's basest instincts were gratified twice. For misogynists, there was the guilty pleasure of seeing a woman subjected to nonconsensual sex as payback for all the rejection men experience. They could then cheer self-righteously as the wrongdoer was punished in a humiliating fashion.

Hannie Caulder (1971) was typical. After her station agent husband is murdered for horses, Raquel Welch is raped by three of the meanest curs in any Western: Ernest Borgnine, Jack Elam and Strother Martin. They burn the house down with her in it. Dressed in a poncho and flat-brimmed hat that makes her the female equivalent of Clint Eastwood's Man with No Name, Welch has nothing underneath but the soiled panties she was wearing when she was raped. She engages a bounty hunter (Robert Culp) to teach her how to shoot. He gives her money to buy a pair of men's britches from a snickering general-store owner, who tells her to sit in water until they shrink. This leads to a shot in which she rises from a tub with wet, tight-fitting pants and a bare back. She tracks down and blows away Elam, Martin and Borgnine, in that order.

Burt Kennedy, director of several popular Westerns, including *The Rounders* (1965) with Glenn Ford and Henry Fonda and *The War Wagon* (1967) with John Wayne and Kirk Douglas, had been critical of the violence in "Spaghetti" Westerns. He ended up making one.

Kennedy was not the only respected director to get caught up in the cycle. Lamont Johnson had the misfortune to direct *Lipstick* (1976), in which model Margaux Hemingway, in her screen debut, played a model—not exactly a stretch. She is raped by a musician (Chris Sarandon), who is her younger sister's teacher. After a trial in which her reputation is dirtied up, he is acquitted. He then attempts to rape the sister, played by Margaux's real-life younger sister Mariel. At the movie's end, Margaux shoots him and his car full of holes with a rifle. While she made other movies, Margaux's career never lived up to the hype that surrounded her debut and she committed suicide at the age of 42. Mariel fared better with an Oscar-nominated performance as Woody Allen's preternaturally worldly 17-year-old lover in *Manhattan* (1979). As an Olympian pentathlon aspirant in *Personal Best* (1982), she got into an arm-wrestling contest with her mentor, the real-life track star Patrice Donnelly. It led to nude lovemaking. Although they did not look that much alike, she took on the role of Dorothy Stratten, the *Playboy* Playmate of the Year murdered by her jealous lover-manager just as her movie career was getting started, in Bob Fosse's *Star 80* (1983). (In *Personal Best*, Hemingway made a joke of her small breasts: "Carpenter's dream. Flat as a board." For *Star 80*, she got implants.)

As usual, it was the exploitation pictures with no-name casts where both rape and revenge were the most graphic. In *The Last House on the Left* (1972), Mari celebrates her 17th birthday with her friend, Phyllis. The girls go out and try to buy drugs from a gang who turn out to be crazed killers and kidnap them. Phyllis is stabbed to death, then disemboweled and her hand cut off. Mari is tortured with a knife, raped, forced to walk into a lake and then shot. With both girls dead, it falls to Mari's parents to gain revenge. Her mother promises oral sex to one of the culprits. She bites off his penis and spits it out. The father takes a chainsaw to the rest.

In *I Spit on Your Grave* (1978), Jennifer, a young writer, drives from New York to a house in the country to work. She stirs up the local men when she stops at a gas station. One of the males, a dimwitted grocery boy, reports back, falsely, that she showed him her tits when he went to her house.

Jennifer suns herself in a canoe dressed in a bikini. The canoe is intercepted by four men in a motorboat. Jennifer is gang-raped in the woods. She staggers home and finds them waiting for her. She is gang-raped again and her manuscript destroyed. The grocery boy is given a knife to kill Jennifer but only pretends that he did. Jennifer recovers and comes back a few weeks later, though not before stopping at a church to ask forgiveness for what she is about to do.

She offers the grocery boy sex but hangs him with a rope. The gas-station owner is seduced with the promise of sex in a bathtub. What starts as a hand job turns into castration after she grabs a knife. He protests that he has a wife and children, but she locks the door and leaves him to bleed to death. On the lake, she goes after the other two men with their own motorboat. One is felled with his own axe. The sole remaining rapist's genitals are chopped up by the propeller of an outboard motor. Before pulling the cord to start the motor, she says, "Suck on it, bitch," a repeat of what he said to her during the rape.

Leave it to Russ Meyer to make comedy out of rape. *Up!* (1976) introduced Raven

De La Croix, one of Meyer's most impressive discoveries with her sweet face, long black hair (a wig) and very large breasts. She is seen jogging alone on a country road in tight-fitting clothes that reveal her cleavage and midriff. Warned by a state trooper that she is asking for it, she soon gets it as a pickup truck blocks her path. A redneck type chases her down to a stream, punches her out and rapes her on the bank. After his orgasm, she comes to. Outraged to find him inside her, she kills him. The trooper comes on the scene and is aroused by her beautiful nude body. He proposes to write a report that will show an accidental death if she will have sex with him. They have so much sex that he is left exhausted.

Bernardo Bertolucci's *Last Tango in Paris* is remembered as much for Pauline Kael's review as for the film itself. Writing in *The New Yorker*, Kael compared the exhibition of *Last Tango* on the closing night of the 1972 Lincoln Center Film Festival to the premiere of Stravinsky's *Le Sacre du Printemps* in 1913 as a transformative moment in history of the medium.

As Kael herself acknowledged, there had been sex scenes before in exploitation pictures, but they offered little in the way of emotional complexity. Much of the impact of *Last Tango* came from Marlon Brando's return to form after a decade or more in which he mostly amused himself with accents, makeup and wigs in otherwise dull movies.

Brando's character, Paul, meets Jeanne (Maria Schneider) in an empty flat that they both seek to rent. In a relationship described by Paul as a "flying fuck at a rolling donut," they have sex in the empty room without knowing anything about each other, even first names. In the film's most famous scene, Brando lubricates her with butter and penetrates her anally. Just before her death in 2011, Maria Schneider claimed that Brando and Bertolucci sprang this on her without any warning and that her on-screen discomfort was real. This was confirmed by Bertolucci in 2013.

Kael's claims for *Last Tango* seemed overstated at the time and doubly so in retrospect. *Last Tango* did not usher in a new era of grown-up sexuality on film. If anything, the opportunity had already come and gone with John Schlesinger's *Sunday Bloody Sunday* (1971), written by Penelope Gilliatt, also a *New Yorker* film critic who alternated with Kael in six-month intervals. A divorced woman (Glenda Jackson) and a wealthy doctor (Peter Finch) share the same young man, each aware of the other's existence but willing to live with the situation rather than lose him.

Grown-up sexuality did figure into Nicholas Roeg's *Don't Look Now* (1973). Rather unusually, the sex scene took place between a married couple with children (Donald Sutherland and Julie Christie). Roeg added it at the last minute so that they wouldn't seem to be fighting all the time. Editor Graeme Clifford broke the scene up to evade censorship but to be consistent with the fractured style of the film with its flash-forwards and flashbacks. Roeg also cut a few frames to avoid an "X" rating.

The real legacy of *Last Tango* turned out to be the *Emmanuelle* series of soft-core productions. These played in theaters that would not normally show foreign or sex pictures.

The most influential film of the era was not *Last Tango* but *The Godfather* (1972), the biggest-grossing film since *The Sound of Music* in 1965. Unlike *The Sound of Music*, which was derided by sophisticated opinion—e.g., Pauline Kael who lost her job as movie critic for *McCall's* as a result—*The Godfather* was hailed by the likes of Stanley Kubrick and Orson Welles. Welles said it proved that a big film could also be a good film. *The Godfather* was the first of what might be dubbed "super-genre" movies, based

Julie Christie and Donald Sutherland in *Don't Look Now* portrayed one of the few torrid sex scenes that involved married people. Despite repeated denials from the principals, rumors persist that they "did it." Paramount.

on what the French call *renouvellement du cliché*. They recapitulated old formulas that had fallen into disuse but on a grander scale with bigger budgets, longer running times and better production values. *The Godfather* drew on *Scarface* from the early 1930s and the "syndicate" movies of the 1950s. Stephen Spielberg's *Jaws* (1975) and *Close Encounters of the Third Kind* (1977) recalled the monster and alien-invasion movies of the 1950s. (*Jaws* surpassed *The Godfather* to become the highest-grossing film to that time.)

Martin Scorsese and George Lucas, who had established themselves with the small-scale, semiautobiographical movies *Mean Streets* and *American Graffiti* in 1973, respectively, also turned to the super-genre movie. Scorsese's *New York, New York* (1977) was a pastiche of M-G-M musicals with M-G-M star Judy Garland's daughter, Liza Minnelli. Lucas's *Star Wars* (1977), inspired by the old *Flash Gordon* serials, was the most successful of all. An almost audible sigh of relief was heard from movie theaters. No longer would audiences have to puzzle over "The Meaning of It All" nor debate "what the director was trying to say." They could just sit back and let the dazzling special effects and booming music wash over them.

At the start of the 1970s, titles like *The Last Picture Show* and *The Last Movie* suggested exhaustion and possible extinction. By the end of the decade, Spielberg and Lucas were well on their way to become the cinema's first billionaires. Movies would not die out after all.

Roger Corman had never lost the faith. Corman had a falling out with American-International over their refusal to support one of his "serious" projects, *Von Richtofen and Brown* (1971), ultimately released by United Artists. He formed a new company, New World Pictures. New World distributed Bergman's *Cries & Whispers* and Fellini's *Am-

arcord, but was best known for exploitation pictures about nurses: *The Student Nurses* (1970), *Private Duty Nurses* (1971) and *Candy Stripe Nurses* (1974). Jonathan Kaplan, who directed *Night Call Nurses* (1972), recalled that Corman specified "frontal nudity from the waist up, total nudity from the rear, no pubic hair." (In 1975's *Capone*, directed by Corman himself, Susan Blakely's open crotch while in bed with Ben Gazzara exposed her vulva, a "first" for American movies.)

For all the nudity, Corman's nurses were not just eye candy. They had to struggle against exploitation within a male-dominated medical system. Director Stephanie Rothman brought a feminist edge to *The Student Nurses.* One of the nurses gets pregnant and has to jump through hoops to get an abortion. Another becomes a revolutionary.

Corman's 1970 *Bloody Mama* had former Fox contract player Diane Varsi nude. The death of Ma Barker (Shelley Winters) and her brood at the end ruled out a sequel, so he came up with *Big Bad Mama* (1974). Angie Dickinson was another 1930s bank-robbing matriarch but now with a pair of nubile teenage daughters. All three appeared nude.

Horror movies were an old Corman staple. Even during the strictest years of the Production Code, the sexual subtext of horror movies was hard to miss. In *Dracula's Daughter* (1936), Gloria Holden lures a young streetwalker (Nan Grey) with the promise of payment if she will model for a painting. Holden looks at her longingly as she takes off her blouse. In *The Velvet Vampire* (1971), directed by Corman protégé Stephanie Rothman, the lesbianism was overt. Instead of Eastern Europe or London, the story was set in the Mojave Desert, where a mysterious woman, Diane Le Fanu (Celeste Yarnall in a black wig), presides over an abandoned mining town. (Her name references Sheridan Le Fanu, the 19th-century writer of Gothic novels such as *Camilla*, from which Carl Theodor Dreyer's classic *Vampyr* (1932) was drawn.) In a further break with convention, she drives around in a dune buggy in broad daylight. The horror aspects are subordinate to the sexual, as Diane proceeds to seduce a young couple whom she invites to spend the night.

In the spoof *Abbott and Costello Meet Frankenstein* (1948), Lon Chaney, Jr., in a reprise of his Larry Talbot role from *The Wolf Man* (1941), explains to the duo how he turns into a wolf by the light of the moon. Costello replies that he does, too.

The Howling (1981), one of the commercial jobs that MacArthur genius grant recipient John Sayles wrote for money, updated the werewolf legend, with the sexual element brought to the fore. The film was full of inside jokes. Characters were named Erle C. Kenton, "Charlie" Lamont, "Dr." George Waggner, Sam Newfield, "Bill" (R. William) Neill—all "B" movie directors of the 1940s. Roger Corman made an appearance as a man who probed the coin return slot of a pay telephone. (Corman's penny-pinching ways had already been the subject of *Hollywood Boulevard*, a 1976 satire of low-budget filmmaking from Corman's own New World Pictures.) Actress Elizabeth Brooks had been promised that her full-frontal nudity in an outdoor ceremony would be obscured by smoke and fire. It wasn't and the stills were published by *Playboy* to her embarrassment.

Caged (1950) was the archetypal women's prison movie. The trailer indicted "prisons that need reform more than the prisoners." The warden (Agnes Moorehead) tries to start an education program but the state legislature won't fund it. A doctor complains, "When my dog had distemper, I took him to a cleaner clinic than this." There is only the slightest hint of lesbianism in the form of a brutal, corrupt matron (Hope Emerson) who may play favorites. One character laments that "after a while, you stop thinking about men."

The women's prison movies of the 1970s stand in the same relation to *Caged* as the rape-revenge movies to *Outrage*. *The Big Doll House*, *Women in Cages*, *The Big Bird Cage* and *Caged Heat*, all released by Corman's New World Pictures, made little pretense that they were about anything other than shower scenes, hair-pulling catfights and girl-on-girl action.

One of the more disturbing New World productions was *Jackson County Jail* (1976). It combined elements of the women's prison movies with the rape-revenge cycle. Advertising executive Yvette Mimieux leaves her unfaithful husband and drives alone from Los Angeles to a new job in New York. Somewhere in flyover country, she picks up a young man and his pregnant girlfriend, who hijack the car and make off with her purse. When she goes to a bar and asks to use the phone, the good ol' boy bartender attempts to rape her. When she fights back, she is the one arrested. The night deputy brings her a hot dog and taunts her by waving the meat in front of her face: "All you Hollywood girls like wieners." He rapes her but she is able to grab a stool and beat him to death.

The prisoner in the next cell, awaiting trial on a murder charge (Tommy Lee Jones in one of his first roles), reaches through the bars, takes the keys from the dead deputy and unlocks both cells. They escape in the deputy's pickup truck. The pickup crashes into a roadblock. Jones escapes on foot and runs into a small-town bicentennial parade. The police open fire with a wanton disregard for civilian life. Jones, mortally wounded, knocks over the standard-bearer and dies, spread-eagled over the American flag. The film expressed a derisive, disenchanted post–Vietnam, post–Watergate view of American life that, with a few exceptions—e.g., *Nashville* (1975), *Taxi Driver* (1976)—rarely surfaced in major company releases.

The success of *Star Wars* resulted in further plundering of old "B" movies and serials, most notably by George Lucas himself in *Raiders of the Lost Ark* (1981). There was a revival of the "white girl jungle goddess" subgenre with Tanya Roberts, costar of *The Beastmaster* (1982), as *Sheena* (1984), derived from a 1950s syndicated television series that starred Amazonian pin-up queen Irish McCalla.

For the new version of *Tarzan, the Ape Man* (1981), star Bo Derek was credited as producer. It was directed by her husband, former actor John Derek, who was by then better known for his *Playboy* photo spreads of Bo Derek and former wife Ursula Andress. A critic called it the first live-action calendar. The female lead was billed above the actor who played Tarzan, pretty much reduced to an afterthought. The original "Weissmuller yell" was reused, only to show how far M-G-M had fallen.

The title *Bolero* (1984) evoked the name of its star, Bo Derek, and the piece of music featured prominently in Blake Edwards's *10* (1979), the movie that brought her to prominence. John Derek, again as director, provided a mixture of intentional and unintentional comedy. Bo Derek plays a wealthy heiress who, upon graduation from an all-girl college, is eager for sexual experience. (At 27, Derek was a trifle mature to be a recent graduate.) The time period is the 1920s, which made for some outré costumes. Her first destination is the Casbah, where, en route to meet an Arabian sheik, she admires "As Time Goes By" (which hadn't been written yet), played on the piano in a nightclub. A seduction scene with silent-movie-style intertitles in homage to Rudolph Valentino's *The Sheik* (1921) comes to a disappointing end when the sheik falls asleep after drizzling Bo's body with honey.

In Spain, she becomes enamored with a bullfighter. She makes him a present of her virginity. She gives a little nod, screams on penetration and reflects, "I'm not a virgin anymore." A four-minute bout of intercourse, scored with swelling operatic music, comes to an end as she wraps her legs around her partner. Her face beams in ecstasy. Unfortunately, he comes to be gored in the genitals. She takes over for him in the bullring and makes it her project to restore his manhood. "That thing is going to work," she promises. She arouses him by riding a horse bareback while fully naked. After a second four-minute epic encounter, filmed from multiple angles, with a neon sign that reads "extasy [sic]," they are married.

With no one to stop him, John Derek also displayed 14-year-old Olivia d'Abo. Although she was seen in long shot and her body was partly covered by soap bubbles, she was fully nude in a bath scene. "I am woman," she said to Bo Derek, as she looked down in admiration of her young breasts. Such scenes seemed certain to earn an "X" rating. John Derek refused to cut a frame. M-G-M would not release an X-rated movie. It went out Unrated with a Content Advisory ("Due to the Adult Nature of This Film No One Under 17 Will Be Admitted") under the banner of its producer, Cannon Films, whose distribution agreement with M-G-M had been terminated. Even the young males who were the target audience walked out in disgust or just laughed at it. Bo Derek won the "Razzie" award as Worst Actress of the Year. She didn't work again for five years and thereafter mostly in television.

By the mid–1970s, the Sexual Revolution had triumphed completely, at least in its main objective: the right of unmarried heterosexual adults to engage in consensual relations. That left two areas unresolved. One was the status of same-sex sex, still regarded by many as immoral or with disgust. The other was teenage sex. How young was too young?

"The Bet Is On: Whoever Loses Their Virginity First—Wins!" That was the tagline on the poster for *Little Darlings* (1980). The wealthy Tatum O'Neal and streetwise, blue-collar Kristy McNichol are bunkmates at an upstate summer camp for New York City girls. Although they are only 15, the other girls shame them because they are still virgins. They are goaded into a bet, in which they compete to lose it. The other girls pool their money and form two teams to wager on the contenders. McNichol picks out a boy (Matt Dillon) from a camp across the lake. O'Neal has a crush on a teacher (Armand Assante) from her own camp. O'Neal wins the bet—by lying. The teacher actually discouraged her, but she recounts a night of passion to the eager girls. McNichol actually did have sex, with Dillon, who didn't know she was a virgin. She doesn't tell anybody. She was the real "winner," although she didn't feel like one. She gave it up for nothing. It turns out that the other girls lied; they were still virgins, too.

Porky's (1982), set in a Florida high school in 1955, was the raunchiest comedy released to that time by a major company. In the first scene, Pee Wee measures his penis, as he does every morning, with disappointing results. Pee Wee's desire to get laid is the spine of the film. Pee Wee had a near miss with the trampy Wendy (Kaki Hunter) but blew it by wearing a condom to their date. (Otherwise, there wouldn't be a movie.) Pee Wee and his friends' quest for sex leads them to the cabin of a prostitute, Cherry Forever (Susan Clark, former contract star at Universal). Her "husband," a huge black man, bursts in on the boys and sends them running into the night naked. (This is actually a prank set up by three classmates.)

Further frustration ensues when the boys go to a honky-tonk on the other side of the county line. "Get It at Porky's" advertises a neon sign with cartoon figures of Porky Pig and his girlfriend, Petunia; the male pig moves closer to the female as she exposes

Above and left: Bo Derek eagerly gave her virginity to bullfighter Andrea Occhipinti in *Bolero*. When he was gored in the genitals, she nursed him back to sexual health. The sight of her nude body as she rode bareback was intended to arouse him. Cannon Films.

her backside. The gross owner, Porky (Chuck Mitchell), takes the boys' money but releases a trapdoor that dumps them into the swamp.

In *Porky's*, it's not just kids who are horny. A young male gym teacher pursues a young female gym teacher named Miss Honeywell (Kim Cattrall, the future Samantha of *Sex and the City*). An older coach mysteriously refers to the young woman as "Lassie." He advises his younger colleague to take

10. The Nude Scene 165

The poster for *Little Darlings* left little doubt as to what the movie was about. Kristy McNichol won but didn't feel like a winner. Paramount.

her up to the boys' locker room where everything will become clear. As she climbs the stairs, there is an upskirt shot of her panties. In the locker room, she is so turned on by the smell of sweaty clothes that she strips nude from the waist down and initiates sex. During intercourse, she howls like a dog. The howls are heard throughout the buys' and girls' gyms and attract the attention of an older female coach who has warned Honeywell that she can be fired for "moral turpitude." The male coach silences her by stuffing a sock into her mouth.

In the film's most famous scene, the boys discover that three openings fortuitously exist in the wall of the girls' shower. They see half a dozen nude, lithe bodies, with a glimpse of pubic hair. Pee Wee's view is blocked by a fat girl who has not previ-

The girls of *Porky's* don't really seem to mind that the boys spied on them in the shower. 20th Century–Fox.

ously figured into the movie and will not be seen again. Pee Wee tells her to get out of the way. When the other girls realize that they are being watched, they run off but wrap themselves in towels and come back toward the boys. One of the boys sticks his tongue through the peephole and a girl puts soap from a dish on it. He retaliates by putting his penis through the peephole and speaks in a falsetto voice in the character of Polly the Penis. The girls feign shock but are actually amused. This attracts the girls' gym coach Miss Balbricker (ballbreaker?), who grabs his penis until he can break free.

In a scene in the principal's office, Miss Balbricker proposes they examine the boys for an identifying telltale mole. As the males in the office try to stifle their laughter, the camera slowly zooms into the Norman Rockwell portrait of a smiling President Eisenhower, who is made to seem more approving than the real Eisenhower probably would have been.

In the final scene, as the credits roll, Pee Wee has sex with Wendy in an otherwise empty school bus with an audience of the school band, plus teachers and police.

The picture of Eisenhower, the cars and the songs of Patti Page and Teresa Brewer belong to the 1950s, but there is no re-creation of the cultural ethos of the time as Peter Bogdanovich did in *The Last Picture Show* (1971) or as Mike Leigh did in *Vera Drake* (2004). Usually movies set in the 1950s—*Far from Heaven, Carol, Mona Lisa Smile, Indignation*, et al.—contrast the era's supposed repression with the permissive present. *Porky's* imbues the period with a radical libertinism that didn't really exist. Would teachers have had sex on the premises during school hours? Would students really have had sex in public?

Jennifer Jason Leigh (left) practices her oral sex skills on a carrot under the tutelage of Phoebe Cates in the cafeteria in *Fast Times at Ridgemont High*. Universal.

The other big teen sex comedy of 1982, *Fast Times at Ridgemont High*, was not only far superior to *Porky's* but one of the best films of its era. One of the things that distinguishes this film from others of the time is that it shows high school students working at jobs. Linda (Phoebe Cates) and Stacy (Jennifer Jason Leigh) work at Perry's Pizza in the Ridgemont Mall. Linda's brother (Judge Reinhold) works in a succession of fast-food places, whose kitschy hats and uniforms are a running gag. Mark "Rat" Ratner (Brian Backer) is the assistant manager of the movie theater on the other side of the mall from Perry's Pizza. Linda is in a physical relationship with an airline employee and disdains high school boys. Linda, who claims to have had sex at 13, acts as a mentor to the still virginal but curious Stacy, teaching her how to give a blow job by sucking a carrot in the high school cafeteria to the admiration of the boys.

When Stacy expresses attraction to a male customer (she thinks he looks like Richard Gere and has a nice butt), Linda encourages her to laugh at his pickup lines no matter how lame. Stacy goes on a date with the 25-year-old stereo salesman that isn't really a date. They end up at a deserted field house, where kissing turns to intercourse. William Paul, whose book *Laughing Screaming* offers a detailed exegesis of this brief scene, concludes, "In no film I have seen a sexual scene not specifically a rape which presented such an overwhelming sense of violation." The scene was actually shortened to avoid an "X" rating from the MPAA but also because it made preview audiences uncomfortable. The sex was awkward and took place in a dugout illuminated by a single light bulb with graffiti on the cinder-block walls. The setting was the antithesis of the idyllic island of *The Blue Lagoon*, a popular make-out movie of 1980.

Linda is eager to know the details. Stacy says it was over quickly and that it hurt. Linda promises that it will get better. Stacy is sent roses with a note, "Memories of You," that she hides from her parents. The salesman loses interest and doesn't call again. Linda tells her not to worry; he'll just end up fat and bald.

"Rat," the movie-theater employee, also has a sexual mentor, Mike, who scalps rock-concert tickets and fancies himself a great ladies' man. Under Mike's tutelage, he takes Stacy to a restaurant but finds that he has forgotten his wallet. After they go home, Stacy takes him into her bedroom, but he remembers that he has to take the car back and the opportunity passes.

The film's most notorious scene begins with Linda and Stacy by the pool at Stacy's house. Linda reads a relationship quiz in a magazine and boasts that she and her boyfriend climax simultaneously. "Rat" and Mike invite themselves over and hang out by the pool. The Judge Reinhold character arrives home and goes to the bathroom. Through the window, he ogles Linda and, in his fantasy, Phoebe Cates emerges from the pool in slow motion, takes off her top and comes toward him. The real Linda comes to the bathroom to look for a Q-tip to unclog her ears. She bursts in on him as he masturbates and reacts in horror and disgust.

Fast Times was the first feature directed by Amy Heckerling, a youngish (27) product of the NYU film program and one of very few women then to direct a major studio (Universal) release. She did not deny the male audience the skin they hoped to see but brought a degree of humanity to the young actresses. The friendship of the Phoebe Cates and Jennifer Jason Leigh characters (which continued in their real lives) proved to be more durable and valuable than their transitory male relationships.

The pool figures in again as Stacy tells Mike that he is the one she really likes. He comes to her house and she suggests they go swimming. They get undressed in the changing room. Stacy is nude but for socks and a crucifix. The music is the same Jackson Browne song, "Somebody's Baby," that accompanied her first sexual experience. Mike ejaculates immediately and leaves in embarrassment. Stacy's beautiful body glows in a long shot but her face registers bewilderment and melancholy.

Stacy asks Linda how long her boyfriend lasts. Linda says 20 or 30 minutes. Stacy reminds her that she once claimed an hour and has perhaps come to suspect that Linda's stories are made up. Stacy tells a lie of her own; she claims that Mike lasted 10 to 20 minutes, to which Linda replies, "Pretty good for a high school boy."

Stacy finds out that she is pregnant. Mike promises to pay for half the cost of an abortion but doesn't come through. Instead, she is driven to her appointment by her brother. Linda gets back at Mike by vandalizing his car. Linda herself breaks up with, or is dumped by, her older lover when he refuses to attend her graduation. Stacy tells Linda that she doesn't want sex but a relationship and romance. Linda responds, "You want romance? In Ridgemont? We can't even get cable TV here." At the film's end, Stacy goes over to the movie theater and gives "Rat" her picture and a kiss. An *American Graffiti*–like afterword that updates the characters' fates tells us that "Rat" and Stacy are dating but haven't gone "all the way."

The Last American Virgin (1982) might be considered a clone of *Fast Times* were it not a remake by the original director (Boaz Davidson) of an Israeli film, *Lemon Popsicle*, made in 1978. *Lemon Popsicle* was set in the 1950s and the soundtrack was stuffed with American pop music of the time. It appears not to have been released theatrically in the U.S., even though the producers paid for music rights. In Israel and Europe, it was so popular that it spawned seven sequels and allowed the producing team of Menahem Golan and Yoram Globus to buy The Cannon Group and become players in the American film industry. It may well be the true ancestor of the teen sex comedies of the 1980s. It had a scene in which one of the boys makes a hole in the wall of the locker room to look at the girls as they undress. In the American remake, the girls are nude in the shower. Critics assumed this was stolen from *Porky's*, although the Israeli film got there first. There was a locker-room penis-measuring contest (with a winning entry of 9½ inches), also derived from the Israeli original.

Gary, the main character, drives a pizza delivery truck. When he makes a delivery to the apartment of a sexy stripper, he summons two friends, one handsome and the other obese. She takes the better-looking of the boys into the bedroom and the others watch through the keyhole as they have sex. She then takes on the overweight boy. Before Gary can take his turn, the woman's husband comes home and the fat kid has to run out in his underwear.

Another episode involved a visit to a streetwalker, who comments on Gary's poor performance. He throws up afterward. The boys come down with a case of crabs.

The film takes a turn away from farce as Gary pursues a new girl, Karen, with whom he is infatuated. He deflates the tire of her moped so that he can offer her a ride to school in the pizza truck. In a parallel to the relationships in *Fast Times*, Karen is attracted to the studly Rick. Gary drives to a teen hangout and sees Karen's moped. He asks where Karen is and is told that Rick has taken her to the football field to "bust her cherry." He prowls to the stadium in darkness. It's unclear where he actually is but the audience can see Karen as she takes off her top and lies down. When she gets pregnant, Gary pawns his stereo and pays for an abortion. At the end, she goes back to Rick and Gary is crushed.

Despite the presence of Phoebe Cates and Ray Walston from the earlier film, *Private School* (1983), set in an exclusive girl's school, was not a worthy follow-up to *Fast Times at Ridgemont High*. Nudity was supplied by beautiful newcomer Betsy Russell, whose shirt was torn off by a rival during an equestrian event. That prompted the line, "That is the best example of bareback riding I've ever seen." Sylvia Kristel, star of the soft-porn *Emmanuelle* series, had been brought to Hollywood by Universal for *The Concorde.... Airport '79* and *Private Lessons* (1981), a popular comedy in which she played a French housekeeper who is the object of the fantasies of her employer's 15-year-old son. She had a cameo in *Private School* as "the sex teacher." She fielded such questions as whether the length or girth of a penis mattered more. A boy's academy down the road provided the usual horny males. They stand three high at the window in order to take Polaroid pictures of the girls as they come out of the shower. (This was lifted from *Animal House*, where John Belushi as Bluto climbed a ladder to peer into sorority bedrooms.) Betsy Russell is aware of being watched and, like Kaki Hunter in *Porky's*, doesn't seem to mind. Later, the boys dress up as girls to gain entry to the school.

A more sophisticated form of voyeurism operated in *Revenge of the Nerds* (1984). With a panty raid to the accompaniment of the *Mission Impossible* theme as diversion, the nerds use their computer and high school A.V. club skills to plant a remote-controlled camera in a sorority house. Although they are initially excited by naked breasts, what they really want to see is "bush." They pan the camera down as a girl takes off her panties. "We've got bush!"

The horny nerds at least wanted real women. In John Hughes's *Weird Science* (1985), two teen boys conjure up a cybersex doll (Kelly LeBrock). To get more computing power, they hack into the Defense Department system. Perhaps they got the idea from *WarGames* (1983). In *Mannequin* (1987), Andrew McCarthy falls in love, as in *One Touch of Venus*, with a plastic doll (Kim Cattrall from *Porky's*). The mannequin is somehow inhabited by the spirit of an ancient Egyptian princess who was mummified alive.

Coincident with the teen sex comedies was the "slasher" cycle circa 1978–84. In John Carpenter's *Halloween* (1978), not only was Janet Leigh's daughter Jamie Lee Curtis cast in the lead, but the Donald Pleasance character was given the same name, "Sam Loomis," as John Gavin in *Psycho*. Curtis would also star in *Prom Night* and *Terror Train*, both in 1980. In the "slasher" movies, promiscuous teenaged girls would be killed off. The surviving "final girl" was virginal and somewhat androgynous. As Carol Clover has pointed out, the "gender wall" in these movies is more of a permeable membrane, with male and female spectators able to identify with both the killer and the victims. Although the slashers were usually male, the big reveal in *Friday the 13th* (1980) was that the killer was the mother of "Jason" (Betsy Palmer), who sought revenge for her son's drowning at a summer camp years before.

The proliferation of teen sex comedy and slasher movies owed as much to supply as demand. In a time of rising production costs, they could be made cheaply. Instead of stars with exorbitant demands for salary and "perks," the casts were young hopefuls eager for a break. There were not a lot of elaborate special effects or action sequences. The settings—schools, summer camps, suburban homes—were available nearby. While some of these films were distributed by the "majors," small companies could still get into the game, e.g., *My Tutor* (1982) released by Crown International.

The "nudie cuties," the "roughies" and pornos had played in theaters that enforced an "adults only" policy. R-rated teen sex and horror films were welcome in suburban multiplexes where the staff, usually teenagers themselves, did not enforce the restrictions and it was easy to slip from one auditorium to another.

On a higher level budgetarily and in artistic aspiration were the erotic melodramas aimed at adults. *Body Heat* (1981) owed a lot to *Double Indemnity* (1944). Without the Production Code, it was free to establish the physical relationship between William Hurt and Kathleen Turner, who plot to murder Turner's rich husband (Richard Crenna). The other difference was that punishment was no longer mandatory. Turner got to enjoy the money.

In the 1981 remake of *The Postman Always Rings Twice*, audiences could finally see what the Code forced to be left out in 1946. Jack Nicholson and Jessica Lange had sex on a prep table with much flour tossed into the air. The overall result was less steamy than sleazy. The movie restored the Depression-era setting of James M. Cain's 1934 novel. Nicholson was older (41) than John Garfield (33) in the glossy original. Instead of the improbably lovable (and de-etnicized) Cecil Kellaway, the Greek diner owner was coarse and brutal but closer in age to his rival.

This represented a change. In the *films noirs* of the 1940s and early 1950s, the husband was older than the wife, sometimes old enough to be her father, e.g., Tom Powers in *Double Indemnity*, George Macready in *Gilda* (1946) and Claude Rains in *Where Danger Lives* (1950). This gave the triangle an Oedipal dimension. Everett Sloane in the *The Lady from Shanghai* (1948) was put on crutches to suggest impotence. The young interloper's superior virility made up for his lack of wealth and status.

Dennis Hopper, who had only directed a couple of times since his troubled *The Last Movie* in 1971, returned with the neo-*noir The Hot Spot* in 1990. The title describes the sunbaked Texas town where Don Johnson gets a job as a salesman in a used car dealership and his involvement with two desirable women. Although set in the present, it had a 1950s vibe, with Virginia Madsen as the voracious wife of the dealership's owner dressed, coiffed and made up to resemble Marilyn Monroe. She drives a pink 1959 Cadillac convertible. Johnson drives a Studebaker Hawk. The dealership's accountant is the young Jennifer Connelly. She and Johnson go swimming on what is her 19th birthday. This occasions some admiring shots of her in a bathing suit. In a flashback, she and another actress will be topless as she recounts how a blackmailer took pictures of them nude. (The other actress plays her sister, who commits suicide after exposure as a lesbian.) Madsen takes advantage of her husband's heart condition; she binds and gags him in what he thinks is a sex game. As she recounts sex with Johnson, she announces, "I'm fucking you to death" and does. The not-so-bereaved widow gets away with it. Madsen and Johnson wind up together, which may be punishment enough.

Of the *femmes fatales* in modern *noir*, none was more *fatale* than Linda Fiorentino in John Dahl's *The Last Seduction* (1994). After she makes off with the $750,000 that her husband scores in a drug deal, he hires a private detective who trails her to upstate New York. She retaliates by persuading her new lover to murder her husband. When he chickens out, Fiorentino kills her husband herself by spraying Mace down his throat and frames her lover. At the film's end, she gets into a stretch limousine.

Fatal Attraction (1987) was based on a British television drama. In the original, the mistress places a telephone call to the married man's wife and the story ends. The American version, directed by Adrian Lyne, pumped it full of melodrama. After a one-night stand with the married Dan (Michael Douglas), Manhattan book editor Alex (Glenn

Close) claims to be pregnant. She stalks him obsessively and murders his family's pet rabbit, putting it on the stove to boil. In the original ending, which Lyne has posted to the internet, Douglas is arrested for the murder of Alex. Alex, while in the Douglas home, left a cassette tape in his desk on which she threatens to kill herself. This is found by Douglas's wife Beth (Anne Archer), who can use it to exonerate him. The final shot is of Close slashing her own throat with a kitchen knife in a flashback.

Preview audiences reacted poorly. "They wanted us to terminate the bitch with extreme prejudice," recalled studio executive Ned Tanen.[1] A new ending was filmed (over the objection of Close) in which Alex comes to the home with the intent to kill Beth. Dan drowns her in a bathtub, but she pops up one more time like the monster in a cheap horror film and is shot by Beth. Audiences liked this better and the film was the third top-grossing movie of the year. Feminists complained that the Close character vilified career women. Producer Sherry Lansing, one of the few high-ranking female executives in Hollywood, argued that the character was not all career women but just *this* woman.

Philip Kaufman's *The Unbearable Lightness of Being* (1988) was sophisticated entertainment with highbrow credentials. It was based on a novel by Milan Kundera and set during the "Prague Spring" of 1968, just prior to the Soviet invasion of Czechoslovakia. A surgeon (Daniel Day-Lewis) cheats on his wife (French actress Juliette Binoche), a photographer, with an artist, the beautiful dark-haired Swedish actress Lena Olin. Olin is stunning in black lace bra and panties. The line "Take off your clothes" occurs early and often. No one refuses. Olin and Juliette Binoche photograph each other nude.

The film narrowly missed an "X" rating from the MPAA only because Richard Hef-

Lena Olin was a free-spirited artist who diverted doctor Daniel Day-Lewis from his wife (Juliette Binoche) in *The Unbearable Lightness of Being*. **Political repression in 1968 Communist Czechoslovakia obviously did not equate to sexual repression. The film narrowly escaped an "X" rating. Universal.**

fner, chair of the Code and Ratings Administration, missed the vote. He later stated that he would have supported an "X."

Kaufman's next movie, *Henry & June* (1990), was the first film to earn the NC-17 rating (children under 17 not admitted). In 1931 Paris, the writer Henry Miller, his wife June and the writer Anaïs Nin, also married, become involved in a *menage a trois*. Universal, as a matter of policy, did not release X-rated movies and Kaufman refused to cut a frame, so the new rating was born. The "X" rating had become anathema to theater owners because of its association with pornography.[2] Other than soft-core spoofs such as *Flesh Gordon* (1974) that aimed at a broader audience, porno movies were not rated. (It costs money to submit a film to the ratings process. The "Triple X" rating for hardcore porn was self-applied and not an actual MPAA rating.)

Anaïs Nin became the subject of her own movie, *Delta of Venus*, in 1995. As *Delta of Venus* was a collection of erotic stories that Nin wrote for money and not very good screen material, the script invented a narrative in which an American female writer in 1940 Paris (Audie England) supports herself by modeling in the nude. She also accepts an offer to write pornographic fiction for a wealthy connoisseur as Nin did in reality. She has an on-again, off-again physical relationship with another American expatriate (Costas Mandylor), whom she leaves in anticipation of the Nazi invasion of France. The film was released in "R" and "NC-17" versions, both of which died at the box office. It was directed by soft-core *auteur* Zalman King, producer of cable television's *Red Shoe Diaries* and the feature film *9 ½ Weeks* (1986).

Long before *Fifty Shades of Grey*, released on Valentine's Day in 2015, brought BDSM (bondage and discipline/sadomasochism) into the mainstream, *9 ½ Weeks* gave audiences a taste of it in 1986. An art gallery employee (Kim Basinger) becomes involved in a kinky relationship with a Wall Street arbitrageur (Mickey Rourke). Director Adrian Lyne, previously best-known for *Flashdance* (1983), treated the S&M scenes like music videos or perfume commercials. In the best-known scene, Basinger performs a striptease in silhouette behind a venetian blind with handcuffs and a whip for props. At its end, Rourke goes behind the screen to see Basinger nude from the rear. In another scene, he presses an ice cube to her nipple and guides it down her abdomen.

A few years later, Zalman King cast Mickey Rourke in *Wild Orchid* (1989) opposite Jacqueline Bissett. It was not Bissett who was nude in the film but newcomer Carré Otis. As was increasingly the case, there was an R-rated version for theaters and an unrated version for home video.

A more realistic version of BDSM, and one actually praised by the BDSM community, was *Secretary* (2002). Typist Maggie Gyllenhaal has a sadomasochistic relationship with her lawyer boss (James Spader) that does not include intercourse. She deliberately makes mistakes for which she can be punished. She masturbates to orgasm. He has her bend over a desk. She is told to pull down her panties and expose her buttocks to him. He masturbates, leaving the back of her blouse covered in semen. (This was not Spader's first introduction to weirdness. In David Cronenberg's *Crash* (1996), about people who get a fetishist turn-on from auto accidents, he had a protracted sex scene with the nude Deborah Kara Unger.)

One of the most eagerly awaited movies of 1999 was Stanley Kubrick's *Eyes Wide Shut*. Barely completed by the time of his death, the production consumed a year in the lives of Tom Cruise and Nicole Kidman, then husband and wife.

Greenwich Village was meticulously and expensively re-created at Pinewood Studios, down to graffiti-covered mailboxes. Signs for the nonexistent "Benton" and "Wren" streets perched the setting at the intersection of reality and dream.

If the centerpiece Black Mass/masquerade/orgy seemed to belong to another era and another continent, it was for a good reason. *Eyes Wide Shut* was a surprisingly faithful adaptation of Arthur Schnitzler's 1926 *Traumnovelle* set in 1900 Vienna. (It had already been adapted by West German television in 1969 in a straightforward version that kept the original time and place.) Although Tom Cruise is in almost every scene, Nicole Kidman is the first thing seen on-screen (nude as she sheds her dress) and has the literal last word, which is "Fuck!" The full exchange is:

> ALICE: "I do love you and there is something very important we need to do as soon as possible."
> BILL: "What's that?"
> ALICE: "Fuck!"

Most audiences were left disappointed. The glamorous principals had only a few scenes together and most of the sex in the two-hour and 45-minute film consisted of anonymous couplings in long shot and semidarkness. These were further obscured by computer-generated silhouettes to avoid the dreaded NC-17 rating. Viewers lured by the prospect of a sexy movie felt that they were victims of an elaborate put-on by Kubrick from beyond the grave.

When producer-director Donna Deitch made *Desert Hearts* in 1985, she had trouble casting it. Most actresses were not willing to enact a lesbian sex scene, at least in the context of a realistic drama and not the wink-wink nudity of exploitation pictures, for fear of typecasting.

Then, *Basic Instinct* (1992) lifted Sharon Stone out of a career rut. The bisexuality of her character, the possible murderess Catherine Trammel, only made her more glamorous. For actresses, "lesbian" scenes enhanced their allure. In the stylish, violent *Bound* (1996), Jennifer Tilly, the girlfriend of a Mafioso, and lesbian ex-convict Gina Gershon become lovers and hatch a plot to steal from the mob. In a nude lovemaking scene on a mattress, Tilly puts her hand to Gershon's vulva and brings her to climax. In *Wild Things* (1998), Denise Richards and Neve Campbell have a nude sex scene in a swimming pool and a threesome with Matt Dillon. A scene in *Black Swan* (2010) in which Mila Kunis performs cunnilingus on Natalie Portman did not hurt the careers of either. (Such scenes were so widespread that one entrepreneur published a poster with two very obese women and the text: "LESBIANS. It Ain't Like in the Movies.")

A more realistic lesbian couple figured in Lisa Cholodenko's *The Kids Are All Right* (2010). Fiftyish college professor Annette Bening and would-be landscaper Julianne Moore still have hot sex. Moore performs cunnilingus on Bening under a blanket. When their two children contact the sperm donor who is their biological father (Mark Ruffalo), Moore, the younger and more conventionally feminine of the couple, has sex with him.

Gender fluidity apparently only applies to women. Male stars are generally unwilling to jeopardize their masculine image. Richard Burton and Rex Harrison ("Sexy Rexy") were so securely established as heterosexual that they could camp it up as aging queens in *Staircase* (1969). For Harry Hamlin and Michael Ontkean, young in their careers, *Making Love* (1982), in which they kissed and went to bed, was more of a risk. A more recent exception was Michael Fassbender in *Shame* (2011), who had sex with both men and women. Tom Hanks in *Philadelphia* (1993) and Sean Penn in *Milk* (2008) won Oscars as gay characters, but their sex lives were subordinated to their legal and political battles.

Female impersonation had long been a comic standby, e.g., Jack Benny in *Charley's Aunt* (1941), Ray Bolger in the musical version *Where's Charley?* (1952), Jack Lemmon and Tony Curtis in *Some Like It Hot* (1959), Dustin Hoffman in *Tootsie* (1982) and Robin Williams as *Mrs. Doubtfire* (1993). The reverse was not so funny. *Boys Don't Cry* (1999) told the true story of Teena Brandon, who adopted a male persona as Brandon Teena. Forced by suspicious males to expose her genitalia, Teena was raped and subsequently murdered. Hilary Swank won the Best Actress Oscar.

Fellatio was radical (on-screen) in 1969 when Milton Moses Ginsberg made the independent film *Coming Apart*. A nude Sally Kirkland gives oral sex to therapist Rip Torn, unaware she is being photographed by his hidden camera. Only the back of her bobbing head and shoulders are shown. In *Shampoo* (1975), it was still startling when Julie Christie says about Warren Beatty, seated next to her at a dinner party, "I'd like to suck his cock." By 1987, fellatio was so routine that it could be tossed off in a Disney film, albeit from their Touchstone subsidiary. In *Outrageous Fortune* (1987), Bette Midler grabs Peter Coyote, says "I know what I need" and takes him to a door. In a trick on the audience, the next shot shows two sets of legs entwined on the floor in sex. This dissolves to the back of a chair in which a seated man gasps, "Oh, God!" Shelly Long's head pops into view. Coyote has been two-timing Midler. Long, smiling, kisses him on the mouth.

Artist Miranda July found a way to make fellatio controversial again in her first feature, *Me and You and Everyone We Know* (2005). A 14-year-old boy is used as a guinea pig by two teenage girls who want to perfect their oral skills. They blindfold him and take turns. When they ask him who did it better, he replies that he is unable to tell any difference.

In *Eighth Grade* (2018), 13-year-old Kayla (Elsie Fisher) is asked by a male classmate, "Do you give blow jobs?" She doesn't answer but turns to YouTube videos for instructional tips. (The film was rated "R" so that real eighth graders couldn't see it.)

In 1995, the popular sex columnist Dan Savage wrote, "Anal is the new oral." This wasn't really true. According to one survey, 89 percent of women have performed oral sex by the age of 30 while 50 percent have experienced anal sex.[3] The only impediment to oral sex is psychological. Most women find anal sex painful (72 percent according to the same survey) and there is the heightened threat of HIV/AIDS. That it isn't fully normalized is reflected by the fact that, in movies, it is referred to, usually in a joking way, but rarely depicted. In *Bridget Jones's Diary* (2001), Renee Zellweger and Hugh Grant reflect that what they have just done is illegal in five Southern states. In *Bad Santa* (2003), Billy Bob Thornton tells a woman he has just penetrated in a toilet stall, "You won't shit right for a week." In *Sideways* (2004), Thomas Haden Church tells his buddy how he lost his wallet: "Her husband works nights or something and he comes home early and catches me on the floor with my cock up his wife's ass."

At the 2013 Academy Awards, host Seth MacFarlane performed a song, "We Saw Your Boobs," that name-checked a number of prominent actresses: Meryl Streep, Angelina Jolie, Naomi Watts, Anne Hathaway, Halle Berry, Nicole Kidman, Marisa Tomei, Kristen Stewart, Helen Hunt, Scarlett Johansson, Jessica Chastain, Jodie Foster, Hillary Swank, Penelope Cruz and Kate Winslet. Most were in the audience. The song was poorly received, and he was not asked to host again. His song did touch on a truth. Nudity was not just the province of starlets in Roger Corman movies.

Ann-Margret was nude in *Carnal Knowledge* with Jack Nicholson (rear), for which she got an Academy Award nomination. Avco Embassy.

Starting with Glenda Jackson in 1969, a number of Oscar winners and nominees had been at least partly nude in the movies for which they were recognized. Valerie Perrine as Lenny Bruce's stripper wife, Honey, was nominated in the Best Actress category for *Lenny* (1974). Jane Fonda won her second Oscar for *Coming Home* (1978), in which she, as the wife of an Army captain, is brought to orgasm by cunnilingus from an enlisted man (Jon Voight), paralyzed from the waist down, shown in semidarkness. Holly Hunter, not known as a sexy type, revealed an unexpectedly shapely body as a mute whose urges are awakened in *The Piano* (1993), for which she won the Oscar. Elisabeth Shue was nominated for her role as a prostitute gang-raped by college boys in *Leaving Las Vegas* (1995). Nominee Kate Winslet in *Titanic* (1997) paid artist Leonardo DiCaprio to draw her "like one of your French girls" as she reclined nude on a couch. Jodie Foster, Oscar winner for *The Accused* (1998), exposed her breasts and panties as she was raped by three men on a billiard table. Diane Lane was nominated for *Unfaithful* (2002), a remake of Claude Chabrol's *La Femme Infidèle* (1969), for her role as married woman with a younger lover in Adrian Lyne's gender-reversed (and less successful) follow-up to *Fatal Attraction*.

In the Best Supporting Actress category, Ann-Margret was nominated for *Carnal Knowledge* (1971), with her first nude scene, as Bobbie, a former model who becomes bored and depressed in her relationship with Jack Nicholson after he forces her to give up her career. A fully nude Annette Bening presented herself to the landlord in lieu of rent in *The Grifters* (1990). Married businesswoman Vera Farmiga shared a hotel room with George Clooney in *Up in the Air* (2009), although a body double was used for the rear view.

11

Blue Movie

Coming to a Theater Near You—Pornography

Hollywood's stock in trade was not sex but sexiness. Ad campaigns offered the prospect of seeing something erotic while, in the actual movie, directors and cinematographers created the illusion of something erotic. Even without censorship, actors might have found nudity and sex scenes awkward and much of the public would have been made uncomfortable. By the late 1960s, mores had changed enough that at least part of the audience was primed for something stronger.

"Films Exploiting Interest in Sex and Violence Find Growing Audience Here" was the headline of a January 1968 story by *New York Times* film critic Vincent Canby. The paper reported that "crude 42nd St. fare" had moved from midtown Manhattan to the outer boroughs and the suburbs. It had also spread within midtown. Canby profiled a woman named Chelly Wilson who owned a string of theaters on Eighth Avenue just up from 42nd St. Once, these had shown foreign-language, mostly Greek, films. When the ethnic market dried up, they turned to sex.

Barry Mahon, producer of *Fanny Hill Meets Lady Chatterley* (1967) and *Fanny Hill Meets Dr. Erotico* (1969), asserted his professionalism and bragged to Canby that he employed a NABET (union) crew.

Radley Metzger was another producer who came to prominence as the market for sex films expanded. Metzger's roots were in European art cinema. He made trailers for Janus Films and prepared subtitled versions of foreign films for the U.S. market. He knew that Swedish films were more permissive about nudity and imported them into the U.S. He had a hit with *I, a Woman* (1965), a Swedish-Danish coproduction, even though the lead actress, Essy Persson, was not all that attractive. At a time when American movies were still subject to the Production Code, a few minutes of female nudity or "horizontal" lovemaking could sell a movie. Thanks to Ingmar Bergman, any film from Sweden could be marketed as an "art" film. Jerry Gross's Cinemation Industries imported *Inga* (1968), made in Sweden but directed by American soft-porn pioneer Joe Sarno.

Metzger then directed films of his own. In *Therese and Isabelle* (1968), a woman returns to the Swiss boarding school of her youth to recall the lesbian affair she had with a classmate. (Canby noted that "lesbian" scenes had become *de rigueur*.) Metzger worked in Europe because costs were lower but also because the elegant palaces and gardens provided a backdrop for his jet-set characters. *Camille 2000* (1969) faithfully transported the Alexandre Dumas novel to a modern setting as he had done previously for Prosper Merimee with *Carmen, Baby* (1967). *The Lickerish Quartet* (1970) began with a quotation from Pirandello and the film was suitably Pirandellian. A wealthy Italian couple watches a black-and-white porno with their son. They get bored and go the circus, where they meet a blonde performer who looks like the woman in the film. They bring her back to their castle. The father has sex with her first. In a surrealistic sequence, they roll around on outsize dictionary pages on which words are highlighted: excite; phallus; organ; testicle; copulate; lust; masturbate; fornicate; hole; fuck (repeated four times as they do it); and, finally, ecstasy. The son has sex with her out of doors and then the mother has her turn.

Russ Meyer, Metzger's main rival as a soft-porn *auteur*, had none of his cultural ambitions. He did make a version of the 18th-century erotic classic *Fanny Hill* for Albert Zugsmith with veteran actress Miriam Hopkins in the cast, but it was not a happy experience and Meyer was soon back on his own. His black-and-white melodrama *Faster, Pussycat! Kill! Kill!* (1966) became a midnight-show standby. *Vixen!* (1968) was his most successful film to that time, with a gross of $8 million against a budget of $76,000.

Vixen! was fairly simple in story and execution. "Vixen" is the name of the main character as well as a description. She and her pilot husband live in British Columbia. He is frequently away to pick up the tourists he flies back for vacations. This gives Vixen plenty of time to bed multiple men, among them her own brother. When the pilot brings back a wealthy couple for a fishing trip, Vixen seduces the husband and then the wife. Meyer half-heartedly attempts to give the story some topicality. A member of the Irish Republic Army (in tweed jacket, green turtleneck and flat cap) charters the plane and, at gunpoint, tries to hijack it to Cuba. He expects that the pilot's black friend will defect, as he came to Canada to escape service in Vietnam and has been subjected to nonstop racist abuse by Vixen. Meyer lovingly photographed the bodies of the women; he especially liked to place them outdoors amid trees, rocks and streams. In the title role, Erica Gavin displayed the ample breasts that became a Meyer hallmark, but also painted-on eyebrows that gave her a devilish appearance. (*Vixen!* might have been the first film to get an "X" rating, but it premiered in Chicago before the ratings system went into effect.)

Dialogue was not exactly a strong point for Meyer or his actors, so he reached back into the silent era. He combined the exaggeration and irreverence of Mack Sennett, the crosscutting to climax of D.W. Griffith, and Soviet director and montage theorist Sergei Eisenstein's juxtaposition of images to make a satirical point. Meyer was often his own cinematographer. Low budgets meant that he had to do multiple camera setups on each day of shooting. With no crew to push dollies, lay tracks or operate cranes, Meyer used the editing room to give his films visual style. He began to attract critical attention. Chicago critic Roger Ebert praised him and became his collaborator. Richard Corliss, editor of *Film Comment* and a critic for *Time*, wrote that he had a simple test by which to judge a sexy movie: Did it give him an erection? By that measure, Meyer succeeded.

Today, Greenwich Village is just another overpriced New York neighborhood but, in the 1960s, it was the home of alternative culture. The Village–based Grove Press's owner, Barney Rosset, had successfully challenged the U.S. Post Office ban on *Lady Chatterley's Lover* in 1960. In 1968, he acquired the rights to Swedish director Vilgot Sjöman's 1967 diptych *I Am Curious (Yellow)* and 1968's *I Am Curious (Blue)*. Blue and yellow are the colors of the Swedish flag and the films were intended as some sort of commentary on contemporary Sweden.

I Am Curious (Yellow) was also about its own making. The director and his crew appear at the beginning of the film to introduce Lena Nyman, a 22-year-old drama student who is to play "Lena Nyman." "Lena Nyman" is the founder and sole officer of the "Nyman Institute," housed in the apartment she shares with her parents. Nyman challenges Sweden's failure to realize its social-democratic ideals. She conducts interviews on the street and asks people, "Is Sweden a class society?" She taunts Swedish tourists back from Spain for their support of Francisco Franco's Fascist regime and protests the Vietnam War in front of the American Embassy.

What got the film seized by U.S. Customs and subsequently caused it to be declared obscene by a Massachusetts court was not its politics but its sexual explicitness. In the film's most notorious moment, Nyman kisses her lover's non-erect penis while both lie nude in the grass. In the previous shot, he appeared to go down on her but it was cut short. There are two scenes of intercourse, one in semidarkness and one in daylight, but penetration is not shown. There is frontal male and female nudity. Lena and her partner are washed with DDT after they contract scabies. In place of the Ten Commandments, the film espoused the New Morality: don't rape; don't spread venereal disease; don't bring unwanted children into the world. As long as you use birth control, sex is okay.

The obscenity ruling was overturned on appeal. In 1966, the U.S. Supreme Court had ruled in *Memoirs v. Massachusetts* that material has to be "utterly without redeeming social value" to be subject to prosecution. The film had redeeming social value in abundance. There was an interview with the since-assassinated Martin Luther King, Jr., filmed in Stockholm by Sjöman in 1966 on the subject of nonviolence. Future Prime Minister of Sweden Olof Palme worried about social inequality and Soviet poet Yevgeny Yevtushenko read his famous poem "Babi Yar." Although Lena Nyman disparaged her body, complaining of sagging breasts and a big belly, the nudity sold tickets. The film grossed millions in its 1969 run and enabled Grove Press to start a film distribution company. Audiences lured by sex got a hodgepodge of cinema verité and Godardian self-referentiality in black and white, by then passé even in "art" films. *I Am Curious (Blue)* flopped.

Another kind of "blue" movie brought actual intercourse to the screen of the New Andy Warhol Garrick Theater in Greenwich Village in July 1969, where Warhol's *Lonesome Cowboys* was faltering. *Blue Movie* was cut down to a little over two hours from an epic film called *Fuck*, or ****, a companion to Warhol's *Eat* and *Sleep*. The title, *Blue Movie*, came from an old term for dirty movies but also referred to the bluish cast lent to the tungsten-balanced film stock by the daylight that streamed into the apartment used for the film. A professional cinematographer would have corrected this with sheets of straw-colored gelatin on the windows to "warm up" the color temperature, but Warhol elected to live with it.

In a 30-mintute unbroken take from a single camera angle, Warhol "superstar" Viva and Louis Waldon, photographed head to toe, lie on a mattress in the middle of a room. They talk about the Vietnam War, New York City Mayor John Lindsay, a garbage strike, assassinations and the upcoming 1968 elections. Viva recalls how the East Hampton police arrested her for wearing a see-through blouse with no bra. They have prolonged sex in long shot with no actual penetration shown. Nevertheless, the police seized the film a week after it opened and threatened the theater staff with fines and imprisonment. A municipal court found the film obscene, a ruling that has never been reversed. When the Whitney Museum of American Art revived the seldom-seen film in 2016, Viva, now known as Viva Hoffman, tried to stop it on the grounds that it was not art but pornography.

Penetrative sex came to the screen in 1970. At first, the documentary form provided a useful dodge. Alex de Renzy's *A History of the Blue Movie* incorporated in its entirety *Smart Alec*, an 11-minute "stag" film made in 1951 by future stripper Candy Barr, who was only 16 but looks more mature. A traveling salesman picks up a young woman at the swimming pool of a motel. They go to his room and peel off their bathing suits. Candy Barr reveals an exceptionally beautiful body. Although the dark and blurry images are many generations removed from the original negative, penetration is clearly shown. Barr later claimed that she was forced to make the film at gunpoint.

Denmark's 1969 decision to abolish obscenity laws provided the pretext for *Sexual Freedom in Denmark*. There were interviews with a Danish psychologist and a female journalist, who argued that there had been no increase in sex crimes or they had even gone down. The sex shops and adult book stores in the film seemed to be aimed more at tourists than Danes, with signs in English. Interviews with people (mostly women) on the street confirmed Scandinavians' reputation for liberalism. All endorsed premarital sex. The middle part of the film offered typical sex education, with diagrams of the male and female anatomy and microphotography or animation of the fertilization of the ovum. The final part of the film rewarded the viewer who had hung in this far, with images of an attractive young couple who demonstrated various sexual positions with visible penetration.

The Presidential Commission on Pornography and Obscenity, initiated in 1967, recommended that the United States follow the Danish example and eliminate all restriction on material seen or read by adults. By the time the commission issued its report, Lyndon Johnson had been succeeded by Richard Nixon, avatar of Middle America and the "silent majority." The one member of the commission appointed by Nixon, Charles Keating, a founder of Citizens for Decent Literature (and later the central figure in the savings and loan scandal of the 1980s), persuaded Nixon to disavow the report.

The availability of explicit material from Sweden and Denmark help set off the "pubic wars." When the UK-based *Penthouse* magazine launched in the U.S. in September 1969, it forced *Playboy* to stop airbrushing the pubic hair of its Playmates.

The first scripted sexually explicit film to play in a movie theater was Bill Osco's *Mona the Virgin Nymph* in August 1970. Although the 71-minute film consists almost entirely of sexual acts, it has, just barely, a story line, even if it's one that makes little sense. Mona refuses her fiancé intercourse as she has promised her mother that she will be a virgin until marriage. In compensation, Mona is a prodigious fellatrix. She is so eager to show her skills that she solicits a stranger on the street, who gives her money on the assumption that she must be a prostitute. Mona also engages in mutual cunnilingus with a blonde masseuse.

Mona's boyfriend goes to her mother's house only to be informed that Mona has gone to the movies. Before he joins her there, the boyfriend has the intercourse Mona previously denied him with Mona's mother. At the movie theater, Mona masturbates. (The poster displayed outside the theater is for *One for the Money*, a 1970 soft-porn feature, although the dialogue heard coming from the screen is from *The Taming of the Shrew*.) The boyfriend finds Mona fellating a random patron. To punish her, he arranges a sex party at which she is made to give and receive oral sex, though why she would consider that a punishment is unclear.

As filmmaking, *Mona* was abysmal. The whirring sound of the camera motor could be heard. The only cinematic innovation was the use of extreme close-ups of genitalia.

Unlike porn features to come, there was no "money shot" (ejaculation). The film carried no cast or crew credits, although the cute lead actress who slightly resembled Simone Simon, star of *Cat People* (1942), was later identified as "Fifi Watson."

The term "porno chic" originated in a January 1973 piece by *New York Times* writer Ralph Blumenthal in response to *Deep Throat*. *Deep Throat* opened on June 12, 1972, at the World Theatre on East 49th Street, where *The Orgy at Lil's Place* had set the previous house record of 29 weeks in 1963. Blumenthal noted that those who patronized *Deep Throat* included Mike Nichols, Jack Nicholson and Truman Capote. *Deep Throat*'s fame was only reinforced when it was temporarily shut down. The World Theatre's marquee read: "Judge Cuts 'Throat,' World Mourns." Although sexually explicit films had run without interference in San Francisco since 1970, the Lindsay administration launched legal action against eight venues that showed adult films.

The complaint against *Deep Throat* counted 15 sexual acts in 62 minutes, seven of fellatio, four of cunnilingus and four of vaginal intercourse.

The success of *Deep Throat* did not so much popularize fellatio as confirm a change that had already taken place. One writer has identified 1968–69 as the time when oral sex came into prominence in mainstream culture.[1] A lyric in the musical *Hair* went "Sodomy, Fellatio, Cunnilingus, Pederasty. Father, why do these things sound so nasty?" (*Hair* moved to Broadway in 1968; it had previously been performed at a club called Cheetah, whose sign depicted two felines engaged in *soixante-neuf*.) A character in John Updike's 1968 best-selling novel *Couples* opines, "To f**k is human, to be blown divine." Philip Roth's Alexander Portnoy in *Portnoy's Complaint* (1972) persuades a girl to go down on him. Unfortunately, she gags.

Things had changed in real life, too. In the 1950s or early 1960s, about the only men who could command oral sex were those who could affect women's careers: Broadway or Hollywood producers, male movie stars, studio executives and such. If the average man wanted it, he had to pay a prostitute or let himself be picked up by a homosexual, experiences that were ambiguous at best and degrading at worst.

Journalist Helen Lawrenson recalled that when she first heard as a girl in the 1920s of what was then called "Frenching," it was "something degraded, indulged in by perverts and so out of the ordinary that prostitutes charged extra for it." She reflected, "The women I've known—and I include myself—made oral love to men not for their own pleasure but for that of the men. It was an unselfish act because none of them liked it."[2]

Reluctance weakened amid the Sexual Revolution of the late 1960s and evaporated in the 1970s. At first, it was considered edgy, the province of nude models and rock musicians' girlfriends. After 1970, even "nice" girls did it, urged on by *Cosmopolitan* magazine, whose every cover seemingly promised tips on "how to give him mind-blowing sex."

With porn, it's not easy to separate cause from effect. While there was obviously a large element of fantasy, porn evolved in ways that broadly mirrored changes in society. Up until about 1969, the *sine qua non* of pornography was heterosexual intercourse. Thereafter, the menu became more varied. After the Stonewall rebellion in 1969, gay male features appeared, such as Wakefield Poole's *Boys in the Sand* (1971). For homosexual men, the depiction on-screen of acts that were technically illegal under sodomy laws offered an affirmation of identity and images of liberation.

In 1968, the feminist Anne Koedt wrote a landmark essay, "The Myth of the Vaginal Orgasm," that located the clitoris as the source of female pleasure. The Freudian idea that attributed a woman's resistance to penetration to "frigidity" was debunked. Blame for women's lack of response was shifted to the incompetence of men who failed to understand the female anatomy. Of course, a finger or tongue did not have to belong to a male at all.

"Lesbian" scenes were not aimed at real lesbians but at men who could fantasize sex with either or both of the women without a male rival who got there first. (Some female performers were gay or bisexual in real life. They pretended to be straight so that they could pretend to be gay.)

In 1951's *Smart Alec*, Candy Barr had pointedly refused to perform oral sex despite the forceful demands of her partner. She called in an older, less attractive brunette to do the deed. In the context of *A History of the Blue Movie* in 1970, her reluctance seemed anachronistic. The porn stars of the 1970s would flaunt their oral skills.

Last Tango in Paris opened in the midst of the *Deep Throat* controversy. Some writers extended the term "porno chic" to encompass both. The association was unfair. *Last Tango* was a serious effort by a director who tried to do in film what writers such as D.H. Lawrence and Henry Miller had done in print years earlier. *Deep Throat* was a cheap ($24,000), one-joke movie that even its director (Gerard Damiano, billed as "Jerry Gerard") admitted was not good. The joke wasn't even funny: A woman (Linda Lovelace) is born with a clitoris in her throat. Only after she learns to swallow an entire nine-inch penis can she achieve orgasm. Her increasingly aggressive sucking is intercut with stock footage of a missile launch. For her climax, fireworks fill the screen.

Not surprisingly, there was a *Deep Tango* (1974). It loosely followed the Bertolucci film with a switch in locale from Paris to the San Francisco Bay Area with the BART train in place of the elevated section of the Metro. "Fifi Watson," the star of *Mona* and now billed as "Mona Watson," was cast as "Dr. Pauline Kaelus." In a gender-reversed variation on the "butter scene," Watson shoved a baguette into the rectum of her male costar.

If *Deep Throat* was facetious, Damiano's subsequent *The Devil in Miss Jones* (1973) took itself very seriously. The title was a play on *The Devil and Miss Jones*, a 1941 Jean Arthur comedy that did not deserve to have that happen to it. In film's key scene, "Georgina Spelvin" performs oral sex on a penis in a three-and-a-half-minute close-up. The recipient was again "Harry Reems," the male lead of *Deep Throat*. ("George Spelvin" was the name used in playbills when an actor played more than one role.) Spelvin got to practice her specialty (off-screen) in *Police Academy* (1984) when, concealed in a lectern, she fellated Commandant Lassard as he addressed the graduates. In a "topper," Steve Guttenberg emerged from the lectern first, so Lassard thought he had been sucked by a guy.

In many places, *Deep Throat* and *The Devil in Miss Jones* were double-billed.

In a twist that could have come from a film script, Lou Peraino, the mobbed-up distributor of *Deep Throat*, enjoyed the movie business so much that he went straight (sort of) and invested his profits in a new company, Bryanston Pictures, which released *The Texas Chainsaw Massacre* and John Carpenter's first feature, *Dark Star*, in 1974.

The third big film of the "porno chic" era, *Behind the Green Door* (1972), was produced by the Mitchell Brothers, owners of the O'Farrell Theater in San Francisco. Its selling point was Marilyn Chambers. Linda Lovelace had been just above average in looks. Georgina Spelvin was 37, a little on the mature side to put it kindly. Just shy of 20 when the film was made, Chambers combined youth, WASP-y features and a lithe, almost boyish, body. She somewhat resembled Cybill Shepherd, who had recently made her debut as the high school beauty of *The Last Picture Show* (1971). Like Shepherd, Chambers had been a model. She was on the box of Ivory Snow soap flakes as a young mother holding a baby, as wholesome an image as there could be. (Procter & Gamble redesigned the package in the wake of Chambers's notoriety. The producers bought up the unsold stock, which Chambers autographed in personal appearances.)

Chambers was paid $25,000, more than the entire budget of *Deep Throat*. (Linda Lovelace got only $1,200.) Adult films could be, if not a respectable career for young women, a remunerative one.

Behind the Green Door is a very strange film and the reasons for its popularity are now hard to fathom. There isn't much sexual action for the first 20 minutes. Instead, there is a framing story about a young woman (Chambers) who drives up the Pacific Coast Highway in her red sports car but is abducted. With little effort to resist or escape, she lets herself be groomed to appear onstage in some sort of sex club, where the show includes a (clothed) female mime. The whole performance thus occurs as a flashback. Chambers is brought onstage by black-garbed women who lick her nipples and vulva.

A black man, boxer Johnny Keyes, emerges from the green door of the title wearing white shorts that leave his genitals exposed and a necklace that marks him as some sort of African chieftain. There is a close-up of his large, erect penis.

The United States had a long history of black men lynched for purported rapes of white women. As late as 1955, Emmett Till, age 14, was murdered for an alleged wolf whistle directed at a white woman. Not until 1967, in a case with the deliciously appropriate name of *Loving v. Virginia*, were anti-miscegenation laws overturned. *Guess Who's Coming to Dinner* was a big hit that year, but any intimacy between Sidney Poitier and his white bride, Katharine Houghton, was kept off-screen.

In *The Birth of a Nation* (1915), Mae Marsh threw herself from a cliff rather than submit to a black man. As the title put it, "we should not grieve that she found sweeter the opal gates of death." In *Behind the Green Door*, the racist's nightmare—a black penis in a white vagina—was something to celebrate. In a 10-minute sequence that mostly eschewed "pump" shots to concentrate on Chambers's face in close-up, she was brought to a screaming orgasm. (Otherwise, she did not speak in the film.) The past was left behind, or was it? The stereotype of the oversexed black buck with a huge penis was revived but given a positive spin. The pairing of a black man with a white woman, usually blonde, would become a common trope in porn. (White men were rarely paired with black women, although Latinas and, especially, Asians of the "China Doll" type were popular.)

Chambers is hoisted above the club floor in a large sling that she shares with four men. She masturbates two of them, fellates a third (Johnny Keyes again) and is penetrated by a fourth.

The film turns artsy with a six-minute montage of ejaculations in slow motion, in negative, solarized or silhouetted images amid color separations. Drops of semen remain suspended above Chambers's lips with a little entering her mouth.

Members of the overdressed audience, some of whom wear masks and which also includes a number of transvestites, become aroused themselves and engage in masturbation or sex with each other. Chambers is taken behind the green door for a climactic bout of sex (with a white man) that combines fellatio, cunnilingus and intercourse, all photographed in close-up.

Porn was controversial in the 1970s because it was new. It wasn't really new but it was out in the open in a way that it had not been before. Even people who considered themselves broadminded could not have been pleased when *Hustler* turned up in the magazine rack at the local pharmacy, when an adult bookshop opened on the street their kids took to school or when a title like *Thar She Blows* appeared on the marquee of the neighborhood theater to which they had been taken to Disney features by their parents.

In addition to predictable attacks from religiously oriented watchdog groups like Morality in Media and Citizens for Decent Literature, porn divided feminists. The New York–based organization Women Against Pornography was cofounded by Susan Brownmiller, author of *Against Our Will*, a history of rape. Her ally Robin Morgan declared, "Pornography is the theory, rape is the practice." An offshoot organization, Feminists Fighting Pornography, was really just one person (Page Mellish). The 1980 anthology *Take Back the Night: Women on Pornography*, edited by Laura Lederer, brought together the voices of leading feminists who did not entirely agree among themselves.

Nadine Strossen, NYU law professor and later the first woman to lead the American Civil Liberties Union, defended porn on First Amendment grounds. Some women found positive aspects to porn. *New York Magazine* restaurant critic Gael Greene championed porn star Jamie Gillis, who became her lover. Sallie Tisdale, a registered nurse, confessed in an article for *Harper's Magazine* ("Talk Dirty to Me") to her avid consumption. Academic Linda Williams published the book *Hard Core* in which *The Opening of Misty Beethoven* (1976), a variation on *Pygmalion* directed by Radley Metzger under the name Henry Paris, was treated seriously.

The anti-porn feminists claimed that most of the women in adult films had been sexually abused as children. They got a gift when Linda Lovelace, the star of *Deep Throat*, published the book *Outrage* in 1980, in which she claimed that she was forced to perform at gunpoint. Lovelace, sick and penniless, again posed for men's magazines just before her death. Most female porn stars refused to play the victim. While some were just in it for the money, others such as Nina Hartley, Candida Royalle and Annie Sprinkle held themselves out as educators who could teach women to enjoy sex without shame or guilt.

The porn world certainly had a dark side. A top male star, John C. Holmes a.k.a. Johnny Wadd, was charged with the murder of four people but acquitted. He later died of AIDS. The lovely but cocaine-addicted Shauna Grant shot herself just shy of her 21st birthday. Of course, straight show business had a much longer list of murders and suicides.

Social and religious conservatives were a big part of the coalition that elected Ronald Reagan in 1980. As payback, Reagan ordered the Justice Department to create a new commission, one that would renounce the conclusions of the 1970 report. It became known as the Meese Commission, after Attorney General Edwin Meese, although the key figure was Henry E. Hudson, Commonwealth Attorney of Arlington County, Virginia. He was known for his campaign to shut down adult bookstores and massage parlors. The right-leaning group relied on the insights of radical feminists, who were their adversaries on other issues such as the legality of abortion. Woman Against Pornography supplied the commission with witnesses who claimed to be victims, but it also protested against the commission's conservative slant even as its leader, Dorchen Leidholdt, testified. The commission issued 92 recommendations that mostly involved more vigorous enforcement of existing laws. It also endorsed law professor Catharine MacKinnon's model ordinance that would allow any woman threatened by sexually explicit material to have it removed and claim damages. It was adopted in Indianapolis, rejected in Minneapolis and later declared unconstitutional.

The commission's lack of methodological rigor made it an easy target for ridicule from social scientists and civil libertarians. The ostensible justification for a second presidential commission was the supposed increase in violent pornography. In reality, most of the violence against women on the screen came in the R-rated action and horror films, especially the "slasher" cycle. Rape was one variant of sex that did not figure prominently in porn. Why would it? The women were either nymphomaniacs or shy, repressed virgins who, after a single sexual experience, became nymphomaniacs.

The dire warnings of feminists and social conservatives were not borne out. There was no increase in sex crimes. A 2007 paper, "Pornography, Rape, and the Internet," by Clemson University economics professor Todd Kendall found that rape actually declined as online pornography became readily accessible. A 2010 study of the best-selling porn videos from 2004 and 2005 claimed to find high levels of both physical and verbal aggression against women: "Of 304 scenes analyzed, 82.4% contained physical aggression, principally gagging, spanking and slapping, while 48.7% contained verbal aggression, primarily name-calling."[3] An article in *The Journal of Sex Research* that analyzed the 289 most popular videos uploaded to the internet site Pornhub over the preceding decades found otherwise: "First, we did not find any consistent uptick in aggressive content over the past decade; in fact, the average video today contains shorter segments showing aggression. Second, videos that contain aggressive acts are both less likely to receive views and less likely to be ranked favorably by viewers, who prefer videos where women clearly perform pleasure."[4] (The two studies are not necessarily in conflict. It is possible that those who still purchase porn seek out harder material than do casual surfers of free sites on the internet.) Another article in *The Journal of Sex Research* found that, contrary to 1970s feminist theory, male viewers of pornography actually had more egalitarian views of women and were more supportive of women in nontraditional roles than nonviewers.[5] The most recent research, drawn from extensive studies in Australia and the Netherlands, suggests that exposure to pornography has little, if any, effect on the viewer.[6]

There are still valid reasons to dislike porn. Porn is explicit without being realistic. There are enough close-ups of genitals to fill a lecture in medical school, but sexual activity does not take place in any plausible context. The pool boy or the appliance repairman shows up and the horny housewife immediately takes him to bed, still in her high heels. (The classic encounter was parodied in the film-within-the-film of Kevin Smith's *Zach and Miri Make a Porno* [2008] in which Seth Rogen tells beautiful Elizabeth Banks in her denim shorts and bare midriff, "I'm a deliveryman and I have some cream for you," before dropping a case of bottles on the floor.) There are the omnipresent "facial" scenes with their undercurrent of misogynist hostility, as a man wastes an ejaculation to spurt semen into the nose, eyes and hair of a woman. There is a contradiction at the core of porn. Sex is the end all and be all, the driving force of life. It is also no big deal, engaged in with no forethought and quickly forgotten.

In 1984, Congress passed the Child Protection Act that made it illegal to show persons under the age of 18 engaged in sexual acts even if the material was not otherwise obscene. One result was that the films made by Traci Lords when she was 15 were pulled

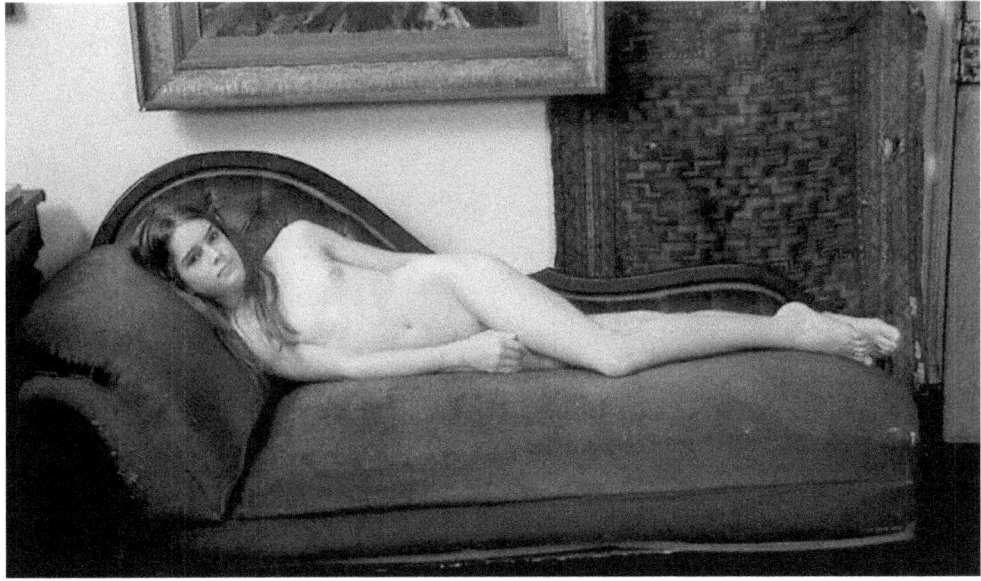

Brooke Shields was a child prostitute in *Pretty Baby*, based on the photography of E.J. Bellocq in New Orleans of 1917. Director Louis Malle was no stranger to controversy. His first feature *The Lovers* in 1958 had a couple share a bathtub and he would provoke again with mother-son masturbation in *Murmur of the Heart* (1971). Paramount.

off the shelves and destroyed even though the damage, if any, had already been done. Some wondered if it would still be possible to make a film like Louis Malle's *Pretty Baby* (1978), set in the Storyville section of New Orleans in 1900, in which the virginity of a 13-year-old prostitute (Brooke Shields) was sold to multiple clients. Shields was nude in the film.

The new climate may have ended the big screen career of director Stanley Donen. His *Blame It on Rio* (1984) was a remake of a 1977 French film. Michael Caine, whose character is 43, has sex with his best friend's 15-year-old daughter (Michelle Johnson, a 17-year-old Brooke Shields look-alike, in her film debut). She is the one who initiates it. He does offer initial resistance but gives in when she takes her top off and puts her impressive breasts in front of him. She takes him to a secluded cove. The sex takes place off-screen, but there is a postcoital shot in which he rests his head on her nude back. (The film was released before the passage of the Child Protection Act but Johnson got permission from a judge for the nudity.) Roger Ebert, Richard Schickel and most other critics found the central situation distasteful. Perhaps it played better in French.

During the "porno chic" era, some critics speculated that mainstream cinema and adult films would converge. This did not really happen.

In its 1973 *Miller* decision, the U.S. Supreme Court held that "community standards" could be invoked in obscenity prosecutions. In the dying days of the Nixon administration, the U.S. Attorney in Memphis brought a case of conspiracy to distribute obscene materials across interstate lines against a group of defendants that included *Deep Throat* star Harry Reems. Reems was convicted, but the conviction was overturned on appeal after a campaign that drew support from Broadway and Hollywood. (Lou Peraino, his brother Joseph and eight others served jail time.) Despite the favorable outcome for Reems, actors may have become more cautious.

Michael Caine finds it hard to resist the 15-year-old daughter (Michele Johnson, actually 17) of his best friend in *Blame It on Rio*. The film got caught in the backlash against "kiddie porn." 20th Century–Fox.

If anything, the availability of hard-core porn may have reduced the pressure on mainstream cinema. The steamy sex scenes of *Last Tango* and *Don't Look Now* became less common as escapism of the Lucas-Spielberg sort ruled the box office.

Adult films continued to feature porn people doing porn things. The industry replicated the old Hollywood studio system. Companies such as Vivid and Caballero had stars under contract. There were awards shows. The films were structured after the old musicals, with sex scenes in place of "numbers." There was a mix of solos (masturbation), duets (oral sex, intercourse) and ensembles (orgies).

Chuck Vincent, a director of adult films, attempted to bridge the gap with *Roommates* (1982), offered in both "hard" and "soft" versions. It brought together three of the top East Coast porn stars—Veronica Hart, Samantha Fox and Kelly Nichols—in a script supposedly drawn from their own experiences as single women in New York City. It was a classic case of falling between two stools and hitting neither. It was too rooted in the porn world for mainstream acceptance and too fraught with complications for the porn audience.

The anal taboo eroded in the 1970s even in non-pornographic films, not only *Last Tango* but also in *Deliverance* (1972), wherein Ned Beatty in his tighty-whities was forced to "squeal like a pig" by a Southern degenerate. In Lina Wertmüller's *Swept Away* (1974), Mariangela Melato took Giancarlo Giannini aback with her request, "Sodomize me," after both were shipwrecked on an island. Anal scenes occasionally figured in 1970s porn, but were either just rear-entry vaginal sex or they involved secondary characters who could easily be cut out to avoid prosecution. In 1980, Veronica Hart became the first "name" performer to do anal for real in *Angel Buns* and *Neon Nights*.

Veronica Hart, the Meryl Streep of porn, was also the star of *Amanda by Night* (1981), photographed and directed by Gary Graver, cinematographer on Orson Welles's last projects, under the pseudonym of Robert McCallum. *Amanda by Night* is considered by some the best porno film ever made, although its merits are only relative; except for the hard-core parts, it resembled an episode of series television. Hart plays a high-class escort (she drives a Mercedes roadster) who passes off a wealthy client to two of her friends. They are both killed. By the "Corliss standard," it wasn't all that arousing. The multiple murders cast a pall of mortality. In a bit of levity, a homicide detective pulls on gun on a corrupt vice squad cop (the ubiquitous Ron Jeremy) who has just extorted a freebie from a massage-parlor girl; as he ejaculates, he is warned that he might be "the first guy to come and go at the same time."

Café Flesh (1985) was an even more ambitious attempt to cross over into the mainstream and one of the last. It had a postapocalyptic story, but the moneymen wanted penetrative sex, so additional footage was shot with doubles for the billed performers. Explicit sex limited it to porn theaters where the sex scenes seemed more like performance art. Nevertheless, there was a sequel. The soundtrack album became a cult favorite.

Clunky home-video equipment had been around in the 1970s, but it wasn't until the early 1980s that the videocassette recorder became a mass-market product. The VHS format became ascendant, in large part because Sony had refused to allow adult films to use Betamax.

Technology accomplished what the Meese Commission could not. Pornography left the public square for the privacy of the home, where, as some quipped, it belonged. By 1987, revenues from home video exceeded that from theaters. By 1990, porno theaters were closing. Even California's Pussycat Theaters, with two dozen screens at its peak in the 1970s, fell on hard times.

If everything was going to end up on video, it made sense to shoot on video. With "gonzo" filmmaking, technical standards collapsed. Porn came full circle, from the plotless loops of 1970 to the so-called Golden Age (c. 1974–81) that emulated Hollywood and back to unscripted sex.

If pornographers no longer aspired to make their movies better, they could make the sex better. With 35mm film, the length of shots was limited by the capacity of the magazine (a maximum of 1,000 feet or 11 minutes). Videotape's one-hour recording capability made it possible to depict a sexual encounter from beginning to end in real time. Lightweight video equipment also facilitated direct sound, instead of the disco-type music and post-dubbed moans and "Oh, Gods" that had become such clichés.

Where porn stars of the 1970s had used black shoe polish to emphasize their pubic hair, the trend of the 1990s was toward a neatly trimmed "landing strip" or even a "full Brazilian" that made an adult woman look like a prepubescent girl.

With the rapid growth of the internet after 1994, pretty much anybody could upload a porn video to the web and pretty much anybody did. Many of the servers were outside the U.S. and beyond the reach of prosecutors. The anti-pornography provisions of the 1996 Communications Decency Act were struck down by the U.S. Supreme Court in *ACLU v. Reno* in 1997. With explicit sex readily available to those who wanted it and easily ignored by those who didn't, it seemed that porn might become a nonissue. During the Clinton administration, the anti-porn groups either disappeared or turned their attention to sex trafficking and the exploitation of minors.

Social conservatives did not entirely give up. Kansas Senator Sam Brownback chaired a hearing of the Subcommittee on Science, Technology and Space in 2005 that heard Dr. Judith Reisman expound her theory that exposure to porn alters the chemistry of the brain through the creation of "erototoxins," a term of her own invention. "Doctor" Reisman held a PhD in Communications and had no clinical research to support her claims. With the Republicans again in power, conservatives pressured the George W. Bush Justice Department to create an Obscenity Prosecution Task Force. Successful prosecutions were brought against "Max Hardcore" and Ira Isaacs, who specialized in extreme fetishist material. Barry Goldman, who dealt in "torture porn," took a plea.

The case against John Stagliano, known as "Buttman," was dismissed by a judge in 2010, who chided prosecutors for their sloppiness. Afterward, Attorney General Eric Holder shut down the task force. Forty-two Senators signed a letter of protest. Holder was named as the number one facilitator of pornography by the group Morality in Media in 2013 in its annual "Dirty Dozen" list. (Holder's role in Operation Delego, an international effort against child pornography that resulted in 72 arrests and 42 guilty pleas, of whom 25 received sentences of 10 years to life, apparently did not count.) Others on the "Dirty Dozen" list included Google, Comcast, Facebook, Twitter and Wikipedia, indicative of the difficulties facing anti-smut crusaders in a time when smart phones potentially put a porno theater in everyone's pocket.

By the dawn of the 21st century, the artistically ambitious pornographic feature was all but extinct. (In 2006, sales of adult DVDs cratered as the first of the free "tube" sites came online.) If the gap between serious cinema and adult films was to be bridged, it would have to be from the other direction.

Michael Winterbottom's *9 Songs* (2004) was often likened to *Last Tango in Paris* but they are actually very different. The sex in *Last Tango* was furtive. The lovers of *9 Songs* live together, go to rock concerts, take day trips together. Sex is simply part of life. It was also real. With Margo Stilley in the "female superior" position, Keiran O'Brien's condom-sheathed penis could clearly be seen stroking her vagina. In an earlier scene, she brought him to climax with her mouth and he ejaculated onto his stomach.

John Cameron Mitchell's *Shortbus* (2005) brought together a group of New Yorkers who are blocked sexually: a couples therapist who is unable to reach orgasm with her husband, though not for lack of trying; an artist turned professional dominatrix who fears that she is losing the capacity to feel anything; a monogamous gay male couple whose sex life is stale. (A controversial scene had one of the gay couple film himself as he performed autofellatio and ejaculated into his mouth.)

A citywide blackout brings them all back to an underground sex salon called Shortbus in hipster Brooklyn that is illuminated by candles. One participant describes the scene as "like the Sixties, but without hope." In a Felliniesque orgy presided over by a drag queen, people of varied ethnicities, body types and sexual orientations are encouraged to express themselves without inhibition. The therapist achieves orgasm in a threesome with a man and another woman. Reminiscent of the ending of *The 40-Year-Old Virgin*, in which Steve Carell's first sexual experience unleashes the Age of Aquarius, the lights of the city come on again.

Opinions of the film varied widely; some called it trash, others praised the performers' bravery in exposing themselves physically and emotionally. Everyone agreed that the stylized panoramas of New York City that linked the characters were brilliantly done.

Neither *9 Songs* nor *Shortbus* was able to break out of the art/indie ghetto.

In 2013, a researcher named Jon Millward entered the vital statistics of 10,000 male and female porn performers from the Internet Adult Film Database into a computer.[7] He also morphed the faces of the 10 most popular female performers to create a composite image. Contrary to stereotype, the average porn star turned out not to be a garishly made-up dyed blonde with surgically enhanced breasts but a conventionally attractive young woman with light brown hair who wears a 34B bra. He also found the average weight to be 117 pounds, not much different from what a woman considered to have a good figure would have weighed five or six decades earlier. The Centers for Disease Control and Prevention reported in 2018 that the average American woman weighed 170.6 pounds. This was more than the average man weighed in 1960. For all its ugly aspects, porn upheld an ideal of beauty that could be traced back to the Aphrodite of Knidos, c. 330 B.C.

12

Girls' Trip

The End of the Double Standard?

> "I Lost My Virginity, but I Still Have the Box It Came In"
> —Available as a T-shirt and on note cards,
> refrigerator magnets and beverage napkins

Sex and the Single Girl, Helen Gurley Brown's best seller of 1962, was one of those books, like John Kenneth Galbraith's *The Affluent Society* a few years earlier, that had an impact more through its title than for its substance. It was not a revelation that single girls had sex. About 15 percent of all brides were pregnant at the altar and another 10 percent had already given birth.[1] Premarital sex was still an issue in relationships; men pushed for it, women resisted what they called "going all the way." It was increasingly condoned "as long as they love each other" and it led to marriage.

The PCA did not see it that way. In the 1960 comedy *Happy Anniversary*, from the 1954 Broadway play *Anniversary Waltz*, a drunken David Niven reveals to the parents of his wife (Mitzi Gaynor) at a party to celebrate their 14th wedding anniversary that he slept with their daughter before they were married. The reverberations almost cause the marriage to break up. It also caused the movie to be denied a Code Seal. A voice-over narration was given to the disconsolate Niven to speak after his wife locked him out of their bedroom: "I was wrong. I never should have taken Alice to that hotel room before we were married. What could I have been thinking of?" It was pretty obvious what he was thinking of, but the unconvincing expression of regret got the producers their Code Seal.

In movies of the early 1960s, young women were presumed to be virgins unless the plot stated otherwise. Fittingly, in the 1964 film of *Sex and the Single Girl*, single girl Natalie Wood does not have sex (just as well as Wood's previous experiences led to madness in *Splendor in the Grass* and unwanted pregnancy in *Love with the Proper Stranger*). As "Dr. Helen Brown," author of the controversial book that gave the movie its title, she is a relationship counselor who has never been married and is still a virgin.

Also in 1964, Jane Fonda, like Wood in her mid-twenties, in a public relationship with Roger Vadim and presumably experienced in real life, had to defend her virginity in *Sunday in New York*.

The joke in *Take Her, She's Mine* (1963) is that James Stewart's efforts to protect the virtue of his college-age daughter (Sandra Dee) get him into embarrassing scrapes while she doesn't really do anything wrong. The screenplay by 66-year-old Nunnally Johnson attempts to give the square material a contemporary gloss. Stewart tells us that the two things his wife hates the most are "racial injustice and excess baggage fees." Dee sings in a coffeehouse where Bob Denver, in his patented beatnik role, is one of the patrons. She participates in a "Ban the Bomb" march and a sit-in at the town library to protest the removal of a book by Henry Miller. In a letter from Paris, she writes that she is still a virgin. Instead of being reassured, Stewart decides he must fly to France. Stewart comes to accept that his daughter has to live her own life. She marries later that day so the threat to her virtue is moot.

A half-century later, things were very different. In *Black Swan* (2010), a dancer (Natalie Portman) is asked by the ballet master if she is a virgin. She answers "no" and is hired. Presumably, a "yes" would have been a disqualification or, at least, something to be explained.

Some of the change can traced to the Vietnam War. It impacted American society much in the way the First World War shattered the Old Europe. Stefan Zweig in *The World of Yesterday* wrote that morality was discredited along with the political leaders who blundered into war and bungled the peace. Young Germans and Austrians of the early 1920s embraced sexual adventurousness, even homosexuality and lesbianism. For a girl, "to be sixteen and still under suspicion of virginity would have been considered a disgrace in any school of Berlin at that time," i.e., during the hyperinflation of 1923.

In 1960, the average age for virginity loss was 20 for males and 19 for females. By 1980, it was 17 for both. In 1960, the average age at first marriage was 22.8 for men and 20.3 for women, so that the interval between first sex and marriage was relatively short. Today, when the average age of marriage is 29.2 for men and 27.3 for women, to speak of "premarital sex" seems quaint.[2] Sociologists have coined the term "pre-premarital sex" to reflect the growing disconnect between the first sex partner(s) and the eventual betrothed.

The teen sex comedy would seem to have played itself out in the 1980s but, in 1999, *American Pie* out-grossed its predecessors in both senses of the word with over $100 million in domestic rentals. Four high school seniors in an upper-middle-class Southern California suburb make a pact that they will lose their virginity on prom might. This is initiated after a classmate claims to have had sex with his girlfriend—falsely, as it turns out. Although copyright credit was given to Don McLean, the title had nothing to do with his song. Jim (Jason Biggs) is told that the female anatomy feels like apple pie, so he sticks his penis into the pie his mother has left for him. *American Pie* added the term MILF (Mom I'd Like to Fuck) to the language. Nudity in the film was provided by a Czech exchange student who masturbates after finding the porn magazines in Biggs's room that his father (Eugene Levy) has sympathetically provided. The girl is unaware that a cam has been planted on a computer connected to the internet. She is summoned home.

The boys mostly realize their goal at an after-prom party, though not in ways they expected. Jim's date, a nerdy band girl, turns out to be sexually voracious and leaves him feeling that he was used as a sex object. An unpopular boy who's paid his prom date $200 ends up with the aforementioned MILF, the mother of his wealthy host. (She asks him, "Are you trying to seduce me?" and we hear the "Mrs. Robinson" song from *The Graduate* quoted on the soundtrack.) A lacrosse player holds off sex when he finds that he has real feelings for his girlfriend. The fourth faces the fact he and his girlfriend will probably not see each other after they leave for college, even though she surrendered sexually in return for his promise of love.

American Pie was one of about a dozen films sent up in *Not Another Teen Movie* (2001). Its foreign exchange student, named "Areola," shows up gratuitously nude, played by an actress who slips in and out of her accent. The trailer for *Not Another Teen Movie* proudly enumerated its stereotypical characters: The Popular Jock, The Cruel Girl, The Token Black Guy. (The latter's function was to interject "Damn!" or "That's wack!" as needed.) The tone can be gauged by its setting as "John Hughes High School." John Hughes was the director of *The Breakfast Club* (1985), the detention hall of which was re-created with the same actor as the principal and a Judd Nelson look-alike. A scene from *Varsity Blues* (1999), in which blonde Ari Larter offered herself as a human sundae with whipped cream over her crotch and breasts (with cherries for nipples), was re-gendered with Chris Evans, who made himself into a banana split with a banana-shaped dildo sticking out like an erect penis from his whipped-cream-swathed buttocks.

The core of the film is a parody/remake of *She's All That* (1999), in which a high school star dumped by his girlfriend bets that he can turn any girl into the prom queen. He fastens on a klutzy girl, Laney, who trips on the stairs. In classic Hollywood "You're beautiful without your glasses" tradition, the nerdy girl (Rachel Leigh Cook) is delicately attractive and would be the best-looking female in the room in most real-life situations. Laney is successfully made over in what she calls "*Pretty Woman* without the hooker part," but is crushed when she learns that she was "just a bet."

The parody version turns Laney into Janey and makes her taller. At the film's end, Janey is stopped at the airport by the popular jock who tries to win her back saying, "I made that bet before I really knew you, before I knew myself." An airline employee (former teen star Molly Ringwald in a gag cameo) announces over the P.A. system, "Please tell me that you didn't just quote Freddie Prinze, Jr." Janey identifies the line as from *She's All That*: "I masturbate to that movie." (She did, earlier, with a comically large vibrating dildo that ended up implanted in her birthday cake.)

At the opposite end of the scale and in a class by themselves are the films of Larry Clark. Even before the opening credits of *Kids* (1995), a teenage boy, Telly, successfully coaxes a 12-year-old girl to give up her virginity. (The actress was actually 18.) We find out later that he is HIV-positive. He appears to come from an affluent background. Although his mother says she has no money to give him, they live in a townhouse in Manhattan. Through the skateboard culture, he becomes involved with a group of street kids—black, white, Latino—from different socioeconomic levels.

Although the film has the raw look of a documentary, it was completely scripted by 18-year-old Harmony Korine. Some of the dialogue in the party scenes was improvised by the actors. The film contrasts the way boys and girls (separately) talk about sex, although the difference is not as great as might be expected. One boy says that "girls like it all romantic and shit." Among the girls, one sticks up for "foreplay, foreplay," while another argues for "hard-core pound fucking." A third says, "That's the only way to do it…. Boom, boom, boom." They come to agree that "there's a difference between making love, sex and fucking," but, whatever you call it, "it's the best thing, nothing better."

Like James Joyce's *Ulysses*, the story takes place in one 24-hour period. Telly has his sights on a 13-year-old girl. Sixteen-year-old Jenny (Chloë Sevigny in her first film) finds out that she is HIV-positive even though she only had sex once, the previous summer, with Telly. Her 17-year-old friend (Rosario Dawson, also in her first film) tests negative even though she admits to sex with "eight or nine" guys and several episodes of anal.

12. Girls' Trip 193

Rosario Dawson (left) and Chloë Sevigny launched their professional acting careers as teenagers in Larry Clark's *Kids*, in which their characters frankly expressed their sexual preferences. Miramax.

Jenny tries to find Telly and tracks him down at a party, where he practices his *modus operandi* on the 13-year-old, his second conquest in one day; he tells her that he loves her, it won't hurt, etc. Jenny comes in as he deflowers the girl and backs away. Jenny passes out from the drugs she took earlier at a downtown club. Telly's friend Casper rapes Jenny in her sleep. Presumably, all now have AIDS.

Kids was intended to shock and it did, with images of young teens smoking dope, drinking and having sex. Boys as young as 11 joked about blow jobs. A black man was beaten nearly to death with a skateboard during a turf fight in the park. For all of the movie's vaunted realism, the AIDS part seemed contrived. The AIDS crisis mostly affected adults, typically gay men caught up in the backroom and bathhouse culture of the 1970s. By the mid–90s, the City of New York had been pushing AIDS awareness for almost a decade. (Larry Clark compared the AIDS plot to the shark in *Jaws*.) Although the performers were nonprofessionals, some went on to acting careers, most notably Chloë Sevigny with a by-now long list of movie and television credits.

Clark's *Ken Park* (2002) takes place in California in a lower-middle-class milieu that contrasts with the affluence of *American Pie*'s Long Beach. Ken Park is not a place but a person: the title character who makes a video of himself at the skateboard rink and blows his brains out on camera. The most normal teen is introduced performing cunnilingus, in close-up, on his girlfriend's MILF-y mother. The most alienated boy performs an act of autoasphyxiation. He masturbates and ejaculates on camera. Later, as the result of an argument over a Scrabble game, he will stab his grandparents to death in their beds. Another boy is sexually abused by his father and runs away from home. A young Latina is discovered by her religious fanatic father having sex with her boyfriend. The boy is beaten. Later the father will dress the girl in the wedding dress of her late mother, whom she resembles, and she will be put through a grotesque "marriage" ceremony.

In the final scene, there is a threesome with the Latina, the cunnilinguist and the boy runaway. One penetrates the girl from behind while she performs oral on the other. She will have intercourse with, and give head to, each boy separately and allow herself to be fingered. She is clearly shown taking both penises into her mouth. (Although they are supposed to be 16, the actress was 22 and the boys 18 and 19.)

The man-hungry female has been a comedy standby since Myrna Loy in *Love Me Tonight* in 1932 and the soubrettes in early talkie musicals. In *Wedding Crashers* (2005), Gloria (Isla Fisher) pursues Vince Vaughn. She tells Vaughn, "I always knew my first time would be on a beach." He is taken aback. Later she tells him, "I'm not wearing any panties." She strokes his crotch and asks, "Where is my little friend?" While nude, she ties him up in bed. Before she tapes a sock to his mouth, he protests: "You were attached to me because I took your virginity." She replies, "I wasn't really a virgin. Far from it. I just thought that's what guys want to hear." Afterward, he suggests taking their relationship to new level, to which she responds, "Do you want to see me with a girl?" He meant that they should get engaged. They marry.

Traditionally, men have gained status from sex while women have seen their reputations tarnished. In comedies of the *Porky's/American Pie* type, male virginity is a stigma that must be erased at the earliest opportunity. It's still "different for girls," but the double standard has eroded. A British survey conducted in 2010–12 found that 42 percent of women regretted the circumstances under which they lost their virginity, while only 20 percent of men did.[3] While chastity is not yet completely devalued, raunchy sex comedies can now have female protagonists. Some are even directed by women.

The To Do List (2013), written and directed by Maggie Carey, was set in her hometown of Boise, Idaho, in the 1990s. Aubrey Plaza plays a high school valedictorian who faces college innocent of sexual experience. She makes a list and applies herself with the same single-minded determination that made her a top student. A check mark appears on-screen as each goal is met. She gives a hand job in a movie theater and allows herself to be fingered. With her face in close-up, she gives detailed direction to a boy who wants to perfect his skills at cunnilingus. His little brother picks an inopportune time to come in. She has her first intercourse in a parked car. She performs oral sex on a grunge rocker in a shower stall and ends up with a mouthful of semen. Finally, she is interrupted in anal sex by her father who admonishes, "Not the back door!"

The To Do List was not a success. Perhaps there is safety in numbers, as sex comedy seems to fare best with multiple protagonists. Nearly two decades after *American Pie*, Universal released *Blockers* (2018). Three high school girls, friends since childhood, make a pact to lose their virginity on prom night. As with the earlier film, things don't go entirely as planned. The girl who initiated the pact reports to her friends that intercourse hurt a bit at first and was over quickly but she still rated the experience as "perfect." A second girl only went as far as receiving oral sex. The third came out to her friends as a lesbian and was embraced by them. The title refers to the intervention of the girls' parents, one mother and two fathers. Their efforts turn out to be ineffectual and ultimately superfluous. Another mother who presumably speaks for the film's female director, Kay Cannon, dissents. She argues against the double standard and she asserts that girls have the same right to decide their sexuality as boys.

One subgenre of the raunchy buddy comedy features an ensemble of adult women

Aubrey Plaza, a nerd in high school, plots her sexual future in *The To Do List*. By the time she is through, she will have explored every anatomical possibility, each with a different partner. CBS Films.

who reunite to recapture their younger days. In Lucia Aniello's *Rough Night* (2017), a woman (Jillian Bell) organizes a bachelorette party for her best friend from college (Scarlett Johansson), now a candidate for office who must keep a squeaky-clean image. Bell orders the man she mistakes for a hired stripper, "Fuck her!" She jumps the man herself and causes him to hit his head and die.

Girls Trip (2017) featured four African American actresses. Tiffany Haddish demonstrates to Jada Pinkett Smith how to deal with a man who has a large penis. She uses a banana encircled by a grapefruit with the ends sliced off and the center reamed out. "You want to squeeze and twist and suck so then it feels like he's getting fucked and sucked all at the same time."

In recent years, virginity loss has been regularly depicted on-screen, sometimes graphically. With *The Dreamers* (2003), Bernardo Bertolucci tried to put himself back at the head of the parade he once led. In 1968 Paris, a twin brother and sister befriend an American student. They go to the Cinematheque and get caught up in street protests. The girl, Eva Green, affects the look and manner of Jeanne Moreau in *Jules and Jim* but she is not as sophisticated as she pretends. When she has sex with the American, it turns out she is a virgin and he has the blood on his fingers to prove it.

In *The Fault in Our Stars* (2014), cancer patients Hazel and Augustus make out in Anne Frank's room to improbable applause from the other visitors. Back at the hotel, there is some fumbling with the cannulas that she takes off and puts aside before removing her bra. They lie entwined in bed. He awakes to find her gone. She has left him a thank-you note with the word "Virgins" inside a circle. An arrow points to a dot on the circle that reads. "18 year old dudes w. one leg." (In the book, it's 17 years.)

If the movies are to be believed, the daughters of Jewish liberals from the Upper West Side of Manhattan treat virginity loss casually. In *Anesthesia* (2015), adolescent sex is actually initiated by the girl who tells her boyfriend, "I think I'm ready. This weekend, my parents will be away." The boy's sister tells their parents that her absent brother is losing his virginity: "He did a risk assessment and the benefits outweigh the potential negatives." During the act, the girl nods her head to signal a readiness for penetration that she marks with a little grunt. After the boy ejaculates, they both laugh.

In Kenneth Lonergan's acclaimed *Margaret* (2011), a bored Lisa Cohen (Anna Paquin) calls up a classmate to ask, "Would you like to meet somewhere and take away my virginity?" She puts on a black dress as she awaits his arrival. He tries to reassure her: "It's basically like the world's greatest activity but it's not worth getting nervous about." He initiates cunnilingus; she is embarrassed but volunteers to do oral sex on him. A brief indication of fellatio ends with a cut. He is obviously experienced. "Are you ready?" "Yeah." "It's probably gonna hurt a little at first but then it will get better. Try to relax." She quietly says "I love you," but he doesn't hear. He pre-ejaculates as the condom slips off. "Did any of it get inside me?" she worries. The scene, dimly lit and mostly in silhouette, may be the most realistic depiction of first-time sex.

In Greta Gerwig's popular *Lady Bird* (2017), Saoirse Ronan, a senior in a Catholic high school, asks her mother when is the best time to lose her virginity. The mother says "in college," but Lady Bird does not wait. Again, it's the girl who takes the initiative. Her virginity loss occasions no regrets but is nothing special either. The boy climaxes and she doesn't. The experience is further diminished when she finds out that he's had sex with six other girls.

Laura M. Carpenter, who literally wrote the book on the subject, *Virginity Lost* published in 2005, gave a presentation at Vanderbilt University, where she is an associate professor of sociology. In it, she traced the evolution of virginity loss in movies.[4] In her first example, *Where the Boys Are* from 1960, virginity loss occurred in college and was traumatic for Yvette Mimieux. (Good girl Dolores Hart held out and was rewarded with a marriage proposal.) By the early 1980s, virginity loss took place in high school. It was still mostly negative. Kristy McNichol in *Little Darlings* experienced disappointment and Jennifer Jason Leigh in *Fast Times at Ridgemont High* experienced both disappointment and an unwanted pregnancy. By the time of 1999's *American Pie*, virginity loss carries no ill effects. It is also contingent on female pleasure. One character tells another that if you don't have an orgasm, why bother losing your virginity?

Carpenter wrestled with the term "virginity loss." Most of the women in her research did not feel that they had lost anything. Rather, they gained entry into a world of grown-up experience, something they saw as a natural step. Feminist scholars argue that virginity is not a physical state but a social construct that serves the interests of the patriarchy and needs to be ditched.

According to Gallup's 2018 Values and Beliefs Survey, a majority still disapproves of teen sex by a margin of 54 to 42, but that is the smallest gap since the question was first asked in 2013. Adults over 65 are the most negative. For the youngest respondents, aged 18 to 29, a majority (59 percent) finds teen sex acceptable.[5]

If attitudes have become more liberal, there is some evidence that actual behavior has become more conservative. Teen sex appears to have peaked in the 1980s and early 1990s. According to the Centers for Disease Control's Youth Risk Survey of high schoolers, the median age of first-time sex went up to almost 18 between 1995 and 1997. In the age of *American Pie*, the average teen graduated high school a virgin.[6]

As the American feature film moved into its second century, a good case could be made that the best movies were not movies at all but the better television shows. Larger budgets and longer shooting schedules still gave theatrical features the edge visually, but even that may not be true much longer. Netflix's *The Crown* and *Babylon Berlin* have cinematography and production values on par with the films of Kubrick, Spielberg and David Lean. People watch Amazon's *The Marvelous Mrs. Maisel* just for the art direction and costumes.

Premium cable can also rival movies when it comes to sexuality. HBO, in particular, has pushed the limits. One episode of *Girls* began with a shot of Allison Williams receiving analingus while bent over a stove. The final episode of season five had an epic apartment-destroying fight between Adam Driver and Jemima Kirke that ended with makeup sex and a high-angle shot that showed both exhausted and Kirke naked from the waist down. In HBO's *Hung*, the teacher-turned-gigolo (Thomas Jane) meets the demanding Lenore (Rebecca Creskoff) and she coaches him in stimulation: "Fingers *and* tongue." *True Detective* offered women willing to enact male fantasies. In the first season, a fortyish Woody Harrelson has some extramarital business with a bosomy court clerk who exposes her beautiful body front and back and handcuffs him before performing oral sex. An ex-prostitute who had given him a freebie comes to orgasm. She calls him up with offer of anal sex. "I think I want you to fuck me in the ass. I've never done it before but I think I want to do it with you."

HBO's smaller rival Showtime offered *Californication* that somehow managed to stretch into seven seasons its saga of a New York novelist transplanted to Los Angeles. Not since William Shatner in the original *Star Trek* found outer space to be populated by many of the most attractive actresses in 1960s Hollywood has the leading actor in a series encountered so many gorgeous women. Every episode had nudity, simulated sex and frank dialogue about sex acts and body parts. It was all improbable, but, then, the show was intended as comedy. Writers apparently like to think that writers are irresistible to women. In Showtime's *The Affair*, a novelist (Dominic West) has to deal with the wife who becomes an ex-wife, the mistress who becomes his new wife and the female professor he meets through a teaching gig. The nonlinear structure combined with multiple viewpoints showed an aspiration to take television to the level of serious literary fiction.

Epilogue

The Reckoning
Weinstein and the #MeToo Movement

On October 5, 2017, *The New York Times* ran a story that charged sexual harassment on the part of producer Harvey Weinstein under the byline of Jodi Kantor and Megan Twohey. Five days later an article appeared in *The New Yorker* by Ronan Farrow that alleged rape. (Kantor, Twohey and Farrow would win the Pulitzer Prize for Public Service journalism.)

French actress Léa Seydoux, costar of *Blue Is the Warmest Color*, revealed how Weinstein attempted to jump her in his hotel room: "He's big and fat so I had to be forceful to resist him."[1] She continued, "Everyone knew what Harvey was up to and no one did anything. It's unbelievable that he has been able to act like this for decades and still keep his career. That's only possible because he has a huge amount of power."

That Weinstein's behavior was an open secret was shown at the 2013 Academy Awards when host Seth MacFarlane, onstage with Emma Stone to present the Oscar for Best Supporting Actress, quipped, "Congratulations, you five ladies no longer have to pretend to be attracted to Harvey Weinstein." Viewers at home were likely mystified but everybody in the Dolby Theatre seemed to get the joke.

Weinstein was expelled from the Academy of Motion Picture Arts and Sciences after the two articles appeared, only the second person in its history to be so punished. The following year, Bill Cosby and Roman Polanski would be expelled also. (In September 2018, Cosby would be found guilty on three counts of aggravated sexual assault and sentenced to three to 10 years in prison, the first celebrity defendant to be convicted in the post–Weinstein era for sexual misconduct.)

Tarana Burke, a social activist, used the phrase "MeToo" on the MySpace social network in 2006 to call attention to sexual abuse against women of color. On October 15, 2017, after the Weinstein stories appeared, actress Alyssa Milano encouraged the use of #MeToo to share experiences of sexual harassment and assault.

In an op-ed for *The New York Times* in December 2017, Salma Hayek revealed that Weinstein forced her to incorporate a nude scene in *Frida* for his gratification.[2] The scene in question occurs when Frida Kahlo picks up a black female singer-dancer (unidentified but presumably Josephine Baker) at a nightclub in Paris. The scene has Hayek frontally nude and two shots of Hayek and the singer entwined, both fully nude.

Ashley Judd brought suit against Weinstein in April 2018. She claimed that he defamed her and damaged her career when he told Peter Jackson, director of *The Lord of the Rings* trilogy, that she was a horror to work with.

The Weinstein Company, in bankruptcy, was sold to Lantern Capital in July 2018.

In a twist of poetic justice, the Weinstein story may itself become a movie. The rights to Kantor and Twohey's reportage of Weinstein was acquired by Plan B Films, a partnership of Brad Pitt, Dede Gardner and Jeremy Kleiner, responsible for the Best Picture Oscar winners *12 Years a Slave* (2013) and *Moonlight* (2016). The picture is expected to resemble *Spotlight* (2015), the exposé of child molestation in the Boston archdiocese by a *Boston Globe* team. A documentary about Weinstein, *Untouchable*, premiered in January 2019 at the Sundance Film Festival, where he was once second only to Robert Redford as a presence.

In January 2018, the Screen Actors Guild Awards served as the coming out party for the Time's Up campaign, a legal defense fund for working women. The nominees and presenters eschewed the usual gowns for all-black attire. Debra Messing, on the red carpet, used the E! Network's own microphone to protest E's underpayment of women. Natalie Portman pointedly presented the Best Director nominees as "all male."

In March 2018, an event on sexual exploitation and harassment was hosted by *Guardian* columnist Polly Toynbee as part of a two-week United Nations Commission on the Status of Women in New York. Actress Sienna Miller in her speech stated, "For me, the strongest significance of the Time's Up movement is that, by bringing to light the darkest moments of some of the most powerful women in Hollywood, it sends a message.... This message is that sexual harassment happens to everyone, even those who we think are untouchable because of their fame or celebrity status."

At the 90th Academy Awards in March, audiences got to hear Ashley Judd invoke "intersectionality," a buzzword of campus social justice warriors that refers to the dual oppression of women and minorities. Best Actress Oscar winner Frances McDormand further puzzled viewers when she called for an "inclusion rider." (An inclusion rider is a provision in a contract that calls for a certain level of diversity in the cast and crew.)

At the 2018 Cannes Film Festival, in early May, 82 women climbed the steps of the Palais des Festivals in a red carpet protest for gender equity in the film industry. The number 82 represented the number of female filmmakers who were selected to compete at Cannes over the festival's seven-decade history. In contrast, there were 1,866 films directed by men. Among the stars and film industry professionals who participated were Salma Hayek and Jane Fonda, *Wonder Woman* director Patty Jenkins and French director Agnès Varda. Also joining were the five female directors of the jury: chairperson Cate Blanchett, Kristen Stewart, Ava DuVernay, French actress Léa Seydoux and Burundian singer Khadja Nin.[3]

On the closing night of the festival, actress Asia Argento told how she was raped by Harvey Weinstein at the 1997 festival when she was 21 years old. "This festival was his hunting ground," she said. Argento was supported by Rose McGowan, who had also accused Weinstein of rape, and Mira Sorvino, who claimed Weinstein sexually harassed her and attempted to force her into a physical relationship. (Argento herself has since been accused of molesting a 17-year-old boy.)

On May 25, 2018, Weinstein surrendered to the New York City police to be charged with rape in the first degree, rape in the third degree and committing a criminal sexual act in the first degree. (One of the six charges was later dropped.) He was released on bail. His lawyer, Benjamin Brafman, said. "Mr. Weinstein did not invent the casting couch in Hollywood." That was true, albeit not much of a defense.

As far back as 1914, *Variety* reported: "In one New York studio it is asserted that no woman can work in that particular place unless countenancing the advances of "the boss," who has nothing to recommend himself to female fancy excepting an official position."[4]

It went both ways. According to Marjorie Rosen, D.W. Griffith was careful of his reputation:

> He would rarely interview a girl without a third party present, and with good reason. Tales were rife of executives hounded by desperate women seeking relief from menial labor and drab routines. Occasionally, one of these girls would corner a producer or director and insist he give her a movie role. If he refused, she cried rape.[5]

Former ingénue Esther Ralston was no longer a major star when she was hired for the second female lead in a Joan Crawford vehicle, *Sadie McKee*, at M-G-M in 1934. In her autobiography, she told how she was summoned to the office of Louis B. Mayer, who wanted sexual favors and issued the classic ultimatum: "I'll blackball you in every studio in Hollywood, and what's more you'll get nothing here."

He didn't quite do that. He sold her contract to Universal, then a second-tier studio. She had leads in some Poverty Row pictures, even a serial. At Paramount, where she had been a top star, she got fifth billing in a "B" picture, *Hollywood Boulevard* (1936). At the end of her movie career, she finally landed an "A" picture at Fox, in the sixth-billed supporting role as singer Nora Bayes in *Tin Pan Alley* (1940).

In her autobiography *Child Star*, Shirley Temple claimed that producer Arthur Freed exposed himself to her at M-G-M, where she would make *Kathleen* (1941). She was only 12. While Temple was in Freed's office, his boss, Louis B. Mayer, attempted to seduce her mother.

According to Elia Kazan in his memoirs, producers had a simple standard for female talent: "Do I want to fuck her?"

A *USA Today* survey in 2018 of 843 women in the entertainment industry found that 94 percent said they had experienced sexual harassment or assault. This included: unwelcome sexual comments, jokes or gestures (94 percent); being touched in a sexual way (69 percent); propositioned for a sexual act/relationship (64 percent); someone flashing/exposing themselves (29 percent); being forced to do a sexual act (21 percent); and ordered unexpectedly to appear naked for auditions (10 percent).[6]

An article in *The Economist* stated:

> Male actors command about twice the screen time of female ones. Men are the heroes and villains and do most of the talking, with (at the last count) two-thirds of speaking parts in successful films, a ratio only slightly better than in the late 1940s. Women, still are often ornaments or victims, love interests or damsels in distress, useful for being disrobed, attacked or both.[7]

The figures came from a study by the Geena Davis Institute on Gender in Media that found that in the 100 highest-grossing live-action films of 2014 and 2015, men appeared on the screen for twice as long as women and spoke for twice as long.[8]

Women actually lost ground in 2017.[9] According to the "Celluloid Ceiling," an annual study by the Center for the Study of Women in Television & Film at San Diego State University, women accounted for 24 percent of protagonists in the 100 top-grossing domestic films of 2017, a decrease of five percentage points from the year before.

On the plus side, more women had speaking roles in those films, accounting for 34 percent of such characters, up two percentage points from the year before. The percentage of major female characters at 37 percent was unchanged.

A more extensive study of inequality in 1,100 popular films by USC Annenberg found female characters (28.4%) were far more likely than male characters (7.5%) to be shown in tight or alluring apparel, and with some nudity (M = 9.6%, F = 24.4%). Females 13–20 years old were just as likely as females 21–39 years old to appear in sexy attire or with some nudity.[10]

The Annenberg study also found "a total of 1,584 individuals worked above the line as directors, writers and producers. 81.7% were male, and 18.2% were female. Of 109 directors, only 7.3% were female. Only 10.1% of writers were female and 18.2% of producers."

According to the "Celluloid Ceiling" report of 2018, women accounted for 8 percent of directors, down from 11 percent in 2017 and even lower than the 9 percent achieved in 1998. However, Annenberg found that 40 of the 100 top-grossing films in 2018 had female leads or coleads, an increase of eight from the previous year.

WarnerMedia, acquired by AT&T in June 2018, put out a statement in September 2018 that committed the company to diversity. WarnerMedia includes Warner Bros., HBO and Turner. The statement reads, in part, "we all must ensure that there is a greater inclusion of women, people of color, the LBGTQ+ community, those with disabilities and other underrepresented groups in greater numbers both in front of and behind the camera."[11]

John Stankey, CEO of WarnerMedia, credited the actor and producer Michael B. Jordan, who costars with Brie Larson in the legal drama *Just Mercy* that had just started filming in Atlanta, for helping to craft the policy. Jordan, in turn, said that he was inspired by Frances McDormand's call for "inclusion riders" at the Oscars. (In March 2019, Stankey accepted the resignation of Kevin Tsujihara as CEO of Warner Bros.' studios after he was accused of favoring actress Charlotte Kirk, with whom he had a sexual relationship, for roles.)

To have more women as directors will bring a wider variety of viewpoints (plural). There is no "woman's angle." Greta Gerwig's semiautobiographical *Lady Bird* is arguably a movie that only a woman could have made or would have wanted to make. Conversely, aside from Kathryn Bigelow's name in the credits, there was nothing in *Detroit* or *Zero Dark Thirty* or *The Hurt Locker* that would have would have identified their maker as a woman.

Suzanne Bier, the Danish director of AMC's *The Night Manager* contends:" We are going to see a more complex description of humanity with more female directors. Female characters have for too long been a sort of love interest, a function of a male main character, whether a mother, a daughter, a girl friend." She added:

> There's no doubt that male characters are more nuanced and interesting than female characters. It isn't just from a feminist, political point of view. It's purely from an artistic point of view. It's just plain boring that women are not allowed to more exciting…. They can be less likable, as long as they're more interesting.

Many support Bier's call for greater and more varied representation of women, but Bier has also taken diversity in a direction that has run into predictable resistance."-Looks are more a taboo than gender or race. If I suggest actors or actresses with unusual looks, I have a much harder time getting them through than anyone else."[12]

Although they may not come out and admit that a particular person is not attractive enough, there is an underlying assumption on the part of the studios that audiences want to look at attractive people.

In December 2018, the Creative Artists Agency (CAA) and tech company shift7 announced the findings of research that examined the correlation of female-led films and box-office success. CAA and shift7 came together through Time's Up and a working group headed by former Sony pictures chairman Amy Pascal that seeks to improve the portrayal of women in media.

The analysis used box-office performance and production data for 350 top-grossing films released between 2017 and 2017. In every budget-level category, films with female leads performed better in worldwide box-office averages.

The analysis also found that films that passed the "Bechdel Test" outperformed films that failed. The "Bechdel Test," created by cartoonist Alison Bechdel, has three criteria: (1) the film has to have at least two women in it; (2) the women speak to one another in the film; and (3) they speak about something other than a man. The research showed that every film that surpassed $1 billion in worldwide gross passed the "Bechdel test."[13]

Patty Jenkins's *Wonder Woman* was the third highest-grossing film of 2017 and the highest-grossing film ever for a female director. Hollywood had been dubious that a female lead could carry an action film. *Supergirl* (1984) with Helen Slater made only a tenth of what the Christopher Reeve *Superman* (1978) grossed and earned even less than the weakest of them, the widely derided *Superman IV: The Quest for Peace* (1987). *Red Sonja* (1985) disappointed even with Arnold Schwarzenegger billed above Brigitte Nielsen in a role subordinate to hers. When producer Nora Jacobson pitched *The Hunger Games* as a possible new franchise, studios passed because the lead was a girl. "I was taught as though it were a common-knowledge truth that girls will identify with a male protagonist, but boys will not identify with a female protagonist," she says. She took the project to Lionsgate, a smaller studio, for whom it became a big hit and made Jennifer Lawrence a major star. A worldwide gross of nearly $600 million could not be gainsaid.

Some of the premiere screenings of *Wonder Woman* were announced as women-only. This was a technical violation of the 1964 Civil Rights Act, under which movie theaters are "public accommodations," so men's rights activists tried to crash them.

Although Wonder Woman was on the cover of the first issue of *Ms.* magazine in 1972, she is a rather ambiguous feminist icon. She is strong and courageous but must also be a sexual fantasy for men. The main, nay only, reason to watch the cheesy 1970s television show was the way Lynda Carter filled out the Wonder Woman costume. Her measurements were listed as 37-25-36, comparable to the Hollywood bombshells of the 1940s and '50s. The new Wonder Woman, Gal Gadot, is beautiful, although there has been some grumbling by men that her breasts are not large enough. (Her measurements are a slender 34-23-34.) In the original comic books, written by Wonder Woman's creator Dr. William Marston, there was an inordinate emphasis on bondage. Dr. Frederic Wertham, whose 1954 *Seduction of the Innocent* decried the sinister influence of comic books on the young, pointed to the image of a woman chained or tied up with rope as a classic sadist's fantasy. The controversy is depicted in *Professor Marston and the Wonder Women* (2017), itself the work of a female director.

The #MeToo era has put pin-up culture on the defensive. *Love*, the British fashion magazine, put its advent video calendar online in December 2017. In a video, directed by Phil Poynter, Emily Ratajkowski writhed suggestively while eating spaghetti in lacy bra and panties. "I love pasta and being greased up in olive oil more than life itself," she was quoted as saying in the video. Addressing the fine line between exploitation and empowerment, Ratajkowski stated, "In the wake of the Harvey fallout and women coming forward with incredible amounts of sexual harassment cases, I have been so disap-

Israeli actress Gal Gadot was *Wonder Woman*, the highest-grossing movie from a female director. Warner Bros.

pointed to hear women talk about 'modesty' and 'our responsibility,' as if we need to, yet again, adjust to make it 'easier' for the rest of the world. I want to do what I want to do."[14]

Even the *Sports Illustrated* swimsuit calendar was forced to change. The 2018 edition added a feature photo shoot in austere black and white, "In Her Own Words," commissioned by a female editor with a female photographer and an all-female crew. As described by Alexandra Schwartz in *The New Yorker*:

> "In Her Own Words" does not feature models wearing swimsuits, but, rather, nude models whose bare flesh has been painted with descriptive words of their own choosing. The model Robin Lawley [had] "MOTHER" printed across her collarbone, "LOVER" down her chest, "NURTURER" on an arm, "CREATIVE" across her inner thigh, "PROGRESSIVE" on a leg, and "HUMAN" just above her pubis.[15]

The Victoria's Secret fashion show has seen its ratings decline to the point where the 2018 edition may the last to be televised. The event has come under attack for the lack of diversity in body types.

In an article for *The New Yorker*, Molly Ringwald, star of three John Hughes teen classics from the 1980s, wrote that she now found elements of those films disturbing, especially as the mother of a teen daughter herself.[16] In *The Breakfast Club*, Judd Nelson looked up her dress and saw her panty-covered crotch. (She was doubled by an adult actress.) That film contained the much-quoted lines spoken by Ally Sheedy in response to a sexual inquiry from a boy: "Well, if you say you haven't, you're a prude. If you say you have, you're a slut. It's a trap."

In *Sixteen Candles* (1984), Ringwald's character, Samantha, is a gawky sophomore who has a crush on senior Jake Ryan, the dreamboat every girl wants. Surprisingly, he reciprocates her interest, even though he has a beautiful blonde girl friend, Caroline. When Caroline gets drunk at a party and passes out, Jake hands her over to a character called The Geek and tells him to "Have fun." When they wake up in the morning in Jake's expensive car, The Geek has the other boys take Polaroids of him with the passed out girl as evidence of his conquest and they hail him, saying, "You're a legend!" That she would never have had sex with an unpopular boy if she had been sober is presented as a joke. Ringwald noted that, essentially, Jake traded his girlfriend for a pair of Samantha's underwear, given by her to The Geek when she felt sorry for his lack of success with girls.

After the confirmation hearings for Brett Kavanaugh to be a Supreme Court Justice, Constance Grady in *Vox* used *Sixteen Candles* to explain the rape culture of the 1980s:

> Girls who drink are asking for it.... Whatever happens to that kind of girl as a result is funny.
> Boys are owed girls. A good guy will help his nerdy bro get a girl. Her consent is not necessary or desired.
> A good guy can participate in this whole system and remained an unsullied dream guy.
> The kind of girl who gets raped has no right to complain about what happens to her.[17]

Wesley Morris in *The New York Times* further connected the ethos of male entitlement in Kavanaugh's high school and college years to the movies of the 1980s:

> In stories envisioned by grown men, boys in movies—smart-ass, horny, fun loving white boys—had it made. They ran brothels (*Risky Business*); punked the principal (*Ferris Bueller's Day Off*); battled the school psycho (*Three O'Clock High*); committed all kinds of battery (*Revenge of the Nerds*); excelled, albeit brutally at juvenile detention (*Bad Boys*); combed the Caribbean for a family vacation (*Hot Pursuit*); invented women to boost their popularity (*Weird Science*); turned into werewolf jocks (*Teen Wolf*); and lied about passing their driving test (*License to Drive*), being a finance executive (*The Secret of My Success*), being cool (*Can't Buy Me Love*) or being black (*Soul Man*).[18]

The girls in most of these were there to be ogled and spied upon. The goal was to get them to bed, not so much because they were so desirable, but to be able to brag to male friends. Kavanaugh himself cited *Animal House, Caddyshack* and *Fast Times* as influences in his high school yearbook.

The #MeToo movement has forced Hollywood to rethink the way sex scenes are negotiated and filmed. HBO hired Alicia Rodis for the position of "intimacy coordinator" for its series *The Deuce* after actress Emily Meade expressed discomfort at having to perform an oral sex scene in front of a crew of people. In October 2018, HBO that there would be an "intimacy coordinator" on all sex scenes.

Actors want better protection and more control both before and after scenes are shot. The issues involve actors, usually actresses, who are pressured to do something that was not negotiated before shooting began. A director might tell an actress to drop a towel, and because it's late at night, and everyone wants to go home, she gives in. In an article for *The Hollywood Reporter*, deputy film editor Tatiana Siegel described the increased use of "nudity riders."[19] The key provisions of a typical "nudity rider" might read something like this:

> 1. The simulated sex scene shall be in accordance with the screenplay as approved by the Artist. There shall be no nudity even if nudity is implied.
> 2. The Artist has an absolute right to an on-set change of heart.

3. The set will be closed to all persons not absolutely necessary for the photography of the scene.

4. No camera will be on the set except for the camera used for the scene. The will be no still cameras, Polaroids or camera-enabled cell phones.

5. No images from the sex scene, including nonphotographic likenesses, shall be used in trailers, stills or posters.

6. The use of a body double must be approved by the Artist and the Artist will have approval over the selection of the body double.

7. Dailies of a simulated sex scene may only be viewed by the Artist, the director, the producer and key personnel whose presence in essential. A written record of the persons present is to be kept and furnished to Artist upon request. No video copies may be made.

Established performers with good lawyers can negotiate provisions that specify how many inches of "gluteal cleft," i.e., butt crack, can be shown. Newcomers are more subject to exploitation. A story January 2018 in the *Los Angeles Times* reported that actor James Franco removed the protective clear plastic vaginal shields from student actresses as he simulated performing oral sex on them in the filming of an orgy scene in the indie drama *The Long Home*.[20]

Perhaps nudity clauses were the reason Rachel Weisz and Rachel McAdams kept their bras on during a sex scene in *Disobedience* (2018), a drama about a lesbian relationship between Orthodox Jewish women. We were back in 1960 when Janet Leigh kept her bra on in a nooner with John Gavin in *Psycho*.

Increasingly, lesbian dramas are directed by women and they do not primarily aim to excite men.

Ellen Page and Kate Mara starred in *My Days of Mercy* (2017) as two women on opposite sides of death-row politics who fall in love. In *Lizzie* (2018), Lizzie Borden (Chloë Sevigny) murders her father and stepmother, partly because the father has molested the housemaid (Kristen Stewart) with whom Lizzie herself has a relationship.

Writer-director Jacquie Lawrence, whose novel *Different for Girls* follows a group of lesbian and bisexual women though their lives, says, "I believe the gaze of a lesbian or bisexual woman director is completely different to the gaze of a straight man."[21]

It's possible for a male director to make a movie that meets with approval from lesbians. Writer-director Stephen Cone, who made the coming-of-age story *Princess Cyd* (2017), sought the advice of gay women. Lawrence says, "If the director is not a lesbian or a bisexual woman, then there have to be lesbian sex consultants on the set."

Tell It to the Bees (2018) presents a love affair between two young women in rural Scotland in the 1950s. In *The Miseducation of Cameron Post* (2018), a girl is sent to a Christian gay conversion camp where she is brought to orgasm by a roommate and, in flashback, remembers her first sexual explorations with her best friend.

Lawrence says, "We have to get over the coming-out sex. I really don't want to watch teenage girls having their first sexual experience. We need to represent older lesbians having sex."

One film that does that is *Vita & Virginia* (2018). It tells how, under the influence of her cross-dressing muse, Vita Sackville-West, Virginia Woolf came to write *Orlando*. (The main character in *Orlando* was both an Elizabethan nobleman and a modern woman three centuries later; Sally Potter directed a 1992 film version that starred Tilda

Swinton.) Director Chanya Button says, "Sex is powerful and interesting and shows human beings at their most vulnerable, but it must always be justified in its detailed approach." She stated that she did not ask herself, "What's hot? What do I imagine two women to do to each other that can titillate an audience?"[22]

Jill Soloway, creator of the Amazon series *I Love Dick*, said of the Chris Kraus novel on which the show is based, "Some people think of this book as the invention of the female gaze in literature."[23]

After his star and girlfriend, the Playmate Dorothy Stratten, was murdered, director Peter Bogdanovich blamed Hugh Hefner and the *Playboy* ethos. In a book, *The Killing of the Unicorn*, he wrote that when women are presented as passive receptacles of male pleasure, what trivializes them can also kill them. He asserted that the real purpose of the Sexual Revolution was to make women available to men. Perhaps so, but as Georges Danton, Leon Trotsky and many others have learned, revolutions have consequences not envisioned by those who initiate them. It was not possible to expand sexual freedom for men without granting it to women. For women, freedom included freedom from harassment and the right to refuse male demands.

As Phoebe Maltz Bovy wrote at the time of the revelations about Weinstein, "Any system that values extreme youth and physical attractiveness winds up being awful, in different ways **for all women**."[24]

Chapter Notes

Prologue

1. Elspeth H. Brown, "Racializing the Virile Body: Eadweard Muybridge's Locomotion Studies, 1883–1887," *Gender and History*, Vol. 17, No. 3, November 2005, pp. 1–30.
2. Rebecca Solnit, *River of Shadows: Eadweard Muybridge and the Technological Wild West* (New York: Viking Press, 2003), p. 220.
3. Gordon Hendricks, *The Kinetoscope: America's First Commercially Successful Motion Picture Exhibitor* (New York: The Beginnings of the American Film, 1966), pp. 77–78.
4. Peter N. Stearns, *Fat History: Bodies and Beauty in the Modern West* (New York: New York University Press, 1997), p. 12.
5. Stearns, p. 12.
6. Stearns, p. 22.

Chapter 1

1. Daniel Czitrom, "The Politics of Performance: Theater Licensing and the Origins of Movie Censorship in New York" in Francis G. Couvares, ed., *Movie Censorship and American Culture* (Amherst: University of Massachusetts Press, 1996), p. 22.
2. The members of the Motion Picture Patents Company were Edison, Biograph, Vitagraph, Essanay, Selig Polyscope, Lubin Manufacturing, Star Film Paris, Kalem Company, George Kleine and Pathé.
3. Samantha Barbas, "How the Movies Became Speech," *Rutgers Law Review*, Vol. 64, No. 3, Spring 2012, pp. 684–85.
4. Nellie Bly, "Champion of Her Sex," *New York Sunday World*, February 2, 1896, p. 10.
5. *Variety*, Vol. XXXVI, No. 10, November 7, 1914, p. 23.
6. *Variety*, November 7, 1915.
7. James Bone, *The Curse of Beauty: The Scandulous & Tragic Life of Audrey Munson, America's First Supermodel* (New York: Regan Arts/Simon & Schuster, 2016), p. 144.
8. Mary Beard, "Sex and Death in the Classical World," *New Statesman*, March 2, 2018.

Chapter 2

1. Quoted in Paula S. Fass, *The Damned and the Beautiful: American Youth in the 1920s* (New York: Oxford University Press, 1977), p. 356.
2. Colleen Moore, *Silent Star* (Garden City: Doubleday, 1968), p. 129.
3. Moore, p. 135.
4. David Hajdu, *Love for Sale: Pop Music in America* (New York: Farrar, Straus and Giroux, 2016), pp. 178–9.
5. Ruth Vasey, *The World According to Hollywood, 1918–1939* (Madison: University of Wisconsin Press, 1997), p. 34.
6. Jill Lepore, *These Truths: A History of the United States* (New York: W.W. Norton, 2018), p. 404.
7. Sarah Churchwell, *Behold, America: The Entangled History of "America First" and "the American Dream"* (New York: Basic Books, 2018), p. 134.
8. *Melvin v. Reid*, Cal. App. 285, 289 (1931).
9. Fass, p. 281.
10. William L. O'Neill, *Feminism in America: A History* (New Brunswick: Transaction, 1998), Chapter Nine.

Chapter 3

1. Barbas, p. 701.
2. Moore, p. 123.
3. Joy to Breen, PCA *Possessed* file, December 15, 1931.
4. Rudy Behlmer, *Inside Warner Bros. (1931–1951)* (New York: Viking Penguin, 1985), p. 15.

Chapter 4

1. "How the Flying Tigers Soared to Glory in World War II," *The Daily Beast*, May 27, 2018. Excerpted from *The Flying Tigers: The Untold Story of the American Pilots Who Waged a Secret War Against Japan* by Sam Kleiner (New York: Viking, 2018).
2. Amanda Littauer, "Sex on the Home Front:

Venereal Disease and the Topography of Heterosexuality," *Notches* (blog), April 5, 2016.

Chapter 5

1. Agnes Poirier, *Left Bank: Art, Passion, and the Rebirth of Paris, 1940–50* (New York: Henry Holt, 2018), p. 184.
2. Press release, quoted in Hortense Powdermaker, *Hollywood, the Dream Factory: An Anthropologist Looks at the Movie Makers* (New York: Little, Brown, 1950).
3. "The Robe: The Evil Empire." *An Historian Goes to the Movies* (blog), April 5, 2015.
4. Stephen Silverman, *Dancing on the Ceiling: Stanley Donen and His Movies* (New York: Alfred A. Knopf, 1998), p. 202.

Chapter 6

1. David V. Jervis and Michael Woulfe, *Glamour and Mischief!* (Palm Springs: David V. Jervis, 2015), p. 153.

Chapter 7

1. Maya Salam, "For Online Daters, Women Peak at 18 While Men Peak at 50, Study Finds. Oy," *The New York Times*, August 15, 2018.
2. Ezra Goodman, *The Fifty-Year Decline and Fall of Hollywood* (New York: Simon & Schuster, 1961), p. 284.

Chapter 8

1. Patricia Bosworth, *The Men in My Life: A Memoir of Love and Art in 1950s Manhattan* (New York: HarperCollins, 2017), p. xiv.

Chapter 9

1. Ed Sikov, *On Sunset Boulevard: The Life and Times of Billy Wilder* (New York: Hyperion, 1998), p. 476.
2. Robert L. Surtees, "*The Graduate*'s Photography," *Films in Review*, Vol. XIX, February 1968, p. 91.
3. Jack Vizzard, *See No Evil: Life Inside a Hollywood Censor* (New York: Simon & Schuster, 1996), pp. 336–341.

Chapter 10

1. Yohana Desta, "Inside the Fight to Keep *Fatal Attraction*'s Original Ending," *Vanity Fair*, March 29, 2017.
2. The NC-17 rating quickly acquired the same stigma. After *Henry & June*, there was not another major studio NC-17 release until Paul Verhoeven's widely derided *Showgirls* (1995), with Elizabeth Berkeley and Gina Gershon nearly naked as rival Las Vegas dancers. Since 1968, only 524 movies out of the over 30,000 submitted received an "X" or "NC-17" rating.
3. "National Survey of Sexual Health and Behavior," *The Journal of Sexual Medicine*, October 2010.

Chapter 11

1. Kevin White, "Tainted Love: The Transformation of Oral-Genital Behavior in the United States, 1970–2000," in Peter Stearns, ed., *American Behavioral History: An Introduction* (New York: New York University Press, 2005), pp. 218–22.
2. Helen Lawrenson, "How Now, Fellatio! Why Dost Thou Tarry?" *Esquire*, May 1977.
3. A.J. Bridges, et al., "Aggression and Sexual Behavior in Best-Selling Pornography Videos: A Content Analysis Update," *Violence Against Women*, Vol. 16, No. 10, October 2010.
4. Eran Shor and Kimberly Heida, "Harder and Harder?" *The Journal of Sex Research*, April 18, 2018.
5. Taylor Kohut, et al., "Is Pornography Really about 'Making Hate to Women'?: Pornography Users Hold More Gender Egalitarian Attitudes Than Nonusers in a Representative American Sample," *The Journal of Sex Research*, Vol. 53, No. 1, 2015.
6. Marty Klein, Taylor Kohut and Nicole Prause, "Why Are We Still So Worried About Watching Porn?" *Slate*, July 30, 2018.
7. Jon Millward, "Deep Inside: A Study of 10,000 Porn Stars and Their Careers," jonmillward.com, February 14, 2013.

Chapter 12

1. Amara Bachu, "Trends in Premarital Childbearing: 1930 to 1994," U.S. Census Bureau, October 1999, Table 1.
2. Annie Gottlieb, *Do You Believe in Magic? The Second Coming of the 60's Generation* (New York: Times Books, 1987), p. 239.
3. University College London, "Summary of Results from the 3rd National Survey of Sexual Attitudes and Lifestyles," November 26, 2013.
4. Laura Carpenter, "*American Pie*: Fact or Fiction? A Closer Look at Virginity Loss in the Movies," talk at Vanderbilt University, March 8, 2010.
5. Gallup, Inc., Annual Values and Beliefs Survey, conducted May 1–10, 2018.
6. Centers for Disease Control and Prevention, "Trends in the Prevalence of Sexual Behaviors and HIV Testing National YRBS: 1991–2013," June 2014.

Epilogue

1. Léa Seydoux, "'I had to defend myself': The night Harvey Weinstein jumped on me," *The Guardian*, October 11, 2017.

2. Salma Hayek, "Harvey Weinstein Is My Monster Too," *The New York Times*, December 13, 2017.

3. Jake Coyle, "82 women walk the red carpet in Cannes film fest protest," *The Washington Times*, May 12, 2018.

4. Quoted in Marjorie Rosen, *Popcorn Venus: Women, Movies & the American Dream* (New York: Coward, McCann & Geoghegan, 1973) p. 30.

5. Rosen, p. 30.

6. Maria Puente and Cara Kelly, "How common is sexual misconduct in Hollywood?" *USA Today*, February 23, 2018.

7. "After the fall: The aftermath of the Weinstein scandal," *The Economist*, March 3, 2018.

8. "The Reel Truth: Women Aren't Seen or Heard," Geena Davis Institute on Gender in Media, September 15, 2016.

9. Cara Buckley, "Film Study Finds Number of Female Protagonists Down 5 Percent," *The New York Times*, February 22, 2018.

10. Stacy Smith, et al., "Inequality in 1,100 Popular Films: Examining Portrayals of Gender, Race/Ethnicity, LGBT & Disability from 2007 to 2017," USC Annenberg, July 2018.

11. Cynthia Littleton, "WarnerMedia Unveils Broad Diversity & Inclusion Policy as Michael B. Jordan's 'Just Mercy' Begins Production," *Variety*, September 5, 2018.

12. Dalya Alberge, "Hollywood must drop fixation with beauty, says Night Manager director," *The Guardian*, December 8, 2018.

13. Press release, "Female-Led Films Outperform at All Budget Levels, Per Research from Creative Artists Agency and shift7," Creative Artists Agency/shift7, December 11, 2018.

14. Vanessa Friedman, "Pinups in the Post-Weinstein World," *The New York Times*, November 27, 2017.

15. Alexandra Schwartz, "Sports Illustrated's Spectacularly Silly #MeToo Swimsuit Issue," *The New Yorker*, February 9, 2018.

16. Molly Ringwald, "What About 'The Breakfast Club'?" *The New Yorker*, April 6, 2018.

17. Constance Grady, "The rape culture of the 1980s, explained by Sixteen Candles," *Vox*, September 27, 2018.

18. Wesley Morris, "In '80s Comedies, Boys Had It Made. Girls Were the Joke," *The New York Times*, October 4, 2018.

19. Tatiana Siegel, "The New Politics of Hollywood Sex Scenes in the #MeToo Era," *The Hollywood Reporter*, August 23, 2018.

20. Daniel Miller and Amy Kaufman, "Five women accuse actor James Franco of inappropriate or sexually exploitative behavior," *Los Angeles Times*, January 11, 2018.

21. Anna Smith, "'Oral sex—and no scissoring!' How the lesbian gaze changed cinema," *The Guardian*, August 10, 2018.

22. *Ibid.*

23. Kristopher Tapley, "Jill Soloway's 'I Love Dick' Brings the 'Female Gaze' to Emmy Voters," *Variety*, April 20, 2017.

24. Phoebe Maltz Bovy, "Yes, I guess, all women," *What Would Phoebe Do?* (blog), October 12, 2017.

Bibliography

Books

Afra, Kia. *The Hollywood Trust: Trade Associations and the Rise of the Studio System*. Lanham: Rowman & Littlefield, 2016.

Barrios, Richard. *A Song in the Dark: The Birth of the Musical Film*. New York: Oxford University Press, 1995.

Bazin, André, *What Is Cinema?* Los Angeles: University of California Press, 1967.

Berger, John. *Ways of Seeing*. London: Penguin, 1972.

Bernstein, Matthew, ed. *Controlling Hollywood: Censorship and Regulation in the Studio Era*. New Brunswick: Rutgers University Press, 1999.

Black, Gregory D. *The Catholic Crusade Against the Movies, 1940–1975*. Cambridge: Cambridge University Press, 1998.

_____. *Hollywood Censored: Morality Codes, Catholics, and the Movies*. Cambridge: Cambridge University Press, 1996.

Bone, James. *The Curse of Beauty: The Scandalous & Tragic Life of Audrey Munson, America's First Supermodel*. New York: Regan Arts/Simon & Schuster, 2016.

Brownlow, Kevin. *Behind the Mask of Innocence*. New York: Alfred A. Knopf, 1990.

Campbell, Russell. *Marked Women: Prostitutes and Prostitution in the Cinema*. Madison: University of Wisconsin Press, 2005.

Clarens, Carlos. *Crime Movies: An Illustrated History*. New York: W.W. Norton, 1980.

_____. *An Illustrated History of the Horror Film*. New York: Capricorn Press, 1967.

Clark, Randall. *At a Theater or Drive-In Near You: The History, Culture, and Politics of the American Exploitation Film*. New York: Garland, 1995.

Clover, Carol J. *Men, Women, and Chain Saws: Gender in the Modern Horror Film*. Princeton: Princeton University Press, 1992.

Couvares, Francis G., ed. *Movie Censorship and American Culture*. Amherst: University of Massachusetts Press, 2006.

Doherty, Thomas. *Hollywood Censor: Joseph I. Breen & The Production Code Administration*. New York: Columbia University Press, 2007.

Ernst, Morris L., and Pare Lorentz. *Censored: The Private Life of the Movie*. New York: Jonathan Cape and Harrison Smith, 1930.

Everson, William K. *American Silent Film*. New York: Oxford University Press, 1978.

Eyman, Scott. *Empire of Dreams: The Epic Life of Cecil B. DeMille*. New York: Simon & Schuster, 2010.

Fass, Paula S. *The Damned and the Beautiful: American Youth in the 1920s*. New York: Oxford University Press, 1977.

Fronc, Jennifer. *Monitoring the Movies: The Fight over Film Censorship in Early Twentieth-Century Urban America*. Austin: University of Texas Press, 2017.

Geltzer, Jeremy. *Dirty Words and Filthy Pictures: Film and the First Amendment*. Austin: University of Texas Press, 2016.

Hajdu, David. *Love for Sale: Pop Music in America*. New York: Farrar, Straus and Giroux, 2016.

Hart, Kylo-Patrick R. *Film and Sexual Politics*. Newcastle-upon-Tyne: Cambridge Scholars, 2006.

Haskell, Molly. *From Reverence to Rape: The Treatment of Women in the Movies*. New York: Holt, Reinhart and Winston, 1974.

Hecht, Ben. *A Child of the Century*. New York: Simon & Schuster, 1954.

Hendricks, Gordon. *The Kinetoscope: America's First Commercially Successful Motion Picture Exhibitor*. New York: The Beginnings of the American Film, 1966.

Jarvie, I.C. *Movies and Society*. New York: Basic Books, 1970.

Jervis, David V., and Michael Woulfe. *Glamour and Mischief!* Palm Springs: David V. Jervis, 2015.

Jurca, Catherine. *Hollywood 1938: Motion Pictures' Greatest Year*. Los Angeles: University of California Press, 2012.

King, Rob. *The Fun Factory: The Keystone Film Company and the Emergence of Mass Culture*. Los Angeles: University of California Press, 2008.

Leff, Leonard J., and Jerold L. Simmons. *The Dame in the Kimono: Hollywood, Censorship, and the Production Code*. New York: Grove Weidenfeld, 1990.

Levy, Emanuel. *George Cukor, Master of Elegance: Hollywood's Legendary Director and His Stars*. New York: William Morrow, 1994.

Lewis, Jon, ed. *Producing*. New Brunswick: Rutgers University Press, 2016.

Maltby, Richard. *Hollywood Cinema*. Malden: Blackwell, 1995.

May, Lary. *Screening Out the Past: The Birth of Mass Culture and the Motion Picture Industry*. New York: Oxford University Press, 1980.

McCarthy, Todd, and Charles Flynn. *Kings of the Bs: Working within the Hollywood System*. New York: Dutton, 1975.

McGilligan, Patrick. *George Cukor: A Double Life*. New York: St. Martin's Press, 1991.

Miller, Don. *"B" Movies: An Informal Survey of the American Low-Budget Film 1933–1945*. New York: Curtis Books, 1973.

Moore, Colleen. *Silent Star*. Garden City: Doubleday, 1968.

O'Neill, William L. *Feminism in America: A History*. New Brunswick: Transaction, 1998.

Paul, William. *Laughing Screaming: Modern Hollywood Horror & Comedy*. New York: Columbia University Press, 1994.

Romanowski, William D. *Reforming Hollywood: How American Protestants Fought for Freedom at the Movies*. New York: Oxford University Press, 2012.

Rosen, Marjorie. *Popcorn Venus: Women, Movies & the American Dream*. New York: Coward, McCann & Geoghegan, 1973.

Schaefer, Eric. *Bold! Daring! Shocking! True!: A History of Exploitation Films, 1919–1959*. Durham: Duke University Press, 1999.

Schumach, Murray. *The Face on the Cutting Room Floor: The Story of Movie and Television Censorship*. New York: William Morrow, 1964.

Sikov, Ed. *On Sunset Boulevard: The Life and Times of Billy Wilder*. New York: Hyperion, 1998.

Sklar, Robert. *Movie-Made America: A Cultural History of American Movies*. New York: Random House, 1975.

Solnit, Rebecca. *River of Shadows: Eadweard Muybridge and the Technological Wild West*. New York: Viking, 2003.

Spring, Joel. *Images of American Life: A History of Ideological Management in School, Movies, Radio, and Television*. Albany: State University of New York Press, 1992.

Stearns, Peter N. *Fat History: Bodies and Beauty in the Modern West*. New York: New York University Press, 1997.

Stearns, Peter N., ed. *American Behavioral History: An Introduction*. New York: New York University Press, 2005.

Stenn, David. *Bombshell: The Life and Death of Jean Harlow*. New York: Doubleday, 1995.

_____. *Clara Bow: Runnin' Wild*. New York: Putnam, 1988.

Uruburu, Paula. *American Eve: Evelyn Nesbit, Stanford White, the Birth of the "It" Girl and the Crime of the Century*. New York: Penguin, 2008.

Vasey, Ruth. *The World According to Hollywood, 1918–1939*. Madison: University of Wisconsin Press, 1997.

Vizzard, Jack. *See No Evil: Life Inside a Hollywood Censor*. New York: Simon & Schuster, 1970.

Wittern-Keller, Laura. *Freedom of the Screen: Legal Challenges to State Film Censorship, 1915–1981*. Lexington: University Press of Kentucky, 2008.

Periodicals

Barbus, Samantha. "How Movies Became Speech." *Rutgers Law Review*, Vol. 64, No. 3, Spring 2012.

Mulvey, Laura. "Visual Pleasure and Narrative Cinema." *Screen*, Vol. XVI, No. 3, October 1975, Pp. 6–18.

Morris, Gary. "Feminism and Exploitation: Roger Corman's New World Pictures." *Bright Lights*, No. 10, July 1993.

_____. "Surf's Up." *Bright Lights*, No. 21, May 1998.

Index

Numbers in ***bold italics*** indicate pages with illustrations

Abbott, Bud 64, 72, 80, 117, 161
Abbott and Costello Go to Mars 81
Abbott and Costello Meet Frankenstein 161
abortion 44, 99, 168
Academy Awards 116, 117, 148, 174, 175, 200; ceremony 146, 174, 199, 200
The Accused 175
Adams, Beverly 144
Adams, Casey (Max Showalter) 105
Adams, Julia/Julie 81
The Admirable Crichton (play) 29
The Adventures of Lucky Pierre 128
The Affair (Showtime) 197
The Affairs of Anatol 31
The Affluent Society (book) 190
Against Our Will (book) 183
Agee, James 72
Aimer, Catherine 5
Aitken, Harry E. 11
Albright, Lola 136
Aldon, Mari 92
Aldrich, Robert 148
Algren, Nelson 136
Ali Baba and the Forty Thieves 80
All About Eve 108
All My Sons 81
All the Loving Couples 148
Allen, Albert Arthur 38
Allen, Corey 137
Allen, Elizabeth 149
Allen, Gene 88
Allen, Woody 97, 124, 158
Amanda By Night 187
Amarcord 160–61
An American in Paris 69
American-International Pictures (AIP) 122, 129, 160
American Pie 191, 194
The American Venus 36, ***38***, ***39***
Ames, Ramsay 67, ***70***
anal sex 174, 186, 192, 194
And God Created Woman (1956) 2, 124
Andress, Ursula 143, 144, ***144***, 162
Anesthesia 196
Angel Buns 186

Aniello, Lucia 195
Animal House 169
Ann-Margret 133, 143, ***143***, 144, 175, ***175***
Anna Christie (1930) 40
Annabella 6
Anniversary Waltz (play) 190
Another Part of the Forest 81
Anthony, Susan B. 13
Antonioni, Michelangelo 146, 149
Aphrodite of Knidos, as Greek ideal 21, 189
Arabian Nights 80, 81
Arbuckle, Fatty (Roscoe) 19, 31
Argento, Asia 200
Arkoff, Samuel Z. 131
Armored Car Robbery 92
Armstrong, R.G. 102
Arnold, Edward 94
Arzner, Dorothy 2, ***40***, 136
Astaire, Fred 58, 64, 65, 68, 69, 85, 86, 87, 89, 107
Astor, Mary 1
At the Foot of the Flatiron 7
Ates, Nejla 100
Auden, W.H. 9
Augenstein, Dr. Isabelle 1
Avalon, Frankie 130
Axelrod, George 106, 112, 131
Ayers, Lemuel 73

Babb, Kroger 124
Babes in Bagdad 80
Baby Doll 117–19, ***118***, 121, 122, 142
Baby Face 56
Babylon Berlin (Netflix) 197
Bachelor in Paradise 137
Back to God's Country (1919) 26, ***26***
The Bad and the Beautiful 92
Bad Boys 205
The Bad Guys (book) 92
Bad Santa 174
Bagdad 80
Baker, Carroll 117, 142
Bakshi, Ralph 148
Balanchine, George 85
Ball, Lucille ***48***, 49, 82
Ball of Fire 136
The Bamboo Blonde 52

Bancroft, Anne 145
The Band Wagon 87, ***91***
Banks, Elizabeth 184
Bara, Theda 14–15, ***15***, 39
Barbarella 145
Bardelys the Magnificent 33
Bardot, Brigitte 96, 123–24, 137
Bardot, Mijanou 123
Barney Oldfield's Race for a Life 12
Barr, Candy 179, 181
Barrie, James M. 29
Barry, Don "Red" 61
Basic Instinct 173
Basinger, Kim 172
Barty, Billy 48
Bates, Alan 149
Battle of the Sexes (1928) 41
Baxter, Warner 50
Bazin, André 63, 74, 79, 82, 124
Beach Party 130, 131
Beard, Mary 22
The Beastmaster 162
The Beat Generation 122
Beatty, Ned 186
Beatty, Warren 174
The Beautiful Blonde from Bashful Bend 71
Bechdel, Alison 203; "Bechdel Test" 203
A Bedroom Blunder 22
Behind the Green Door 181–82
Behold, America (book) 34
Belafonte, Harry 136
Bell, Jillian 195
Belushi, John 169
Benchley, Robert 47
Benglis, Lynda 68
Bening, Annette 173, 175
Bennett, Constance 40
Benny, Jack 174
Berger, John 1
Bergman, Ingmar 124, 160, 176
Berkeley, Busby 46, 47–49, 62, 85
Berlin, Irving 47
Berman, Pandro S. 69
Bernhardt, Sarah 7
Bernstein, Leonard 9
Berry, Halle 174
Berry, John 136
Bertolucci, Bernardo 159, 195

215

Index

The Best Things in Life Are Free 110
Bettis, Valerie 67
Betty Boop's Rise to Fame 57
Betty's Bath 37
Beyond the Forest **73**
Beyond the Valley of the Dolls 150
Bier, Suzanne 202
Big Bad Mama 161
The Big Bird Cage 162
The Big Doll House 162
The Big Operator 122
The Big Sleep 157
Bigelow, Kathryn 202
Bigger Than Life 117
Binford, Lloyd T. 73
Binoche, Juliet 171
Bird of Paradise (1932) 55, **55**
The Birth of a Nation 18, 182
Bishop, Joey 140
Bisset, Jacqueline 146, 172
Bitzer, Billy 41
Black Oxen 34, 39
Black Swan 173, 191
Blackboard Jungle 116, 122, 132
Blakely, Susan 161
Blame It on Rio 185
Blanchard, Mari 80, 81
Blanchett, Cate 200
Blockers 194
Blonde Comet 52
Blonde Ice 52
Blondell, Joan 52, 53, 56, 133
Blood and Sand (1941) 115
Bloody Mama 161
Bloom, Claire 139
Blore, Eric 59
Blow-Up 146
Blue Denim 133
Blue Is the Warmest Color 199
Blue Movie 178
Blumenthal, Ralph 180
Bly, Nellie (Elizabeth Cochrane) 13
Bob & Carol & Ted & Alice 142, 148
The Bob Cummings Show (TV series) 114
Body Heat 170
body type, ideal 9, 20–21, 54, 78
Boetticher, Budd 114
Bogdanovich, Peter 166, 207
Bolero (1934) 140
Bolero (1984) 162
Bolger, Ray 85, 174
Bolshevism on Trial 27
Borgnine, Ernest 157
Bovy, Phoebe Maltz 207
Bow, Clara 37, 39–41, **40**, 61
The Boxing Cats 6
Boyd, Stephen 115, 137
Boys Don't Cry 174
Boys in the Sand 180
Boy's Night Out 137
Bracken, Eddie 72, 89
Bracken's World (TV series) 149
Bradley, James 6

Brando, Marlon 116, 159
Breakfast at Tiffany's 134
The Breakfast Club 192, 204
Breathless 121
Breen, Joseph 54, 56, 61, 62, 74, 98, 117, 157; "Breen Office" 61, 69, 84, 89, 126
Brendel, El 45
The Bribe 94
Bridget Jones's Diary 175
Brief Encounter 139
Briggs, Joe Bob 58
The Bright Road 135
The Broadway Melody 45
Broderick, Helen 59
Bronson, Charles 142
Brooks, Elizabeth 161
Brooks, Louise 36, 86
Brown, Helen Gurley 190
Brownback, Sen. Sam 187–88
Browning, Tod 61
Brownmiller, Susan 183
Brute Force 81
Bryanston Pictures 181
Buck Privates 64
Buckley, William F., Jr. 116
Buetel, Jack 74, 95
Burke, Tarana 199
Burke's Law (TV series) 144
burlesque 8, 79–80, 36–37
Burr, Raymond 108
Burton, Richard (actor) 142, 173
Burton, Sir Richard 80
Bush, George W. 188
BUtterfield 8 134
Button, Chanya 207
Bye Bye Birdie 143

The Cabinet of Dr. Caligari (1919)
Café Flesh 187
Caffaro, Cheri 156–57
Caged 161–62
Caged Heat 162
Cagney, James 51, 52, 98, 92
Cahiers du Cinéma (periodical) 63, 124
Caine, Michael 145, 185, **186**
Calamity Jane 92
Calder, Alexander 16
Calendar Girl 73
Californication (Showtime) 197
Call Her Savage 41
Camille 2000 176
Campbell, Neve 173
Campus Confessions 69
Canby, Vincent 176
Candy Stripe Nurses 161
Cannon, Dyan 148
Cannon, Kay 194
Cannon Films 163, 168
Cantor, Eddie 46, 47, 72
Capone 161
Capp, Al 121
Capra, Frank 52
Captain from Castile 115
Carefree 65
Carell, Steve 188
Carey, Macdonald 100

Carey, Maggie 194
Carmen, Baby 176
Carmen Jones 135
Carmencita 6
Carnal Knowledge 143
Carnal Knowledge 175, **175**
Carol 166
Carol, Martine 124
Carpenter, John 169, 181
Carpenter, Laura 196
The Carpetbaggers 142
Carradine, John 68, 150
Carroll, Earl 36, 56
Carter, Janis 95
Carter, Lynda 203
Castle, Peggie 87
Cat on a Hot Tin Roof 121
Cat People (1942) 72, 189
Cates, Phoebe **166**, 167–68
Cattrall, Kim 164, 169
Caught in the Draft 64
Caulfield, Joan 76, **78**
Ceballos, Larry 49
censor boards 52, 58, 119; Chicago 10, 23, 98; Kansas 11, 99, 101, 147; Maryland 12, 147; New York 10, 12, 19, 75, 120, 147; Ohio 11, 98; Pennsylvania 11, 45; Virginia 32, 147
Censored: The Private Life of the Movies (book) 32
Chabrol, Claude 175
Chaikin, Joe 149
Chambers, Marilyn 181–82
Chamion 6
Chandler, Jeff 81
Chaney, Lon 26
Chaney, Lon, Jr. 68, 161
Chapin, Martha 60
Chaplin, Charlie 33
The Chapman Report 137
Charisse, Cyd 60, 79, 86–87, **90, 91**, 144
Charley's Aunt 174
Charlie Bubbles 146
Chase, Barrie 88–89, 140
Chase, Canon William Sheafe 10, 22
Chastain, Jessica 174
Chatterton, Ruth 1
Chayefsky, Paddy 80
Cheating Blondes 52
Chevalier, Maurice 47
Child Bride 61
Child Star (autobiography) 201
Cholodenko, Lisa 173
Chorus Girls and the Salvation Army 8
Christie, Julie 159, **160**, 174
Christy, Howard Chandler 37
Church, Thomas Haden 174
The Churchman (periodical) 45
Churchwell, Sarah 34
The Circus 33
City That Never Sleeps 94
Clark, Larry 192
Clark, Susan 163
Clarke, Shirley 127

Index

Cleopatra (1917) 14, **15**
Cleopatra (1963) 114–15,
Clifton, Elmer 60–61
Clinton, Bill 187
A Clockwork Orange 153
Clooney, George 175
Close, Glenn 170–71
Clover, Carol 169
Clyde, June 45
Cobra Woman 81
Coburn, Charles 105
Cocaine Fiends see *The Pace That Kills*
The Cock-Eyed World 45
The Cocoanuts 46
Cogley, John 116
Cohn, Harry 67, 106
Colbert, Claudette 55, 58, 109
A Cold Wind in August 136
Cole, Jack 85, 96
College Confidential 122
Collier's Weekly 7
Collins, Joan 114–15
Colorado Territory 77
Columbia Pictures 65, 106
Coming Apart 174
Compson, Betty 60
Cone, Stephen 206
Confessions of a Vice Baron 60
The Connection 127
Connelly, Jennifer 170
The Conqueror 103
Conrad, William 103
Conried, Hans 82
Contempt 137
The Contrast 28
Convention City 56
Cook, Elisha, Jr. **93**, 94
Cook, Rachel Leigh 192
Cool Hand Luke 146
Coolidge, Calvin 34
Cooper, Gary 107, 113
Cooper, Jackie 62
Cooper, Miriam 25
Corio, Ann 80, 136
Corliss, Richard 177; "Corliss standard" 177, 187
Corman, Roger 131, 132, 160, 161, 162, 175
Cornell Daily Sun 29
Cosby, Bill 199
Cosmopolitan Magazine 180
Costello, Lou 64, 72, 80, 117, 161
Couples (novel) 180
Courtenay, Tom 146
Cover Girl 66
Coward, Noel 56
Coyote, Peter 174
Crabbe, Larry "Buster" 56, 58
Crafts, Wilbur 10
Crawford, Joan 1, 108
Crenna, Richard 170
Creskoff, Rebecca 197
Cries and Whispers 160
Crime Does Not Pay (short subject series) 92
The Crimson Kimono 137
Crosby, Bing 72

The Crown (Netflix) 197
Crown International 170
Cruise, Tom 172–72
Cruz, Penelope 174
The Cuckoos 46
Cukor, George 87, 137
Culp, Robert 157
Cummings, Robert (Bob) 89, 114, 130
Cummins, Peggy 92
La Cureé 145
Curtis, Jamie Lee 169
Curtis, Tony 81, 174

d'Abo, Olivia 163
Dahl, Arlene 110, **110**, **111**
Dahl, John 170
Dailey, Dan 70
Dall, John 92
Damaged Goods 58
d'Amboise, Jacques 110, **112**
Dames 51
Damiano, Gerard 181
Dance, Girl, Dance 136
Dandridge, Dorothy 135
Dangerous Blondes 52
Dangerous Hours 27
Dangerous Mission 95
Dante's Inferno (1935) 57
Danton, Georges 207
Danton, Ray 122, 140
Darcy, Georgine 107
Dark Star 181
Darley, Gabrielle 36
Darnell, Linda 82, 95
Darren, James 129
Dassin, Jules 124
Daves, Delmer 133
David and Bathsheba 84
Davies, Marion 33
Davis, Bette 73, 108, 133
Dawson, Rosario 192, **193**
Day, Doris 92, 110, 137
Day, Marceline **40**
Days of Thrills and Laughter 33
Dead Men Don't Wear Plaid 2
Dean, James 116, 117
de Beauvoir, Simone 1
De Carlo, Yvonne 81
de Corsia, Ted 103
de Dienes, Andre 79
Dee, Sandra 129, 133, 190
Deep in My Heart 39, 87, **91**
Deep Tango 181
Deep Throat 180, 181
De Havilland, Olivia 139
Deitch, Donna 173
De La Croix, Raven 158–59
De Lennart, Sonja 110
Deliverance 186
del Rio, Dolores 54, 55
Delta of Venus 172
Demetrius and the Gladiators 104
De Mille, Cecil B. 29, 32–33, 54–55, 83–84, 119
De Niro, Robert 148
Dennis, Sandy 149

Denver, Bob 116, 146, 191
De Palma, Brian 148
Derek, Bo 162, **164**
Derek, John 162
de Renzy, Alex 179
Dern, Bruce 132
The Desert Hawk 81
Desert Hearts 173
The Desert Song (operetta) 39
Design for Living 56
De Sylva (Buddy), Brown (Lew) and Henderson (Ray) 110
Detective Story 99
Detroit 202
The Deuce (HBO) 205
The Devil and Miss Jones 181
The Devil in Miss Jones 181
Devil's Angels 132
Devil's Canyon 96
The Devil's Daughter 13
Devry, Elaine 140
deWilde, Brandon 133
Diamond Lil (play) 56
Diary of a Nudist 127
DiCaprio, Leonardo 175
Dickinson, Angie 107, 115, 146, 161
Dietrich, Marlene 40
Different for Girls (novel) 206
Dillinger (1945) 102
Dillman, Bradford 121
Dillon, Matt 163, 173
Dineen, Fr. FitzGeorge 51
Disobedience 206
Distant Drums 92
Dr. Goldfoot and the Bikini Machine 129
Dr. No 143
Dodsworth 1
Donen, Stanley 87
Donohue, Troy 133
Donovan, Casey 156
Donovan, King 141
Don't Bet on Blondes 52
Don't Change Your Husband 29
Don't Look Now 159, **160**, 186
Don't Make Waves 144
Dorn, Philip 62
Dors, Diana 114
Double Indemnity 170
Dougan, Vikki 114
Dougherty, Dennis Cardinal 56
Douglas, Kirk 158
Douglas, Michael 170–71
Down to the Sea in Ships (1922) 61
Dracula's Daughter 161
Drake, Dona 72–73, **75**
Dreamers 195
Dreifuss, Arthur 131
Dressler, Marie 22
Driver, Adam 197
DuBarry Was a Lady (film) 70
DuBarry Was a Lady (stage) 70
Duchamp, Marcel
Duel in the Sun 77, 86, 115
Dunham, Katharine 72
Durbin, Deanna 71

Index

Duvall, Robert 151
DuVernay Ava 200
Dvorak, Ann 54, 133
Dwan, Allan 73

Eakins, Thomas, 5–6
East of Eden 117
Eastwood, Clint 157
Eaton, Mary, 46
Ebert, Roger 150, 177, 185
The Economist (periodical) 201
Ecstasy 63, 124
Eden, Barbara 144
Edge of the City 117
Edison, Thomas A. 6–8
Edwards, Margaret 14, *15*
Egan, Richard 94
Eighth Grade 174
Eisenhower, Dwight D.
Eisenstein, Sergei 177
Ekberg, Anita 113, ***114***, 137, 144
Elam, Jack 157
Elg, Taina 87
Elmer Gantry 134
Elvgren, Gil 80, 107
Emerson, Hope 161
Emmanuelle 159, 169
Employees' Entrance 55
England, Audie 172
Epler, Blanche 5
Ernst, Morris L. 32
Escort Girl 60
Esper, Dwain 61
Esquire magazine 63, 70–71
Evans, Chris 192
Everett, Chad 137
Everson, William K. 92
Ex-Lady 55
Excuse My Dust 100
Eyes Wide Shut 172–73

A Face in the Crowd 121
The Facts of Life 139
Fanny Hill 177
Fanny Hill Meets Dr. Erotico 176
Fanny Hill Meets Lady Chatterley 176
Far from Heaven 166
Farmer, Mimsy 131, 132
Farmiga, Vera 175
Farrell, Glenda 53
Farrow, Ronan 199
Fashions of 1934 ***50***
Fassbender, Michael 173
Fast Times at Ridgemont High ***166***, 167–68
Faster Pussycat! Kill! Kill! 177
Fatal Attraction 170–71, 175
Fatima's Coochee-Coochee Dance
Faulkner, William 56, 121
The Fault in Our Stars 195
Fawcett, Farrah 151
Fazenda, Louise, 22
Female 55
Female on the Beach 129
feminism 29, 79, 152–53, 183
Feminism in America (book) 42
La Femme Infidèle 175

Ferris Bueller's Day Off 205
Fifty Shades of Grey 172
Film Comment (periodical) 177
film noir 170
Finch, Peter 115, 159
Fineman, Irving 133
Finney, Albert 146
Fiorentino, Linda 170
Fire Down Below 109
Fisher, Eddie 135, ***135***
Fisher, Elsie 175
Fisher, Isla 194
Fitzgerald, F. Scott 33
Flaming Passion 34
Flaming Youth 33–34, 42
The Flapper 33
Flash Gordon (1936 serial) 58, ***59***, 160
Flashdance 172
Fleischer, Max 57
Fleming, Rhonda 81, 110, ***110***, ***111***, 126
Fleming, Victor 53
Flesh Gordon 172
Florey, Robert 46
Flower Drum Song 135
Flying Down to Rio 50–51
Flynn, Errol 117
Fonda, Henry 92
Fonda, Jane 136, 139, 145, 175, 190, 200
Fonda, Peter 131, 132
Fontaine, Joan 136
A Fool There Was 13
Foolish Wives 30–31
Footlight Parade 48
Footlight Serenade 69
Forbidden Daughters 38
Ford, Glenn 67, 158
Ford, John 103
Forrest, Sally 100–101, ***102***, ***103***
42nd St. 47
The 40-Year Old Virgin 188
Fosse, Bob 158
Foster, Helen 42, 44
Foster, Jodie 174, 175
4 for Texas 144
The Fox 149
Fox, Samantha 186
Fox, William 11, 12
Fox Film 12, 55
Fox Movietone Follies 45
Franciosa, Anthony 146
Francis, Anne 1, 136
Francis, Connie 130
Franco, James 206
Frank, Melvin 139
Frank, Robert 116
Franz, Arthur 94
Frazee, Jane 73
Freaks 61
Frechette, Mark 149
Frederick's of Hollywood 79
Freed, Arthur 201
French, Daniel Chester, 16
The French Line 96–99, 106, 126, 129
Freud, Sigmund 180–81

Frida 199
Friday the 13th 169
Friedhofer, Hugo 87
Fritz the Cat 148
From Here to Eternity 118, 129
From Reverence to Rape (book) 151
From Show Girl to Burlesque Queen 8
Fuller, Samuel 137
Fun in Acapulco 144
Funicello, Annette 130, 132
Funkhouser, Metellus Lucullus Cicero 23
Funny Face 107
Furneaux, Yvonne 124
The Fuzzy Pink Nightgown 109

Gable, Clark 53, 58, 63, 87, 108, 109, 117
Gable and Lombard 2
Gabriel Over the White House 54
Gadot, Gal 203, ***204***
Gaines, William 116
Galbraith, John K. 190
Gallup Poll 63–64; Values and Beliefs survey 196
Gambling with Souls 60
The Gang's All Here 81
Garbo, Greta 40, 56, 89
Garden of Eden (1954) 102, 127
Garfield, John 170
Garland, Judy 62, 69, 160
Gardner, Ava 67, ***69***, 92, 93, 109
Gavin, Erica 150, 177
Gavin, John 169,
The Gay Shoe Clerk 6
Gaynor, Mitzi 87, 88, 190
Gaynor, William 11
Gazzara, Ben 161
Geena Davis Institute 201
Genghis Khan 103
Gentlemen Prefer Blondes (film) 96, 105, 141
Gentlemen Prefer Blondes (novel) 52
George, Susan 153–56, ***154***, ***155***
The George Raft Story 140
The Gerry Society Makes a Mistake 8
Gershon, Gina 173
Gershwin, George 85
Gerwig, Greta 196, 202
Geva, Tamara 85
Ghost in the Invisible Bikini 129
Giannini, Giancarlo 186
Gibbons, Cedric 56–57
Gibson, Charles Dana 7
Gidget (film) 129
Gilda 67, ***68***, 92, 96, 170
Gilliat, Penelope 159
Gilligan's Island (TV series) 144
Gillis, Jamie 183
Ginger (1971) 156–57
Ginsberg, Allen 116
The Girl Can't Help It 112
Girl from Jones Beach 72

Index

The Girl in the Red Velvet Swing 114
Girl of the Night 136
Girls (HBO) 187
Girls About Town 53
Girls, Guns and Gangsters 122
Girls Town 122
Girls Trip 196
Gish, Dorothy 13
Gish, Lillian 13
Globus, Yoran 168
Glorifying the American Girl 46
Glyn, Elinor 38–40
God Is the Bigger Elvis 130
Godard, Jean-Luc 137, 178
Goddard, Paulette 67, 80
The Godfather 159
God's Little Acre 121
Golan, Menachem 168
Gold Diggers of 1933 47
The Gold Rush 33
Goldie 52
Goldman, Barry 188
Goldstein, Leonard 126
Goldwyn, Samuel 31, 46, 49, 85
Gomez, Thomas 103
Gone with the Wind 85, 117
Goodman, Ezra 112
Gordon, Leo 148
Gordon, Mack **49**
Gowland, Peter 80, 143
Grable, Betty 47, 63, 68–70, **71**, 78, 110, 117, 140
The Graduate 137, 146, 191
Grady, Constance 205
Graham, Martha 85
Grahame, Gloria 137
Grant, Cary 105, 107
Grant, Shauna 183
Graver, Gary 187
Gray, Lawrence **38**
The Great Bank Robbery 107
The Great Ziegfeld 62
Green, Eva 195
Greene, Gael 183
Greer, Howard 52, 96
Greetings 148
Grey, Nan 161
Griffith, Andy 121
Griffith, D.W. 12, 18, 25–26, **25**, 27, 41, 60, 177, 201
The Grifters 175
The Grit of the Girl Telegrapher 13
Gross, Jerry 176
Grove Press 177
Guess Who's Coming to Dinner 182
A Guide for the Married Man 139
Guilty Parents 60
Gun Crazy (1950) 92
Guttenberg, Steve 181
Gwynne, Anne 68
Gyllenhaal, Maggie 172
Gypsy 136

Haas, Hugo 94, 106
Haddish, Tiffany 195
Hair (musical) 180
Hajdu, David 34
Hale, Barbara 1
Hall, Jon 80, **82**
Haller, Daniel 132
Halprin, Daria 149
Hamilton, George 130
Hamilton, Neil 42
Hamlet (1948) 81
Hamlin, Harry 173
Hammerstein, Oscar 134
Hampton, Benjamin 45
Hanks, Tom 173
Hannie Caulder 157
Happy Anniversary 190
Happy Days (film) 46
Hard Core (book) 183
Hardin, Ty 139
Harding, Warren G. 29, 34
Hardy, Oliver 53
Harkrider, John, 46
Harlow, Jean, 40, 52, **53**
Harmon, Joy 146
Harper's Magazine 183
Harrelson, Woody 197
Harrison, Linda 140
Harrison, P.S. 37
Harrison, Rex 173
Harron, Robert 26
Hart, Dolores 130, 196
Hart, Lorenz 85
Hart, Veronica 186–87
Hartley, Nina 183
Haskell, Molly 114, 151
Hatari! 107
Hatcher, Teri, 45
Hathaway, Anne 174
The Haunted Palace 131
Haver, Phyllis 41–42
Hawks, Howard 105, 107, 143
Hayek, Salma 199, 200
Hays, Will H. 31, 45, 51, 54, 63, 74; "Hays Office" 37, 72
Hayward, Susan 84, 104, **106**, **107**
Hayworth, Rita 63, 64, 66–67, **68**, 78, 96, 106, 110, 115, 145
HBO 197, 205
Head, Edith 2
The Heavenly Body 63
Hecht, Ben 59–60, 84
Heckerling, Amy 167
Heffner, Richard 171–72
Hefner, Hugh 78, 142, 207
Heindorf, Ray 89
Hello, Dolly! 150
Hell's Angels 52, 96
Helton, Percy 94
Hemingway, Margaux 158
Hemingway, Mariel 158
Hemmings, David 146
Henning, Paul 114
Henry & June 172
Hepburn, Audrey 107, 110
Hepburn, Katharine 153
Herbert, Hugh 51
Here Come the Girls 82
Here Comes Mr. Jordan 67
Herren, Roger 151
Hersholt, Jean 41
Heywood, Anne 149
Higham, Charles 104
His Kind of Woman 96
A History of the Blue Movie 179, 181
Hitchcock, Alfred 107, 117, 142
Hoffman, Dustin 146, 153–156, 174
Holden, Gloria 161
Holder, Eric 187
A Hole in the Head 114
Hollywood Boulevard (1936) 201
Hollywood Boulevard (1976) 161
Hollywood or Bust 113
The Hollywood Reporter 205
The Hollywood Revue 45
Holmes, John C. 183
Holmes, John Clellon 116
Hoop-la 41
Hope, Bob 64, 67, 78, 82, 139, 146
Hopkins, Miriam 177
Hopper, Dennis 131, 170
Horne, Lena 73, 135
Horror of Dracula 54
Horton, Edward Everett 58, 68
Hot Pursuit 205
Hot Rhythm 72–73
Hot Rods to Hell 132
The Hot Spot 170
Houghton, Katharine 182
A House Is Not a Home 135
How to Be Very, Very Popular 110
How to Marry a Millionaire 105
How to Photograph Women (book) 80
How to Stuff a Wild Bikini 129
"Howl" (poem) 115
The Howling 161
Hoyningen-Huene, George 88
Hudson, Henry 183
Hudson, Rock 109, 137
Hughes, Rep. Dudley 12
Hughes, Howard 52, 64, 74–75, 76, 95, 100, 102, 103, 104, 117
Hughes, John 169, 191, 204
Hula 40
Hula Hula Land 23
Human Sexual Response (book) 145
Human Wreckage 34
Hung (HBO) 197
The Hunger Games 203
Hunt, Helen 174
Hunter, Holly 175
Hunter, Kaki 163, 169
Hurrell, George 64–65, 71
Hurry Sundown 145
Hurt, William 170
The Hurt Locker 202
Hustler magazine 183
Huston, John **152**
Huston, Walter 1, 54, 77
Hutton, Betty 72
Hyatt, Ann, 36
Hypocrites 14–15, **15**

Index

I, a Woman 176
I Am Curious (Blue) 177, 178
I Am Curious (Yellow) 2, 177–78
I Dream of Jeannie (TV series) 144
I Love Dick (Amazon) 207
I Spit on Your Grave (1978)
I, the Jury (film) 87
I, the Jury (novel) 87
I'll Cry Tomorrow 104
I'll Never Forget What's-is-name 146
The Immoral Mr. Teas 126–27, 128
In the Tombs 9
Incendiary Blonde 52
Incorrect Entertainment (book) 51
Indignation 166
Inga 176
Inge, William 136
The Innocent Years (TV documentary) 9
The Inside of the White Slave Traffic 24
Inspiration 16
Intolerance **25**, 25–26
Intrator, Jerald 127
Invasion of the Body Snatchers (1956) 141
Iron Man 52
Irma La Douce 136, 137
Is Any Girl Safe? 25
Isaacs, John D. 5
Island in the Sun 135
It (1927) 39–40
It Happened in Athens 140
It Happened One Night 58
It's a Bikini World 129

Jackson, Glenda 149, 159, 175
Jackson, Peter 199
Jackson County Jail 162
Jacobson, Nora 203
Jane, Thomas 197
Jarrett, Arthur **49**
Jarvie, I.C. 58
Jaws 160
The Jazz Singer (1927) 45
Jeanne Eagels 107
Jenkins, Charles Francis 6
Jenkins, Patty 200
Jensen, Karen 149
Jeremy, Ron 187
Jergens, Adele 92
Jet Pilot 103
Joanna 150
Johann, Zita 54
Johansson, Scarlett 174, 195
Johnny Guitar 108–109
Johns, Glynis 139
Johnson, Don 170
Johnson, James P. 34
Johnson, Lamont 158
Johnson, Lyndon B. 179
Johnson, Michele 185, **186**
Johnson, Nunnally 110, 190
Johnson, Virginia 145

Jolie, Angelina 174
Jolson, Al 45
Jones, Carolyn 115
Jones, Dorothy B. 58
Jones, Jennifer 77, 115
Jones, Shirley 134
Jones, Tommy Lee 162
Jordan, Michael B. 202
The Journal of Sex Research 184
Journey to the Lost City 126
Joy, Col. Jason S. 51, 54
Joy, Leatrice 32
Joyner, Joyzelle 55
Judd, Ashley 199, 200
Jules and Jim 195
Jupiter's Darling 83
Jurado, Katy 115
Jürgens, Curd 124, 136
Just Mercy 202

Kael, Pauline 159
Kalantan 100
Kantor, Jodi 199
Kaplan, Jonathan 161
Karloff, Boris 54, 131
Karlson, Phil 127
Kathleen 201
Katzman, Sam 82, 131
Kaufman, Boris 102
Kaufman, Philip 171
Kaufmann, Christine 144
Kavanaugh, Brett 205
Kazan, Elia 99, 117–19, 121, 135, 137, 142, 201
Keaton, Buster 33, 53
Keeler, Ruby 47
Kefauver, Sen. Estes 80
Kellaway, Cecil 170
Kellerman, Annette 19–21, **21**, 22, **22**, 82, 90
Kellerman, Sally 151
Kelly, Gene 85–86, 88, **88**, 139
Kelly, Grace 107
Kelly, Patsy 53
Ken Park 193
Kendall, Kay 87
Kendall, Todd 184
Kendis, J.D. 60
Kennedy, Burt 158
Kent, Willis 60
Kenton, Erle C. 72, 161
Kerouac, Jack 116
Keyes, Johnny 182
The Kid 33
The Kid from Spain 47
Kidd, Michael 87
Kidman, Nicole 172–73, 174
Kids 192
The Killers (1946) 92
The Killing 94
The Killing of Sister George 148
The Killing of the Unicorn (book) 207
King, Martin Luther, Jr. 178
King, Zalman 172
The King and Four Queens 109
Kirkland, Sally 174
Kiss Me, Kate 89

Kiss Me, Stupid 107, 146
Kiss Them for Me 107
Kiss Tomorrow Goodbye 92
Klaw, Irving 80
Klute 136
Knapp, Dorothy 36
Knute Rockne, All-American 58
Koedt, Anne 180–81
Koenekamp, Fred 150
Kohner, Frederic 129
Korda, Alexander 80
Korine, Harmony 192
Kovack, Nancy 144
Kramer, Larry 149
Kreuger, Miles 47
Kristel, Sylvia 169
Kubrick, Stanley 94, 133, 153, 159, 172–73, 197
Kulp, Nancy 114
Kundera, Milan 171
Kunis, Mila 173
Kwan, Nancy 135
Kyrou, Ado 124

Ladd, Diane 132
Ladies They Talk About 63
Lady Bird 196, 202
Lady Chatterley's Lover (novel) 149, 177
Lady for a Day 54
The Lady from Shanghai 170
Lady Godiva (of Coventry) 109
Lady of Burlesque 136
LaGuardia, Fiorello 79, 136
Lake, Veronica 62
Lamarr, Hedy 62–63, **64**, **65**, 84
Lamont, Charles 161
Lamour, Dorothy 81
Land of the Pharaohs 114
Landi, Elissa 54
Landis, Carole 63
Landis, Kenesaw Mountain 31
Landry, Robert 63
Lane, Diane 175
Lang, Fritz 126
Langdon, Sue Ann 139
Lange, Jessica 170
Lanphier, Fay 36–37, 38, **39**
Lansing, Joi 114
Lansing, Sherry 171
Larsen, A.E. 85
Larson, Brie 202
Larter, Ari 192
Lasky, Jesse L. 27, 29, 37
The Last American Virgin 168
Last Exit to Brooklyn (novel) 100
The Last House on the Left (1972) 158
The Last Movie 160, 170
The Last Picture Show 160, 166
The Last Seduction 170
Last Tango in Paris 2, 159, 181, 186
Laughton, Charles 54
Laurel, Stan 53
Laurie, Piper 81, 95, 100
Lawrence, D.H. 149, 181
Lawrence, Jacquie 206

Lawrence, Jennifer 203
Lawrenson, Helen 180
Lawson, Priscilla 58, **59**
Lazar, John 150
Lean, David 197
Leaving Las Vegas 175
Lee, Gypsy Rose 80, 136
The Legend of Lylah Clare 107
Legion of Decency 56, 58, 74, 100, 101, 102, 104, 107, 119, 122, 137, 139, 142; name change 142
Leidhold, Dorchen 183
Leigh, Janet 103, 108, 142
Leigh, Jennifer Jason **166**, 167–68, 196
Leigh, Mike 166
Leites, Nathan 92
Lembeck, Harvey 132
Lemmon, Jack 174
Lemon Popsicle 168
Lenny 175
Lepore, Jill 64
Lerner, Alan Jay 87
lesbians 173, 176, 206–7
Lester, Richard
Let's Face It 72
Levant, Oscar 137
Levine, Joseph E. 137
Levy, Eugene 191
Lewis, Daniel Day 171
Lewis, Herschell Gordon 128
Lewis, Jerry 113, **120**
Lewis, Sylvia 82, 104
Liane, Jungle Goddess 124
License to Drive 205
The Lickerish Quartet 176
Life magazine 63, 67, 103
Li'l Abner **120**, 121
Linden, Jennie 149
Lindsay, John V. 178, 180
A Lion Is in the Streets 6
Lipstick 158
Lisbon 124
Little Darlings 163, **165**, 196
"Little Egypt" (Fatima Djemille) 6
Living It Up 110
Lizzie (2018) 206
Lloyd, Harold 33
Lockheed, Alan 18
Lo Duca, Joseph 124
Loew's Inc. 98, 117
Lola Montes 124
Lolita (1962) 133
Lollobrigida, Gina 115
Lombard, Carole 140
London, Julie 113, **113**, 115
London, Samuel 24
The Lonely Villa 12
Lonergan, Kenneth 196
Lonesome Cowboys 148, 178
Long, Shelley 174
The Long Home 206
Loos, Anita 25, 52
Lord, Fr. Daniel 51
Lord, Jack 113
Lord Love a Duck 131
Lords, Traci 184
Loren, Sophia 115, 137

Lorentz, Pare 32
Loring, Eugene 87
The Los Angeles Times 206
Lost in a Harem 80
Louis, Jean 67
The Love-Ins 131
Love Me or Leave Me 92
Love with the Proper Stranger 142, 190
Lovelace, Linda 181, 183
Lover Come Back 137
Lovers Must Learn (novel) 133
The Loves of Carmen 115
Lowery, Robert 68
Loy, Myrna 194
Lubitsch, Ernst 47, 56, 70
Lucas, George 160, 162, 186
Lucretia Lombard 34
Lupino, Ida 1, 61, 100, 157
Lynd, Helen 33
Lynd, Robert 33
Lyne, Adrian 175
Lynley, Carol 133
Lyon, Ben 52
Lyon, Cliff 103
Lyon, Sue 133

Macao 96
MacDonald, Jeanette 71
Macfadden, Barnarr 36
MacFarlane, Seth 174, 199
Macgowan, Kenneth, 46
Machaty, Gustav 63
MacKinnon, Catherine 184
MacLaine, Shirley 136
MacRae, Gordon 92
Macready, George 170
Mad (periodical) 116
Madsen, Virginia 170
The Magic Carpet 82
Mahon, Barry 176
Making Love 172
Malden, Karl 121
Male and Female 29, 54
The Male Animal 92
"male gaze" 71, 153
Malle, Louis 185
Malone, Dorothy 109, **109**, 130
"mammary madness" 114
Man of the West 113
Mandylor, Costas 172
Manhattan 158
Maniac (1934) 61
Mankiewicz, Joseph L. 1
Mannequin 169
Man's Favorite Sport 143
Mansfield, Jayne 99, 107, 111–12, 140, 141
Manslaughter (1922) 32–33, 54
Many Loves of Dobie Gillis (TV series) 115
Mara, Kate 206
Margaret 196
Marjorie Morningstar 142
Marsh, Mae, 13, 26, 42, 182
Marston, William 203
Martin, Dean 114
Martin, Strother 157

Martin, Tony 62, **64**, 82, **84**
Martinelli, Elsa 107
Marty (1953 TV drama; 1955 film) 80
The Marvelous Mrs. Maisel (Amazon) 197
Marvin, Lee 146
Marx Brothers 46, 53
MASH 151
Mason, James 117, 133, 136
Masters, Dr. William 145
Matthau, Walter 139, **141**
Mature, Victor 96, 114
"Max Hardcore" 188
Maxwell, Marilyn 70
May, Elaine 115
Mayer, Louis B. 69, 95, 201
Mayo, Virginia 77, 89–90, 96, **97**, 114
McAdam, Rachel 206
McCambridge, Mercedes 109
McCarten, John C. 99
McCarthy, Andrew 169
McCarthy, Sen. Joe 115
McClellan, George B., Jr. 10, 11
McCrea, Joel 55, 153
McDonald, Marie 141
McDormand, Frances 200, 202
McDowell, Malcolm 153
McGowan, Rose 200
McGuire, Dorothy 94
McLaglen, Victor, 45, 73
McNichol, Kristy 163, **165**, 196
Me and You and Everyone We Know 174
Me Too (#MeToo) 199
Meade, Emily 205
Mean Streets 160
Medina, Patricia 80, 82
Meese, Edwin III 183; Meese Commission 183, 187
Meighan, Thomas 30, 32
Melato, Mariangela 186
Mellinger, Frederick 79
Menzies, William Cameron, 41
Mercer, Johnny 78, 136
Mercouri, Melina 134
Merrick, David 136
Messing, Debra 200
Metalious, Grace 116
Metzger, Radley 176
Meyer, Russ 126, 150, 158–59, 177
M-G-M 55, 117, 162, 163
Michael, Marion 124
Michaels, Beverly 94, 106
Middleton, Charles **59**
Middletown (book) 33
Midler, Bette 174
Midnight Cowboy 148
Milano, Alyssa 199
Mildred Pierce 76, 129
Milestone, Lewis 61
Milk 183
Milland, Ray 107, 124
Miller, Ann 39, 58, 72
Miller, Arthur 81, 117
Miller, Henry 172, 181, 191

Miller, Sienna 200
Million Dollar Legs (1939) 62, 69
Million Dollar Mermaid 83
Millward, Jon 189
Milner, Martin 129
Mimieux, Yvette 130, 133, 162, 196
Minnelli, Liza 146, 160
Minnelli, Vincente 69, 87
Minsky Brothers 80, 136
Minter, Mary Miles 32
The Miracle (1951) 119
"*Miracle*" case *see* Supreme Court, U.S.
The Miracle of Morgan's Creek 72
Miracle on 34th St. (1947) 142
The Miseducation Of Cameron Post 206
Mishkin, William 128
Miss America pageant 36–37; contestants 78, 109
Mitchell, James 87
Mitchell, John Cameron 188
Mitchell, Thomas 77
Mitchell Brothers 181
Mitchum, Robert 95
Modern Man (periodical) 80
Mona Lisa Smile 166
Mona, the Virgin Nymph 179
Monika (*Summer with Monika*) 124
Monkey Business (1952) 105
Monogram Pictures 60, 72
Monroe, Marilyn 80, 81, 96, 105–6, *108*, 109, 110, 111, 142
Montalban, Ricardo 86
Montez, Maria 80–81, *82*
Montiel, Sarita 115
The Moon Is Blue 99
Moon Over Miami 63
Moore, Cleo 106
Moore, Colleen 33–34, *43*, 51, 53
Moore, Julianne 173
Moore, Terry 95
Moorehead, Agnes 103, 161
Mooring, William H. 80
The More the Merrier 58
Moreau, Jeanne 195
Moreno, Antonio, 40
Morgan, Robin 183
Morris, Gary 130
Morris, Wesley 205
Morse, Robert 140
Mother Wore Tights 70
Motion Picture Association of American (MPAA) 74, 99, 117
Motion Picture Patents Company 10, 23
Motion Picture Producers and Distributors Association (MPPDA) 31, 51, 54, 74
Movies: A Psychological Study (book) 93
Movies in the Age of Innocence (book) 9
Mozert, Zoë 74, *76*
Mrs. Doubtfire 174
Ms. magazine **203**

Muhl, Ed 81
Mulvey, Laura 153
The Mummy (1932) 54
The Mummy's Ghost 67
Muni, Paul 54
Munson, Audrey 16–19, *17*
The Muppet Movie 147
Murder at the Vanities 56, *57*
Murder by the Clock 53
Mutual decision *see* Supreme Court, U.S.
Mutual Weekly 11
Muybridge, Eadweard 5–6
My Days of Mercy 206
My Gal Sal 66–67
My Tutor 169
Myles, Meg 127
Myra Breckenridge 150
"The Myth of the Vaginal Orgasm" (essay) 180–81

Naked Alibi 137
The Naked Maja 109
Naldi, Nita 39
Napier, Charles 150
Narcotic 61
The Narrow Margin (1952) 94
Nashville 162
National Board of Review 17
National Review 116
Navy Blues 65
Neill, R. William 161
Nielsen, Brigitte 203
Nielsen, Leslie 149
Nelson, Gene 92
Nelson, Judd 192, 204
Nelson, Lori 81, *83*, 122
Neon Nights 186
Neptune's Daughter (1914) 20, 83
Nesbit, Evelyn 9, 10, 22, 66, 114
Nettleton, Lois 149
Never on Sunday 121, 134
The New York Daily Mirror 53
The New York Herald Tribune 34, 102
New York, New York 160
The New York Times 22, 99, 176
The New York Times Magazine 166
The New Yorker 47, 99, 204
Newfield, Sam 161
Newmar, Julie *120*, 121
Niagara 105
Nichols, Barbara 114
Nichols, Kelly 186
Nichols, Mike 115
Nicholson, Jack 131, 132, 170, 175, 180
Night Call Nurses 161
Night of the Generals 146
The Night Manager (AMC) 202
The Night World 47
Nilsson, Anna Q. 13
Nin, Anaïs 172
Nin, Khadja 200
9 Songs 188
9½ Weeks 172
Ninotchka 63, 89

Niven, David 190
Nixon, Richard 179
No Man's Woman 94
Noonan, Tommy 141
Normand, Mabel 12, 22
Norris, Kathleen 34
North, Sheree 110–11, *112*
Nosseck, Max 102
Not Another Teen Movie 192
Not Wanted 61
Novak, Kim 106–7, 112
Nude on the Moon 127
"The Nude Scene" (TV episode) 149
nudist films 102, 127
nudity: banned by Production Code 142; in non-theatrical films 37–39; in silent films 16–22, 23
"nudity rider" 205–206
Nye, Sen. Gerald 64
Nyman, Lena 177–78

Oakman, Wheeler 60
O'Brien, Keiran 188
O' Brien, Pat 53, 58, 121
Of Human Bondage 107
Of Mice and Men (1939) 61
O'Hara, Jamie 102
O'Hara, John 134
O'Hara, Maureen 80, 109, 136
O'Hara, Quinn 130
Olin, Lena 171, *171*
Oliver, Susan 132
Olivier, Laurence 81
On the Road (novel) 116
On the Town (film) 66
On the Waterfront 117
On Your Toes (1936 stage; 1939 film) 85–86
Once Upon a Honeymoon 136
One for the Money 179
One Hour with You 47
One Million B.C. (1966) 145
One Touch of Venus 67, *69*
O'Neal, Tatum 163, *165*
O'Neil, Sally 41
O'Neil family, and RKO 102
O'Neill, William 42
Ontkean, Michael 173
The Opening of Misty Beethoven 183
oral sex 174, 180; cunnilingus 146, 180, 182, 193; fellatio 142, 174, 180, 182, 193, 194
The Orgy at Lil's Place 128, 180
Orlando (novel, film) 206
Orphans of the Storm 27
Orry-Kelly 88
The Oscar 137
Osco, Bill 179
Our Movie Made Children (book) 56
The Outlaw 64, 74–77, *76*, 77
Outrage (book) 183
Outrage (1950) 157
Outrageous Fortune 174
Over-Exposed 106

Index

The Pace That Kills 60
Page, Bettie 80
Page, Ellen 206
Pageant (periodical) 79
Paget, Debra 126, *126*
Paige, Janis 89
Paige, Robert 72
Painting the Clouds with Sunshine 92
Pal Joey 107
Palance, Jack 95
The Paleface 77
Palme, Olof 178
Palmer, Betsy 169
Palmer, Peter *120*, 121
Pan, Hermes 66
Panama, Norman 139
Paquin, Anna
Paramount 27, 32, 55
Paramount on Parade 45
Pardon My Sarong 72, *73*
Parker, Jean 68, 96
Parker, Suzy 107
Parrish 133
Parrish, Leslie *120*, 121
Party Girl 89
Patrick, John 88
Paul, William 167
The Pawnbroker 142
Payne, John 110, *110*, *111*
Payton, Barbara 92
Peckinpah, Sam 153–56
Penn, Sean 173
Pennington, Ann 47
Penthouse Magazine 179
Peraino, Lou 181
The Perils of Pauline (1914 serial) 13
Perkins, Anthony 142
Perrine, Valerie 175
Personal Best 158
Peters, Jean 115
Petty, George 63, 76, 89
The Petty Girl 76, *78*
Pevney, Joseph 81
Peyton Place (novel) 116
The Phenix City Story 127
Phffft! 106
Philadelphia 173
Photoplay magazine 17, 54
Phyrne, 22
The Piano 175
Pickford, Mary 13
Pickup 94
Picnic 106
Pigskin Parade 69
Pillow Talk 137
Pin-Up Girl 68
pin-ups 63, 64, pin-up culture 73, 203
Pirandello, Luigi 176
Plan 9 from Outer Space 125
Planet of the Apes (1968) 140
Platinum Blonde 52
Platt, Marc 67
Playboy magazine 79, 80, 141, 142, 144, 161, 162, 207; Playmates 78, 128

Plaza, Aubrey 194, ***195***
Pleshette, Suzanne 133
Point Blank 146
Poitier, Sidney 182
Polanski, Roman 199
Police Academy 181
Police Gazette (periodical) 7
Polowney, Frank 68
Ponti, Carlo 137
Poole, Wakefield 181
Popcorn Venus (book) 153, 201
Porgy and Bess 135
Porky's 163–66, ***165***, 169, 194
pornography 179–83, 187–89
Porter, Cole 70, 88, 89
Portman, Natalie 173, 191, 200
Portnoy's Complaint 180
Portrait of Madame X (painting) 7, 67
The Postman Always Rings Twice (1946) 94, 170
The Postman Always Rings Twice (1981) 170
Potter, Sally 206
Powell, Dick 47, 95
Powers, Mala 157
Powers, Tom 170
Praxiteles 21
Preisser, June 62
premarital sex: in 1920s 42; in 1940s 72; in 1960s 146, 190; "pre-pre marital sex" 191
Preminger, Otto 70, 99
Presley, Elvis 116
Pretty Baby 185, ***185***
Pretty Woman 192
Previn, André 136
Price, Vincent 96, 99, 131
The Pride and the Passion 115
The Prince Who Was a Thief 81
Princess Cyd 206
Prinz, LeRoy 89
Private Duty Nurses 161
Private Lessons 169
The Private Lives of Adam and Eve 129
Private School 169
The Prodigal 85
Professor Marston and the Wonder Women 203
Prom Night 169
Production Code 1, 85, 90, 99, 133, 140
Production Code Administration (PCA) 1, 57, 61, 89, 98, 142, 146, 172, 190; Code Seal 98, 99, 102, 104, 117, 137, 146, 190
Project XX (TV series) 9
Promises, Promises 141
prostitution 10, 23–25, 35, 134–36
Psych-Out 132
Psycho (1960) 121, 142, 206
The Public Enemy 52
Purity 16–17, 19
The Purple Rose of Cairo 97
Pushover 106

Queen Christina 56
Quigley, Martin 51, 119

Race Suicide 60
The Racket (1928) 54
Radio City Revels 58
Raft, George 86
Raiders of the Lost Ark 162
Rains, Claude 170
Ralston, Esther 36, 201
rape 79; rape scenes, 154–55, 156–59, 184
Rappe, Virginia 31
Ratajkowski, Emily 203
Rathbone, Basil 131
ratings system, MPAA 1, 147, 148, 171–72
Ray, Aldo ***119***, 121, 131
Raymond, Gene 51
Reaching for the Moon 47
Reagan, Ronald 89–90, 92, 183
Rear Window (1954) 107–8
Rebel Without a Cause 116, 142
Red Hair 40
The Red Kimono ***35***, 36
Red Shoe Diaries 172
Red Sonja 203
Red-Headed Woman 52
Reed, Oliver 146, 149
Reed, Rex 150
Reefer Madness 61, 131
Reems, Harry 181, 185
Reeve Christopher 203
Reid, Beryl 148
Reid, Dorothy Davenport (Mrs. Wallace) 34, ***35***, 36, 42, 60
Reid, Wallace, 31, 34
Renfro, Marli 142
Report on Blacklisting (book) 115
Republic Pictures, 72, 73, 122
Revenge of the Creature ***83***
Revenge of the Nerds 169, 205
Rhodes, Erik 59
Richards, Denise 173
The Richest Girl in the World 96
Ride the High Country 153
Rififi 124
Ringwald, Molly 192
Riot on the Sunset Strip 131
The Rise and Fall of Legs Diamond 114
Risky Business 205
Ritter, Joseph (Archbishop) 98
RKO Radio Pictures 45, 95, 98, 114, 122; RKO Theaters 76, 98
Road to Morocco 72
The Road to Rome (play) 83
The Road to Ruin (1928) 42
The Road to Ruin (1934) 44, 60
The Robe 85, ***86***
Roberts, Tanya 162
Robertson, Cliff 129
Robertson, Dale 100, 101
Rodgers, Richard 85, 134
Rodriguez, Estelita 115
Roeg, Nicholas 159
Rogen, Seth 184

224 Index

Rogers, Earl 36
Rogers, Ginger *49*, 50, 51, 58, 65, 68, 69, 71, 85, 105, 136
Rogers, Jean 58, *59*
Roman, Ruth 79
Roman Scandals 49
Romberg, Sigmund 39, 87
Rome Adventure 133
Romeo and Juliet (1916) 13
Romero, Cesar 135
Ronan, Soairse 196
Roommates 186
Rosalie 65
Rose, David 136
Rose, Helen 2, 88, 121, 134
Rosen, Marjorie 151–53, 201
Rosie the Riveter 71
Roth, Philip 180
Rothman, Stephanie 161
Rough Night 195
"roughies" 128–29, 156
Rourke, Mickey 172
Rowland, Henry 150
The Royal Family of Broadway 45
Royalle, Candida 183
Rush, Richard 132
Russell, Betsy 169
Russell, Jane 65, *66*, 71, 74, 75, *76*, *77*, 96–99, *100*, *101*, 117, *118*, 129, 145
Russell, Lillian 7
Russell, Rosalind 153
Ryan, Robert 121

Sachse, Salli 132
Sackville-West, Vita 206
Sadie McKee 201
Sahl, Mort 115
St. Cyr, Lili 99
St. John, Betta 96
St. John, Jill 137
St. Johns, Adela Rogers 36
Salinger, Conrad 73
Salome (1954) 85
Salome, Where She Danced 81
Samson and Delilah 84–84, 85, 103
Sanctuary (film) 121
Sanctuary (novel) 56
The Sandpiper 142
Sargent, Dr. Dudley Andrew 19–21
Sargent, John Singer 7, 67
Sarne, Mike 150
Sarno, Joe 176
Sarris, Andrew 96, 153
Satan in High Heels 127
The Saturday Evening Post 7
Savage, Dan 174
Scarface (1932) 54, 86, 160
The Scarlet Empress 56
Schain, Don 156
Schary, Dore 117
Schenck, Nicholas 117
Schiaffino, Rosanna 144
Schickel, Richard 185
Schilt, Thibault 124
Schlesinger, John 159

Schneider, Maria 159
Schnitzler, Arthur 31, 173
Schulberg, B.P. 39
Schwartz, Alexandra 204
Schwarzenegger, Arnold 203
Scorsese, Martin 160
Scott, Lizabeth 92
Scott, Randolph 114, 153
Scribner's Magazine 7
Scum of the Earth 128
The Searchers 103–4
Second Chance 95
The Secret of My Success 205
Secretary 172
Sedoux, Léa 199, 200
Seduction of the Innocent (book) 203
See No Evil 146
Seinfeld (TV) 45
Selby, Hubert, Jr. 100
Sellers, Peter 133
Selznick, David O. 31, 41, 117
Selznick, Lewis J. 31
Sennett, Mack 12, 22–23, 37, 129, 177
Sevigny, Chloë 192, *193*, 206
Sex and the Single Girl (book) 190
Sex and the Single Girl (film) 137, 190
Sexual Freedom in Denmark 179
Shampoo 174
Shapiro, Stanley 137
Sharif, Omar 103
Shatner, William 197
Shawlee, Joan 132
She Done Him Wrong 56
Shearer, Norma 51
Sheedy, Ally 204
Sheena 162
The Sheik 162
Shepherd, Cybill 182
Sheridan, Ann 62
The Sheriff of Fractured Jaw 140
She's All That 192
She's Back on Broadway 92
She's Working Her Way through College 92
Shields, Brooke 185, *185*
Shipman, Nell 26
Shock Corridor 137, *138*
The Shocking Miss Pilgrim 70
Shoes 24
Shortbus 188
The Show of Shows 45
Show People 33
Shue, Elisabeth 175
Shurlock, Geoffrey 117, 146
Sideways 174
Sidney, George 112, 143
Siegel, Tatiana 205
The Sign of the Cross (1932)
Sign of the Pagan 81
Silk Stockings 88
Silverman, Stephen 87
Simmons, Jean 85, 95
Simon, John 147
Simon, Simone 72, 189
Sin 13

The Sin Syndicate 156
Sinatra, Frank 107
Sinatra, Nancy 132
Sinbad the Sailor 99
Singh, Devendra 78
Singin' in the Rain 86, **90**
Siren of Bagdad 80, 82
Sixteen Candles 204–5
Sjöman, Vilgot 177–78
Skelton, Red 100
Skouras, Spyros 14, 139
Slate, Jeremy 137
Slater, Helen 203
Slave Girl 81
Slide, Anthony 51
Slightly Scarlet 109–110
Sloane, Everett 170
Smalley, Phillips 12
Smart Alec 179, 181
The Smiling Lieutenant 47
Smith, Sen. Hoke 12
Smith, Keely 115
Smith, Kevin 184
The Sniper 94
Snowden, Leigh 81
So This Is New York 73
Solnit, Rebecca 5
Soloway, Jill 207
Some Like It Hot 110, 121
Something's Got to Give 142
Sommer, Elke 142
Son of Ali Baba 81
Son of Paleface 96
Son of Sinbad 99–102, 103, 106
Song of Scheherezade 81
Soubrettes in a Bachelor's Flat 8
Soul Man 205
The Sound of Music 159
Spader, James 172
Spain, Fay 129
Spartacus 121
Spellman, Francis Cardinal 118
Spelvin, Georgina 181
Spielberg, Steven 160, 186, 197
Splendor in the Grass 142, 190
Split Second 95
Sports Illustrated (periodical) 204
Spottiswoode, Roger 153, 155
Sprinkle, Annie 183
Stagliano, John ("Buttman") 188
Stankey, John 202
Stanwyck, Barbara 63, 108, 136
Star! 150
Star 80 158
A Star Is Born (1954) 141
Star Trek 197
Star Wars 160
Stars and Stripes Forever 126
Steele, Karen 114
Steiner, Max 133
Sterling, Jan **125**
Stevens, Connie 133, ***134***
Stevens, George 58
Stevens, Inger 140, ***141***
Stevens, Stella 142
Stewart, Elaine 142
Stewart, James 63, 107, 137, 190

Stewart, Kristen 174, 200, 206
Stilley, Margo 188
Stone, Emma 199
Stone, George E. 50
Stone, Sharon 173
The Story of Temple Drake 56
Stratten, Dorothy 158, 207
Straw Dogs (1971) 153
Streep, Meryl 187
Streetcar Chivalry 7
A Streetcar Named Desire 119
Strike Me Pink 72
Striporama 99
The Stripper 136
Strossen, Nadine 183
Struss, Karl, 41
The Student Nurses 161
Studio Relations Committee 51, 56
The Stunt Man 132
Sturges, Preston 70, 72
Sudan 81
Sullivan, Barry 109
The Sultan's Daughter 80
A Summer Place 133
Sunday, Bloody Sunday 159
Sunday in New York 190
Sunny Side Up 46
Supergirl 203
Superman 203
Superman IV 203
Supreme Court, U.S.: *ACLU v. Reno* 187; *Bush v. Gore* 143; *Loving v. Virginia* 182; *Miller* decision 185; "*Miracle*" case 120; *Mutual* decision 12; "redeeming social value" 178
Susan Slade 133
Suspense (1913) 12
Sutherland, Donald 159, **160**
Swank, Hilary 174
Swanson, Gloria 30, 108
Sweater Girl 62
The Sweet Ride 146
Sweet Rosie O'Grady 69
Swept Away 186
Swing Time 69
The Swinger 143

Tadd, Mrs. J. Liberty 5
Tahiti Honey 72
Take Back the Night (anthology) 183
Take Her, She's Mine 190
The Talk of the Town 58
Tally, Thomas 10
Talmadge, Constance 30
Talman, William 92, 94
Tamango 136
Tamblyn, Russ **125**
The Taming of the Shrew 189
Tanned Legs 45
Tarzan and His Mate 56
Tarzan, the Ape Man (1982) 162
Tashlin, Frank 112, 113
A Taste of Flesh 156
Tate, Sharon 144, **145**
Taurog, Norman 85

Taxi Driver 162
Taylor, Elizabeth 121, 134, **135**, 142
Taylor, William Desmond 32
Tea and Sympathy 122, 132
Tearle, Conway 39
Teen Wolf 205
Tell It to the Bees 206
Tell Your Children see *Reefer Madness*
Temple, Shirley 57, 203
The Temptation of St. Anthony 15 10 162
Ten Broeck, Franklin 6
The Ten Commandments (1956) 119
Tender Comrade 71
Terror Train 169
Terry-Thomas 140
The Texas Chainsaw Massacre (1974) 181
Texas Lady 109
Thalberg, Irving 52
Thanhouser, Edwin 16
That Lady in Ermine 70
That Touch of Mink 137
Thaw, Harry K. 9–10, 66
The Thaw-White Tragedy 9
Thaxter, Phyllis 94
There's No Business Like Show Business 106
Therese and Isabelle 176
They Drive by Night 62
They Won't Forget 62
The Thief of Baghdad (1940) 80
This Day and Age 54
This Side of Paradise (novel) 34
This Was Burlesque (revue) 136
Thomas, Jane 18
Thomas, Norman 80
Thomas, Olive 33
Thomson, David 39, 141
Thornton, Billy Bob 174
A Thousand and One Nights 81
3 Nuts and a Bolt 141
Three O'Clock High 205
Three on a Match 133
Three Smart Girls 71
Three Smart Girls Grow Up 71
Three Weeks 34
Thunder Alley 132
Thurman, Mary 22
Thyssen, Greta 114
Till, Emmett 182
Tillie's Punctured Romance 23
Tilly, Jennifer 173
Time magazine 118, 177
"Time's Up" 203
Tin Pan Alley 69, 201
Tina Louise **119**, 121, 144
Titanic (1997) 175
The To Do List 194, **195**
Tobacco Road (novel) 121
Todd, Thelma 53
Tomei, Marisa 174
Tomlin, Lily 93
Tommy 143
Tonight and Every Night 67
Tootsie 174

Top Hat 47, 58
Tora! Tora! Tora! 150
Towers, Constance 137, **138**
Town Without Pity 144
Toynbee, Polly 200
Tracy, Spencer 121
Traffic in Souls 23–24
Trapeze 115
Trapeze Disrobing Act 6
Travilla, William "Billy" 105, 111
Treloar and Miss Marshall 7
The Trial of Mary Dugan 51
Trilling, Lionel 98
The Trip 132
Trotsky, Leon 207
True Detective (HBO) 197
Trumbo, Dalton 115
Turner, Kathleen 170
Turner, Lana 70
Turpin, Ben 22
Tuten, Frederic 87
Tuttle, Frank 36, **38**
20th Century–Fox 149–51
2001: A Space Odyssey 153
Two Weeks in Another Town 144
Twohey, Megan 199

Under the Yom Yum Tree 137
undergarments 13, 54, 62, 79
Underwater! 99, **118**
Underworld 54
The Unearthly 123
Unfaithful 175
Unger, Deborah Kara 172
United Nations Commission on the Status of Women 200
Universal Pictures 81; Universal-International 82, 122
An Unseen Enemy 12
Untamed Youth 122
Untouchable 200
The Unwritten Law 9–10, **11**
Up! 158–59
Updike, John 180

Vadim, Roger 123, 144, 190
Valenti, Jack 146
Valentino, Rudolph 31, 162
Valley of the Dolls 150
Vampyr 161
Van Doren, Mamie 81, 122–23, **125**, 129, 141
Van Fleet, Jo 109
Van Sant, Gus 142
Vanzetti, Bartolomeo 92
Varda, Agnés 200
"Varga girl" 63, 70, 71,
Vargas, Alberto 63, 70, 89
Variety (periodical) 16, 200
Varsity Blues 192
Vaughn, Vince 194
Veils of Bagdad 80
Velez, Lupe 115
The Velvet Vampire 161
Venus de Milo, as ideal 21, 36, **38**, 67, **69**
Vera Drake 166
Vera-Ellen 86, **88**

Vertigo 106, 107
Vice Raid 123
The Victors 142
Vidal, Gore 150
Vidor, King 33
Vincent, Chuck 186
virginity 42, 191, 196
Virginity Lost (book) 196
Visconti, Luchino 137
Vita and Virginia 206
Viva (Viva Hoffman) 178
Vixen! 150, 177
Vizzard, Jack 98, 146
von Sternberg, Josef 48
Von Stroheim, Erich 25–26, 30–31
Vox (online publication) 205

Wagenknecht, Edward 9
Waldon, Louis 178
Wallach, Eli 118
Wallis, Hal B. 56, 136
Walk on the Wild Side 136
Walker, James J. 42
Walker, Robert 67
Walsh, Raoul 45, 89, 140
Wanger, Walter 14
The War Wagon 158
WarGames 168
Warhol, Andy 148, 178
Warner, David 153
Warner, Jack L. 56, 117, 139
Warner Bros. 47, 55–56, 89, 139; Warner Media 202
A Water Nymph 22
Waters, John 112
Watson, Fifi/Mona 180, 181
Watts, Naomi 174
Wayne, John 103–4, *107*, 158
Weber, Lois 12, *15*, 24
Wedding Crashers 194
Weed, A.E. 8
Weill, Kurt 67
Weinstein, Harvey 199–200
Weird Science 169, 205
Weisz, Rachel 206
Welch, Raquel 135, 145, 150–51, *152*, 157
Weld, Tuesday 127
Welles, Orson 159, 187
Wells, Dawn 144
Wendkos, Paul 129
Wertham, Frederic 203
Wertmüller, Lina 186

West, Domenic 197
West, Mae 54, 56, 150
Westbound 114
Wharton, Edith 9
What Happened on 23rd St. 7
What Price Glory (1926) 45
What Price Hollywood? 41
Wheeler, Bert 53
Wheeler, Sen. Burton K. 64
Where Danger Lives 170
Where the Boys Are (1960) 130, 196
White, Carol 146
White, Pearl 13
White, Stanford 9, 16, 66
White Cargo 63
White Heat 89
White Savage 81
"white slave" cycle 23–25, 36
Whitney Museum of American Art 178
Whoopee! (1928 stage, 1930 film) 46
Why Be Good? 42, *43*
Why Change Your Wife? 29
Wicked Woman 94
The Widow Jones 6
Wild Angels 132
The Wild Bunch 153
The Wild One 116
Wild Orchids 172
Wild Things 173
Wilder, Anna Kelton 71
Wilder, Billy 105, 136
Wilkins, Dr. Walter 18
Will Success Spoil Rock Hunter? 112
Williams, Allison 197
Williams, Chili 67
Williams, Edy 150, ***151***
Williams, Esther 82–83, 89
Williams, Kenny 137
Williams, Linda 183
Williams, Robin 174
Williams, Tennessee 117, 118, 121
Wilson, Chelly 176
Wilson, Woodrow 12, 27, 29
Windsor, Marie *93*, 94
Wing, Toby 47
Wings 40
Winslet, Kate 174, 175
Winters, Shelley 135, 137, 139, 161
Wishman, Doris 127

Wives and Lovers 137
The Wolf Man 161
Wolfenstein, Martha 92
Woman of the Year 58
Woman on the Beach 129
Women Against Pornography 183
Women in Love 149
Wong, Anna May 135
Wood, Ed 124
Wood, Natalie 136, 142, 148, 190
Woodward, Joanne 115, 136
Woolf, Virginia 206
Woolsey, Robert 53
The World of Suzie Wong 135
The World of Yesterday (book) 191
World Theatre 180
Woulfe, Michael 95, 96–97, 104
Written on the Wind 109
The Wrong Man 117
Wyatt, Jane 58
Wyler, William 99
Wynn, Keenan 114
Wynn, Nan *73*

Yamaguchi, Shirley 135
Yankee Pasha 81
Yarnall, Celeste 161
Yevtushenko, Yevgeny 178
York, Susannah 148
You Were Never Lovelier 65
You'll Never Get Rich 64
Young, Clara Kimball 60
Young, Victor 103

Zabriskie Point 149
Zach and Miri Make a Porno 184
Zanuck, Darryl F. 104, 135, 139
Zanuck, Richard 150
Zarak 114, ***114***
Zellweger, Renee 174
Zero Dark Thirty 202
Ziegfeld, Florenz, Jr. 46, 62
Ziegfeld Follies (film) 73
Ziegfeld Follies (stage) 36, 102
Ziegfeld Girl 62
Zimbalist, Efrem, Jr. 139
Zinsser, William K. 102
Zorina, Vera 85
Zugsmith, Albert 122–23, 129, 177
Zukor, Adolph 26–27
Zweig, Stefan 191

www.ingramcontent.com/pod-product-compliance
Lightning Source LLC
Chambersburg PA
CBHW060342010526
44117CB00017B/2927